I0836852

LANDS OF THE SARACEN.

BAYARD TAYLOR.

Ruins of Baalbec

NEW YORK: G. P. PUTNAM.

1860.

THE

LANDS OF THE SARACEN:

OR,

PICTURES OF PALESTINE, ASIA MINOR, SICILY, AND SPAIN.

BY

BAYARD TAYLOR.

Twentieth Edition.

NEW YORK:
G. P. PUTNAM, 532 BROADWAY.
1863.

R. CRAIGHEAD,
Printer, Stereotyper, and Electrotyper,
Caxton Building,
81, 83, and 85 Centre Street.

TO

WASHINGTON IRVING,

THIS book—the chronicle of my travels through lands once occupied by the Saracens—naturally dedicates itself to you, who, more than any other American author, have revived the traditions, restored the history, and illustrated the character of that brilliant and heroic people. Your cordial encouragement confirmed me in my design of visiting the East, and making myself familiar with Oriental life; and though I bring you now but imperfect returns, I can at least unite with you in admiration of a field so rich in romantic interest, and indulge the hope that I may one day pluck from it fruit instead of blossoms. In Spain, I came upon your track, and I should hesitate to exhibit my own gleanings where you have harvested, were it not for the belief that the rapid sketches I have given will but enhance, by the contrast, the charm of your finished picture.

BAYARD TAYLOR.

PREFACE.

THIS volume comprises the second portion of a series of travels, of which the "JOURNEY TO CENTRAL AFRICA," already published, is the first part. I left home, intending to spend a winter in Africa, and to return during the following summer; but circumstances afterwards occurred, which prolonged my wanderings to nearly two years and a half, and led me to visit many remote and unexplored portions of the globe. To describe this journey in a single work, would embrace too many incongruous elements, to say nothing of its great length, and as it falls naturally into three parts, or episodes, of very distinct character, I have judged it best to group my experiences under three separate heads, merely indicating the links which connect them. This work includes my travels in Palestine, Syria, Asia Minor, Sicily and Spain, and will be followed by a third and concluding volume, containing my adventures in India, China, the Loo-Choo Islands, and Japan. Although many of the letters, contained in this volume, describe beaten tracks of travel, I have always given my own individual impressions, and may claim for them the merit of entire sincerity. The journey from Aleppo to Constantinople, through the heart of Asia Minor, illustrates regions rarely traversed by tourists, and will, no doubt, be new to most of my readers. My aim, throughout the work, has been to give correct pictures of Oriental life and scenery, leaving antiquarian research and speculation to abler hands. The scholar, or the man of science, may complain with reason that I have neglected valuable opportunities for adding something to the stock of human knowledge: but if a few of the many thousands, who can only travel by their firesides, should find my pages answer the purpose of a series of cosmoramic views—should in them behold with a clearer inward eye the hills of Palestine, the sun-gilded minarets of Damascus, or the lonely pine-forests of Phrygia—should feel, by turns, something of the inspiration and the indolence of the Orient—I shall have achieved all I designed, and more than I can justly hope.

NEW YORK, *October*, 1854.

CONTENTS.

CHAPTER I.

LIFE IN A SYRIAN QUARANTINE.

CHAPTER II.

THE COAST OF PALESTINE.

CHAPTER III.

FROM JAFFA TO JERUSALEM.

CHAPTER IV.

THE DEAD SEA AND THE RIVER JORDAN.

CHAPTER V.

THE CITY OF CHRIST.

CHAPTER VI.

THE HILL-COUNTRY OF PALESTINE.

CHAPTER VII.

THE COUNTRY OF GALILEE.

CHAPTER XIII.

CHAPTER XIV.

JOURNEY TO ANTIOCH AND ALEPPO.

CHAPTER XV.

LIFE IN ALEPPO.

CHAPTER XVI.

THROUGH THE SYRIAN GATES.

CHAPTER XVII.

ADANA AND TARSUS.

CHAPTER XVIII.

THE PASS OF MOUNT TAURUS.

CHAPTER XIX.

THE PLAINS OF KARAMANIA.

CHAPTER XX.

SCENES IN KONIA.

CHAPTER XXI.

THE HEART OF ASIA MINOR.

CHAPTER XXII.

THE FORESTS OF PHRYGIA.

CHAPTER XXIII.

KIUTAHYA, AND THE RUINS OF ŒZANI.

CHAPTER XXIV.

THE MYSIAN OLYMPUS.

CHAPTER XXV.

BROUSA AND THE SEA OF MARMORA.

CHAPTER XXVI.

THE NIGHT OF PREDESTINATION.

CHAPTER XXVII.

THE SOLEMNITIES OF BAIRAM.

CHAPTER XXVIII.

THE MOSQUES OF CONSTANTINOPLE.

CHAPTER XXIX.

FAREWELL TO THE ORIENT—MALTA.

CHAPTER XXX.

THE FESTIVAL OF ST. AGATHA.

CHAPTER XXXI.

THE ERUPTION OF MOUNT ETNA.

CHAPTER XXXII.

GIBRALTAR.

CHAPTER XXXIII.

CADIZ AND SEVILLE.

CHAPTER XXXIV.

JOURNEY IN A SPANISH DILIGENCE.

CHAPTER XXXV.

GRANADA AND THE ALHAMBRA.

CHAPTER XXXVI.

THE BRIDLE-ROADS OF ANDALUSIA.

CHAPTER XXXVII.

THE MOUNTAINS OF RONDA.

THE LANDS OF THE SARACEN.

CHAPTER I.

LIFE IN A SYRIAN QUARANTINE.

Voyage from Alexandria to Beyrout—Landing at Quarantine—The Guardiano—Our Quarters—Our Companions—Famine and Feasting—The Morning—The Holy Man of Timbuctoo—Sunday in Quarantine—Islamism—We are Registered—Love through a Grating—Trumpets—The Mystery Explained—Delights of Quarantine—Oriental *vs.* American Exaggeration—A Discussion of Politics—Our Release—Beyrout—Preparations for the Pilgrimage.

"The mountains look on Quarantine,
And Quarantine looks on the sea."

QUARANTINE MS.

IN QUARANTINE, BEYROUT,
Saturday, April 17, 1852.

EVERYBODY has heard of Quarantine, but in our favored country there are many untravelled persons who do not precisely know what it is, and who no doubt wonder why it should be such a bugbear to travellers in the Orient. I confess I am still somewhat in the same predicament myself, although I have already been twenty-four hours in Quarantine. But, as a peculiarity of the place is, that one can do nothing, however good a will he has, I propose to set down my experiences each day, hoping that I and my readers may obtain some insight into the nature of Quarantine, before the term of my probation is over.

I left Alexandria on the afternoon of the 14th inst., in company with Mr. Carter Harrison, a fellow-countryman, who had joined me in Cairo, for the tour through Palestine. We had a head wind, and rough sea, and I remained in a torpid state during most of the voyage. There was rain the second night; but, when the clouds cleared away yesterday morning, we were gladdened by the sight of Lebanon, whose summits glittered with streaks of snow. The lower slopes of the mountains were green with fields and forests, and Beyrout, when we ran up to it, seemed buried almost out of sight, in the foliage of its mulberry groves. The town is built along the northern side of a peninsula, which projects about two miles from the main line of the coast, forming a road for vessels. In half an hour after our arrival, several large boats came alongside, and we were told to get our baggage in order and embark for Quarantine. The time necessary to purify a traveller arriving from Egypt from suspicion of the plague, is five days, but the days of arrival and departure are counted, so that the durance amounts to but three full days. The captain of the Osiris mustered the passengers together, and informed them that each one would be obliged to pay six piastres for the transportation of himself and his baggage Two heavy lighters are now drawn up to the foot of the gangway, but as soon as the first box tumbles into them, the men tumble out. They attach the craft by cables to two smaller boats, in which they sit, to tow the infected loads. We are all sent down together, Jews, Turks, and Christians—a confused pile of men, women, children, and goods. A little boat from the city, in which there are representatives from the two hotels, hovers around us, and cards are thrown to us. The zealous agents wish to supply us immediately with tables, beds, and all other household appliances; but we decline their help until we arrive at the mysterious spot. At last we float off—two lighters full of infected, though respectable, material, towed by oarsmen of most scurvy appearance, but free from every suspicion of taint.

The sea is still rough, the sun is hot, and a fat Jewess becomes sea-sick. An Italian Jew rails at the boatmen ahead, in the Neapolitan patois, for the distance is long, the Quarantine being on the land-side of Beyrout. We see the rows of little yellow houses on the cliff, and with great apparent risk of being swept upon the breakers, are tugged into a small cove, where there is a landing-place. Nobody is there to receive us; the boatmen jump into the water and push the lighters against the stone stairs, while we unload our own baggage. A tin cup filled with sea-water is placed before us, and we each drop six piastres into it—for money, strange as it may seem, is infectious. By this time, the *guardianos* have had notice of our arrival, and we go up with them to choose our habitations. There are several rows of one-story houses overlooking the sea, each containing two empty rooms, to be had for a hundred piastres; but a square two-story dwelling stands apart from them, and the whole of it may be had for thrice that sum. There are seven Frank prisoners, and we take it for ourselves. But the rooms are bare, the kitchen empty, and we learn the important fact, that Quarantine is durance vile, without even the bread and water. The guardiano says the agents of the hotel are at the gate, and we can order from them whatever we want. Certainly; but at their own price, for we are wholly at their mercy. However, we go down stairs, and the chief officer, who accompanies us, gets into a corner as we pass, and holds a stick before him to keep us off. He is now clean, but if his garments brush against ours, he is lost. The people we meet in the grounds step aside with great respect to let us pass, but if we offer them our hands, no one would dare to touch a finger's tip.

Here is the gate: a double screen of wire, with an interval between, so that contact is impossible. There is a crowd of individuals outside, all anxious to execute commissions. Among them is the agent of the hotel, who proposes to fill our bare rooms with furniture, send us a servant and cook, and charge us the same as if we lodged with him. The bargain is closed at once, and he hurries off to make the arrangements. It is now four o'clock, and the bracing air of the headland gives a terrible appetite to those of us who, like me, have been sea-sick and fasting for forty-eight hours. But there is no food within the Quarantine except a patch of green wheat, and a well in the limestone rock. We two Americans join company with our room-mate, an Alexandrian of Italian parentage, who has come to Beyrout to be married, and make the tour of our territory. There is a path along the cliffs overhanging the sea, with glorious views of Lebanon, up to his snowy top, the pine-forests at his base, and the long cape whereon the city lies at full length, reposing beside the waves. The Mahommedans and Jews, in companies of ten (to save expense), are lodged in the smaller dwellings, where they have already aroused millions of fleas from their state of torpid expectancy. We return, and take a survey of our companions in the pavilion: a

French woman, with two ugly and peevish children (one at the breast), in the next room, and three French gentlemen in the other—a merchant, a young man with hair of extraordinary length, and a *filateur*, or silk-manufacturer, middle-aged and cynical. The first is a gentleman in every sense of the word, the latter endurable, but the young Absalom is my aversion. I am subject to involuntary likings and dislikings, for which I can give no reason, and though the man may be in every way amiable, his presence is very distasteful to me.

We take a pipe of consolation, but it only whets our appetites. We give up our promenade, for exercise is still worse; and at last the sun goes down, and yet no sign of dinner. Our pavilion becomes a Tower of Famine, and the Italian recites Dante. Finally a strange face appears at the door. By Apicius! it is a servant from the hotel, with iron bedsteads, camp-tables, and some large chests, which breathe an odor of the Commissary Department. We go stealthily down to the kitchen, and watch the unpacking. Our dinner is there, sure enough, but alas! it is not yet cooked. Patience is no more; my companion manages to filch a raw onion and a crust of bread, which we share, and roll under our tongues as a sweet morsel, and it gives us strength for another hour. The Greek dragoman and cook, who are sent into Quarantine for our sakes, take compassion on us; the fires are kindled in the cold furnaces; savory steams creep up the stairs; the preparations increase, and finally climax in the rapturous announcement: "Messieurs, dinner is ready." The soup is liquified bliss; the *cotelettes d'agneau* are *cotelettes de bonheur;* and as for that broad dish of Syrian larks—Heaven forgive us the regret that more songs had not been silenced for our sake! The meal is all nectar and ambrosia, and now, filled and contented, we subside into sleep on comfortable couches. So closes the first day of our incarceration.

This morning dawned clear and beautiful. Lebanon, except his snowy crest, was wrapped in the early shadows, but the Mediterranean gleamed like a shield of sapphire, and Beyrout, sculptured against the background of its mulberry groves, was glorified beyond all other cities. The turf around our pavilion fairly blazed with the splendor of the yellow daisies and crimson poppies that stud it. I was satisfied with what I saw, and felt no wish to leave Quarantine to-day. Our Italian friend, however, is more impatient. His betrothed came early to see him, and we were edified by the great alacrity with which he hastened to the grate, to renew his vows at two yards' distance from her. In the meantime, I went down to the Turkish houses, to cultivate the acquaintance of a singular character I met on board the steamer. He is a negro of six feet four, dressed in a long scarlet robe. His name is Mahommed Senoosee, and he is a *fakeer*, or holy man, from Timbuctoo. He has been two years absent from home, on a pilgrimage to Mecca and Medina, and is now on his way to Jerusalem and Damascus. He has travelled extensively in all parts of Central Africa, from Dar-Fur to Ashantee, and professes to be on good terms with the Sultans of Houssa and Bornou. He has even been in the great kingdom of Waday, which has never been explored by Europeans, and as far south as Iola, the capital of Adamowa. Of the correctness of his narrations I have not the least doubt, as they correspond geographically with all that we know of the interior of Africa. In answer to my question whether a European might safely make the same tour, he replied that there would be no difficulty, provided he was accompanied by a native, and he offered to take me even to Timbuctoo, if I would return with him. He was very curious to obtain information about America, and made notes of all that I told him, in the quaint character used by the Mughrebbins, or Arabs of the West, which has considerable resemblance to the ancient Cufic. He wishes to join company with me for the journey to Jerusalem, and perhaps I shall accept him.

Sunday, April 18.

As Quarantine is a sort of limbo, without the pale of civilized society, we have no church service to-day. We have done the best we could, however, in sending one of the outside dragomen to purchase a Bible, in which we succeeded. He brought us a very handsome copy, printed by the American Bible Society in New York. I tried vainly in Cairo and Alexandria to find a missionary who would supply my heathenish destitution of the Sacred Writings; for I had reached the East through Austria, where they are prohibited, and to travel through Palestine without them, would be like sailing without pilot or compass. It gives a most impressive reality to Solomon's "house of the forest of Lebanon," when you can look up from the page to those very forests and those grand mountains, "excellent with the cedars." Seeing the holy man of Timbuctoo praying with his face towards Mecca, I went down to him, and we conversed for a long time on religious matters. He is tolerably well informed, having read the Books of Moses and the Psalms of David, but, like all Mahommedans, his ideas of religion consist mainly of forms, and its reward is a sensual paradise. The more intelligent of the Moslems give a spiritual interpretation to the nature of the Heaven promised by the Prophet, and I have heard several openly confess their disbelief in the seventy houries and the palaces of pearl and emerald. Shekh Mahommed Senoosee scarcely ever utters a sentence in which is not the word "Allah," and "La illah il' Allah" is repeated at least every five minutes. Those of his class consider that there is a peculiar merit in the repetition of the names and attributes of God. They utterly reject the doctrine of the Trinity, which they believe implies a sort of partnership, or God-firm (to use their own words), and declare that all who accept it are hopelessly damned. To deny Mahomet's prophetship would excite a violent antagonism, and I content myself with making them acknowledge that God is greater than all Prophets or Apostles, and that there is but one God for all the human race. I have never yet encountered that bitter spirit of bigotry which is so frequently ascribed to them; but on the contrary, fully as great a tolerance as they would find exhibited towards them by most of the Christian sects.

This morning a paper was sent to us, on which we were requested to write our names, ages, professions, and places of nativity. We conjectured that we were subjected to the suspicion of political as well as physical taint, but happily this was not the case. I registered myself as a *voyageur*, the French as *negocians*, and when it came to the woman's turn, Absalom, who is a partisan of female progress, wished to give her the same profession as her husband—a machinist. But she declared that her only profession was that of a "married woman," and she was so inscribed. Her peevish boy rejoiced in the title of "*pleuricheur*," or "weeper," and the infant as "*titeuse*," or "sucker." While this was going on, the guardiano of our room came in very mysteriously, and beckoned to my companion, saying that " Mademoiselle was at the gate." But it was the Italian who was wanted, and again, from the little window of our pavilion, we watched his hurried progress over the lawn. No sooner had she departed, than he took his pocket telescope, slowly sweeping the circuit of the bay as she drew nearer and nearer Beyrout. He has succeeded in distinguishing, among the mass of buildings, the top of the house in which she lives, but alas! it is one story too low, and his patient espial has only been rewarded by the sight of some cats promenading on the roof.

I have succeeded in obtaining some further particulars in relation to Quarantine. On the night of our arrival, as we were about getting into our beds, a sudden and horrible gush of brimstone vapor came up stairs, and we all fell to coughing like patients in a pulmonary hospital. The odor increased till we were obliged to open the windows and sit beside them in order to breathe comfortably. This was the preparatory fumigation, in order to remove the ranker seeds of plague, after which the milder symptoms will of themselves vanish in the pure air of the place. Several times a day we are stunned and overwhelmed with the cracked brays of three discordant trumpets, as grating and doleful as the last gasps of a dying donkey. At first I supposed the object of this was to give a greater agitation to the air, and separate and shake down the noxious exhalations we emit; but since I was informed that the soldiers outside would shoot us in case we attempted to escape, I have concluded that the sound is meant to alarm us, and prevent our approaching too near the walls. On inquiring of our guardiano whether the wheat growing within the grounds was subject to Quarantine, he informed me that it did not ccovey infection, and that three old geese, who walked out past the guard with impunity, were free to go and come, as they had never been known to have the plague. Yesterday evening the medical attendant, a Polish physician, came in to inspect us, but he made a very hasty review, looking down on us from the top of a high horse.

Monday, April 19.

Eureka! the whole thing is explained. Talking to day with the guardiano, he happened to mention that he had been three years in Quarantine, keeping watch over infected travellers. "What!" said I, "you have been sick three years." "Oh no," he replied; "I have never been sick at all." "But are not people sick in Quarantine?" "*Stafferillah!*" he exclaimed; 'they are always in better health than the people outside." "What is Quarantine for, then?" I persisted. "What is it for?" he repeated, with a pause of blank amazement at my ignorance, "why, to get money from the travellers!" Indiscreet guardiano! It were better to suppose ourselves under suspicion of the plague, than to have such an explanation of the mystery. Yet, in spite of the unpalatable knowledge, I almost regret that this is our last day in the establishment. The air is so pure and bracing, the views from our windows so magnificent, the colonized branch of the Beyrout Hotel so comfortable, that I am content to enjoy this pleasant idleness—the more pleasant since, being involuntary, it is no weight on the conscience. I look up to the Maronite villages, perched on the slopes of Lebanon, with scarce a wish to climb to them, or turning to the sparkling Mediterranean, view

"The speronara's sail of snowy hue
Whitening and brightening on that field of blue,"

and have none of that unrest which the sight of a vessel in motion suggests.

To-day my friend from Timbuctoo came up to have another talk. He was curious to know the object of my travels, and as he would not have comprehended the exact truth, I was obliged to convey it to him through the medium of fiction. I informed him that I had been dispatched by the Sultan of my country to obtain information of the countries of Africa; that I wrote in a book accounts of everything I saw, and on my return, would present this book to the Sultan, who would reward me with a high rank—perhaps even that of Grand Vizier. The Orientals deal largely in hyperbole, and scatter numbers and values with the most reckless profusion. The Arabic, like the Hebrew, its sister tongue, and other old original tongues of Man, is a language of roots, and abounds with the boldest metaphors. Now, exaggeration is but the imperfect form of metaphor. The expression is always a splendid amplification of the simple fact. Like skilful archers, in order to hit the mark, they aim above it. When you have once learned his standard of truth, you can readily gauge an Arab's expressions, and regulate your own accordingly. But whenever I have attempted to strike the key-note myself, I generally found that it was below, rather than above, the Oriental pitch.

The Shekh had already informed me that the King of Ashantee, whom he had visited, possessed twenty-four houses full of gold, and that the Sultan of Houssa had seventy thousand horses always standing saddled before his palace, in order that he might take his choice, when he wished to ride out. By this he did not mean that the facts were precisely so, but only that the King was very rich, and the Sultan had a great many horses. In order to give the Shekh an idea of the great wealth and power of the American Nation, I was obliged to adopt the same plan. I told him, therefore, that our country was two years' journey in extent, that the Treasury consisted of four thousand houses filled to the roof with gold, and that two hundred thousand soldiers on horseback kept continual guard around Sultan Fillmore's palace. He received these tremendous statements with the utmost serenity and satisfaction, carefully writing them in his book, together with the name of Sultan Fillmore, whose fame has ere this reached the remote regions of Timbuctoo. The Shekh, moreover, had the desire of visiting England, and wished me to give him a letter to the English Sultan. This rather exceeded my powers, but I wrote a simple certificate explaining who he was, and whence he came, which I sealed with an immense display of wax, and gave him. In return, he wrote his name in my book, in the Mughrebbin character, adding the sentence : "There is no God but God."

This evening the forbidden subject of politics crept into our quiet community, and the result was an explosive contention which drowned even the braying of the agonizing trumpets outside. The gentlemanly Frenchman is a sensible and consistent republican, the old *filateur* a violent monarchist, while Absalom, as I might have foreseen, is a Red, of the schools of Proudhon and Considerant. The first predicted a Republic in France, the second a Monarchy in America, and the last was in favor of a general and total demolition of all existing systems. Of course, with such elements, anything like a serious discussion was impossible ; and, as in most French debates, it ended in a bewildering confusion of cries and gesticulations In the midst of it, I was struck by the cordiality with which the Monarchist and the Socialist united in their denunciations of England and the English laws. As they sat side by side, pouring out anathemas against "perfide Albion," I could not help exclaiming: "*Voilà, comme les extrêmes se rencontrent!*" This turned the whole current of their wrath against me, and I was glad to make a hasty retreat.

The physician again visited us to-night, to promise a release to-morrow morning. He looked us all in the faces, to be certain that there were no signs of pestilence, and politely regretted that he could not offer us his hand. The husband of the "married woman" also came, and relieved the other gentlemen from the charge of the "weeper." He was a stout, ruddy Provençal, in a white blouse, and I commiserated him sincerely for having such a disagreeable wife.

To-day, being the last of our imprisonment, we have received many tokens of attention from dragomen, who have sent their papers through the grate to us, to be returned to-morrow after our liberation. They are not very prepossessing specimens of their class, with the exception of Yusef Badra, who brings a recommendation from my friend, Ross Browne. Yusef is a handsome, dashing fellow, with something of the dandy in his dress and air, but he has a fine, clear, sparkling eye, with just enough of the devil in it to make him attractive. I think, however, that the Greek dragoman, who has been our companion in Quarantine, will carry the day. He is by birth a Bœotian, but now a citizen of Athens, and calls himself François Vitalis. He speaks French, German, and Italian, besides Arabic and Turkish, and as he has been for twelve or fifteen years vibrating between Europe and the East, he must by this time have amassed sufficient experience to answer the needs of rough-and-tumble travellers like ourselves. He has not asked us for the place, which displays so much penetration on his part, that we shall end by offering it to him. Perhaps he is content to rest his claims upon the memory of our first Quarantine dinner. If so, the odors of the cutlets and larks—even of the raw onion, which we remember with tears—shall not plead his cause in vain.

BEYROUT (out of Quarantine), *Wednesday, May* 21.

The handsome Greek, Diamanti, one of the proprietors of the "Hotel de Belle Vue," was on hand bright and early yesterday morning, to welcome us out of Quarantine. The gates were thrown wide, and forth we issued between two files of soldiers, rejoicing in our purification. We walked through mulberry orchards to the town, and through its steep and crooked streets to the hotel, which stands beyond, near the extremity of the Cape, or Ras Beyrout. The town is small, but has an active population, and a larger commerce than any other port in Syria. The anchorage, however, is an open road, and in stormy weather it is impossible for a boat to land. There are two picturesque old castles on some rocks near the shore, but they were almost destroyed by the English bombardment in 1841. I noticed two or three granite columns, now used as the lintels of some of the arched ways in the streets, and other fragments of old masonry, the only remains of the ancient Berytus.

Our time, since our release, has been occupied by preparations for the journey to Jerusalem. We have taken François as dragoman, and our *mukkairee*, or muleteers, are engaged to be in readiness to-morrow morning. I learn that the Druses are in revolt in Djebel Hauaran and parts of the Anti-Lebanon, which will prevent my forming any settled plan for the tour through Palestine and Syria. Up to this time, the country has been considered quite safe, the only robbery this winter having been that of the party of Mr. Degen, of New York, which was plundered near Tiberias. Dr. Robinson left here two weeks ago for Jerusalem, in company with Dr. Eli Smith, of the American Mission at this place.

CHAPTER II.

THE COAST OF PALESTINE

The Pilgrimage Commences—The Muleteers—The Mules—The Donkey—Journey to Sidon—The Foot of Lebanon—Pictures—The Ruins of Tyre—A Wild Morning—The Tyrian Surges—Climbing the Ladder of Tyre—Panorama of the Bay of Acre—The Plain of Esdraelon—Camp in a Garden—Acre—the Shore of the Bay—Haifa—Mount Carmel and its Monastery—A Deserted Coast—The Ruins of Cæsarea—The Scenery of Palestine—We become Robbers—El Haram—Wrecks—the Harbor and Town of Jaffa.

"Along the line of foam, the jewelled chain,
The largesse of the ever-giving main."

R. H. STODDARD.

RAMLEH, *April* 27, 1852.

WE left Beyrout on the morning of the 22d. Our caravan consisted of three horses, three mules, and a donkey, in charge of two men—Dervish, an erect, black-bearded, and most impassive Mussulman, and Mustapha, who is the very picture of patience and good-nature. He was born with a smile on his face, and has never been able to change the expression. They are both masters of their art, and can load a mule with a speed and skill which I would defy any Santa Fé trader to excel. The animals are not less interesting than their masters. Our horses, to be sure, are slow, plodding beasts, with considerable endurance, but little spirit; but the two baggage-mules deserve gold medals from the Society for the Promotion of Industry. I can overlook any amount of waywardness in the creatures, in consideration of the steady, persevering energy, the cheerfulness and even enthusiasm with which they perform their duties. They seem to be conscious that they are doing well, and to take a delight in the consciousness. One of them has a band of white shells around his neck, fastened with a tassel and two large blue beads; and you need but look at him to see that he is aware how becoming it is. He thinks it was given to him for good conduct, and is doing his best to merit another. The little donkey is a still more original animal. He is a practical humorist, full of perverse tricks, but all intended for effect, and without a particle of malice. He generally walks behind, running off to one side or the other to crop a mouthful of grass, but no sooner does Dervish attempt to mount him, than he sets off at full gallop, and takes the lead of the caravan. After having performed one of his feats, he turns around with a droll glance at us, as much as to say: "Did you see that?" If we had not been present, most assuredly he would never have done it. I can imagine him, after his return to Beyrout, relating his adventures to a company of fellow-donkeys, who every now and then burst into tremendous brays at some of his irresistible dry sayings.

I persuaded Mr. Harrison to adopt the Oriental costume, which, from five months' wear in Africa, I greatly preferred to the Frank. We therefore rode out of Beyrout as a pair of Syrian Beys, while François, with his belt, sabre, and pistols had much the aspect of a Greek brigand. The road crosses the hill behind the city, between the Forest of Pines and a long tract of red sand-hills next the sea. It was a lovely morning, not too bright and hot, for light, fleecy vapors hung along the sides of Lebanon. Beyond the mulberry orchards, we entered on wild, half-cultivated tracts, covered with a bewildering maze of blossoms. The hill-side and stony shelves of soil overhanging the sea fairly blazed with the brilliant dots of color which were rained upon them. The pink, the broom, the poppy, the speedwell, the lupin, that beautiful variety of the cyclamen, called by the Syrians "*deek e-djebel*" (cock o' the mountain), and a number of unknown plants dazzled the eye with their profusion, and loaded the air with fragrance as rare as it was unfailing. Here and there, clear, swift rivulets came down from Lebanon, coursing their way between thickets of blooming oleanders. Just before crossing the little river Damoor, François pointed out, on one of the distant heights, the residence of the late Lady Hester Stanhope. During the afternoon we crossed several offshoots of the Lebanon, by paths incredibly steep and stony, and towards evening reached Saïda, the ancient Sidon, where we obtained permission to pitch our tent in a garden. The town is built on a narrow point of land, jutting out from the centre of a bay, or curve in the coast, and contains about five thousand inhabitants. It is a quiet, sleepy sort of a place, and contains nothing of the old Sidon except a few stones and the fragments of a mole, extending into the sea. The fortress in the water, and the Citadel, are remnants of Venitian sway. The clouds gathered after nightfall, and occasionally there was a dash of rain on our tent. But I heard it with the same quiet happiness, as when, in boyhood, sleeping beneath the rafters, I have heard the rain beating all night upon the roof. I breathed the sweet breath of the grasses whereon my carpet was spread, and old Mother Earth, welcoming me back to her bosom, cradled me into calm and refreshing sleep. There is no rest more grateful than that which we take on the turf or the sand, except the rest below it.

We rose in a dark and cloudy morning, and continued our way between fields of barley, completely stained with the bloody hue of the poppy, and meadows turned into golden mosaic by a brilliant yellow daisy. Until noon our road was over a region of alternate meadow land and gentle though stony elevations, making out from Lebanon. We met continually with indications of ancient power and prosperity. The ground was strewn with hewn blocks, and the foundations of buildings remain in many places. Broken sarcophagi lie half-buried in grass, and the gray rocks of the hills are pierced with tombs. The soil, though stony, appeared to be naturally fertile, and the crops of wheat, barley, and lentils were very flourishing. After rounding the promontory which forms the southern boundary of the Gulf of Sidon, we rode for an hour or two over a plain near the sea, and then came down to a valley which ran up among the hills, terminating in a natural amphitheatre. An ancient barrow, or tumulus, nobody knows of whom, stands near the sea. During the day I noticed two charming little pictures. One, a fountain gushing into a broad square basin of masonry, shaded by three branching cypresses. Two Turks sat on its edge, eating their bread and curdled milk, while their horses drank out of the stone trough below. The other, an old Mahommedan, with a green turban and white robe, seated at the foot of a majestic sycamore, over the high bank of a stream that tumbled down its bed of white marble rock to the sea.

The plain back of the narrow, sandy promontory on which

the modern Soor is built, is a rich black loam, which a little proper culture would turn into a very garden. It helped me to account for the wealth of ancient Tyre. The approach to the town, along a beach on which the surf broke with a continuous roar, with the wreck of a Greek vessel in the foreground, and a stormy sky behind, was very striking. It was a wild, bleak picture, the white minarets of the town standing out spectrally against the clouds. We rode up the sand-hills, back of the town, and selected a good camping-place among the ruins of Tyre. Near us there was an ancient square building, now used as a cistern, and filled with excellent fresh water The surf roared tremendously on the rocks, on either hand, and the boom of the more distant breakers came to my ear like the wind in a pine forest. The remains of the ancient sea-wall are still to be traced for the entire circuit of the city, and the heavy surf breaks upon piles of shattered granite columns. Along a sort of mole, protecting an inner harbor on the north side, are great numbers of these columns. I counted fifteen in one group, some of them fine red granite, and some of the marble of Lebanon. The remains of the pharos and the fortresses strengthening the sea-wall, were pointed out by the Syrian who accompanied us as a guide, but his faith was a little stronger than mine. He even showed us the ruins of the jetty built by Alexander, by means of which the ancient city, then insulated by the sea, was taken. The remains of the causeway gradually formed the promontory by which the place is now connected with the main land. These are the principal indications of Tyre above ground, but the guide informed us that the Arabs, in digging among the sand-hills for the stones of the old buildings, which they quarry out and ship to Bey rout, come upon chambers, pillars, arches, and other objects. The Tyrian purple is still furnished by a muscle found upon the coast, but Tyre is now only noted for its tobacco and millstones. I saw many of the latter lying in the streets of the town, and an Arab was selling a quantity at auction in the square, as we passed. They are cut out from a species of dark volcanic rock, by the Bedouins of the mountains. There were half a dozen small coasting vessels lying in the road, but the old harbors are entirely destroyed. Isaiah's prophecy is literally fulfilled: "Howl, ye ships of Tarshish; for it is laid waste, so that there is no house, no entering in."

On returning from our ramble we passed the house of the Governor, Daood Agha, who was dispensing justice in regard to a lawsuit then before him. He asked us to stop and take coffee, and received us with much grace and dignity. As we rose to leave, a slave brought me a large bunch of choice flowers from his garden.

We set out from Tyre at an early hour, and rode along the beach around the head of the bay to the Ras-el-Abiad, the ancient Promontorium Album. The morning was wild and cloudy, with gleams of sunshine that flashed out over the dark violet gloom of the sea. The surf was magnificent, rolling up in grand billows, which broke and formed again, till the last of the long, falling fringes of snow slid seething up the sand. Something of ancient power was in their shock and roar, and every great wave that plunged and drew back again, called in its solemn bass: "Where are the ships of Tyre? where are the ships of Tyre?" I looked back on the city, which stood advanced far into the sea, her feet bathed in thunderous spray. By and by the clouds cleared away, the sun came out bold and bright, and our road left the beach for a meadowy plain, crossed by fresh streams, and sown with an inexhaustible wealth of flowers. Through thickets of myrtle and mastic, around which the rue and lavender grew in dense clusters, we reached the foot of the mountain, and began ascending the celebrated Ladder of Tyre. The road is so steep as to resemble a staircase, and climbs along the side of the promontory, hanging over precipices of naked white rock, in some places three hundred feet in height. The mountain is a mass of magnesian limestone, with occasional beds of marble. The surf has worn its foot into hollow caverns, into which the sea rushes with a dull, heavy boom, like distant thunder. The sides are covered with thickets of broom, myrtle, arbutus, ilex, mastic and laurel, overgrown with woodbine, and interspersed with patches of sage, lavender, hyssop, wild thyme, and rue. The whole mountain is a heap of balm; a bundle of sweet spices.

Our horses' hoofs clattered up and down the rounds of the ladder, and we looked our last on Tyre, fading away behind the white hem of the breakers, as we turned the point of the promontory. Another cove of the mountain-coast followed, terminated by the Cape of Nakhura, the northern point of the Bay of Acre. We rode along a stony way between fields of wheat and barley, blotted almost out of sight by showers of scarlet poppies and yellow chrysanthemums. There were frequent ruins: fragments of sarcophagi, foundations of houses, and about half way between the two capes, the mounds of Alexandro-Schœnæ. We stopped at a khan, and breakfasted under a magnificent olive tree, while two boys tended our horses to see that they ate only the edges of the wheat field. Below the house were two large cypresses, and on a little tongue of land the ruins of one of those square towers of the corsairs, which line all this coast. The intense blue of the sea, seen close at hand over a broad field of goldening wheat, formed a dazzling and superb contrast of color. Early in the afternoon we climbed the Ras Nakhura, not so bold and grand, though quite as flowery a steep as the Promontorium Album. We had been jogging half an hour over its uneven summit, when the side suddenly fell away below us, and we saw the whole of the great gulf and plain of Acre, backed by the long ridge of Mount Carmel. Behind the sea, which makes a deep indentation in the line of the coast, extended the plain, bounded on the east, at two leagues' distance, by a range of hills covered with luxuriant olive groves, and still higher, by the distant mountains of Galilee. The fortifications of Acre were visible on a slight promontory near the middle of the Gulf. From our feet the line of foamy surf extended for miles along the red sand-beach, till it finally became like a chalk-mark on the edge of the field of blue.

We rode down the mountain and continued our journey over the plain of Esdraelon—a picture of summer luxuriance and bloom. The waves of wheat and barley rolled away from our path to the distant olive orchards; here the water gushed from a stone fountain and flowed into a turf-girdled pool, around which the Syrian women were washing their garments; there, a garden of orange, lemon, fig, and pomegranate trees in blossom, was a spring of sweet odors, which overflowed the whole land. We rode into some of these forests, for they were no less, and finally pitched our tent in one of them, belonging to the palace of the former Abdallah Pasha, within a mile of Acre. The old Saracen aqueduct, which still conveys water to the town, overhung our tent. For an hour before reaching our destination, we had seen it on the left, crossing the hollows on light stone arches. In one place I counted fifty-eight, and in another one hundred and three of these arches, some of which were fifty feet high. Our camp was a charming place : a nest of deep herbage, under two enormous fig-trees, and surrounded by a balmy grove of orange and citron. It was doubly beautiful when the long line of the aqueduct was lit up by the moon, and the orange trees became mounds of ambrosial darkness.

In the morning we rode to Acre, the fortifications of which have been restored on the land-side. A ponderous double gate way of stone admitted us into the city, through what was once, apparently, the court-yard of a fortress. The streets of the town are narrow, terribly rough, and very dirty, but the bazaars are extensive and well stocked. The principal mosque, whose heavy dome is visible at some distance from the city, is surrounded with a garden, enclosed by a pillared corridor, paved with marble. All the houses of the city are built in the most massive style, of hard gray limestone or marble, and this circumstance alone prevented their complete destruction during the English bombardment in 1841. The marks of the shells are everywhere seen, and the upper parts of the lofty buildings are completely riddled with cannon-balls, some of which remain embedded in the stone. We made a rapid tour of the town on horseback, followed by the curious glances of the people, who were in doubt whether to consider us Turks or Franks. There were a dozen vessels in the harbor, which is considered the best in Syria.

The baggage-mules had gone on, so we galloped after them along the hard beach, around the head of the bay. It was a brilliant morning ; a delicious south-eastern breeze came to us over the flowery plain of Esdraelon ; the sea on our right shone blue, and purple, and violet-green, and black, as the shadows or sunshine crossed it, and only the long lines of roaring foam, for ever changing in form, did not vary in hue. A fisherman stood on the beach in a statuesque attitude, his handsome bare legs bathed in the frothy swells, a bag of fish hanging from his shoulder, and the large square net, with its sinkers of lead in his right hand, ready for a cast. He had good luck, for the waves brought up plenty of large fish, and cast them at our feet, leaving them to struggle back into the treacherous brine. Between Acre and Haifa we passed six or eight wrecks, mostly of small trading vessels. Some were half buried in sand, some so old and mossy that they were fast rotting away, while a few had been recently hurled there. As we rounded the deep curve of the bay, and approached the line of palm-trees girding the foot of Mount Carmel, Haifa, with its wall and Saracenic town in ruin on the hill above, grew more clear and bright in the sun, while Acre dipped into the blue of the Mediterranean. The town of Haifa, the ancient Caiapha, is small, dirty, and beggarly looking ; but it has some commerce, sharing the trade of Acre in the productions of Syria. It was Sunday, and all the Consular flags were flying. It was an unexpected delight to find the American colors in this little Syrian town, flying from one of the tallest poles. The people stared at us as we passed, and I noticed among them many bright Frankish faces, with eyes too clear and gray for Syria. O ye kind brothers of the monastery of Carmel ! forgive me if I look to you for an explanation of this phenomenon.

We ascended to Mount Carmel. The path led through a

grove of carob trees, from which the beans, known in Germany as St. John's bread, are produced. After this we came into an olive grove at the foot of the mountain, from which long fields of wheat, giving forth a ripe summer smell, flowed down to the shore of the bay. The olive trees were of immense size, and I can well believe, as Fra Carlo informed us, that they were probably planted by the Roman colonists, established there by Titus. The gnarled, veteran boles still send forth vigorous and blossoming boughs. There were all manner of lovely lights and shades chequered over the turf and the winding path we rode. At last we reached the foot of an ascent, steeper than the Ladder of Tyre. As our horses slowly climbed to the Convent of St. Elijah, whence we already saw the French flag floating over the shoulder of the mountain, the view opened grandly to the north and east, revealing the bay and plain of Acre, and the coast as far as Ras Nakhura, from which we first saw Mount Carmel the day previous. The two views are very similar in character, one being the obverse of the other. We reached the Convent—Dayr Mar Elias, as the Arabs call it—at noon, just in time to partake of a bountiful dinner, to which the monks had treated themselves. Fra Carlo, the good Franciscan who receives strangers, showed us the building, and the Grotto of Elijah, which is under the altar of the Convent Church, a small but very handsome structure of Italian marble. The sanctity of the Grotto depends on tradition entirely, as there is no mention in the Bible of Elijah having resided on Carmel, though it was from this mountain that he saw the cloud, "like a man's hand," rising from the sea. The Convent, which is quite new—not yet completed, in fact—is a large, massive building, and has the aspect of a fortress.

As we were to sleep at Tantura, five hours distant, we were obliged to make a short visit, in spite of the invitation of the hospitable Fra Carlo to spend the night there. In the afternoon we passed the ruins of Athlit, a town of the Middle Ages, and the Castel Pellegrino of the Crusaders. Our road now followed the beach, nearly the whole distance to Jaffa, and was in many places, for leagues in extent, a solid layer of white, brown, purple and rosy shells, which cracked and rattled under our horses' feet. Tantura is a poor Arab village, and we had some difficulty in procuring provisions. The people lived in small huts of mud and stones, near the sea. The place had a thievish look, and we deemed it best to be careful in the disposal of our baggage for the night.

In the morning we took the coast again, riding over millions of shells. A line of sandy hills, covered with thickets of myrtle and mastic, shut off the view of the plain and meadows between the sea and the hills of Samaria. After three hours' ride we saw the ruins of ancient Cæsarea, near a small promontory. The road turned away from the sea, and took the wild plain behind, which is completely overgrown with camomile, chrysanthemum and wild shrubs. The ruins of the town are visible at a considerable distance along the coast. The principal remains consist of a massive wall, flanked with pyramidal bastions at regular intervals, and with the traces of gateways, draw-bridges and towers. It was formerly surrounded by a deep moat. Within this space, which may be a quarter of a mile square, are a few fragments of buildings, and toward the sea, some high arches and masses of masonry. The plain around abounds with traces of houses, streets, and court-yards Cæsarea was one of the Roman colonies, but owed its prosperity principally to Herod. St. Paul passed through it on his way from Macedon to Jerusalem, by the very road we were travelling.

During the day the path struck inland over a vast rolling plain, covered with sage, lavender and other sweet-smelling shrubs, and tenanted by herds of gazelles and flocks of large storks. As we advanced further, the landscape became singularly beautiful. It was a broad, shallow valley, swelling away towards the east into low, rolling hills, far back of which rose the blue line of the mountains—the hill-country of Judea. The soil, where it was ploughed, was the richest vegetable loam. Where it lay fallow it was entirely hidden by a bed of grass and camomile. Here and there great herds of sheep and goats browsed on the herbage. There was a quiet pastoral air about the landscape, a soft serenity in its forms and colors, as if the Hebrew patriarchs still made it their abode. The district is famous for robbers, and we kept our arms in readiness, never suffering the baggage to be out of our sight.

Towards evening, as Mr. H. and myself, with François, were riding in advance of the baggage mules, the former with his gun in his hand, I with a pair of pistols thrust through the folds of my shawl, and François with his long Turkish sabre, we came suddenly upon a lonely Englishman, whose companions were somewhere in the rear. He appeared to be struck with terror on seeing us making towards him, and, turning his horse's head, made an attempt to fly. The animal, however, was restive, and, after a few plunges, refused to move. The traveller gave himself up for lost; his arms dropped by his side; he stared wildly at us, with pale face and eyes opened wide with a look of helpless fright. Restraining with difficulty a snout of laughter, I said to him : "Did you leave Jaffa to-day ?" but so completely was his ear the fool of his imagination, that he thought I was speaking Arabic, and made a faint attempt to get out the only word or two of that language which he knew. I then repeated, with as much distinctness as I could command : "Did—you—leave —Jaffa—to-day ?" He stammered mechanically, through his chattering teeth, "Y-y-yes !" and we immediately dashed off at a gallop through the bushes. When we last saw him, he was standing as we left him, apparently not yet recovered from the shock.

At the little village of El Haram, where we spent the night, I visited the tomb of Sultan Ali ebn-Aleym, who is now revered as a saint. It is enclosed in a mosque, crowning the top of a hill. I was admitted into the court-yard without hesitation, though, from the porter styling me "Effendi," he probably took me for a Turk. At the entrance to the inner court, I took off my slippers and walked to the tomb of the Sultan—a square heap of white marble, in a small marble enclosure. In one of the niches in the wall, near the tomb, there is a very old iron box, with a slit in the top. The porter informed me that it contained a charm, belonging to Sultan Ali, which was of great use in producing rain in times of drouth.

In the morning we sent our baggage by a short road across the country to this place, and then rode down the beach towards Jaffa. The sun came out bright and hot as we paced along the line of spray, our horses' feet sinking above the fetlocks in pink and purple shells, while the droll sea-crabs scampered away from our path, and the blue gelatinous sea-nettles were tossed before us by the surge. Our view was confined to the sand-hills—sometimes covered with a flood of scarlet poppies—on one hand; and to the blue, surf-fringed sea on the other. The terrible coast was still lined with wrecks, and just before reaching the town, we passed a vessel of some two hundred tons, recently cast ashore, with her strong hull still unbroken. We forded the rapid stream of El Anjeh, which comes down from the Plain of Sharon, the water rising to our saddles. The low promontory in front now broke into towers and white domes, and great masses of heavy walls. The aspect of Jaffa is exceedingly picturesque. It is built on a hill, and the land for many miles around it being low and flat, its topmost houses overlook all the fields of Sharon. The old harbor, protected by a reef of rocks, is on the north side of the town, but is now so sanded up that large vessels cannot enter. A number of small craft were lying close to the shore. The port presented a different scene when the ships of Hiram, King of Tyre, came in with the materials for the Temple of Solomon. There is but one gate on the land side, which is rather strongly fortified. Outside of this there is an open space, which we found filled with venders of oranges and vegetables, camel-men and the like, some vociferating in loud dispute, some given up to silence and smoke, under the shade of the sycamores.

We rode under the heavily arched and towered gateway, and entered the bazaar. The street was crowded, and there was such a confusion of camels, donkeys, and men, that we made our way with difficulty along the only practicable street in the city, to the sea-side, where François pointed out a hole in the wall as the veritable spot where Jonah was cast ashore by the whale. This part of the harbor is the receptacle of all the offal of the town; and I do not wonder that the whale's stomach should have turned on approaching it. The sea-street was filled with merchants and traders, and we were obliged to pick our way between bars of iron, skins of oil, heaps of oranges, and piles of building timber. At last we reached the end, and, as there was no other thoroughfare, returned the same way we went, passed out the gate, and took the road to Ramleh and Jerusalem.

But I hear the voice of François, announcing, "*Messieurs, le diner est prêt.*" We are encamped just beside the pool of Ramleh, and the mongrel children of the town are making a great noise in the meadow below it. Our horses are enjoying their barley; and Mustapha stands at the tent-door tying up his sacks. Dogs are barking and donkeys braying all along the borders of the town, whose filth and dilapidation are happily concealed by the fig and olive gardens which surround it. I have not curiosity enough to visit the Greek and Latin Convents embedded in its foul purlieus, but content myself with gazing from my door upon the blue hills of Palestine, which we must cross to-morrow, on our way to Jerusalem.

CHAPTER III.

FROM JAFFA TO JERUSALEM.

The Garden of Jaffa—Breakfast at a Fountain—The Plain of Sharon—The Ruined Mosque of Ramleh—A Judean Landscape—The Streets of Ramleh—Am I in Palestine?—A Heavenly Morning—The Land of Milk and Honey—Entering the Hill-Country—The Pilgrim's Breakfast—The Father of Lies—A Church of the Crusaders—The Agriculture of the Hills—The Valley of Elah—Day-Dreams—The Wilderness—The Approach—We see the Holy City.

——" Through the air sublime,
Over the wilderness and o'er the plain;
Till underneath them fair Jerusalem,
The Holy City, lifted high her towers."

PARADISE REGAINED.

JERUSALEM, *Thursday, April* 29, 1852.

LEAVING the gate of Jaffa, we rode eastward between delightful gardens of fig, citron, orange, pomegranate and palm. The country for several miles around the city is a complete level—part of the great plain of Sharon—and the gray mass of building crowning the little promontory, is the only landmark seen above the green garden-land, on looking towards the sea The road was lined with hedges of giant cactus, now in blossom, and shaded occasionally with broad-armed sycamores. The orange trees were in bloom, and at the same time laden down with ripe fruit. The oranges of Jaffa are the finest in Syria, and great numbers of them are sent to Beyrout and other ports further north. The dark foliage of the pomegranate fairly blazed with its heavy scarlet blossoms, and here and there a cluster of roses made good the Scriptural renown of those of Sharon. The road was filled with people, passing to and fro, and several families of Jaffa Jews were having a sort of pic-nic in the choice shady spots.

Ere long we came to a fountain, at a point where two roads met. It was a large square structure of limestone and marble, with a stone trough in front, and a delightful open chamber at the side. The space in front was shaded with immense sycamore trees, to which we tied our horses, and then took our seats in the window above the fountain, where the Greek brought us our breakfast. The water was cool and delicious, as were our Jaffa oranges. It was a charming spot, for as we sat we could look under the boughs of the great trees, and down between the gardens to Jaffa and the Mediterranean. After leaving the gardens, we came upon the great plain of Sharon, on which we could see the husbandmen at work far and near, ploughing and sowing their grain. In some instances, the two operations were made simultaneously, by having a sort of funnel attached to the plough-handle, running into a tube which entered the earth just behind the share. The man held the plough with one hand, while with the other he dropped the requisite quantity of seed through the tube into the furrow. The people are ploughing now for their summer crops, and the wheat and barley which they sowed last winter are already in full head. On other parts of the plain, there were large flocks of sheep and goats, with their attendant shepherds. So ran the rich landscape, broken only by belts of olive trees, to the far hills of Judea.

Riding on over the long, low swells, fragrant with wild thyme and camomile, we saw at last the tower of Ramleh, and down the valley, an hour's ride to the north-east, the minaret of Ludd, the ancient Lydda. Still further, I could see the houses of the village of Sharon, embowered in olives. Ramleh is built along the crest and on the eastern slope of a low hill, and at a distance appears like a stately place, but this impression is immediately dissipated on entering it. West of the town is a large square tower, between eighty and ninety feet in height. We rode up to it through an orchard of ancient olive trees, and over a field of beans. The tower is evidently a minaret, as it is built in the purest Saracenic style, and is surrounded by the ruins of a mosque. I have rarely seen anything more graceful than the ornamental arches of the upper portions. Over the door is a lintel of white marble, with an Arabic inscription. The mosque to which the tower is attached is almost entirely destroyed, and only part of the arches of a corridor around three sides of a court-yard, with the fountain in the centre, still remain. The subterranean cisterns, under the court-yard, amazed me with their extent and magnitude. They are no less than twenty-four feet deep, and covered by twenty-four vaulted ceilings, each twelve feet square, and resting on massive pillars. The mosque, when entire, must have been one of the finest in Syria.

We clambered over the broken stones cumbering the entrance, and mounted the steps to the very summit. The view reached from Jaffa and the sea to the mountains near Jerusalem, and southward to the plain of Ascalon—a great expanse of grain and grazing land, all blossoming as the rose, and dotted, especially near the mountains, with dark, luxuriant olive-groves.

The landscape had something of the green, pastoral beauty of England, except the mountains, which were wholly of Palestine. The shadows of fleecy clouds, drifting slowly from east to west, moved across the landscape, which became every moment softer and fairer in the light of the declining sun.

I did not tarry in Ramleh. The streets are narrow, crooked, and filthy as only an Oriental town can be. The houses have either flat roofs or domes, out of the crevices in which springs a plentiful crop of weeds. Some yellow dogs barked at us as we passed, children in tattered garments stared, and old turbaned heads were raised from the pipe, to guess who the two brown individuals might be, and why they were attended by such a fierce *cawass*. Passing through the eastern gate, we were gladdened by the sight of our tents, already pitched in the meadow beside the cistern. Dervish had arrived an hour before us, and had everything ready for the sweet lounge of an hour, to which we treat ourselves after a day's ride. I watched the evening fade away over the blue hills before us, and tried to convince myself that I should reach Jerusalem on the morrow. Reason said : " You certainly will !"—but to Faith the Holy City was as far off as ever. Was it possible that I was in Judea ? Was this the Holy Land of the Crusades, the soil hallowed by the feet of Christ and his Apostles ? I must believe it. Yet it seemed once that if I ever trod that earth, then beneath my feet, there would be thenceforth a consecration in my life, a holy essence, a purer inspiration on the lips, a surer faith in the heart. And because I was not other than I had been, I half doubted whether it was the Palestine of my dreams.

A number of Arab cameleers, who had come with travellers

across the Desert from Egypt, were encamped near us. François was suspicious of some of them, and therefore divided the night into three watches, which were kept by himself and our two men. Mustapha was the last, and kept not only himself, but myself, wide awake by his dolorous chants of love and religion. I fell sound asleep at dawn, but was roused before sunrise by François, who wished to start betimes, on account of the rugged road we had to travel. The morning was mild, clear, and balmy, and we were soon packed and in motion. Leaving the baggage to follow, we rode ahead over the fertile fields. The wheat and poppies were glistening with dew, birds sang among the fig-trees, a cool breeze came down from the hollows of the hills, and my blood leaped as nimbly and joyously as a young hart on the mountains of Bether.

Between Ramleh and the hill-country, a distance of about eight miles, is the rolling plain of Arimathea, and this, as well as the greater part of the plain of Sharon, is one of the richest districts in the world. The soil is a dark-brown loam, and, without manure, produces annually superb crops of wheat and barley. We rode for miles through a sea of wheat, waving far and wide over the swells of land. The tobacco in the fields about Ramleh was the most luxuriant I ever saw, and the olive and fig attain a size and lusty strength wholly unknown in Italy. Judea cursed of God! what a misconception, not only of God's mercy and beneficence, but of the actual fact! Give Palestine into Christian hands, and it will again flow with milk and honey. Except some parts of Asia Minor, no portion of the Levant is capable of yielding such a harvest of grain, silk, wool, fruits, oil, and wine. The great disadvantage under which the country labors, is its frequent drouths, but were the soil more generally cultivated, and the old orchards replanted, these would neither be so frequent nor so severe.

We gradually ascended the hills, passing one or two villages, imbedded in groves of olives. In the little valleys, slanting down to the plains, the Arabs were still ploughing and sowing, singing the while an old love-song, with its chorus of "*ya, ghazalee! ya, ghazalee!*" (oh, gazelle! oh, gazelle!) The valley narrowed, the lowlands behind us spread out broader, and in half an hour more we were threading a narrow pass, between stony hills, overgrown with ilex, myrtle, and dwarf oak. The wild purple rose of Palestine blossomed on all sides, and a fragrant white honeysuckle in some places hung from the rocks. The path was terribly rough, and barely wide enough for two persons on horseback to pass each other. We met a few pilgrims returning from Jerusalem, and a straggling company of armed Turks, who had such a piratical air, that without the solemn asseveration of François that the road was quite safe, I should have felt uneasy about our baggage. Most of the persons we passed were Mussulmen, few of whom gave the customary "Peace be with you!" but once a Syrian Christian saluted me with, "God go with you, O Pilgrim!" For two hours after entering the mountains, there was scarcely a sign of cultivation. The rock was limestone, or marble, lying in horizontal strata, the broken edges of which rose like terraces to the summits. These shelves were so covered with wild shrubs—in some places even with rows of olive trees—that to me they had not the least appearance of that desolation so generally ascribed to them.

In a little dell among the hills there is a small ruined mosque, or chapel (I could not decide which), shaded by a group of magnificent terebinth trees. Several Arabs were resting in its shade, and we hoped to find there the water we were looking for, in order to make breakfast. But it was not to be found, and we climbed nearly to the summit of the first chain of hills, where in a small olive orchard, there was a cistern, filled by the late rains. It belonged to two ragged boys, who brought us an earthen vessel of the water, and then asked, "Shall we bring you milk, O Pilgrims!" I assented, and received a small jug of thick buttermilk, not remarkably clean, but very refreshing. My companion, who had not recovered from his horror at finding that the inhabitants of Ramleh washed themselves in the pool which supplied us and them, refused to touch it. We made but a short rest, for it was now nearly noon, and there were yet many rough miles between us and Jerusalem. We crossed the first chain of mountains, rode a short distance over a stony upland, and then descended into a long cultivated valley, running to the eastward. At the end nearest us appeared the village of Aboo 'l Ghosh (the Father of Lies), which takes its name from a noted Bedouin shekh, who distinguished himself a few years ago by levying contributions on travellers. He obtained a large sum of money in this way, but as he added murder to robbery, and fell upon Turks as well as Christians, he was finally captured, and is now expiating his offences in some mine on the coast of the Black Sea.

Near the bottom of the village there is a large ruined building, now used as a stable by the inhabitants. The interior is divided into a nave and two side-aisles by rows of square pillars, from which spring pointed arches. The door-way is at the side, and is Gothic, with a dash of Saracenic in the ornamental mouldings above it. The large window at the extremity of the nave is remarkable for having round arches, which circumstance, together with the traces of arabesque painted ornaments on the columns, led me to think it might have been a mosque; but Dr. Robinson, who is now here, considers it a Christian church, of the time of the Crusaders. The village of Aboo 'l Ghosh is said to be the site of the birth-place of the Prophet Jeremiah, and I can well imagine it to have been the case. The aspect of the mountain-country to the east and north-east would explain the savage dreariness of his lamentations. The whole valley in which the village stands, as well as another which joins it on the east, is most assiduously cultivated. The stony mountain sides are wrought into terraces, where, in spite of soil which resembles an American turnpike, patches of wheat are growing luxuriantly, and olive trees, centuries old, hold on to the rocks with a clutch as hard and bony as the hand of Death. In the bed of the valley the fig tree thrives, and sometimes the vine and fig grow together, forming the patriarchal arbor of shade familiar to us all. The shoots of the tree are still young and green, but the blossoms of the grape do not yet give forth their goodly savor. I did not hear the voice of the turtle, but a nightingale sang in the briery thickets by the brook side, as we passed along.

Climbing out of this valley, we descended by a stony staircase, as rugged as the Ladder of Tyre, into the Wady Beit-Hanineh. Here were gardens of oranges in blossom, with orchards of quince and apple, overgrown with vines, and the fragrant hawthorn tree, snowy with its bloom. A stone bridge, the only one on the road, crosses the dry bed of a winter stream, and, looking up the glen, I saw the Arab village of Kulonieh, at the entrance of the valley of Elah, glorious with the memories of the shepherd-boy, David. Our road turned off to the right, and commenced ascending a long, dry glen between mountains which grew more sterile the further we went. It was nearly two hours past noon, the sun fiercely hot, and our horses were nigh jaded out with the rough road and our impatient spurring. I began to fancy we could see Jerusalem from the top of the pass, and tried to think of the ancient days of Judea. But it was in vain. A newer picture shut them out, and banished even the diviner images of Our Saviour and His Disciples. Heathen that I was, I could only think of Godfrey and the Crusaders, toiling up the same path, and the ringing lines of Tasso vibrated constantly in my ear:

'Ecco apparir Gierusalemm' si vede ;
Ecco additar Gierusalemm' si scorge ;
Ecco da mille voci unitamente,
Gierusalemme salutar si sente !"

The Palestine of the Bible—the Land of Promise to the Israelites, the land of Miracle and Sacrifice to the Apostles and their followers—still slept in the unattainable distance, under a sky of bluer and more tranquil loveliness than that to whose cloudless vault I looked up. It lay as far and beautiful as it once seemed to the eye of childhood, and the swords of Seraphim kept profane feet from its sacred hills. But these rough rocks around me, these dry, fiery hollows, these thickets of ancient oak and ilex, had heard the trumpets of the Middle

Ages, and the clang and clatter of European armor--I could feel and believe that. I entered the ranks ; I followed the trumpets and the holy hymns, and waited breathlessly for the moment when every mailed knee should drop in the dust, and every bearded and sunburned cheek be wet with devotional tears.

But when I climbed the last ridge, and looked ahead with a sort of painful suspense, Jerusalem did not appear. We were two thousand feet above the Mediterranean, whose blue we could dimly see far to the west, through notches in the chain of hills. To the north, the mountains were gray, desolate, and awful. Not a shrub or a tree relieved their frightful barrenness. An upland tract, covered with white volcanic rock, lay before us. We met peasants with asses, who looked (to my eyes) as if they had just left Jerusalem. Still forward we urged our horses, and reached a ruined garden, surrounded with hedges of cactus, over which I saw domes and walls in the distance. I drew a long breath and looked at François. He was jogging along without turning his head ; he could not have been so indifferent if that was really the city. Presently, we reached another slight rise in the rocky plain. He began to urge his panting horse, and at the same instant we both lashed the spirit into ours, dashed on at a break-neck gallop, round the corner of an old wall on the top of the hill, and lo ! the Holy City ! Our Greek jerked both pistols from his holsters, and fired them into the air, as we reined up on the steep.

From the descriptions of travellers, I had expected to see in Jerusalem an ordinary modern Turkish town ; but that before me, with its walls, fortresses, and domes, was it not still the

City of David ? I saw the Jerusalem of the New Testament, as I had imagined it. Long lines of walls crowned with a notched parapet and strengthened by towers; a few domes and spires above them; clusters of cypress here and there; this was all that was visible of the city. On either side the hill sloped down to the two deep valleys over which it hangs. On the east, the Mount of Olives, crowned with a chapel and mosque, rose high and steep, but in front, the eye passed directly over the city, to rest far away upon the lofty mountains of Moab, beyond the Dead Sea. The scene was grand in its simplicity. The prominent colors were the purple of those distant mountains, and the hoary gray of the nearer hills. The walls were of the dull yellow of weather-stained marble, and the only trees, the dark cypress and moonlit olive. Now, indeed, for one brief moment, I knew that I was in Palestine ; that I saw Mount Olivet and Mount Zion; and—I know not how it was—my sight grew weak, and all objects trembled and wavered in a watery film. Since we arrived, I have looked down upon the city from the Mount of Olives, and up to it from the Valley of Jehosaphat; but I cannot restore the illusion of that first view.

We allowed our horses to walk slowly down the remaining half-mile to the Jaffa gate. An Englishman, with a red silk shawl over his head, was sketching the city, while an Arab held an umbrella over him. Inside the gate we stumbled upon an Italian shop with an Italian sign, and after threading a number of intricate passages under dark archways, and being turned off from one hotel, which was full of travellers, reached another, kept by a converted German Jew, where we found Dr. Robinson and Dr. Ely Smith, who both arrived yesterday. It sounds strange to talk of a hotel in Jerusalem, but the world is progressing, and there are already three. I leave to-morrow for Jericho, the Jordan, and the Dead Sea, and shall have more to say of Jerusalem on my return.

CHAPTER IV.

THE DEAD SEA AND THE RIVER JORDAN.

Bargaining for a Guard—Departure from Jerusalem—The Hill of Offence—Bethany—The Grotto of Lazarus—The Valley of Fire—Scenery of the Wilderness—The Hills of Engaddi—The shore of the Dead Sea—A Bituminous Bath—Gallop to the Jordan—A watch for Robbers—The Jordan—Baptism—The Plains of Jericho—The Fountain of Elisha—The Mount of Temptation—Return to Jerusalem.

"And the spoiler shall come upon every city, and no city shall escape; the valley also shall perish and the plain shall be destroyed, as the Lord hath spoken."—JEREMIAH, xlviii. 8.

JERUSALEM, *May* 1, 1852.

I RETURNED this afternoon from an excursion to the Dead Sea, the River Jordan, and the site of Jericho. Owing to the approaching heats, an early visit was deemed desirable, and the shekhs, who have charge of the road, were summoned to meet us on the day after we arrived. There are two of these gentlemen, the Shekh el-Aràb (of the Bedouins), and the Shekh el-Fellaheen (of the peasants, or husbandmen), to whom each traveller is obliged to pay one hundered piastres for an escort. It is, in fact, a sort of compromise, by which the shekhs agree not to rob the traveller, and to protect him against other shekhs. If the road is not actually safe, the Turkish garrison here is a mere farce, but the arrangement is winked at by the Pasha, who, of course, gets his share of the

100,000 piastres which the two scamps yearly levy upon travellers. The shekhs came to our rooms, and after trying to postpone our departure, in order to attach other tourists to the same escort, and thus save a little expense, took half the pay and agreed to be ready the next morning. Unfortunately for my original plan, the Convent of San Saba has been closed within two or three weeks, and no stranger is now admitted. This unusual step was caused by the disorderly conduct of some Frenchmen who visited San Saba. We sent to the Bishop of the Greek Church, asking a simple permission to view the interior of the Convent; but without effect.

We left the city yesterday morning by St. Stephen's Gate, descended to the Valley of Jehosaphat, rode under the stone wall which encloses the supposed Gethsemane, and took a path leading along the Mount of Olives, towards the Hill of Offence, which stands over against the southern end of the city, opposite the mouth of the Vale of Hinnon. Neither of the shekhs made his appearance, but sent in their stead three Arabs, two of whom were mounted and armed with sabres and long guns. Our man, Mustapha, had charge of the baggage-mule, carrying our tent and the provisions for the trip. It was a dull, sultry morning; a dark, leaden haze hung over Jerusalem, and the *khamseen*, or sirocco-wind, came from the south-west, out of the Arabian Desert. We had again resumed the Oriental costume, but in spite of an ample turban, my face soon began to scorch in the dry heat. From the crest of the Hill of Offence there is a wide view over the heights on both sides of the valley of the Brook Kedron. Their sides are worked into terraces, now green with springing grain, and near the bottom planted with olive and fig trees. The upland ridge or watershed of Palestine is cultivated for a considerable distance around Jerusalem. The soil is light and stony, yet appears to yield a good return for the little labor bestowed upon it.

Crossing the southern flank of Mount Olivet, in half an hour we reached the village of Bethany, hanging on the side of the hill. It is a miserable cluster of Arab huts, with not a building which appears to be more than a century old. The Grotto of Lazarus is here shown, and, of course, we stopped to see it. It belongs to an old Mussulman, who came out of his house with a piece of waxed rope, to light us down. An aperture opens from the roadside into the hill, and there is barely room enough for a person to enter. Descending about twenty steps at a sharp angle, we landed in a small, damp vault, with an opening in the floor, communicating with a short passage below. The vault was undoubtedly excavated for sepulchral purposes, and the bodies were probably deposited (as in many Egyptian tombs) in the pit under it. Our guide, however, pointed to a square mass of masonry in one corner as the tomb of Lazarus, whose body, he informed us, was still walled up there. There was an arch in the side of the vault, once leading to other chambers, but now closed up, and the guide stated that seventy-four Prophets were interred therein. There seems to be no doubt that the present Arab village occupies the site of Bethany; and if it could be proved that this pit existed at the beginning of the Christian Era, and there never had been any other, we might accept it as the tomb of Lazarus. On the crest of a high hill, over against Bethany, is an Arab village on the site of Bethpage.

We descended into the valley of a winter stream, now filled

with patches of sparse wheat, just beginning to ripen. The mountains grew more bleak and desolate as we advanced, and as there is a regular descent in the several ranges over which one must pass, the distant hills of the lands of Moab and Ammon were always in sight, rising like a high, blue wall against the sky. The Dead Sea is 4,000 feet below Jerusalem, but the general slope of the intervening district is so regular that from the spires of the city, and the Mount of Olives, one can look down directly upon its waters. This deceived me as to the actual distance, and I could scarcely credit the assertion of our Arab escort, that it would require six hours to reach it. After we had ridden nearly two hours, we left the Jericho road, sending Mustapha and a staunch old Arab direct to our resting-place for the night, in the Valley of the Jordan. The two mounted Bedouins accompanied us across the rugged mountains lying between us and the Dead Sea.

At first, we took the way to the Convent of Mar Saba, following the course of the Brook Kedron down the Wady en-Nar (Valley of Fire). In half an hour more we reached two large tanks, hewn out under the base of a limestone cliff, and nearly filled with rain. The surface was covered with a greenish vegetable scum, and three wild and dirty Arabs of the hills were washing themselves in the principal one Our Bedouins immediately dismounted and followed their example, and after we had taken some refreshment, we had the satisfaction of filling our water-jug from the same sweet pool. After this, we left the San Saba road, and mounted the height east of the valley. From that point, all signs of cultivation and habitation disappeared. The mountains were grim, bare, and frightfully rugged. The scanty grass, coaxed into life by the winter rains, was already scorched out of all greenness; some bunches of wild sage, gnaphalium, and other hardy aromatic herbs spotted the yellow soil, and in sheltered places the scarlet poppies burned like coals of fire among the rifts of the gray limestone rock. Our track kept along the higher ridges and crests of the hills, between the glens and gorges which sank on either hand to a dizzy depth below, and were so steep as to be almost inaccessible. The region is so scarred, gashed and torn, that no work of man's hand can save it from perpetual desolation. It is a wilderness more hopeless than the Desert. If I were left alone in the midst of it, I should lie down and await death, without thought or hope of rescue.

The character of the day was peculiarly suited to enhance the impression of such scenery. Though there were no clouds, the sun was invisible: as far as we could see, beyond the Jordan, and away southward to the mountains of Moab and the cliffs of Engaddi, the whole country was covered as with the smoke of a furnace; and the furious sirocco, that threatened to topple us down the gulfs yawning on either hand, had no coolness on its wings. The horses were sure-footed, but now and then a gust would come that made them and us strain against it, to avoid being dashed against the rock on one side, or hurled off the brink on the other. The atmosphere was painfully oppressive, and by and by a dogged silence took possession of our party. After passing a lofty peak which François called Djebel Nuttar, the Mountain of Rain, we came to a large Moslem building, situated on a bleak eminence, overlooking part of the valley of the Jordan. This is the tomb called Nebbee Moussa by the Arabs, and believed by them to stand upon the spot where Moses died. We halted at the gate, but no one came to admit us, though my companion thought he saw a man's head at one of the apertures in the wall. Arab tradition here is as much at fault as Christian tradition in many other places. The true Nebo is somewhere in the chain of Pisgah; and though, probably, I saw it, and all see it who go down to the Jordan, yet "no man knoweth its place unto this day."

Beyond Nebbee Moussa, we came out upon the last heights overlooking the Dead Sea, though several miles of low hills remained to be passed. The head of the sea was visible as far as the Ras-el-Feshka on the west, and the hot fountains of Callirhoë on the eastern shore. Farther than this, all was vapor and darkness. The water was a soft, deep purple hue, brightening into blue. Our road led down what seemed a vast sloping causeway from the mountains, between two ravines, walled by cliffs several hundred feet in height. It gradually flattened into a plain, covered with a white, saline incrustation, and grown with clumps of sour willow, tamarisk, and other shrubs, among which I looked in vain for the osher, or Dead Sea apple. The plants appeared as if smitten with leprosy; but there were some flowers growing almost to the margin of the sea. We reached the shore about 2 P. M. The heat by this time was most severe, and the air so dense as to occasion pains in my ears. The Dead Sea is 1,300 feet below the Mediterranean, and without doubt the lowest part of the earth's surface. I attribute the oppression I felt to this fact and to the sultriness of the day, rather than to any exhalation from the sea itself. François remarked, however, that had the wind—which by this time was veering round to the north-east—blown from the south, we could scarcely have endured it. The sea resembles a great cauldron, sunk between mountains from three to four thousand feet in height; and probably we did not experience more than a tithe of the summer heat.

I proposed a bath, for the sake of experiment, but François endeavored to dissuade us. He had tried it, and nothing could be more disagreeable; we risked getting a fever, and, besides, there were four hours of dangerous travel yet before us. But by this time we were half undressed, and soon were floating on the clear bituminous waves. The beach was fine gravel and shelved gradually down. I kept my turban on my head, and was careful to avoid touching the water with my face. The sea was moderately warm and gratefully soft and soothing to the skin. It was impossible to sink; and even while swimming, the body rose half out of the water. I should think it possible to dive for a short distance, but prefer that some one else would try the experiment. With a log of wood for a pillow, one might sleep as on one of the patent mattresses. The taste of the water is salty and pungent, and stings the tongue like saltpetre. We were obliged to dress in all haste, without even wiping off the detestable liquid; yet I experienced very little of that discomfort which most travellers have remarked. Where the skin had been previously bruised, there was a slight smarting sensation, and my body felt clammy and glutinous, but the bath was rather refreshing than otherwise.

We turned our horses' heads towards the Jordan, and rode on over a dry, barren plain. The two Bedouins at first dashed ahead at 'ull gallop, uttering cries, and whirling their long guns in the air. The dust they raised was blown in our faces, and contained so much salt that my eyes began to smart painfully. Thereupon I followed them at an equal rate of speed, and we left a long cloud of the accursed soil whirling behind us. Presently, however, they fell to the rear, and continued to keep at some distance from us. The reason of this was soon explained. The path turned eastward, and we already saw a line of dusky green winding through the wilderness. This was the Jordan, and the mountains beyond, the home of robber Arabs, were close at hand. Those robbers frequently cross the river and conceal themselves behind the sand-hills on this side. Our brave escort was, therefore, inclined to put us forward as a forlorn-hope, and secure their own retreat in case of an attack. But as we were all well armed, and had never considered their attendance as anything more than a genteel way of buying them off from robbing us, we allowed them to lag as much as they chose. Finally, as we approached the Pilgrims' Ford, one of them took his station at some distance from the river, on the top of a mound, while the other got behind some trees near at hand ; in order, as they said, to watch the opposite hills, and alarm us whenever they should see any of the Beni Sukrs, or the Beni Adwams, or the Tyakh, coming down upon us.

The Jordan at this point will not average more than ten yards in breadth. It flows at the bottom of a gully about fifteen feet deep, which traverses the broad valley in a most tortuous course. The water has a white, clayey hue, and is very swift. The changes of the current have formed islands and beds of soil here and there, which are covered with a dense growth of ash, poplar, willow, and tamarisk trees. The banks of the river are bordered with thickets, now overgrown with wild vines, and fragrant with flowering plants. Birds sing continually in the cool, dark coverts of the trees. I found a singular charm in the wild, lonely, luxuriant banks, the tangled undergrowth, and the rapid, brawling course of the sacred stream, as it slipped in sight and out of sight among the trees. It is almost impossible to reach the water at any other point than the Ford of the Pilgrims, the supposed locality of the passage of the Israelites and the baptism of Christ. The plain near it is still blackened by the camp-fires of the ten thousand pilgrims who went down from Jerusalem three weeks ago, to bathe. We tied our horses to the trees, and prepared to follow their example, which was necessary, if only to wash off the iniquitous slime of the Dead Sea. François, in the meantime, filled two tin flasks from the stream and stowed them in the saddle-bags. The current was so swift, that one could not venture far without the risk of being carried away; but I succeeded in obtaining a complete and most refreshing immersion. The taint of Gomorrah was not entirely washed away, but I rode off with as great a sense of relief as if the baptism had been a moral one, as well, and had purified me from sin.

We rode for nearly two hours, in a north-west direction, to the Bedouin village of Rihah, near the site of ancient Jericho. Before reaching it, the gray salt waste vanishes, and the soil is covered with grass and herbs. The barren character of the first region is evidently owing to deposits from the vapors of the Dea Sea, as they are blown over the plain by the south wind. The channels of streams around Jericho are filled with nebbuk trees, the fruit of which is just ripening. It is apparently indigenous, and grows more luxuriantly than on the

White Nile. It is a variety of the *rhamnus*, and is set down by botanists as the Spina Christi, of which the Saviour's mock crown of thorns was made. I see no reason to doubt this, as the twigs are long and pliant, and armed with small, though most cruel, thorns. I had to pay for gathering some of the fruit, with a torn dress and bleeding fingers. The little apples which it bears are slightly acid and excellent for alleviating thirst. I also noticed on the plain a variety of the night-shade, with large berries of a golden color. The spring flowers, so plentiful now in all other parts of Palestine, have already disappeared from the Valley of the Jordan.

Rihah is a vile little village of tents and mud-huts, and the only relic of antiquity near it is a square tower, which may possibly be of the time of Herod. There are a few gardens in the place, and a grove of superb fig-trees. We found our tent already pitched beside a rill which issues from the Fountain of Elisha. The evening was very sultry, and the musquitoes gave us no rest. We purchased some milk from an old man who came to the tent, but such was his mistrust of us that he refused to let us keep the earthen vessel containing it until morning. As we had already paid the money to his son, we would not let him take the milk away until he had brought the money back. He then took a dagger from his waist and threw it before us as security, while he carried off the vessel and returned the price. I have frequently seen the same mistrustful spirit exhibited in Egypt. Our two Bedouins, to whom I gave some tobacco in the evening, manifested their gratitude by stealing the remainder of our stock during the night.

This morning we followed the stream to its source, the

Fountain of Elisha, so called as being probably that healed by the Prophet. If so, the healing was scarcely complete. The water, which gushes up strong and free at the foot of a rocky mound, is warm and slightly brackish. It spreads into a shallow pool, shaded by a fine sycamore tree. Just below, there are some remains of old walls on both sides, and the stream goes roaring away through a rank jungle of canes fifteen feet in height. The precise site of Jericho, I believe, has not been fixed, but "the city of the palm trees," as it was called, was probably on the plain, near some mounds which rise behind the Fountain. Here there are occasional traces of foundation walls, but so ruined as to give no clue to the date of their erection. Further towards the mountain there are some arches, which appear to be Saracenic. As we ascended again into the hill-country, I observed several traces of cisterns in the bottoms of ravines, which collect the rains. Herod, as is well known, built many such cisterns near Jericho, where he had a palace. On the first crest, to which we climbed, there is part of a Roman tower yet standing. The view, looking back over the valley of Jordan, is magnificent, extending from the Dead Sea to the mountains of Gilead, beyond the country of Ammon. I thought I could trace the point where the River Yabbok comes down from Mizpeh of Gilead to join the Jordan.

The wilderness we now entered was fully as barren, but less rugged than that through which we passed yesterday. The path ascended along the brink of a deep gorge, at the bottom of which a little stream foamed over the rocks. The high, bleak summits towards which we were climbing, are considered by some Biblical geographers to be Mount Quarantana, the scene of Christ's fasting and temptation. After two hours we reached the ruins of a large khan or hostlery, under one of the peaks, which François stated to be the veritable "high mountain" whence the Devil pointed out all the kingdoms of the earth. There is a cave in the rock beside the road, which the superstitious look upon as the orifice out of which his Satanic Majesty issued. We met large numbers of Arab families, with their flocks, descending from the mountains to take up their summer residence near the Jordan. They were all on foot, except the young children and goats, which were stowed together on the backs of donkeys. The men were armed, and appeared to be of the same tribe as our escort, with whom they had a good understanding.

The morning was cold and cloudy, and we hurried on over the hills to a fountain in the valley of the Brook Kedron, where we breakfasted. Before we had reached Bethany a rain came down, and the sky hung dark and lowering over Jerusalem, as we passed the crest of Mount Olivet. It still rains, and the filthy condition of the city exceeds anything I have seen, even in the Orient.

CHAPTER V.

THE CITY OF CHRIST.

Modern Jerusalem—The Site of the City—Mount Zion—Mount Moriah—The Temple—The Valley of Jehosaphat—The Olives of Gethsemane—The Mount of Olives—Moslem Tradition—Panorama from the Summit—The Interior of the City—The Population—Missions and Missionaries—Christianity in Jerusalem—Intolerance—The Jews of Jerusalem—The Face of Christ—The Church of the Holy Sepulchre—The Holy of Holies—The Sacred Localities—Visions of Christ—The Mosque of Omar—The Holy Man of Timbuctoo—Preparations for Departure.

"Cut off thy hair, O Jerusalem, and cast it away, and take up a lamentation in high places; for the Lord hath rejected and forsaken the generation of his wrath."—JEREMIAH vii. 29.

"Here pilgrims roam, that strayed so far to seek
In Golgotha him dead, who lives in Heaven."
MILTON.

JERUSALEM, *Monday, May* 3, 1852.

SINCE travel is becoming a necessary part of education, and a journey through the East is no longer attended with personal risk, Jerusalem will soon be as familiar a station on the grand tour as Paris or Naples. The task of describing it is already next to superfluous, so thoroughly has the topography of the city been laid down by the surveys of Robinson and the drawings of Roberts. There is little more left for Biblical research. The few places which can be authenticated are now generally accepted, and the many doubtful ones must always be the subjects of speculation and conjecture. There is no new light which can remove the cloud of uncertainties wherein one continually wanders. Yet, even rejecting all these with the most skeptical spirit, there still remains enough to make the place sacred in the eyes of every follower of Christ. The city stands on the ancient site ; the Mount of Olives looks down upon it ; the foundations of the Temple of Solomon are on Mount Moriah ; the Pool of Siloam has still a cup of water for those who at noontide go down to the Valley of Jehosaphat ; the ancient gate yet looketh towards Damascus, and of the Palace of Herod, there is a tower which Time and Turk and Crusader have spared.

Jerusalem is built on the summit ridge of the hill-country of Palestine, just where it begins to slope eastward. Not half a mile from the Jaffa Gate, the waters run towards the Mediterranean. It is about 2,700 feet above the latter, and 4,000 feet above the Dead Sea, to which the descent is much more abrupt. The hill, or rather group of small mounts, on which Jerusalem stands, slants eastward to the brink of the Valley of Jehosaphat, and the Mount of Olives rises opposite, from the sides and summit of which, one sees the entire city spread out like a map before him. The Valley of Hinnon, the bed of which is on a much higher level than that of Jehosaphat, skirts the south-western and southern part of the walls, and drops into the latter valley at the foot of Mount Zion, the most southern of the mounts. The steep slope at the junction of the two valleys is the site of the city of the Jebusites, the most ancient part of Jerusalem. It is now covered with garden-terraces, the present wall crossing from Mount Zion on the south to Mount Moriah on the east. A little glen, anciently called the Tyropeon, divides the mounts, and winds through to the Damascus Gate, on the north, though from the height of the walls and the position of the city, the depression which it causes in the mass of buildings is not very perceptible, except from the latter point. Moriah is the lowest of the mounts, and hangs directly over the Valley of Jehosaphat. Its summit was built up by Solomon so as to form a quadrangular terrace, five hundred by three hundred yards in dimension. The lower courses of the grand wall, composed of huge blocks of gray conglomerate limestone, still remain, and there seems to be no doubt that they are of the time of Solomon. Some of the stones are of enormous size ; I noticed several which were fifteen, and one twenty-two feet in length. The upper part of the wall was restored by Sultan Selim, the conqueror of Egypt, and the level of the terrace now supports the great Mosque of Omar, which stands on the very site of the temple. Except these foundation walls, the Damascus Gate and the Tower of Hippicus, there is nothing left of the ancient city. The length of the present wall of circumference is about two miles, but the circuit of Jerusalem, in the time of Herod, was probably double that distance.

The best views of the city are from the Mount of Olives, and the hill north of it, whence Titus directed the siege which resulted in its total destruction. The Crusaders under Godfrey of Bouillon encamped on the same hill. My first walk after reaching here, was to the summit of the Mount of Olives. Not far from the hotel we came upon the Via Dolorosa, up which, according to Catholic tradition, Christ toiled with the cross upon his shoulders. I found it utterly impossible to imagine that I was walking in the same path, and preferred doubting the tradition. An arch is built across the street at the spot where they say he was shown to the populace. (*Ecce Homo.*) The passage is steep and rough, descending to St. Stephen's Gate by the Governor's Palace, which stands on the site of the house of Pontius Pilate. Here, in the wall forming the northern part of the foundation of the temple, there are some very fine remains of ancient workmanship. From the city wall, the ground descends abruptly to the Valley of Jehosaphat. The Turkish residents have their tombs on the city side, just under the terrace of the mosque, while thousands of Jews find a peculiar beatitude in having themselves interred on the opposite slope of the Mount of Olives, which is in some places quite covered with their crumbling tombstones. The bed of the Brook Kedron is now dry and stony. A sort of chapel, built in the bottom of the valley, is supposed by the Greeks to cover the tomb of the Virgin—a claim which the Latins consider absurd. Near this, at the very foot of the Mount of Olives, the latter sect have lately built a high stone wall around the Garden of Gethsemane, for the purpose, apparently, of protecting the five aged olives. I am ignorant of the grounds wherefore Gethsemane is placed here. Most travellers have given their faith to the spot, but Dr. Robinson, who is more reliable than any amount of mere tradition, does not coincide with them. The trees do not appear as ancient as some of those at the foot of Mount Carmel, which are supposed to date from the Roman colony established by Titus. Moreover, it is well known that at the time of the taking of Jerusalem by that Emperor, all the trees, for many miles around, were destroyed. The olive-trees, therefore, cannot be those under which Christ rested, even supposing this to be the true site of Gethsemane.

The Mount of Olives is a steep and rugged hill, dominating over the city and the surrounding heights. It is still covered with olive orchards, and planted with patches of grain, which do not thrive well on the stony soil. On the summit is a mosque, with a minaret attached, which affords a grand panoramic view. As we reached it, the Chief of the College of Dervishes, in the court of the Mosque of Omar, came out with a number of attendants. He saluted us courteously, which would not have been the case had he been the Superior of the Latin Convent, and we Greek Monks. There were some Turkish ladies in the interior of the mosque, so that we could not gain admittance, and therefore did not see the rock containing the foot-prints of Christ, who, according to Moslem tradition, ascended to heaven from this spot. The Mohammedans, it may not be generally known, accept the history of Christ, except his crucifixion, believing that he passed to heaven without death, another person being crucified in his stead. They call him the *Roh-Allah*, or Spirit of God, and consider him, after Mahomet, as the holiest of the Prophets.

We ascended to the gallery of the minaret. The city lay opposite, so fairly spread out to our view that almost every house might be separately distinguished. It is a mass of gray buildings, with dome-roofs, and but for the mosques of Omar and El Aksa, with the courts and galleries around them, would be exceedingly tame in appearance. The only other prominent points are the towers of the Holy Sepulchre, the citadel, enclosing Herod's Tower, and the mosque on mount Zion. The

Turkish wall, with its sharp angles, its square bastions, and the long, embrasured lines of its parapet, is the most striking feature of the view. Stony hills stretch away from the city on all sides, at present cheered with tracts of springing wheat, but later in the season, brown and desolate. In the south, the convent of St. Elias is visible, and part of the little town of Bethlehem. I passed to the eastern side of the gallery, and looking thence, deep down among the sterile mountains, beheld a long sheet of blue water, its southern extremity vanishing in a hot, sulphury haze. The mountains of Ammon and Moab, which formed the back-ground of my first view of Jerusalem, leaned like a vast wall against the sky, beyond the mysterious sea and the broad valley of the Jordan. The great depression of this valley below the level of the Mediterranean gives it a most remarkable character. It appears even deeper than is actually the case, and resembles an enormous chasm or moat, separating two different regions of the earth. The *khamseen* was blowing from the south, from out the deserts of Edom, and threw its veil of fiery vapor over the landscape. The muezzin pointed out to me the location of Jericho, of Kerak in Moab, and Es-Salt in the country of Ammon. Ere long the shadow of the minaret denoted noon, and, placing his hands on both sides of his mouth, he cried out, first on the South side, towards Mecca, and then to the West, and North, and East: "God is great: there is no God but God, and Mohammed is His Prophet! Let us prostrate ourselves before Him: and to Him alone be the glory!"

Jerusalem, internally, gives no impression but that of filth, ruin, poverty, and degradation. There are two or three streets in the western or higher portion of the city which are tolerably clean, but all the others, to the very gates of the Holy Sepulchre, are channels of pestilence. The Jewish Quarter, which is the largest, so sickened and disgusted me, that I should rather go the whole round of the city walls than pass through it a second time. The bazaars are poor, compared with those of other Oriental cities of the same size, and the principal trade seems to be in rosaries, both Turkish and Christian, crosses, seals, amulets, and pieces of the Holy Sepulchre. The population, which may possibly reach 20,000, is apparently Jewish, for the most part; at least, I have been principally struck with the Hebrew face, in my walks. The number of Jews has increased considerably within a few years, and there is also quite a number who, having been converted to Protestantism, were brought hither at the expense of English missionary societies for the purpose of forming a Protestant community. Two of the hotels are kept by families of this class. It is estimated that each member of the community has cost the Mission about £4,500: a sum which would have Christianized tenfold the number of English heathen. The Mission, however, is kept up by its patrons, as a sort of religious luxury. The English have lately built a very handsome church within the walls, and the Rev. Dr. Gobat, well known by his missionary labors in Abyssinia, now has the title of Bishop of Jerusalem. A friend of his in Central Africa gave me a letter of introduction for him, and I am quite disappointed in finding him absent. Dr. Barclay, of Virginia, a most worthy man in every respect, is at the head of the American Mission here. There is, besides, what is called the "American Colony," at the village of Artos, near Bethlehem: a little community of religious enthusiasts, whose experiments in cultivation have met with remarkable success, and are much spoken of at present.

Whatever good the various missions here may, in time, accomplish (at present, it does not amount to much), Jerusalem is the last place in the world where an intelligent heathen would be converted to Christianity. Were I cast here, ignorant of any religion, and were I to compare the lives and practices of the different sects as the means of making my choice—in short, to judge of each faith by the conduct of its professors—I should at once turn Mussulman. When you consider that in the Holy Sepulchre there are *nineteen* chapels, each belonging to a different sect, calling itself Christian, and that a Turkish police is always stationed there to prevent the bloody quarrels which often ensue between them, you may judge how those who call themselves followers of the Prince of Peace practice the pure faith he sought to establish. Between the Greek and Latin churches, especially, there is a deadly feud, and their contentions are a scandal, not only to the few Christians here, but to the Moslems themselves. I believe there is a sort of truce at present, owing to the settlement of some of the disputes—as, for instance, the restoration of the silver star, which the Greeks stole from the shrine of the Nativity, at Bethlehem. The Latins, however, not long since, demolished, *vi et armis*, a chapel which the Greeks commenced building on Mount Zion. But, if the employment of material weapons has been abandoned for the time, there is none the less a war of words and of sounds still going on. Go into the Holy Sepulchre, when mass is being celebrated, and you can scarcely endure the din. No sooner does the Greek choir begin its shrill chant, than the Latins fly to the assault.

They have an organ, and terribly does that organ strain its bellows and labor its pipes to drown the rival singing. You think the Latins will carry the day, when suddenly the cymbals of the Abyssinians strike in with harsh brazen clang, and, for the moment, triumph. Then there are Copts, and Maronites, and Armenians, and I know not how many other sects, who must have their share; and the service that should be a many-toned harmony pervaded by one grand spirit of devotion, becomes a discordant orgie, befitting the rites of Belial.

A long time ago—I do not know the precise number of years—the Sultan granted a firman, in answer to the application of both Jews and Christians, allowing the members of each sect to put to death any person belonging to the other sect, who should be found inside of their churches or synagogues. The firman has never been recalled, though in every place but Jerusalem it remains a dead letter. Here, although the Jews freely permit Christians to enter their synagogue, a Jew who should enter the Holy Sepulchre would be lucky if he escaped with his life. Not long since, an English gentleman, who was taken by the monks for a Jew, was so severely beaten that he was confined to his bed for two months. What worse than scandal, what abomination, that the spot looked upon by so many Christians as the most awfully sacred on earth, should be the scene of such brutish intolerance! I never pass the group of Turkish officers, quietly smoking their long pipes and sipping their coffee within the vestibule of the Church, without a feeling of humiliation. Worse than the money-changers whom Christ scourged out of the Temple, the guardians of this edifice make use of His crucifixion and resurrection as a means of gain. You may buy a piece of the stone covering the Holy Sepulchre, duly certified by the Greek Patriarch of Jerusalem, for about $7. At Bethlehem, which I visited this morning, the Latin monk who showed us the manger, the pit where 12,000 innocents were buried, and other things, had much less to say of the sacredness or authenticity of the place, than of the injustice of allowing the Greeks a share in its possession.

The native Jewish families in Jerusalem, as well as those in other parts of Palestine, present a marked difference to the Jews of Europe and America. They possess the same physical characteristics—the dark, oblong eye, the prominent nose, the strongly-marked cheek and jaw—but in the latter, these traits have become harsh and coarse. Centuries devoted to the lowest and most debasing forms of traffic, with the endurance of persecution and contumely, have greatly changed and vulgarized the appearance of the race. But the Jews of the Holy City still retain a noble beauty, which proved to my mind their descent from the ancient princely houses of Israel The forehead is loftier, the eye larger and more frank in its expression, the nose more delicate in its prominence, and the face a purer oval. I have remarked the same distinction in the countenances of those Jewish families of Europe, whose members have devoted themselves to Art or Literature. Mendelssohn's was a face that might have belonged to the House of David.

On the evening of my arrival in the city, as I set out to walk through the bazaars, I encountered a native Jew, whose face will haunt me for the rest of my life. I was sauntering slowly along, asking myself "Is this Jerusalem?" when, lifting my eyes, they met those of Christ! It was the very face which Raphael has painted—the traditional features of the Saviour, as they are recognised and accepted by all Christendom. The waving brown hair, partly hidden by a Jewish cap, fell clustering about the ears ; the face was the most perfect oval, and almost feminine in the purity of its outline ; the sereno, child-like mouth was shaded with a light moustache, and a silky brown beard clothed the chin ; but the eyes—shall I ever look into such orbs again ? Large, dark, unfathomable, they beamed with an expression of divine love and divine sorrow, such as I never before saw in human face. The man had just emerged from a dark archway, and the golden glow of the sunset, reflected from a white wall above, fell upon his face. Perhaps it was this transfiguration which made his beauty so unearthly ; but, during the moment that I saw him, he was to me a revelation of the Saviour. There are still miracles in the Land of Judah. As the dusk gathered in the deep streets, I could see nothing but the ineffable sweetness and benignity of that countenance, and my friend was not a little astonished, if not shocked, when I said to him, with the earnestness of belief, on my return : "I have just seen Christ."

I made the round of the Holy Sepulchre on Sunday, while the monks were celebrating the festival of the Invention of the Cross, in the chapel of the Empress Helena. As the finding of the cross by the Empress is almost the only authority for the places inclosed within the Holy Sepulchre, I went there inclined to doubt their authenticity, and came away with my doubt vastly strengthened. The building is a confused labyrinth of chapels, choirs, shrines, staircases, and vaults—without any definite plan or any architectural beauty, though very rich in parts and full of picturesque effects. Golden lamps continually burn before the sacred places, and you rarely visit the church without seeing some procession of monks, with crosses, censers, and tapers, threading the shadowy passages, from shrine to shrine It is astonishing how many localities are assembled under one roof. At first, you are shown the stone on which Christ rested from the burden of the cross; then, the place where the soldiers cast lots for His garments, both of them adjoining the Sepulchre. After seeing this, you are taken to the Pillar of Flagellation; the stocks; the place of crowning with thorns; the spot where He met His mother; the cave where the Empress Helena found the cross; and, lastly, the summit of Mount Calvary. The Sepulchre is a small marble building in the centre of the church. We removed our shoes at the entrance, and were taken by a Greek monk, first into a sort of ante-chamber, lighted with golden lamps, and having in the centre, inclosed in a case of marble, the stone on which the angel sat. Stooping through a low door, we entered the Sepulchre itself. Forty lamps of gold burn unceasingly above the white marble slab, which, as the monks say, protects the stone whereon the body of Christ was laid. As we again emerged, our guide led us up a flight of steps to a second story, in which stood a shrine, literally blazing with gold. Kneeling on the marble floor, he removed a golden shield, and showed us the hole in the rock of Calvary, where the cross was planted. Close beside it was the fissure produced by the earthquake which followed the Crucifixion. But, to my eyes, aided by the light of the dim wax taper, it was no violent rupture, such as an earthquake would produce, and the rock did not appear to be the same as that of which Jerusalem is built. As we turned to leave, a monk appeared with a bowl of sacred rose-water, which he sprinkled on our hands, bestowing a double portion on a rosary of sandal-wood which I carried But it was a Mohammedan rosary, brought from Mecca, and containing the sacred number of ninety nine beads.

I have not space here to state all the arguments for and against the localities in the Holy Sepulchre. I came to the conclusion that none of them were authentic, and am glad to have the concurrence of such distinguished authority as Dr. Robinson. So far from this being a matter of regret, I, for one, rejoice that those sacred spots are lost to the world. Christianity does not need them, and they are spared a daily profanation in the name of religion. We know that Christ has walked on the Mount of Olives, and gone down to the Pool of Siloam, and tarried in Bethany; we know that here, within the circuit of our vision, He has suffered agony and death, and that from this little point went out all the light that has made the world greater and happier and better in its later than in its earlier days.

Yet, I must frankly confess, in wandering through this city —revered alike by Christians, Jews and Turks as one of the holiest in the world—I have been reminded of Christ, the Man, rather than of Christ, the God. In the glory which overhangs Palestine afar off, we imagine emotions which never come, when we tread the soil and walk over the hallowed sites. As I toiled up the Mount of Olives, in the very footsteps of Christ, panting with the heat and the difficult ascent, I found it utterly impossible to conceive that the Deity, in human form, had walked there before me. And even at night, as I walk on the terraced roof, while the moon, "the balmy moon of blessed Israel," restores the Jerusalem of olden days to my imagination, the Saviour who then haunts my thoughts is the Man Jesus, in those moments of trial when He felt the weaknesses of our common humanity; in that agony of struggle in the garden of Gethsemane, in that still more bitter cry of human doubt and human appeal from the cross: "My God, my God, why hast Thou forsaken me!" Yet there is nc reproach for this conception of the character of Christ. Better the divinely-inspired Man, the purest and most perfect of His race, the pattern and type of all that is good and holy in Humanity, than the Deity for whose intercession we pray, while we trample His teachings under our feet. It would be well for many Christian sects, did they keep more constantly before their eyes the sublime humanity of Christ. How much bitter intolerance and persecution might be spared the world, if, instead of simply adoring Him as a Divine Mediator, they would strive to walk the ways He trod on earth. But Christianity is still undeveloped, and there is yet no sect which represents its full and perfect spirit.

It is my misfortune if I give offence by these remarks. I cannot assume emotions I do not feel, and must describe Jerusalem as I found it. Since being here, I have read the accounts of several travellers, and in many cases the devotional rhapsodies—the ecstacies of awe and reverence—in which they indulge, strike me as forced and affected. The pious writers have described what was expected of them, not what they found. It was partly from reading such accounts that my anticipations were raised too high, for the view of the city from the Jaffa road and the panorama from the Mount of Olives are the only things wherein I have been pleasantly disappointed

By far the most interesting relic left to the city is the foundation wall of Solomon's Temple. The Mosque of Omar, according to the accounts of the Turks, and Mr. Catherwood's examination, rests on immense vaults, which are believed to be the substructions of the Temple itself. Under the dome of the mosque there is a large mass of natural rock, revered by the Moslems as that from which Mahomet mounted the beast Borak when he visited the Seven Heavens, and believed by Mr. Catherwood to have served as part of the foundation of the Holy of Holies. No Christian is allowed to enter the mosque, or even its enclosure, on penalty of death, and even the firman of the Sultan has failed to obtain admission for a Frank. I have been strongly tempted to make the attempt in my Egyptian dress, which happens to resemble that of a mollah or Moslem priest, but the Dervishes in the adjoining college have sharp eyes, and my pronunciation of Arabic would betray me in case I was accosted. I even went so far as to buy a string of the large beads usually carried by a mollah, but unluckily I do not know the Moslem form of prayer, or I might carry out the plan under the guise of religious abstraction. This morning we succeeded in getting a nearer view of the mosque from the roof of the Governor's palace. François, by assuming the character of a Turkish *cawass*, gained us admission. The roof overlooks the entire enclosure of the Haram, and gives a complete view of the exterior of the mosque and the paved court surrounding it. There is no regularity in the style of the buildings in the enclosure, but the general effect is highly picturesque. The great dome of the mosque is the grandest in all the Orient, but the body of the edifice, made to resemble an octagonal tent, and covered with blue and white tiles, is not high enough to do it justice. The first court is paved with marble, and has four porticoes, each of five light Saracenic arches, opening into the green park, which occupies the rest of the terrace. This park is studded with cypress and fig trees, and dotted all over with the tombs of shekhs. As we were looking down on the spacious area, behold! who should come along but Shekh Mohammed Senoosee, the holy man of Timbuctoo, who had laid off his scarlet robe and donned a green one. I called down to him, whereupon he looked up and recognised us. For this reason I regret our departure from Jerusalem, as I am sure a little persuasion would induce the holy man to accompany me within the mosque.

We leave to-morrow for Damascus, by way of Nazareth and Tiberius. My original plan was to have gone to Djerash, the ancient Geraza, in the land of Gilead, and thence to Bozrah, in Djebel Hauaran. But Djebel Adjeloun, as the country about Djerash is called, is under a powerful Bedouin shekh, named Abd-el Azeez, and without an escort from him, which involves considerable delay and a fee of $150, it would be impossible to make the journey. We are therefore restricted to the ordinary route, and in case we should meet with any difficulty by the way, Mr. Smith, the American Consul, who is now here, has kindly procured us a firman from the Pasha of Jerusalem. All the travellers here are making preparations to leave, but there are still two parties in the Desert.

CHAPTER VI.

THE HILL-COUNTRY OF PALESTINE.

Leaving Jerusalem—The Tombs of the Kings—El Bireh—The Hill-Country—First View of Mount Hermon—The Tomb of Joseph—Ebal and Gerizim—The Gardens of Nablous—The Samaritans—The Sacred Book—A Scene in the Synagogue—Mentor and Telemachus—Ride to Samaria—The Ruins of Sebaste—Scriptural Landscapes—Halt at Genin—The Plain of Esdraelon—Palestine and California—The Hills of Nazareth—Accident—Fra Joachim—The Church of the Virgin—The Shrine of the Annunciation—The Holy Places.

"Blest land of Judea! thrice hallowed of song,
Where the holiest of memories pilgrim-like throng:
In the shade of thy palms, by the shores of thy sea,
On the hills of thy beauty, my heart is with thee!"

J. G. Whittier.

Latin Convent, Nazareth, *Friday, May* 7, 1852.

We left Jerusalem by the Jaffa Gate, because within a few months neither travellers nor baggage are allowed to pass the Damascus Gate, on account of smuggling operations having been carried on there. Not far from the city wall there is a superb terebinth tree, now in the full glory of its shining green leaves. It appears to be bathed in a perpetual dew; the rounded masses of foliage sparkle and glitter in the light, and the great spreading boughs flood the turf below with a deluge of delicious shade. A number of persons were reclining on the grass under it, and one of them, a very handsome Christian boy, spoke to us in Italian and English. I scarcely remember a brighter and purer day than that of our departure. The sky was a sheet of spotless blue ; every rift and scar of the distant hills was retouched with a firmer pencil, and all the outlines, blurred away by the haze of the previous few days, were restored with wonderful distinctness. The temperature was hot, but not sultry, and the air we breathed was an elixir of immortality.

Through a luxuriant olive grove we reached the Tombs of the Kings, situated in a small valley to the north of the city. Part of the valley, if not the whole of it, has been formed by quarrying away the crags of marble and conglomerate limestone for building the city. Near the edge of the low cliffs overhanging it, there are some illustrations of the ancient mode of cutting stone, which, as well as the custom of excavating tombs in the rock, was evidently borrowed from Egypt. The upper surface of the rocks was first made smooth, after which the blocks were mapped out and cut apart by grooves chiselled between them. I visited four or five tombs, each of which had a sort of vestibule or open portico in front. The door was low, and the chambers which I entered, small and black, without sculptures of any kind. The tombs bear some resemblance in their general plan to those of Thebes, except that they are without ornaments, either sculptured or painted. There are fragments of sarcophagi in some of them. On the southern side of the valley is a large quarry, evidently worked for marble, as the blocks have been cut out from below, leaving a large overhanging mass, part of which has broken off and fallen down. Some pieces which I picked up were of a very fine white marble, somewhat resembling that of Carrara. The opening of the quarry made a striking picture, the soft pink hue of the weather-stained rock contrasting exquisitely with the vivid green of the vines festooning the entrance.

From the long hill beyond the Tombs, we took our last view of Jerusalem, far beyond whose walls I saw the Church of the Nativity, at Bethlehem. The Jewish synagogue on the top of the mountain called Nebbee Samwil, the highest peak in Palestine, was visible at some distance to the west. Notwithstanding its sanctity, I felt little regret at leaving Jerusalem, and cheerfully took the rough road northward, over the stony hills. There were few habitations in sight, yet the hill-sides were cultivated, wherever it was possible for anything to grow. The wheat was just coming into head, and the people were at work, planting maize. After four hours' ride, we reached El Bireh, a little village on a hill, with the ruins of a convent and a large khan. The place takes its name from a fountain of excellent water, beside which we found our tents already pitched. In the evening, two Englishmen, an ancient Mentor, with a wild young Telemachus in charge, arrived, and camped near us. The night was calm and cool, and the full moon poured a flood of light over the bare and silent hills.

We rose long before sunrise, and rode off in the brilliant morning—the sky unstained by a speck of vapor. In the valley, beyond El Bireh, the husbandmen were already at their ploughs, and the village boys were on their way to the uncultured parts of the hills, with their flocks of sheep and goats. The valley terminated in a deep gorge, with perpendicular walls of rock on either side. Our road mounted the hill on the eastern side, and followed the brink of the precipice through the pass, where an enchanting landscape opened upon us. The village of Yebrood crowned a hill which rose oppo site, and the mountain slopes leaning towards it on all sides were covered with orchards of fig trees, and either rustling with wheat or cleanly ploughed for maize. The soil was a dark brown loam, and very rich. The stones have been laboriously built into terraces; and, even where heavy rocky boulders almost hid the soil, young fig and olive trees were planted in the crevices between them. I have never seen more thorough and patient cultivation. In the crystal of the morning air, the very hills laughed with plenty, and the whole landscape beamed with the signs of gladness on its countenance.

The site of ancient Bethel was not far to the right of our road. Over hills laden with the olive, fig, and vine, we passed to Ain el-Haramiyeh, or the Fountain of the Robbers. Here there are tombs cut in the rock on both sides of the valley. Over another ridge, we descended to a large, bowl-shaped valley, entirely covered with wheat, and opening eastward towards the Jordan. Thence to Nablous (the Shechem of the Old and Sychar of the New Testament) is four hours through a winding dell of the richest harvest land. On the way, we first caught sight of the snowy top of Mount Hermon, distant at least eighty miles in a straight line. Before reaching Nablous, I stopped to drink at a fountain of clear and sweet water, beside a square pile of masonry, upon which sat two Moslem dervishes. This, we were told, was the Tomb of Joseph, whose body, after having accompanied the Israelites in all their wanderings, was at last deposited near Shechem. There is less reason to doubt this spot than most of the sacred places of Palestine, for the reason that it rests, not on Christian, but on Jewish tradition. The wonderful tenacity with which the Jews cling to every record or memento of their early history, and the fact that from the time of Joseph a portion of them have always lingered near the spot, render it highly probable that the locality of a spot so sacred should have been preserved from generation to generation to the present time. It has been recently proposed to open this tomb, by digging under it from the side. If the body of Joseph was actually deposited here, there are, no doubt, some traces of it remaining. It must have been embalmed, according to the Egyptian custom, and placed in a coffin of the Indian sycamore, the wood of which is so nearly incorruptible, that thirty-five centuries would not suffice for its decomposition. The singular interest of such a discovery would certainly justify the experiment. Not far from the tomb is Jacob's Well, where Christ met the Woman of Samaria. This place is also considered as authentic, for the same reasons. If not wholly convincing to all, there is, at least, so much probability in them that one is freed from that painful coldness and incredulity with which he beholds the sacred shows of Jerusalem.

Leaving the Tomb of Joseph, the road turned to the west, and entered the narrow pass between Mounts Ebal and Gerizim. The former is a steep, barren peak, clothed with terraces of cactus, standing on the northern side of the pass. Mount Gerizim is cultivated nearly to the top, and is truly a mountain of blessing, compared with its neighbor. Through an orchard of grand old olive-trees, we reached Nablous, which presented a charming picture, with its long mass of white, dome-topped stone houses, stretching along the foot of Gerizim through a sea of bowery orchards. The bottom of the valley resembles some old garden run to waste. Abundant streams, poured from the generous heart of the Mount of Blessing, leap and gurgle with pleasant noises through thickets of orange, fig, and pomegranate, through bowers of roses and tangled masses of briars and wild vines. We halted in a grove of olives, and, after our tent was pitched, walked upward through the orchards to the Ras-el-Ain (Promontory of the Fountain), on the side of Mount Gerizim. A multitude of beggars sat at the city gate; and, as they continued to clamor after I had given sufficient alms, I paid them with "*Allah deelek!*"—(God give it to you!)—the Moslem's reply to such importunity—and they ceased in an instant. This exclamation, it seems, takes away from them the power of demanding a second time.

From under the Ras-el-Ain gushes forth the Fountain of Honey, so called from the sweetness and purity of the water. We drank of it, and I found the taste very agreeable, but my companion declared that it had an unpleasant woolly flavor. When we climbed a little higher, we found that the true source from which the fountain is supplied was above, and that an Arab was washing a flock of sheep in it! We continued our walk along the side of the mountain to the other end of the city, through gardens of almond, apricot, prune, and walnut-trees, bound each to each by great vines, whose heavy arms they seemed barely able to support. The interior of the town is dark and filthy; but it has a long, busy bazaar extending its whole length, and a café, where we procured the best coffee in Syria.

Nablous is noted for the existence of a small remnant of the ancient Samaritans. The stock has gradually dwindled away, and amounts to only forty families, containing little more than a hundred and fifty individuals. They live in a particular quarter of the city, and are easily distinguished from the other inhabitants by the cast of their features. After our guide, a native of Nablous, had pointed out three or four, I had no difficulty in recognising all the others we met. They have long, but not prominent noses, like the Jews; small, oblong eyes, narrow lips, and fair complexions, most of them having brown hair. They appear to be held in considerable obloquy by the Moslems. Our attendant, who was of the low class of Arabs, took the boys we met very unceremoniously by the head, calling out: "Here is another Samaritan!" He then conducted us to their synagogue, to see the celebrated Pentateuch, which is there preserved. We were taken to a small, open court, shaded by an apricot-tree, where the priest, an old man in a green robe and white turban, was seated in meditation. He had a long grey beard, and black eyes, that lighted up with a sudden expression of eager greed when we promised him backsheesh for a sight of the sacred book. He arose and took us into a sort of chapel, followed by a number of Samaritan boys. Kneeling down at a niche in the wall, he produced from behind a wooden case a piece of ragged parchment, written with Hebrew characters. But the guide was familiar with this deception, and rated him so soundly that, after a little hesitation, he laid the fragment away, and produced a large tin cylinder, covered with a piece of green satin embroidered in gold. The boys stooped down and reverently kissed the blazoned cover, before it was removed. The cylinder, sliding open by two rows of hinges, opened at the same time the parchment scroll, which was rolled at both ends. It was, indeed, a very ancient manuscript, and in remarkable preservation. The rents have been carefully repaired and the scroll neatly stitched upon another piece of parchment, covered on the outside with violet satin. The priest informed me that it was written by the son of Aaron; but this does not coincide with the fact that the Samaritan Pentateuch is different from that of the Jews. It is, however, no doubt one of the oldest parchment records in the world, and the Samaritans look upon it with unbounded faith and reverence. The Pentateuch, according to their version, contains their only form of religion. They reject everything else which the Old Testament contains. Three or four days ago was their grand feast of sacrifice, when they made a burnt offering of a lamb, on the top of Mount Gerizim. Within a short time, it is said they have shown some curiosity to become acquainted with the New Testament, and the High Priest sent to Jerusalem to procure Arabic copies.

I asked one of the wild-eyed boys whether he could read the sacred book. "Oh, yes," said the priest, "all these boys can read it;" and the one I addressed immediately pulled a volume from his breast, and commenced reading in fluent Hebrew. It appeared to be a part of their church service, for both the priest and *boab*, or door-keeper, kept up a running series of responses, and occasionally the whole crowd shouted out some deep-mouthed word in chorus. The old man leaned forward with an expression as fixed and intense as if the text had become incarnate in him, following with his lips the sound of the boy's voice. It was a strange picture of religious enthusiasm, and was of itself sufficient to convince me of the legitimacy of the Samaritan's descent. When I rose to leave I gave him the promised fee, and a smaller one to the boy who read the service. This was the signal for a general attack from the door-keeper and all the boys who were present. They s rounded me with eyes sparkling with the desire of gain, kissed the border of my jacket, stroked my beard coaxingly with their hands, which they then kissed, and, crowding up with a boisterous show of affection, were about to fall on my neck in a heap, after the old Hebrew fashion. The priest, clamorous for more, followed with glowing face, and the whole group had a riotous and bacchanalian character, which I should never have imagined could spring from such a passion as avarice.

On returning to our camp, we found Mentor and Telemachus arrived, but not on such friendly terms as their Greek prototypes. We were kept awake for a long time that night by their high words, and the first sound I heard the next morning came from their tent. Telemachus, I suspect, had found some island of Calypso, and did not relish the cold shock of the plunge into the sea, by which Mentor had forced him away. He insisted on returning to Jerusalem, but as Mentor would not allow him a horse, he had not the courage to try it on foot. After a series of altercations, in which he took a pistol to shoot the dragoman, and applied very profane terms to everybody in the company, his wrath dissolved into tears, and when we left, Mentor had decided to rest a day at Nablous, and let him recover from the effects of the storm.

We rode down the beautiful valley, taking the road to Sebaste (Samaria), while our luggage-mules kept directly over the mountains to Jenin. Our path at first followed the course of the stream, between turfy banks and through luxuriant orchards. The whole country we overlooked was planted with olive-trees, and, except the very summits of the mountains, covered with grain-fields. For two hours our course was north-east, leading over the hills, and now and then dipping into beautiful dells. In one of these a large stream gushes from the earth in a full fountain, at the foot of a great olive-tree. The hill-side above it was a complete mass of foliage, crowned with the white walls of a Syrian village. Descending the valley, which is very deep, we came in sight of Samaria, situated on the summit of an isolated hill. The sanctuary of the ancient Christian church of St. John towers high above the mud walls of the modern village. Riding between olive-orchards and wheat-fields of glorious richness and beauty, we passed the remains of an acqueduct, and ascended the hill The ruins of the church occupy the eastern summit. Part of them have been converted into a mosque, which the Christian foot is not allowed to profane. The church, which is in the Byzantine style, is apparently of the time of the Crusaders. It had originally a central and two side-aisles, covered with groined Gothic vaults. The sanctuary is semi-circular, with a row of small arches, supported by double pillars. The church rests on the foundations of some much more ancient building—probably a temple belonging to the Roman city.

Behind the modern village, the hill terminates in a long, eliptical mound, about one-third of a mile in length. We made the tour of it, and were surprised at finding a large number of columns, each of a single piece of marble. They had once formed a double colonnade, extending from the church to a gate on the western side of the summit. Our native guide said they had been covered with an arch, and constituted a long market or bazaar—a supposition in which he may be correct. From the gate, which is still distinctly marked, we overlooked several deep valleys to the west, and over them all, the blue horizon of the Mediterranean, south of Cæsarea. On the northern side of the hill there are upwards of twenty more pillars standing, besides a number hurled down, and the remains of a quadrangular colonnade, on the side of the hill below. The total number of pillars on the summit cannot be less than one hundred, from twelve to eighteen feet in height. The hill is strewn, even to its base, with large hewn blocks and fragments of sculptured stone. The present name of the city was given to it by Herod, and it must have been at that time a most stately and beautiful place.

We descended to a valley on the east, climbed a long ascent, and after crossing the broad shoulder of a mountain beyond, saw below us a landscape even more magnificent than that of Nablous. It was a great winding valley, its bottom rolling in waves of wheat and barley, while every hill-side, up to the bare rock, was mantled with groves of olive. The very summits which looked into this garden of Israel, were green with fragrant plants—wild thyme and sage, gnaphalium and camomile. Away to the west was the sea, and in the north-west the mountain chain of Carmel. We went down to the gardens and pasture-land, and stopped to rest at the Village of Geba, which hangs on the side of the mountain. A spring of whitish but delicious water gushed out of the soil, in the midst of a fig orchard. The women passed us, going back and forth with tall water-jars on their heads. Some herd-boys brought down a flock of black goats, and they were all given drink in a large wooden bowl. They were beautiful animals, with thick curved horns, white eyes, and ears a foot long. It was a truly Biblical picture in every feature.

Beyond this valley we passed a circular basin, which has no outlet, so that in winter the bottom of it must be a lake. After winding among the hills an hour more, we came out upon the town of Jenin, a Turkish village, with a tall white minaret, at the head of the great plain of Esdraelon. It is supposed to be the ancient Jezreel, where the termagant Jezebel was thrown out of the window. We pitched our tent in a garden near the town, under a beautiful mulberry tree, and, as the place is in very bad repute, engaged a man to keep guard at night. An English family was robbed there two or three weeks ago. Our guard did his duty well, pacing back and forth, and occasionally grounding his musket to keep up his courage by the sound. In the evening, François caught a chameleon, a droll-looking little creature, which changed color in a marvellous manner.

Our road, next day, lay directly across the Plain of Esdraelon, one of the richest districts in the world. It is now a green sea, covered with fields of wheat and barley, or great grazing tracts, on which multitudes of sheep and goats are wandering. In some respects it reminded me of the Valley of San José, and if I were to liken Palestine to any other country I have seen, it would be California. The climate and succession of the seasons are the same, the soil is very similar in quality, and the landscapes present the same general features. Here, in spring, the plains are covered with that deluge of floral bloom, which makes California seem a paradise. Here there are the same picturesque groves, the same rank fields of wild oats clothing the mountain-sides, the same aromatic herbs impregnating the air with balm, and above all, the same blue, cloudless days and dewless nights. While travelling here, I am constantly reminded of our new Syria on the Pacific.

Towards noon, Mount Tabor separated itself from the chain of hills before us, and stood out singly, at the extremity of the plain. We watered our horses at a spring in a swamp, were some women were collected, beating with sticks the rushes they had gathered to make mats. After reaching the mountains on the northern side of the plain, an ascent of an hour and a-half, through a narrow glen, brought us to Nazareth, which is situated in a cul-de-sac, under the highest peaks of the range. As we were passing a rocky part of the road, Mr. Harrison's horse fell with him and severely injured his leg. We were fortunately near our destination, and on reach- the Latin Convent, Fra Joachim, to whose surgical abilities the traveller's book bore witness, took him in charge. Many others besides ourselves have had reason to be thankful for the good offices of the Latin monks in Palestine. I have never met with a class more kind, cordial, and genial. All the convents are bound to take in and entertain all applicants—of whatever creed or nation—for the space of three days.

In the afternoon, Fra Joachim accompanied me to the Church of the Virgin, which is inclosed within the walls of the convent. It is built over the supposed site of the house in which the mother of Christ was living, at the time of the angelic annunciation. Under the high altar, a flight of steps leads down to the shrine of the Virgin, on the threshold of the house, where the Angel Gabriel's foot rested, as he stood, with a lily in his hand, announcing the miraculous conception. The shrine, of white marble and gold, gleaming in the light of golden lamps, stands under a rough arch of the natural rock, from the side of which hangs a heavy fragment of a granite pillar, suspended, as the devout believe, by divine power. Fra Joachim informed me that, when the Moslems attempted to obliterate all tokens of the holy place, this pillar was preserved by a miracle, that the locality might not be lost to the Christians. At the same time, he said, the angels of God carried away the wooden house which stood at the entrance of the grotto; and, after letting it drop in Marseilles, while they rested, picked it up again and set it down in Loretto, where it still remains. As he said this, there was such entire, absolute belief in the good monk's eyes, and such happiness in that belief, that not for ten times the gold on the shrine would I have expressed a doubt of the story. He then bade me kneel, that I might see the spot where the angel stood, and devoutly repeated a paternoster while I contemplated the pure plate of snowy marble, surrounded with vases of fragrant flowers, between which hung cressets of gold, wherein perfumed oils were burning. All the decorations of the place conveyed the idea of transcendent purity and sweetness; and, for the first time in Palestine, I wished for perfect faith in the spot. Behind the shrine, there are two or three chambers in the rock, which served as habitations for the family of the Virgin.

A young Christian Nazarene afterwards conducted me to the House of Joseph, the Carpenter, which is now inclosed in a little chapel. It is merely a fragment of wall, undoubtedly as old as the time of Christ, and I felt willing to consider it a genuine relic. There was an honest roughness about the large stones, inclosing a small room called the carpenter's shop, which I could not find it in my heart to doubt. Besides, in a quiet country town like Nazareth, which has never known such vicissitudes as Jerusalem, much more dependence can be placed on popular tradition. For the same reason, I looked with reverence on the Table of Christ, also inclosed within a chapel. This is a large, natural rock, about nine feet by twelve, nearly square, and quite flat on the top. It is said that it once served as a table for Christ and his Disciples. The building called the School of Christ, where he went with other children of his age, is now a church of the Syrian Christians, who were performing a doleful mass, in Arabic, at the time of my visit. It is a vaulted apartment, about forty feet long, and only the lower part of the wall is ancient. At each of these places, the Nazarene put into my hand a piece of pasteboard, on which was printed a prayer in Latin, Italian, and Arabic, with the information that whoever visited the place, and made the prayer, would be entitled to seven years' indulgence. I duly read all the prayers, and, accordingly, my conscience ought to be at rest for twenty-one years.

CHAPTER VII.

THE COUNTRY OF GALILEE.

Departure from Nazareth—A Christian Guide—Ascent of Mount Tabor—Wallachian Hermits—The Panorama of Tabor—Ride to Tiberias—A Bath in Genesareth—The Flowers of Galilee—The Mount of Beatitude—Magdala—Joseph's Well—Meeting with a Turk—The Fountain of the Salt-Works—The Upper Valley of the Jordan—Summer Scenery—The Rivers of Lebanon—Tell el-Kadi—An Arcadian Region—The Fountains of Banias.

"Beyond are Bethulia's mountains of green,
And the desolate hills of the wild Gadarene;
And I pause on the goat-crags of Tabor to see
The gleam of thy waters, O dark Galilee!"—WHITTIER.

BANIAS (Cæsarea Philippi), *May* 10, 1852.

WE left Nazareth on the morning of the 8th inst. My companion had done so well under the care of Fra Joachim that he was able to ride, and our journey was not delayed by his accident. The benedictions of the good Franciscans accompanied us as we rode away from the Convent, past the Fountain of the Virgin, and out of the pleasant little valley where the boy Jesus wandered for many peaceful years. The Christian guide we engaged for Mount Tabor had gone ahead, and we did not find him until we had travelled for more than two hours among the hills. As we approached the sacred mountain, we came upon the region of oaks—the first oak I had seen since leaving Europe last autumn. There are three or four varieties, some with evergreen foliage, and in their wild luxuriance and the picturesqueness of their forms and group ings, they resemble those of California. The sea of grass and flowers in which they stood was sprinkled with thick tufts of wild oats—another point of resemblance to the latter country. But here, there is no gold; there, no sacred memories.

The guide was waiting for us beside a spring, among the trees. He was a tall youth of about twenty, with a mild, submissive face, and wore the dark-blue turban, which appears to be the badge of a native Syrian Christian. I found myself involuntarily pitying him for belonging to a despised sect. There is no disguising the fact that one feels much more respect for the Mussulman rulers of the East, than for their oppressed subjects who profess his own faith. The surest way to make a man contemptible is to treat him contemptuously, and the Oriental Christians, who have been despised for centuries, are, with some few exceptions, despicable enough. Now, however, since the East has become a favorite field of travel, and the Frank possesses an equal dignity with the Moslem, the native Christians are beginning to hold up their heads, and the return of self-respect will, in the course of time, make them respectable.

Mount Tabor stands a little in advance of the hill-country, with which it is connected only by a low spur or shoulder, its base being the Plain of Esdraelon. This is probably the reason why it has been fixed upon as the place of the Transfiguration, as it is not mentioned by name in the New Testament. The words are: "an high mountain apart," which some suppose to refer to the position of the mountain, and not to the remoteness of Christ and the three Disciples from men. The sides of the mountain are covered with clumps of oak, hawthorn and other trees, in many places overrun with the white honeysuckle, its fingers dropping with odor of nutmeg and cloves. The ascent, by a steep and winding path, occu pied an hour. The summit is nearly level, and resembles some overgrown American field, or "oak opening." The grass is more than knee-deep ; the trees grow high and strong, and there are tangled thickets and bowers of vines without end. The eastern and highest end of the mountain is covered with the remains of an old fortress-convent, once a place of great strength, from the thickness of its walls. In a sort of cell formed among the ruins we found two monk-hermits. I addressed them in all languages of which I know a salutation, without effect, but at last made out that they were Wallachians. They were men of thirty-five, with stupid faces, dirty garments, beards run to waste, and fur caps. Their cell was a mere hovel, without furniture, except a horrid caricature of the Virgin and Child, and four books of prayers in the Bulgarian character. One of them walked about knitting a stocking, and paid no attention to us ; but the other, after giving us some deliciously cold water, got upon a pile of rubbish, and stood regarding us with open mouth while we took breakfast. So far from this being a cause of annoyance, I felt really glad that our presence had agitated the stagnant waters of his mind.

The day was hazy and sultry, but the panoramic view from Mount Tabor was still very fine. The great Plain of Esdraelon lay below us like a vast mosaic of green and brown—jasper and verd-antique. On the west, Mount Carmel lifted his head above the blue horizon line of the Mediterranean. Turning to the other side, a strip of the Sea of Galilee glimmered deep down among the hills, and the Ghor, or the Valley of the Jordan, stretched like a broad gash through them. Beyond them, the country of Djebel Adjeloun, the ancient Decapolis, which still holds the walls of Gadara and the temples and theatres of Djerash, faded away into vapor, and, still further to the south, the desolate hills of Gilead, the home of Jephthah. Mount Hermon is visible when the atmosphere is clear but we were not able to see it.

From the top of Mount Tabor to Tiberias, on the Sea of Galilee, is a journey of five hours, through a wild country, with but one single miserable village on the road. At first we rode through lonely dells, grown with oak and brilliant with flowers, especially the large purple mallow, and then over broad, treeless tracts of rolling land, but partially cultivated. The heat was very great ; I had no thermometer, but should judge the temperature to have been at least 95° in the shade. From the edge of the upland tract, we looked down on the Sea of Galilee—a beautiful sheet of water sunk among the mountains, and more than 300 feet below the level of the Mediterranean. It lay unruffled in the bottom of the basin, reflecting the peaks of the bare red mountains beyond it. Tiberias was at our very feet, a few palm trees alone relieving the nakedness of its dull walls. After taking a welcome drink at the Fountain of Fig-trees, we descended to the town, which has a desolate and forlorn air. Its walls have been partly thrown down by earthquakes, and never repaired. We found our tents already pitched on the bank above the lake, and under one of the tottering towers.

Not a breath of air was stirring ; the red hills smouldered in the heat, and the waters of Genesareth at our feet glimmered with an oily smoothness, unbroken by a ripple. We untwisted our turbans, kicked off our baggy trowsers, and speedily releasing ourselves from the barbarous restraints of dress, dipped into the tepid sea and floated lazily out until we could feel the exquisite coldness of the living springs which sent up their jets from the bottom. I was lying on my back, moving my fins just sufficiently to keep afloat, and gazing dreamily through half-closed eyes on the forlorn palms of Tiberias, when a shrill voice hailed me with: "O Howadji, get out of our way!" There, at the old stone gateway below our tent, stood two Galilean damsels, with heavy earthen jars upon their heads. "Go away yourselves, O maidens!" I answered, "if you want us to come out of the water." "But we must fill our pitchers," one of them replied. "Then fill them at once, and be not afraid; or leave them, and we will fill them for you." Thereupon they put the pitchers down, but remained watching us very complacently while we sank the vessels to the bottom of the lake, and let them fill from the colder and purer tide of the springs. In bringing them back through the water to the gate, the one I propelled before me happened to strike against a stone, and its fair owner, on receiving it, immediately pointed to a crack in the side, which she declared I had made, and went off lamenting. After we had resumed our garments, and were enjoying the pipe of indolence and the coffee of contentment, she returned and made such an outcry, that I was fain to purchase peace by the price of a new pitcher. I passed the first hours of the night in looking out of my tent-door, as I lay, on the stars sparkling in the bosom of Galilee, like the sheen of Assyrian spears, and the glare of the great fires kindled on the opposite shore.

The next day, we travelled northward along the lake, passing through continuous thickets of oleander, fragrant with its heavy pink blossoms. The thistles were more abundant and beautiful than ever. I noticed, in particular, one with a superb globular flower of a bright blue color, which would make a choice ornament for our gardens at home. At the north-western head of the lake, the mountains fall back and leave a large tract of the richest meadow-land, which narrows away into a deep dell, overhung by high mountain headlands, faced with naked cliffs of red rock. The features of the landscape are magnificent. Up the dell, I saw plainly the Mount of Beatitude, beyond which lies the village of Cana of Galilee. In coming up the meadow, we passed a miserable little village of thatched mud huts, almost hidden by the rank weeds which grew around them. A withered old crone sat at one of the doors, sunning herself. "What is the name of this village?" I asked. "It is Mejdel," was her reply. This was the ancient Magdala, the home of that beautiful but sinful Magdalene, whose repentance has made her one of the brightest of the Saints. The crystal waters of the lake here lave a shore of the cleanest pebbles. The path goes winding through oleanders, nebbuks, patches of hollyhock, anise-seed, fennel, and other spicy plants, while, on the west, great fields of barley stand ripe for the cutting. In some places, the Fellahs, men and women, were at work, reaping and binding the sheaves. After crossing this tract, we came to the hill, at the foot of which was a ruined khan, and on the summit, other undistinguishable ruins, supposed by some to be those of Capernaum The site of that exalted town, however, is still a matter of discussion.

We journeyed on in a most sweltering atmosphere over the ascending hills, the valley of the Upper Jordan lying deep on our right. In a shallow hollow, under one of the highest peaks, there stands a large deserted khan, over a well of very cold, sweet water, called *Bir Youssuf* by the Arabs. Somewhere near it, according to tradition, is the field where Joseph was sold by his brethren; and the well is, no doubt, looked upon by many as the identical pit into which he was thrown. A stately Turk of Damascus, with four servants behind him, came riding up as we were resting in the gateway of the khan, and, in answer to my question, informed me that the well was so named from Nebbee Youssuf (the Prophet Joseph), and not from Sultan Joseph Saladin. He took us for his countrymen, accosting me first in Turkish, and, even after I had talked with him some time in bad Arabic, asked me whether I had been making a pilgrimage to the tombs of certain holy Moslem saints, in the neighborhood of Jaffa. He joined company with us, however, and shared his pipe with me, as we continued our journey. We rode for two hours more over hills bare of trees, but covered thick with grass and herbs, and finally lost our way. François went ahead, dashing through the fields of barley and lentils, and we reached the path again, as the Waters of Merom came in sight. We then descended into the Valley of the Upper Jordan, and encamped opposite the lake, at Ain el-Mellaha (the Fountain of the Salt-Works), the first source of the sacred river. A stream of water, sufficient to turn half-a-dozen mills, gushes and gurgles up at the foot of the mountain. There are the remains of an ancient dam, by which a large pool was formed for the irrigation of the valley. It still supplies a little Arab mill below the fountain. This is a frontier post, between the jurisdictions of the Pashas of Jerusalem and Damascus, and the *mukkairee* of the Greek Caloyer, who left us at Tiberias, was obliged to pay a duty of seven and a half piastres on fifteen mats, which he had bought at Jerusalem for one and a half piastres each. The poor man will perhaps make a dozen piastres (about half a dollar) on these mats at Damascus, after carrying them on his mule for more than two hundred miles.

We pitched our tents on the grassy meadow below the mill—a charming spot, with Tell el-Khanzir (the hill of wild boars) just in front, over the Waters of Merom, and the snow-streaked summit of Djebel esh-Shekh—the great Mount Hermon—towering high above the valley. This is the loftiest peak of the Anti-Lebanon, and is 10,000 feet above the sea. The next morning, we rode for three hours before reaching the second spring of the Jordan, at a place which François called Tell el-Kadi, but which did not at all answer with the description given me by Dr. Robinson, at Jerusalem. The upper part of the broad valley, whence the Jordan draws his waters, is flat, moist, and but little cultivated. There are immense herds of sheep, goats, and buffaloes wandering over it. The people are a dark Arab tribe, and live in tents and miserable clay huts. Where the valley begins to slope upward towards the hills, they plant wheat, barley, and lentils. The soil is the fattest brown loam, and the harvests are wonderfully rich. I saw many tracts of wheat, from half a mile to a mile in extent, which would average forty bushels to the acre. Yet the ground is never manured, and the Arab plough scratches up but a few inches of the surface. What a paradise might be made of this country, were it in better hands!

The second spring is not quite so large as Ain el-Mellaha; but, like it, pours out a strong stream from a single source The pool was filled with women, washing the heavy fleeces of their sheep, and beating the dirt out of their striped camel's-hair abas with long poles. We left it, and entered on a slope of stony ground, forming the head of the valley. The view extended southward, to the mountains closing the northern cove of the Sea of Galilee. It was a grand, rich landscape—so rich that its desolation seems forced and unnatural. High on the summit of a mountain to the west, the ruins of a large Crusader fortress looked down upon us. The soil, which slowly climbs upward through a long valley between Lebanon and Anti-Lebanon, is cut with deep ravines. The path is very difficult to find; and while we were riding forward at random, looking in all directions for our baggage mules, we started up a beautiful gazelle. At last, about noon, hot, hungry, and thirsty, we reached a swift stream, roaring at the bottom of a deep ravine, through a bed of gorgeous foliage. The odor of the wild grape-blossoms, which came up to us, as we rode along the edge, was overpowering in its sweetness. An old bridge of two arches crossed the stream. There was a pile of rocks against the central pier, and there we sat and took breakfast in the shade of the maples, while the cold green waters foamed at our feet. By all the Naiads and Tritons, what a joy there is in beholding a running stream! The rivers of Lebanon are miracles to me, after my knowledge of the Desert. A company of Arabs, seven in all, were gathered under the bridge: and, from a flute which one of them blew, I judged they were taking a pastoral holiday. We kept our pistols beside us; for we did not like their looks. Before leaving, they told us that the country was full of robbers, and advised us to be on the lookout. We rode more carefully, after this, and kept with our baggage on reaching it. An hour after leaving the bridge, we came to a large circular, or rather annular mound, overgrown with knee-deep grass and clumps of oak-trees. A large stream, of a bright blue color, gushed down the north side, and after half embracing the mound swept off across the meadows to the Waters of Merom. There could be no doubt that this was Tell el-Kadi, the site of Dan, the most northern town of ancient Israel. The mound on which it was built is the crater of an extinct volcano. The Hebrew word *Dan* signifies "judge," and Tell el-Kadi, in Arabic, is "The Hill of the Judge."

The Anti-Lebanon now rose near us, its northern and western slopes green with trees and grass. The first range, perhaps 5,000 feet in height, shut out the snowy head of Hermon; but still the view was sublime in its large and harmonious outlines. Our road was through a country resembling Arcadia—the earth hidden by a dense bed of grass and flowers; thickets of blossoming shrubs; old, old oaks, with the most gnarled of trunks, the most picturesque of boughs, and the glossiest of green leaves; olive-trees of amazing antiquity; and, threading and enlivening all, the clear-cold floods of Lebanon. This was the true haunt of Pan, whose altars are now before me, graven on the marble crags of Hermon. Looking on those altars, and on the landscape, lovely as a Grecian dream, I forget that the lament has long been sung: "Pan, Pan is dead!"

In another hour, we reached this place, the ancient Cæsarea Philippi, now a poor village, embowered in magnificent trees, and washed by glorious waters. There are abundant remains of the old city: fragments of immense walls; broken granite columns; traces of pavements; great blocks of hewn stone; marble pedestals, and the like. In the rock at the foot of the mountain, there are several elegant niches, with Greek inscriptions, besides a large natural grotto. Below them, the water gushes up through the stones, in a hundred streams, forming a flood of considerable size. We have made our camp in an olive grove near the end of the village, beside an immense terebinth tree, which is inclosed in an open court, paved with stone. This is the town-hall of Banias, where the Shekh dispenses justice, and at the same time, the resort of all the idlers of the place. We went up among them, soon after our arrival, and were given seats of honor near the Shekh, who talked with me a long time about America. The people exhibit a very sensible curiosity, desiring to know the extent of our country, the number of inhabitants, the amount of taxation, the price of grain, and other solid information.

The Shekh and the men of the place inform us that the Druses are infesting the road to Damascus. This tribe is in rebellion in Djebel Hauaran, on account of the conscription, and some of them, it appears, have taken refuge in the fastnesses of Hermon, where they are beginning to plunder travellers. While I was talking with the Shekh, a Druse came down from the mountains, and sat for half an hour among the villagers, under the terebinth, and we have just heard that he has gone back the way he came. This fact has given us some anxiety, as he may have been a spy sent down to gather news; and, if so, we are almost certain to be waylaid. If we were well armed, we should not fear a dozen, but all our weapons consist of a sword and four pistols. After consulting together, we decided to apply to the Shekh for two armed men, to accompany us. I accordingly went to him again, and exhibited the firman of the Pasha of Jerusalem, which he read, stating that, even without it, he would have felt it his duty to grant our request. This is the graceful way in which the Orientals submit to a peremptory order. He thinks that one man will be sufficient, as we shall probably not meet with any large party.

The day has been, and still is, excessively hot. The atmosphere is sweltering, and all around us, over the thick patches of mallow and wild mustard, the bees are humming with a continuous sultry sound. The Shekh, with a number of lazy villagers, is still seated under the terebinth, in a tent of shade, impervious to the sun. I can hear the rush of the fountains of Banias—the holy springs of Hermon, whence Jordan is born. But what is this? The odor of the velvety weed of Shiraz meets my nostrils; a dark-eyed son of Pan places the narghileh at my feet; and, bubbling more sweetly than the streams of Jordan, the incense most dear to the god dims the crystal censer, and floats from my lips in rhythmic ejaculations. I, too, am in Arcadia!

CHAPTER VIII.

CROSSING THE ANTI-LEBANON.

The Harmless Guard—Cæsarea Philippi—The Valley of the Druses—The Sides of Mount Hermon—An Alarm—Threading a Defile—Distant view of Djebel Hauaran—Another Alarm—Camp at Katana—We Ride into Damascus.

DAMASCUS, *May* 12, 1852.

WE rose early, so as to be ready for a long march. The guard came—a mild-looking Arab—without arms; but on our refusing to take him thus, he brought a Turkish musket, terrible to behold, but quite guiltless of any murderous intent. We gave ourselves up to fate, with true Arab-resignation, and began ascending the Anti-Lebanon. Up and up, by stony paths, under the oaks, beside the streams, and between the wheat-fields, we climbed for two hours, and at last reached a comb or dividing ridge, whence we could look into a valley on the other side, or rather inclosed between the main chain and the offshoot named Djebel Heish, which stretches away towards the south-east. About half-way up the ascent, we passed the ruined acropolis of Cæsarea Philippi, crowning the summit of a lower peak. The walls and bastions cover a great extent of ground, and were evidently used as a stronghold in the Middle Ages.

The valley into which we descended lay directly under one of the peaks of Hermon and the rills that watered it were fed from his snow-fields. It was inhabited by Druses, but no men were to be seen, except a few poor husbandmen, ploughing on the mountain-sides. The women, wearing those enormous horns on their heads which distinguish them from the Mohammedan females, were washing at a pool below. We crossed the valley, and slowly ascended the height on the opposite side, taking care to keep with the baggage-mules. Up to this time, we met very few persons; and we forgot the anticipated perils in contemplating the rugged scenery of the Anti-Lebanon. The mountain-sides were brilliant with flowers, and many new and beautiful specimens arrested our attention. The asphodel grew in bunches beside the streams, and the large scarlet anemone outshone even the poppy, whose color here is the quintessence of flame. Five hours after leaving Banias, we reached the highest part of the pass—a dreary volcanic region, covered with fragments of lava. Just at this place, an old Arab met us, and, after scanning us closely, stopped and accosted Dervish. The latter immediately came running ahead, quite excited with the news that the old man had seen a company of about fifty Druses descend from the sides of Mount Hermon, towards the road we were to travel. We immediately ordered the baggage to halt, and Mr. Harrison, François, and myself rode on to reconnoitre. Our guard, the valiant man of Banias, whose teeth already chattered with fear, prudently kept with the baggage. We crossed the ridge and watched the stony mountain-sides for some time; but no spear or glittering gun-barrel could we see. The caravan was then set in motion; and we had not proceeded far before we met a second company of Arabs, who informed us that the road was free.

Leaving the heights, we descended cautiously into a ravine with walls of rough volcanic rock on each side. It was a pass where three men might have stood their ground against a hundred; and we did not feel thoroughly convinced of our safety till we had threaded its many windings and emerged upon a narrow valley. A village called Beit Jenn nestled under the rocks; and below it, a grove of poplar-trees shaded the banks of a rapid stream. We had now fairly crossed the Anti-Lebanon. The dazzling snows of Mount Hermon overhung us on the west; and, from the opening of the valley, we looked across a wild, waste country, to the distant range of Djebel Hauaran, the seat of the present rebellion, and one of the most interesting regions of Syria. I regretted more than ever not being able to reach it. The ruins of Bozrah, Ezra, and other ancient cities, would well repay the arduous character of the journey, while the traveller might succeed in getting some insight into the life and habits of that singular people, the Druses. But now, and perhaps for some time to come, there is no chance of entering the Hauaran.

Towards the middle of the afternoon, we reached a large village, which is usually the end of the first day's journey from Banias. Our men wanted to stop here, but we considered that to halt then would be to increase the risk, and decided to push on to Katana, four hours' journey from Damascus. They yielded with a bad grace; and we jogged on over the stony road, crossing the long hills which form the eastern base of the Anti-Lebanon. Before long, another Arab met us with the news that there was an encampment of Druses on the plain between us and Katana. At this, our guard, who had recovered sufficient spirit to ride a few paces in advance, fell back, and the impassive Dervish became greatly agitated. Where there is an uncertain danger, it is always better to go ahead than to turn back ; and we did so. But the guard reined up on the top of the first ridge, trembling as he pointed to a distant hill, and cried out: "*Ahò, ahò henàk!*" (There they are!) There were, in fact, the shadows of some rocks, which bore a faint resemblance to tents. Before sunset, we reached the last declivity of the mountains, and saw far in the dusky plain, the long green belt of the gardens of Damascus, and here and there the indistinct glimmer of a minaret. Katana, our resting-place for the night, lay below us, buried in orchards of olive and orange. We pitched our tents on the banks of a beautiful stream, enjoyed the pipe of tranquillity, after our long march, and soon forgot the Druses, in a slumber that lasted unbroken till dawn.

In the morning we sent back the man of Banias, left the baggage to take care of itself, and rode on to Damascus, as fast as our tired horses could carry us. The plain, at first barren and stony, became enlivened with vineyards and fields of wheat, as we advanced. Arabs were everywhere at work, ploughing and directing the water-courses. The belt of living green, the bower in which the great city, the Queen of the Orient, hides her beauty, drew nearer and nearer, stretching out a crescent of foliage for miles on either hand, that gradually narrowed and received us into its cool and fragrant heart. We sank into a sea of olive, pomegranate, orange, plum, apricot, walnut, and plane trees, and were lost. The sun sparkled in the rolling surface above ; but we swam through the green depths, below his reach, and thus, drifted on through miles of shade, entered the city.

Since our arrival, I find that two other parties of travellers, one of which crossed the Anti-Lebanon on the northern side of Mount Hermon, were obliged to take guards, and saw several Druse spies posted on the heights, as they passed. A Russian gentleman travelling from here to Tiberias, was stopped three times on the road, and only escaped being plundered from the fact of his having a Druse dragoman. The disturbances are more serious than I had anticipated. Four regiments left here yesterday, sent to the aid of a company of cavalry, which is surrounded by the rebels in a valley of Dejebel Hauaran, and unable to get out.

CHAPTER IX.

PICTURES OF DAMASCUS.

Damascus from the Anti-Lebanon—Entering the City—A Diorama of Bazaars—An Oriental Hotel—Our Chamber—The Bazaars—Pipes and Coffee—The Rivers of Damascus—Palaces of the Jews—Jewish Ladies—A Christian Gentleman—The Sacred Localities—Damascus Blades—The Sword of Haroun Al-Raschid—An Arrival from Palmyra.

"Are not Abana and Pharpar, rivers of Damascus, better than all the waters of Israel?"—2 KINGS, v. 12.

DAMASCUS, *Wednesday, May* 19, 1852.

DAMASCUS is considered by many travellers as the best remaining type of an Oriental city. Constantinople is semi-European; Cairo is fast becoming so; but Damascus, away from the highways of commerce, seated alone between the Lebanon and the Syrian Desert, still retains, in its outward aspect and in the character of its inhabitants, all the pride and fancy and fanaticism of the times of the Caliphs. With this judgment, in general terms, I agree; but not to its ascendancy, in every respect, over Cairo. True, when you behold Damascus from the Salahiyeh, the last slope of the Anti-Lebanon, it is the realization of all that you have dreamed of Oriental splendor; the world has no picture more dazzling. It is Beauty carried to the Sublime, as I have felt when overlooking some boundless forest of palms within the tropics. From the hill, whose ridges heave behind you until in the south they rise to the snowy head of Mount Hermon, the great Syrian plain stretches away to the Euphrates, broken at distances of ten and fifteen miles, by two detached mountain chains. In a terrible gorge at your side, the river Barrada, the ancient Pharpar, forces its way to the plain, and its waters, divided into twelve different channels, make all between you and those blue island-hills of the desert, one great garden, the boundaries of which your vision can barely distinguish. Its longest diameter cannot be less than twenty miles. You look down on a world of foliage, and fruit, and blossoms, whose hue, by contrast with the barren mountains and the yellow rim of the desert which incloses it, seems brighter than all other gardens in the world. Through its centre, following the course of the river, lies Damascus; a line of white walls, topped with domes and towers and tall minarets, winding away for miles through the green sea. Nothing less than a city of palaces, whose walls are marble and whose doors are ivory and pearl, could keep up the enchantment of that distant view.

We rode for an hour through the gardens before entering the gate. The fruit-trees, of whatever variety—walnut, olive, apricot, or fig—were the noblest of their kind. Roses and pomegranates in bloom starred the dark foliage, and the scented jasmine overhung the walls. But as we approached the city, the view was obscured by high mud walls on either side of the road, and we only caught glimpses now and then of the fragrant wilderness. The first street we entered was low and mean, the houses of clay. Following this, we came to an uncovered bazaar, with rude shops on either side, protected by mats stretched in front and supported by poles.

Here all sorts of common stuffs and utensils were sold, and the street was filled with crowds of Fellahs and Desert Arabs. Two large sycamores shaded it, and the Seraglio of the Pasha of Damascus, a plain two-story building, faced the entrance of the main bazaar, which branched off into the city. We turned into this, and after passing through several small bazaars stocked with dried fruits, pipes and pipe-bowls, groceries, and all the primitive wares of the East, reached a large passage, covered with a steep wooden roof, and entirely occupied by venders of silk stuffs. Out of this we passed through another, devoted to saddles and bridles; then another, full of spices, and at last reached the grand bazaar, where all the richest stuffs of Europe and the East were displayed in the shops. We rode slowly along through the cool twilight, crossed here and there by long pencils of white light, falling through apertures in the roof, and illuminating the gay turbans and silk caftans of the lazy merchants. But out of this bazaar, at intervals, opened the grand gate of a khan, giving us a view of its marble court, its fountains, and the dark arches of its store-rooms; or the door of a mosque, with its mosaic floor and pillared corridor. The interminable lines of bazaars, with their atmospheres of spice and fruit and fragrant tobacco, the hushed tread of the slippered crowds; the plash of falling fountains and the bubbling of innumerable narghilehs; the picturesque merchants and their customers, no longer in the big trowsers of Egypt, but the long caftans and abas of Syria; the absence of Frank faces and dresses—in all these there was the true spirit of the Orient, and so far, we were charmed with Damascus.

At the hotel in the Soog el-Haràb, or Frank quarter, the

illusion was not dissipated. It had once been the house of some rich merchant. The court into which we were ushered is paved with marble, with a great stone basin, surrounded with vases of flowering plants, in the centre. Two large lemon trees shade the entrance, and a vine, climbing to the top of the house, makes a leafy arbor over the flat roof. The walls of the house are painted in horizontal bars of blue, white, orange and white—a gay grotesqueness of style which does not offend the eye under an eastern sun. On the southern side of the court is the *liwan*, an arrangement for which the houses of Damascus are noted. It is a vaulted apartment, twenty feet high, entirely open towards the court, except a fine pointed arch at the top, decorated with encaustic ornaments of the most brilliant colors. In front, a tesselated pavement of marble leads to the doors of the chambers on each side. Beyond this is a raised floor covered with matting, and along the farther end a divan, whose piled cushions are the most tempting trap ever set to catch a lazy man. Although not naturally indolent, I find it impossible to resist the fascination of this lounge. Leaning back, cross-legged, against the cushions, with the inseparable pipe in one's hand, the view of the court, the water-basin, the flowers and lemon trees, the servants and dragomen going back and forth, or smoking their narghilehs in the shade—all framed in the beautiful arched entrance, is so perfectly Oriental, so true a tableau from the times of good old Haroun Al-Raschid, that one is surprised to find how many hours have slipped away while he has been silently enjoying it.

Opposite the *liwan* is a large room paved with marble, with a handsome fountain in the centre. It is the finest in the hotel, and now occupied by Lord Dalkeith and his friends. Our own room is on the upper floor, and is so rich in decorations that I have not yet finished the study of them. Along the side, looking down on the court, we have a mosaic floor of white, red, black and yellow marble. Above this is raised a second floor, carpeted and furnished in European style. The walls, for a height of ten feet, are covered with wooden panelling, painted with arabesque devices in the gayest colors, and along the top there is a series of Arabic inscriptions in gold. There are a number of niches or open closets in the walls, whose arched tops are adorned with pendent wooden ornaments, resembling stalactites, and at the corners of the room the heavy gilded and painted cornice drops into similar grotesque incrustations. A space of bare white wall intervenes between this cornice and the ceiling, which is formed of slim poplar logs, laid side by side, and so covered with paint and with scales and stripes and network devices in gold and silver, that one would take them to be clothed with the skins of the magic serpents that guard the Valley of Diamonds. My most satisfactory remembrance of Damascus will be this room.

My walks through the city have been almost wholly confined to the bazaars, which are of immense extent. One can walk for many miles, without going beyond the cover of their peaked wooden roofs, and in all this round will find no two precisely alike. One is devoted entirely to soap ; another to tobacco, through which you cough and sneeze your way to the bazaar of spices, and delightedly inhale its perfumed air. Then there is the bazaar of sweetmeats ; of vegetables ; of red slippers ; of shawls ; of caftans ; of bakers and ovens ; of wooden ware ; of jewelry—a great stone building, covered with vaulted passages ; of Aleppo silks ; of Baghdad carpets ; of Indian stuffs ; of coffee ; and so on, through a seemingly endless variety. As I have already remarked, along the line of the bazaars are many khans, the resort of merchants from all parts of Turkey and Persia, and even India. They are large, stately buildings, and some of them have superb gateways of sculptured marble. The interior courts are paved with stone, with fountains in the centre, and many of them are covered with domes resting on massive pillars. The largest has a roof of nine domes, supported by four grand pillars, which inclose a fountain. The mosques, into which no Christian is allowed to enter, are in general inferior to those of Cairo, but their outer courts are always paved with marble, adorned with fountains, and surrounded by light and elegant corridors. The grand mosque is an imposing edifice, and is said to occupy the site of a former Christian church.

Another pleasant feature of the city is its coffee shops, which abound in the bazaars and on the outskirts of the gardens, beside the running streams. Those in the bazaars are spacious rooms with vaulted ceilings, divans running around the four walls, and fountains in the centre. During the afternoon they are nearly always filled with Turks, Armenians and Persians, smoking the narghileh, or water-pipe, which is the universal custom in Damascus. The Persian tobacco, brought here by the caravans from Baghdad, is renowned for this kind of smoking. The most popular coffee-shop is near the citadel, on the banks and over the surface of the Pharpar. It is a rough wooden building, with a roof of straw mats, but the sight and sound of the rushing waters, as they shoot away with arrowy swiftness under your feet, the shade of the trees that line the banks, and the cool breeze that always visits the spot, beguile you into a second pipe ere you are aware. "*El mà, wa el khòdra, wa el widj el hàssan*—water, verdure and a beautiful face," says an old Arab proverb, "are three things which delight the heart," and the Syrians avow that all three are to be found in Damascus. Not only on the three Sundays of each week, but every day, in the gardens about the city, you may see whole families (and if Jews or Christians, many groups of families) spending the day in the shade, beside the beautiful waters. There are several gardens fitted up purposely for these pic-nics, with kiosks, fountains and pleasant seats under the trees. You bring your pipes, your provisions and the like with you, but servants are in attendance to furnish fire and water and coffee, for which, on leaving, you give them a small gratuity. Of all the Damascenes I have yet seen, there is not one but declares his city to be the Garden of the World, the Pearl of the Orient, and thanks God and the Prophet for having permitted him to be born and to live in it.

But, except the bazaars, the khans and the baths, of which there are several most luxurious establishments, the city itself is neither so rich nor so purely Saracenic in its architecture as Cairo. The streets are narrow and dirty, and the houses, which are never more than two low stories in height, are built of sun-dried bricks, coated with plaster. I miss the solid piles of stone, the elegant doorways, and, above all, the exquisite hanging balconies of carved wood, which meet one in the old streets of Cairo. Damascus is the representative of all that is gay, brilliant, and picturesque, in Oriental life; but for stately magnificence, Cairo, and, I suspect, Baghdad, is its superior.

We visited the other day the houses of some of the richest Jews and Christians. Old Abou-Ibrahim, the Jewish servant of the hotel, accompanied and introduced us. It is customary for travellers to make these visits, and the families, far from being annoyed, are flattered by it. The exteriors of the houses are mean; but after threading a narrow passage, we emerged into a court, rivalling in profusion of ornament and rich contrast of colors one's early idea of the Palace of Aladdin. The floors and fountains are all of marble mosaic; the arches of the *liwan* glitter with gold, and the walls bewilder the eye with the intricacy of their adornments. In the first house, we were received by the family in a room of precious marbles, with niches in the walls, resembling grottoes of silver stalactites. The cushions of the divan were of the richest silk, and a chandelier of Bohemian crystal hung from the ceiling. Silver narghilehs were brought to us, and coffee was served in heavy silver *zerfs*. The lady of the house was a rather corpulent lady of about thirty-five, and wore a semi-European robe of embroidered silk and lace, with full trowsers gathered at the ankles, and yellow slippers. Her black hair was braided, and fastened at the end with golden ornaments, and the light scarf twisted around her head blazed with diamonds. The lids of her large eyes were stained with *kohl*, and her eyebrows were plucked out and shaved away so as to leave only a thin, arched line, as if drawn with a pencil, above each eye. Her daughter, a girl of fifteen, who bore the genuine Hebrew name of Rachel, had even bigger and blacker eyes than her mother; but her forehead was low, her mouth large, and the expression of her face exceedingly stupid. The father of the family was a middle-aged man, with a well-bred air, and talked with an

Oriental politeness which was very refreshing. An English lady, who was of our party, said to him, through me, that if she possessed such a house she should be willing to remain in Damascus. "Why does she leave, then?" he immediately answered: "this is her house, and everything that is in it." Speaking of visiting Jerusalem, he asked me whether it was not a more beautiful city than Damascus. "It is not more beautiful," I said, "but it is more holy," an expression which the whole company received with great satisfaction.

The second house we visited was even larger and richer than the first, but had an air of neglect and decay. The slabs of rich marble were loose and broken, about the edges of the fountains; the rich painting of the wood-work was beginning to fade; and the balustrades leading to the upper chambers were broken off in places. We were ushered into a room, the walls and ceilings of which were composed entirely of gilded arabesque frame-work, set with small mirrors. When new, it must have had a gorgeous effect; but the gold is now tarnished, and the glasses dim. The mistress of the house was seated on the cushions, dividing her time between her pipe and her needle-work. She merely made a slight inclination of her head as we entered, and went on with her occupation. Presently her two daughters and an Abyssinian slave appeared, and took their places on the cushions at her feet, the whole forming a charming group, which I regretted some of my artist friends at home could not see. The mistress was so exceedingly dignified, that she bestowed but few words on us. She seemed to resent our admiration of the slave, who was a most graceful creature; yet her jealousy, it afterwards appeared, had reference to her own husband, for we had scarcely left, when a servant followed to inform the English lady that if she was willing to buy the Abyssinian, the mistress would sell her at once for two thousand piastres.

The last visit we paid was to the dwelling of a Maronite, the richest Christian in Damascus. The house resembled those we had already seen, except that, having been recently built, it was in better condition, and exhibited better taste in the ornaments. No one but the lady was allowed to enter the female apartments, the rest of us being entertained by the proprietor, a man of fifty, and without exception the handsomest and most dignified person of that age I have ever seen. He was a king without a throne, and fascinated me completely by the noble elegance of his manner. In any country but the Orient, I should have pronounced him incapable of an unworthy thought: here, he may be exactly the reverse.

Although Damascus is considered the oldest city in the world, the date of its foundation going beyond tradition, there are very few relics of antiquity in or near it. In the bazaar are three large pillars, supporting half the pediment, which are said to have belonged to the Christian Church of St. John, but, if so, that church must have been originally a Roman temple. Part of the Roman walls and one of the city gates remain; and we saw the spot where, according to tradition, Saul was let down from the wall in a basket. There are two localities pointed out as the scene of his conversion, which, from his own account, occurred near the city. I visited a subterranean chapel claimed by the Latin monks to be the cellar of the house of Ananias, in which the Apostle was concealed. The cellar is, undoubtedly, of great antiquity; but as the whole quarter was for many centuries inhabited wholly by Turks, it would be curious to know how the monks ascertained which was the house of Ananias. As for the "street called Straight," it would be difficult at present to find any in Damascus corresponding to that epithet.

The famous Damascus blades, so renowned in the time of the Crusaders, are made here no longer. The art has been lost for three or four centuries. Yet genuine old swords, of the true steel, are occasionally to be found. They are readily distinguished from modern imitations by their clear and silvery ring when struck, and by the finely watered appearance of the blade, produced by its having been first made of woven wire, and then worked over and over again until it attained the requisite temper. A droll Turk, who is the *shekh ed-dellàl*, or Chief of the Auctioneers, and is nicknamed Abou-Anteeka (the Father of the Antiques), has a large collection of sabres, daggers, pieces of mail, shields, pipes, rings, seals, and other ancient articles. He demands enormous prices, but generally takes about one-third of what he first asks. I have spent several hours in his curiosity shop, bargaining for turquoise rings, carbuncles, Persian amulets, and Circassian daggers. While looking over some old swords the other day, I noticed one of exquisite temper, but with a shorter blade than usual. The point had apparently been snapped off in fight, but owing to the excellence of the sword, or the owner's affection for it, the steel had been carefully shaped into a new point. Abou-Anteeka asked five hundred piastres, and I, who had taken a particular fancy to possess it, offered him two hundred in an indifferent way, and then laid it aside to examine other articles. After his refusal to accept my offer, I said nothing more, and was leaving the shop, when the old fellow called me back, saying: "You have forgotten your sword,"—which I thereupon took at my own price. I have shown it to Mr. Wood, the British Consul, who pronounced it an extremely fine specimen of Damascus steel; and, on reading the inscription enamelled upon the blade, ascertains that it was made in the year of the Hegira, 181, which corresponds to A.D. 798. This was during the Caliphate of Haroun Al-Raschid, and who knows but the sword may have once flashed in the presence of that great and glorious sovereign—nay, been drawn by his own hand! Who knows but that the Milan armor of the Crusaders may have shivered its point, on the field of Askalon! I kiss the veined azure of thy blade, O Sword of Haroun! I hang the crimson cords of thy scabbard upon my shoulder, and thou shalt henceforth clank in silver music at my side, singing to my ear, and mine alone, thy chants of battle, thy rejoicing songs of slaughter!

Yesterday evening, three gentlemen of Lord Dalkeith's party arrived from a trip to Palmyra. The road thither lies through a part of the Syrian Desert belonging to the Aneyzeh tribe, who are now supposed to be in league with the Druses, against the Government. Including this party, only six persons have succeeded in reaching Palmyra within a year, and two of them, Messrs. Noel and Cathcart, were imprisoned four days by the Arabs, and only escaped by the accidental departure of a caravan for Damascus. The present party was obliged to travel almost wholly by night, running the gauntlet of a dozen Arab encampments, and was only allowed a day's stay at Palmyra. They were all disguised as Bedouins, and took nothing with them but the necessary provisions. They made their appearance here last evening, in long, white abas, with the Bedouin *keffie* bound over their heads, their faces burnt, their eyes inflamed, and their frames feverish with seven days and nights of travel. The shekh who conducted them was not an Aneyzeh, and would have lost his life had they fallen in with any of that tribe.

CHAPTER X.

THE VISIONS OF HASHEESH.

"Exulting, trembling, raging, fainting,
Possessed beyond the Muse's painting."
COLLINS.

DURING my stay in Damascus, that insatiable curiosity which leads me to prefer the acquisition of all lawful knowledge through the channels of my own personal experience, rather than in less satisfactory and less laborious ways, induced me to make a trial of the celebrated *Hasheesh*—that remarkable drug which supplies the luxurious Syrian with dreams more alluring and more gorgeous than the Chinese extracts from his darling opium pipe. The use of Hasheesh—which is a preparation of the dried leaves of the *cannabis indica*—has been familiar to the East for many centuries. During the Crusades, it was frequently used by the Saracen warriors to stimulate them to the work of slaughter, and from the Arabic term of "*Hasha-sheën*," or Eaters of Hasheesh, as applied to them, the word "assassin" has been naturally derived. An infusion of the same plant gives to the drink called "*bhang*," which is in common use throughout India and Malaysia, its peculiar properties. Thus prepared, it is a more fierce and fatal stimulant than the paste of sugar and spices to which the Turk resorts, as the food of his voluptuous evening reveries. While its immediate effects seem to be more potent than those of opium, its habitual use, though attended with ultimate and permanent injury to the system, rarely results in such utter wreck of mind and body as that to which the votaries of the latter drug inevitably condemn themselves.

A previous experience of the effects of hasheesh—which I took once, and in a very mild form, while in Egypt—was so peculiar in its character, that my curiosity, instead of being satisfied, only prompted me the more to throw myself, for once, wholly under its influence. The sensations it then produced were those, physically, of exquisite lightness and airiness—mentally, of a wonderfully keen perception of the ludicrous, in the most simple and familiar objects. During the half hour in which it lasted, I was at no time so far under its control, that I could not, with the clearest perception, study the changes through which I passed. I noted, with careful attention, the fine sensations which spread throughout the whole tissue of my nervous fibre, each thrill helping to divest my frame of its earthy and material nature, until my substance appeared to me no grosser than the vapors of the atmosphere, and while sitting in the calm of the Egyptian twilight, I expected to be lifted up and carried away by the first breeze that should ruffle the Nile. While this process was going on, the objects by which I was surrounded assumed a strange and whimsical expression. My pipe, the oars which my boatmen plied, the turban worn by the captain, the water-jars and culinary implements, became in themselves so inexpressibly absurd and comical, that I was provoked into a long fit of laughter. The hallucination died away as gradually as it came, leaving me overcome with a soft and pleasant drowsiness, from which I sank into a deep, refreshing sleep.

My companion and an English gentleman, who, with his wife, was also residing in Antonio's pleasant caravanserai—agreed to join me in the experiment. The dragoman of the latter was deputed to procure a sufficient quantity of the drug. He was a dark Egyptian, speaking only the *lingua franca* of the East, and asked me, as he took the money and departed on his mission, whether he should get hasheesh *"per ridere, o per dormire?"* "Oh, *per ridere*, of course," I answered; "and see that it be strong and fresh." It is customary with the Syrians to take a small portion immediately before the evening meal, as it is thus diffused through the stomach and acts more gradually, as well as more gently, upon the system. As our dinner-hour was at sunset, I proposed taking hasheesh at that time, but my friends, fearing that its operation might be more speedy upon fresh subjects, and thus betray them into some absurdity in the presence of the other travellers, preferred waiting until after the meal. It was then agreed that we should retire to our room, which, as it rose like a tower one story higher than the rest of the building, was in a manner isolated, and would screen us from observation.

We commenced by taking a tea-spoonful each of the mixture which Abdallah had procured. This was about the quantity I had taken in Egypt, and as the effect then had been so slight, I judged that we ran no risk of taking an over-dose. The strength of the drug, however, must have been far greater in this instance, for whereas I could in the former case distinguish no flavor but that of sugar and rose leaves, I now found the taste intensely bitter and repulsive to the palate. We allowed the paste to dissolve slowly on our tongues, and sat some time, quietly waiting the result. But, having been taken upon a full stomach, its operation was hindered, and after the lapse of nearly an hour, we could not detect the least change in our feelings. My friends loudly expressed their conviction of the humbug of hasheesh, but I, unwilling to give up the experiment at this point, proposed that we should take an additional half spoonful, and follow it with a cup of hot tea, which, if there were really any virtue in the preparation, could not fail to call it into action. This was done, though not without some misgivings, as we were all ignorant of the precise quantity which constituted a dose, and the limits within which the drug could be taken with safety. It was now ten o'clock ; the streets of Damascus were gradually becoming silent, and the fair city was bathed in the yellow lustre of the Syrian moon. Only in the marble court-yard below us, a few dragomen and *mukkairee* lingered under the lemon-trees, and beside the fountain in the centre.

I was seated alone, nearly in the middle of the room, talking with my friends, who were lounging upon a sofa placed in a sort of alcove, at the farther end, when the same fine nervous thrill, of which I have spoken, suddenly shot through me. But this time it was accompanied with a burning sensation at the pit of the stomach ; and, instead of growing upon me with the gradual pace of healthy slumber, and resolving me, as before, into air, it came with the intensity of a pang, and shot throbbing along the nerves to the extremities of my body. The sense of limitation—of the confinement of our senses within the bounds of our own flesh and blood—instantly fell away. The walls of my frame were burst outward and tumbled into ruin ; and, without thinking what form I wore—losing sight even of all idea of form—I felt that I existed throughout a vast extent of space. The blood, pulsed from my heart, sped through uncounted leagues before it reached my extremities; the air drawn into my lungs expanded into seas of limpid ether, and the arch of my skull was broader than the vault of heaven. Within the concave that held my brain, were the fathomless deeps of blue; clouds floated there, and the winds of heaven rolled them together, and there shone the orb of the sun. It was—though I thought not of that at the time—like a revelation of the mystery of omnipresence. It is difficult to describe this sensation, or the rapidity with which it mastered me. In the state of mental exaltation in which I was then plunged, all sensations, as they rose, suggested more or less coherent images. They presented themselves to me in a double form: one physical, and therefore to a certain extent tangible; the other spiritual, and revealing itself in a succession of splendid metaphors. The physical feeling of extended being was accompanied by the image of an exploding meteor, not subsiding into darkness, but continuing to shoot from its centre or nucleus—which corresponded to the burning spot at the pit of my stomach—incessant adumbrations of light that finally lost themselves in the infinity of space. To my mind, even now, this image is still the best illustration of my sensations, as I recall them; but I greatly doubt whether the reader will find it equally clear.

My curiosity was now in a way of being satisfied; the Spirit (demon, shall I not rather say?) of Hasheesh had entire possession of me. I was cast upon the flood of his illusions, and drifted helplessly whithersoever they might choose to bear me. The thrills which ran through my nervous system became more rapid and fierce, accompanied with sensations that steeped my whole being in unutterable rapture. I was encompassed by a sea of light, through which played the pure, harmonious colors that are born of light. While endeavoring, in broken expressions, to describe my feelings to my friends, who sat looking upon me incredulously—not yet having been affected by the drug—I suddenly found myself at the foot of the great Pyramid of Cheops. The tapering courses of yellow limestone gleamed like gold in the sun, and the pile rose so high that it seemed to lean for support upon the blue arch of the sky. I wished to ascend it, and the wish alone placed me immediately upon its apex, lifted thousands of feet above the wheat-fields and palm-groves of Egypt. I cast my eyes downward, and, to my astonishment, saw that it was built, not of limestone, but of huge square plugs of Cavendish tobacco! Words cannot paint the overwhelming sense of the ludicrous which I then experienced. I writhed on my chair in an agony of laughter, which was only relieved by the vision melting away like a dissolving view; till, out of my confusion of indistinct images and fragments of images, another and more wonderful vision arose.

The more vividly I recall the scene which followed, the more carefully I restore its different features, and separate the many threads of sensation which it wove into one gorgeous web, the more I despair of representing its exceeding glory. I was moving over the Desert, not upon the rocking dromedary, but seated in a barque made of mother-of-pearl, and studded with jewels of surpassing lustre. The sand was of grains of gold, and my keel slid through them without jar or sound. The air was radiant with excess of light, though no sun was to be seen. I inhaled the most delicious perfumes; and harmonies, such as

Beethoven may have heard in dreams, but never wrote, floated around me. The atmosphere itself was light, odor, music; and each and all sublimated beyond anything the sober senses are capable of receiving. Before me—for a thousand leagues, as it seemed—stretched a vista of rainbows, whose colors gleamed with the splendor of gems—arches of living amethyst, sapphire, emerald, topaz, and ruby. By thousands and tens of thousands, they flew past me, as my dazzling barge sped down the magnificent arcade; yet the vista still stretched as far as ever before me. I revelled in a sensuous elysium, which was perfect, because no sense was left ungratified. But beyond all, my mind was filled with a boundless feeling of triumph. My journey was that of a conqueror—not of a conqueror who subdues his race, either by Love or by Will, for I forgot that Man existed—but one victorious over the grandest as well as the subtlest forces of Nature. The spirits of Light, Color, Odor, Sound, and Motion were my slaves; and, having these, I was master of the universe.

Those who are endowed to any extent with the imaginative faculty, must have at least once in their lives experienced feelings which may give them a clue to the exalted sensuous raptures of my triumphal march. The view of a sublime mountain landscape, the hearing of a grand orchestral symphony, or of a choral upborne by the "full-voiced organ," or even the beauty and luxury of a cloudless summer day, suggests emotions similar in kind, if less intense. They took a warmth and glow from that pure animal joy which degrades not, but spiritualizes and ennobles our material part, and which differs from cold, abstract, intellectual enjoyment, as the flaming diamond of the Orient differs from the icicle of the

North. Those finer senses, which occupy a middle ground between our animal and intellectual appetites, were suddenly developed to a pitch beyond what I had ever dreamed, and being thus at one and the same time gratified to the fullest extent of their preternatural capacity, the result was a single harmonious sensation, to describe which human language has no epithet. Mahomet's Paradise, with its palaces of ruby and emerald, its airs of musk and cassia, and its rivers colder than snow and sweeter than honey, would have been a poor and mean terminus for my arcade of rainbows. Yet in the character of this paradise, in the gorgeous fancies of the Arabian Nights, in the glow and luxury of all Oriental poetry, I now recognize more or less of the agency of hasheesh.

The fulness of my rapture expanded the sense of time; and though the whole vision was probably not more than five minutes in passing through my mind, years seemed to have elapsed while I shot under the dazzling myriads of rainbow arches. By and by, the rainbows, the barque of pearl and jewels, and the desert of golden sand, vanished; and, still bathed in light and perfume, I found myself in a land of green and flowery lawns, divided by hills of gently undulating outline. But, although the vegetation was the richest of earth, there were neither streams nor fountains to be seen; and the people who came from the hills, with brilliant garments that shone in the sun, besought me to give them the blessing of water. Their hands were full of branches of the coral honeysuckle, in bloom. These I took; and, breaking off the flowers one by one, set them in the earth. The slender, trumpet-like tubes immediately became shafts of masonry, and sank deep into the earth; the lip of the flower changed into a circular mouth of rose-colored marble, and the people, leaning over its brink, lowered their pitchers to the bottom with cords, and drew them up again, filled to the brim, and dripping with honey.

The most remarkable feature of these illusions was, that at the time when I was most completely under their influence, I knew myself to be seated in the tower of Antonio's hotel in Damascus, knew that I had taken hasheesh, and that the strange, gorgeeus and ludicrous fancies which possessed me, were the effect of it. At the very same instant that I looked upon the Valley of the Nile from the pyramid, slid over the Desert, or created my marvellous wells in that beautiful pastoral country, I saw the furniture of my room, its mosaic pavement, the quaint Saracenic niches in the walls, the painted and gilded beams of the ceiling, and the couch in the recess before me, with my two companions watching me. Both sensations were simultaneous, and equally palpable. While I was most given up to the magnificent delusion, I saw its cause and felt its absurdity most clearly. Metaphysicians say that the mind is incapable of performing two operations at the same time, and may attempt to explain this phenomenon by supposing a rapid and incessant vibration of the perceptions between the two states. This explanation, however, is not satisfactory to me; for not more clearly does a skilful musician with the same breath blow two distinct musical notes from a bugle, than I was conscious of two distinct conditions of being in the same moment. Yet, singular as it may seem, neither conflicted with the other. My enjoyment of the visions was complete and absolute, undisturbed by the faintest doubt of their reality, while, in some other chamber of my brain, Reason sat coolly watching them, and heaping the liveliest ridicule on their fantastic features. One set of nerves was thrilled with the bliss of the gods, while another was convulsed with unquenchable laughter at that very bliss. My highest ecstacies could not bear down and silence the weight of my ridicule, which, in its turn, was powerless to prevent me from running into other and more gorgeous absurdities. I was double, not "swan and shadow," but rather, Sphinx-like, human and beast. A true Sphinx, I was a riddle and a mystery to myself.

The drug, which had been retarded in its operation on account of having been taken after a meal, now began to make itself more powerfully felt. The visions were more grotesque than ever, but less agreeable ; and there was a painful tension throughout my nervous system—the effect of over-stimulus. I was a mass of transparent jelly, and a confectioner poured me into a twisted mould. I threw my chair aside, and writhed and tortured myself for some time to force my loose substance into the mould. At last, when I had so far succeeded that only one foot remained outside, it was lifted off, and another mould, of still more crooked and intricate shape, substituted. I have no doubt that the contortions through which I went, to accomplish the end of my gelatinous destiny, would have been extremely ludicrous to a spectator, but to me they were painful and disagreeable. The sober half of me went into fits of laughter over them, and through that laughter, my vision shifted into another scene. I had laughed until my eyes overflowed profusely. Every drop that fell, immediately became a large loaf of bread, and tumbled upon the shop-board of a baker in the bazaar at Damascus. The more I laughed, the faster the loaves fell, until such a pile was raised about the baker, that I could hardly see the top of his head. "The man will be suffocated," I cried, "but if he were to die, I cannot stop!"

My perceptions now became more dim and confused. I felt that I was in the grasp of some giant force; and, in the glimmering of my fading reason, grew earnestly alarmed, for the terrible stress under which my frame labored increased every moment. A fierce and furious heat radiated from my stomach throughout my system; my mouth and throat were as dry and hard as if made of brass, and my tongue, it seemed to me, was a bar of rusty iron. I seized a pitcher of water, and drank long and deeply; but I might as well have drunk so much air, for not only did it impart no moisture, but my palate and throat gave me no intelligence of having drunk at all. I stood in the centre of the room, brandishing my arms convulsively, and heaving sighs that seemed to shatter my whole being. "Will no one," I cried in distress, "cast out this devil that has possession of me?" I no longer saw the room nor my friends, but I heard one of them saying, "It must be real; he could not counterfeit such an expression as that. But it don't look much like pleasure." Immediately afterwards there was a scream of the wildest laughter, and my countryman sprang upon the floor, exclaiming, "O, ye gods! I am a locomotive!" This was his ruling hallucination; and, for the space of two or three hours, he continued to pace to and fro with a measured stride, exhaling his breath in violent jets, and when he spoke, dividing his words into syllables, each of which he brought out with a jerk, at the same time turning his hands at his sides, as if they were the cranks of imaginary wheels. The Englishman, as soon as he felt the dose beginning to take effect, prudently retreated to his own room, and what the nature of his visions was, we never learned, for he refused to tell, and, moreover, enjoined the strictest silence on his wife.

By this time it was nearly midnight. I had passed through the Paradise of Hasheesh, and was plunged at once into its fiercest Hell. In my ignorance I had taken what, I have since learned, would have been a sufficient portion for six men, and was now paying a frightful penalty for my curiosity. The excited blood rushed through my frame with a sound like the roaring of mighty waters. It was projected into my eyes until I could no longer see ; it beat thickly in my ears, and so throbbed in my heart, that I feared the ribs would give way under its blows. I tore open my vest, placed my hand over the spot, and tried to count the pulsations ; but there were two hearts, one beating at the rate of a thousand beats a minute, and the other with a slow, dull motion. My throat, I thought, was filled to the brim with blood, and streams of blood were pouring from my ears. I felt them gushing warm down my cheeks and neck. With a maddened, desperate feeling, I fled from the room, and walked over the flat, terraced roof of the house. My body seemed to shrink and grow rigid as I wrestled with the demon, and my face to become wild, lean and haggard. Some lines which had struck me, years before, in reading Mrs. Browning's "Rhyme of the Duchess May," flashed into my mind :—

"And the horse, in stark despair, with his front hoofs poised in air,
  On the last verge, rears amain ;
And he hangs, he rocks between—and his nostrils curdle in—
And he shivers, head and hoof, and the flakes of foam fall off ;
  And his face grows fierce and thin."

That picture of animal terror and agony was mine. I was the horse, hanging poised on the verge of the giddy tower, the next moment to be borne sheer down to destruction. Involuntarily, I raised my hand to feel the leanness and sharpness of my face. Oh horror! the flesh had fallen from my bones, and it was a skeleton head that I carried on my shoulders! With one bound I sprang to the parapet, and looked down into the silent courtyard, then filled with the shadows thrown into it by the sinking moon. Shall I cast myself down headlong? was the question I proposed to myself; but though the horror of that skeleton delusion was greater than my fear of death, there was an invisible hand at my breast which pushed me away from the brink.

I made my way back to the room, in a state of the keenest suffering. My companion was still a locomotive, rushing to and fro, and jerking out his syllables with the disjointed accent peculiar to a steam-engine. His mouth had turned to brass, like mine, and he raised the pitcher to his lips in the attempt to moisten it, but before he had taken a mouthful, set the pitcher down again with a yell of laughter, crying out: "How can I take water into my boiler, while I am letting off steam?"

But I was now too far gone to feel the absurdity of this, or his other exclamations. I was sinking deeper and deeper into a pit of unutterable agony and despair. For, although I was not conscious of real pain in any part of my body, the cruel tension to which my nerves had been subjected filled me through and through with a sensation of distress which was far more severe than pain itself. In addition to this, the remnant of will with which I struggled against the demon, became gradually weaker, and I felt that I should soon be powerless in his hands. Every effort to preserve my reason was accompanied by a pang of mortal fear, lest what I now experienced was insanity, and would hold mastery over me for ever. The thought of death, which also haunted me, was far less bitter than this dread. I knew that in the struggle which was going on in my frame, I was borne fearfully near the dark gulf, and the thought that, at such a time, both reason and will were leaving my brain, filled me with an agony, the depth and blackness of which I should vainly attempt to portray. I threw myself on my bed, with the excited blood still roaring wildly in my ears, my heart throbbing with a force that seemed to be rapidly wearing away my life, my throat dry as a potsherd, and my stiffened tongue cleaving to the roof of my mouth—resisting no longer, but awaiting my fate with the apathy of despair.

My companion was now approaching the same condition, but as the effect of the drug on him had been less violent, so his stage of suffering was more clamorous. He cried out to me that he was dying, implored me to help him, and reproached me vehemently, because I lay there silent, motionless, and apparently careless of his danger. "Why will he disturb me?" I thought; "he thinks he is dying, but what is death to madness? Let him die; a thousand deaths were more easily borne than the pangs I suffer." While I was sufficiently conscious to hear his exclamations, they only provoked my keen anger; but after a time, my senses became clouded, and I sank into a stupor. As near as I can judge, this must have been three o'clock in the morning, rather more than five hours after the hasheesh began to take effect. I lay thus all the following day and night, in a state of gray, blank oblivion, broken only by a single wandering gleam of consciousness. I recollect hearing François' voice. He told me afterwards that I arose, attempted to dress myself, drank two cups of coffee, and then fell back into the same death-like stupor ; but of all this, I did not retain the least knowledge. On the morning of the second day, after a sleep of thirty hours, I awoke again to the world, with a system utterly prostrate and unstrung, and a brain clouded with the lingering images of my visions. I knew where I was, and what had happened to me, but all that I saw still remained unreal and shadowy. There was no taste in what I ate, no refreshment in what I drank, and it required a painful effort to comprehend what was said to me and return a coherent answer. Will and Reason had come back, but they still sat unsteadily upon their thrones.

My friend, who was much further advanced in his recovery, accompanied me to the adjoining bath, which I hoped would assist in restoring me. It was with great difficulty that I preserved the outward appearance of consciousness. In spite of myself, a veil now and then fell over my mind, and after wandering for years, as it seemed, in some distant world, I awoke with a shock, to find myself in the steamy halls of the bath, with a brown Syrian polishing my limbs. I suspect that my language must have been rambling and incoherent, and that the menials who had me in charge understood my condition, for as soon as I had stretched myself upon the couch which follows the bath, a glass of very acid sherbet was presented to me, and after drinking it I experienced instant relief. Still the spell was not wholly broken, and for two or three days I continued subject to frequent involuntary fits of absence, which made me insensible, for the time, to all that was passing around me. I walked the streets of Damascus with a strange consciousness that I was in some other place at the same time, and with a constant effort to reunite my divided perceptions.

Previous to the experiment, we had decided on making a bargain with the shekh for the journey to Palmyra. The state, however, in which we now found ourselves, obliged us to relinquish the plan. Perhaps the excitement of a forced march across the desert, and a conflict with the hostile Arabs, which was quite likely to happen, might have assisted us in throwing off the baneful effects of thé drug ; but all the charm which lay in the name of Palmyra and the romantic interest of the trip, was gone. I was without courage and without energy, and nothing remained for me but to leave Damascus.

Yet, fearful as my rash experiment proved to me, I did not regret having made it. It revealed to me deeps of rapture and of suffering which my natural faculties never could have sounded. It has taught me the majesty of human reason and of human will, even in the weakest, and the awful peril of tampering with that which assails their integrity. I have here faithfully and fully written out my experience, on account of the lesson which it may convey to others. If I have unfortunately failed in my design, and have but awakened that restless curiosity which I have endeavored to forestall, let me beg all who are thereby led to repeat the experiment upon themselves, that they be content to take the portion of hasheesh which is considered sufficient for one man, and not, like me, swallow enough for six.

CHAPTER XI.

A DISSERTATION ON BATHING AND BODIES.

"No swan-soft woman, rubbed with lucid oils,
The gift of an enamored god, more fair."
BROWNING.

WE shall not set out from Damascus—we shall not leave the Pearl of the Orient to glimmer through the seas of foliage wherein it lies buried—without consecrating a day to the Bath, that material agent of peace and good-will unto men. We have bathed in the Jordan, like Naaman, and been made clean; let us now see whether Abana and Pharpar, rivers of Damascus, are better than the waters of Israel.

The Bath is the "peculiar institution" of the East. Coffee has become colonized in France and America; the Pipe is a cosmopolite, and his blue, joyous breath congeals under the Arctic Circle, or melts languidly into the soft airs of the Polynesian Isles; but the Bath, that sensuous elysium which cradled the dreams of Plato, and the visions of Zoroaster, and the solemn meditations of Mahomet, is only to be found under an Oriental sky. The naked natives of the Torrid Zone are amphibious; they do not bathe, they live in the water. The European and Anglo-American wash themselves and think they have bathed; they shudder under cold showers and perform laborious antics with coarse towels. As for the Hydropathist, the Genius of the Bath, whose dwelling is in Damascus, would be convulsed with scornful laughter, could he behold that aqueous Diogenes sitting in his tub, or stretched out in his wet wrappings, like a sodden mummy, in a cata comb of blankets and feather beds. As the rose in the East has a rarer perfume than in other lands, so does the Bath bestow a superior purification and impart a more profound enjoyment.

Listen not unto the lamentations of travellers, who complain of the heat, and the steam, and the dislocations of their joints. They belong to the stiff-necked generation, who resist the processes, whereunto the Oriental yields himself body and soul. He who is bathed in Damascus, must be as clay in the hands of a potter. The Syrians marvel how the Franks can walk, so difficult is it to bend their joints. Moreover, they know the difference between him who comes to the Bath out of a mere idle curiosity, and him who has tasted its delight and holds it in due honor. Only the latter is permitted to know all its mysteries. The former is carelessly hurried through the ordinary forms of bathing, and, if any trace of the cockney remain in him, is quite as likely to be disgusted as pleased. Again, there are many second and third-rate baths, whither cheating dragomen conduct their victims, in consideration of a division of spoils with the bath-keeper. Hence it is, that the Bath has received but partial justice at the hands of tourists in the East. If any one doubts this, let him clothe himself with Oriental passiveness and resignation, go to the Hamman el-Khyateën, at Damascus, or the Bath of Mahmoud Pasha, at Constantinople, and demand that he be perfectly bathed.

Come with me, and I will show you the mysteries of the perfect bath. Here is the entrance, a heavy Saracenic arch, opening upon the crowded bazaar. We descend a few steps to the marble pavement of a lofty octagonal hall, lighted by a dome. There is a jet of sparkling water in the centre, falling into a heavy stone basin. A platform about five feet in height runs around the hall, and on this are ranged a number of narrow couches, with their heads to the wall, like the pallets in a hospital ward. The platform is covered with straw matting, and from the wooden gallery which rises above it are suspended towels, with blue and crimson borders. The master of the bath receives us courteously, and conducts us to one of the vacant couches. We kick off our red slippers below, and mount the steps to the platform. Yonder traveller, in Frank dress, who has just entered, goes up with his boots on, and we know, from that fact, what sort of a bath he will get.

As the work of disrobing proceeds, a dark-eyed boy appears with a napkin, which he holds before us, ready to bind it about the waist, as soon as we regain our primitive form. Another attendant throws a napkin over our shoulders and wraps a third around our head, turban-wise. He then thrusts a pair of wooden clogs upon our feet, and, taking us by the arm, steadies our tottering and clattering steps, as we pass through a low door and a warm ante-chamber into the first hall of the bath. The light, falling dimly through a cluster of bull's-eyes in the domed ceiling, shows, first, a silver thread of water, playing in a steamy atmosphere; next, some dark motionless objects, stretched out on a low central platform of marble. The attendant spreads a linen sheet in one of the vacant places, places a pillow at one end, takes off our clogs, deposits us gently on our back, and leaves us. The pavement is warm beneath us, and the first breath we draw gives us a sense of suffocation. But a bit of burning aloe-wood has just been carried through the hall, and the steam is permeated with fragrance. The dark-eyed boy appears with a narghileh, which he places beside us, offering the amber mouth-piece to our submissive lips. The smoke we inhale has an odor of roses; and as the pipe bubbles with our breathing, we feel that the dews of sweat gather heavily upon us. The attendant now reappears, kneels beside us, and gently kneads us with dexterous hands. Although no anatomist, he knows every muscle and sinew whose suppleness gives ease to the body, and so moulds and manipulates them that we lose the rigidity of our mechanism, and become plastic in his hands. He turns us upon our face, repeats the same process upon the back, and leaves us a little longer to lie there passively, glistening in our own dew.

We are aroused from a reverie about nothing by a dark-brown shape, who replaces the clogs, puts his arm around our waist and leads us into an inner hall, with a steaming tank in the centre. Here he slips us off the brink, and we collapse over head and ears in the fiery fluid. Once—twice—we dip into the delicious heat, and then are led into a marble alcove, and seated flat upon the floor. The attendant stands behind us, and we now perceive that his hands are encased in dark hair-gloves. He pounces upon an arm, which he rubs until, like a serpent, we slough the worn-out skin, and resume our infantile smoothness and fairness. No man can be called clean until he has bathed in the East. Let him walk directly from his accustomed bath and self-friction with towels, to the Hammam el-Khyateën, and the attendant will exclaim, as he shakes out his hair-gloves: "O Frank! it is a long time since you have bathed." The other arm follows, the back, the breast, the legs, until the work is complete, and we know precisely how a horse feels after he has been curried.

Now the attendant turns two cocks at the back of the alcove, and holding a basin alternately under the cold and hot streams, floods us at first with a fiery dash, that sends a delicious warm shiver through every nerve; then, with milder applications, lessening the temperature of the water by semi-tones, until, from the highest key of heat which we can bear, we glide rapturously down the gamut until we reach the lowest bass of coolness. The skin has by this time attained an exquisite sensibility, and answers to these changes of temperature with thrills of the purest physical pleasure. In fact, the whole frame seems purged of its earthy nature and transformed into something of a finer and more delicate texture.

After a pause, the attendant makes his appearance with a large wooden bowl, a piece of soap, and a bunch of palm-fibres. He squats down beside the bowl, and speedily creates a mass of snowy lather, which grows up to a pyramid and topples over the edge. Seizing us by the crown-tuft of hair upon our shaven head, he plants the foamy bunch of fibres full in our face. The world vanishes; sight, hearing, smell, taste (unless we open our mouth), and breathing, are cut off; we have become nebulous. Although our eyes are shut, we seem to see a blank whiteness; and, feeling nothing but a soft fleeciness, we doubt whether we be not the Olympian cloud which visited Io. But the cloud clears away before strangulation begins, and the velvety mass descends upon the body. Twice we are thus "slushed" from head to foot, and made more slippery than the anointed wrestlers of the Greek games. Then the basin comes again into play, and we glide once more musically through the scale of temperature.

The brown sculptor has now nearly completed his task. The figure of clay which entered the bath is transformed into polished marble. He turns the body from side to side, and lifts the limbs to see whether the workmanship is adequate to his conception. His satisfied gaze proclaims his success. A skilful bath-attendant has a certain æsthetic pleasure in his occupation. The bodies he polishes become to some extent his own workmanship, and he feels responsible for their symmetry or deformity. He experiences a degree of triumph in contemplating a beautiful form, which has grown more airily light and beautiful under his hands. He is a great connoisseur of bodies, and could pick you out the finest specimens with as ready an eye as an artist.

I envy those old Greek bathers, into whose hands were delivered Pericles, and Alcibiades, and the perfect models of Phidias. They had daily before their eyes the highest types of Beauty which the world has ever produced; for of all things that are beautiful, the human body is the crown. Now, since the delusion of artists has been overthrown, and we know that Grecian Art is but the simple reflex of Nature—that the old masterpieces of sculpture were no miraculous embodiments of a *beau ideal*, but copies of living forms—we must admit that in no other age of the world has the physical Man been so perfectly developed. The nearest approach I have ever seen to the symmetry of ancient sculpture was among the Arab tribes of Ethiopia. Our Saxon race can supply the athlete, but not the Apollo.

Oriental life is too full of repose, and the Ottoman race has become too degenerate through indulgence, to exhibit many striking specimens of physical beauty. The face is generally fine, but the body is apt to be lank, and with imperfect muscular development. The best forms I saw in the baths were those of laborers, who, with a good deal of rugged strength, showed some grace and harmony of proportion. It may be received as a general rule, that the physical development of the European is superior to that of the Oriental, with the exception of the Circassians and Georgians, whose beauty well entitles them to the distinction of giving their name to our race.

So far as female beauty is concerned, the Circassian women have no superiors. They have preserved in their mountain home the purity of the Grecian models, and still display the perfect physical loveliness, whose type has descended to us in the Venus de Medici. The Frank who is addicted to wandering about the streets of Oriental cities can hardly fail to be favored with a sight of the faces of these beauties. More than once it has happened to me, in meeting a veiled lady, sailing along in her balloon-like feridjee, that she has allowed the veil to drop by a skilful accident, as she passed, and has startled me with the vision of her beauty, recalling the line of the Persian poet: "Astonishment! is this the dawn of the glorious sun, or is it the full moon?" The Circassian face is a pure oval; the forehead is low and fair, "an excellent thing in woman," and the skin of an ivory whiteness, except the faint pink of the cheeks and the ripe, roseate stain of the lips. The hair is dark, glossy, and luxuriant, exquisitely outlined on the temples; the eyebrows slightly arched, and drawn with a delicate pencil; while lashes like "rays of darkness" shade the large, dark, humid orbs below them. The alabaster of the face, so pure as scarcely to show the blue branching of the veins on the temples, is lighted by those superb eyes—

"Shining eyes, like antique jewels set in Parian statue-stone,"

—whose wells are so dark and deep, that you are cheated into the belief that a glorious soul looks out of them.

Once, by an unforeseen chance, I beheld the Circassian form, in its most perfect development. I was on board an Austrian steamer in the harbor of Smyrna, when the harem of a Turkish pasha came out in a boat to embark for Alexandria. The sea was rather rough, and nearly all the officers of the steamer were ashore. There were six veiled and swaddled women, with a black eunuch as guard, in the boat, which lay tossing for some time at the foot of the gangway ladder, before the frightened passengers could summon courage to step out. At last the youngest of them—a Circassian girl of not more than fifteen or sixteen years of age—ventured upon the ladder, clasping the hand-rail with one hand, while with the other she held together the folds of her cumbrous feridjee. I was standing in the gangway, watching her, when a slight lurch of the steamer caused her to loose her hold of the garment, which, fastened at the neck, was blown back from her shoulders, leaving her body screened but by a single robe of light, gauzy silk. Through this, the marble whiteness of her skin, the roundness, the glorious symmetry of her form, flashed upon me, as a vision of Aphrodite, seen

"Through leagues of shimmering water, like a star."

It was but a momentary glimpse ; yet that moment convinced me that forms of Phidian perfection are still nurtured in the vales of Caucasus.

The necessary disguise of dress hides from us much of the beauty and dignity of Humanity. I have seen men who appeared heroic in the freedom of nakedness, shrink almost into absolute vulgarity, when clothed. The soul not only sits at the windows of the eyes, and hangs upon the gateway of the lips ; she speaks as well in the intricate, yet harmonious lines of the body, and the ever-varying play of the limbs. Look at the torso of Ilioneus, the son of Niobe, and see what an agony of terror and supplication cries out from that headless and limbless trunk ! Decapitate Laocoön, and his knotted muscles will still express the same dreadful suffering and resistance. None knew this better than the ancient sculptors ; and hence it was that we find many of their statues of distinguished men wholly or partly undraped. Such a view of Art would be considered transcendental now-a-days, when our dress, our costumes, and our modes of speech either ignore the existence of our bodies, or treat them with little of that reverence which is their due.

But, while we have been thinking these thoughts, the attendant has been waiting to give us a final plunge into the seething tank. Again we slide down to the eyes in the fluid heat, which wraps us closely about until we tingle with exquisite hot shiverings. Now comes the graceful boy, with clean, cool, lavendered napkins, which he folds around our waist and wraps softly about the head. The pattens are put upon our feet, and the brown arm steadies us gently through the sweating-room and ante-chamber into the outer hall, where we mount to our couch. We sink gently upon the cool linen, and the boy covers us with a perfumed sheet. Then, kneeling beside the couch, he presses the folds of the sheet around us, that it may absorb the lingering moisture and the limpid perspiration shed by the departing heat. As fast as the linen becomes damp, he replaces it with fresh, pressing the folds about us as tenderly as a mother arranges the drapery of her sleeping babe; for we, though of the stature of a man, are now infantile in our helpless happiness. Then he takes our passive hand and warms its palm by the soft friction of his own; after which, moving to the end of the couch, he lifts our feet upon his lap, and repeats the friction upon their soles, until the blood comes back to the surface of the body with a misty glow, like that which steeps the clouds of a summer afternoon.

We have but one more process to undergo, and the attendant already stands at the head of our couch. This is the course of passive gymnastics, which excites so much alarm and resistance in the ignorant Franks. It is only resistance that is dangerous, completely neutralizing the enjoyment of the process. Give yourself with a blind submission into the arms of the brown Fate, and he will lead you to new chambers of delight. He lifts us to a sitting posture, places himself behind us, and folds his arms around our body, alternately tightening and relaxing his clasp, as if to test the elasticity of the ribs. Then seizing one arm, he draws it across the opposite shoulder, until the joint cracks like a percussion-cap. The shoulder-blades, the elbows, the wrists, and the finger-joints are all made to fire off their muffled volleys; and then, placing one knee between our shoulders, and clasping both hands upon our forehead, he draws our head back until we feel a great snap of the vertebral column. Now he descends to the hip-joints, knees, ankles, and feet, forcing each and all to discharge a salvo *de joie.* The slight languor left from the bath is gone, and an airy, delicate exhilaration, befitting the winged Mercury, takes its place.

The boy, kneeling, presents us with a *finjan* of foamy coffee, followed by a glass of sherbet cooled with the snows of Lebanon. He presently returns with a narghileh, which we smoke by the effortless inhalation of the lungs. Thus we lie in perfect repose, soothed by the fragrant weed, and idly watching the silent Orientals, who are undressing for the bath or reposing like ourselves. Through the arched entrance, we see a picture of the bazaars : a shadowy painting of merchants seated amid their silks and spices, dotted here and there with golden drops and splashes of sunshine, which have trickled through the roof. The scene paints itself upon our eyes, yet wakes no slightest stir of thought. The brain is a becalmed sea, without a ripple on its shores. Mind and body are drowned in delicious rest ; and we no longer remember what we are. We only know that there is an Existence somewhere in the air, and that wherever it is, and whatever it may be, it is happy.

More and more dim grows the picture. The colors fade and blend into each other, and finally merge into a bed of rosy clouds, flooded with the radiance of some unseen sun. Gentlier than "tired eyelids upon tired eyes," sleep lies upon our senses : a half-conscious sleep, wherein we know that we behold light and inhale fragrance. As gently, the clouds dissipate into air, and we are born again into the world. The Bath is at an end. We arise and put on our garments, and walk forth into the sunny streets of Damascus. But as we go homewards, we involuntarily look down to see whether we are really treading upon the earth, wondering, perhaps, that we should be content to do so, when it would be so easy to soar above the house-tops.

CHAPTER XII.

BAALBEC AND LEBANON.

Departure from Damascus—The Fountains of the Pharpar—Pass of the Anti-Lebanon—Adventure with the Druses—The Range of Lebanon—The Demon of Hasheesh departs—Impressions of Baalbec—The Temple of the Sun—Titanic Masonry—The Ruined Mosque—Camp on Lebanon—Rascality of the Guide—The Summit of Lebanon—The Sacred Cedars—The Christians of Lebanon—An Afternoon in Eden—Rugged Travel—We Reach the Coast—Return to Beyrout.

"Peor and Baälim
Forsake their temples dim."
MILTON.

"The cedars wave on Lebanon,
But Judah's statelier maids are gone."
BYRON.

BEYROUT, *Thursday, May* 27, 1852.

AFTER a stay of eight days in Damascus, we called our men, Dervish and Mustapha, again into requisition, loaded our enthusiastic mules, and mounted our despairing horses. There were two other parties on the way to Baalbec—an English gentleman and lady, and a solitary Englishman, so that our united forces made an imposing caravan. There is always a custom-house examination, not on entering, but on issuing from an Oriental city, but travellers can avoid it by procuring the company of a Consular Janissary as far as the gate. Mr. Wood, the British Consul, lent us one of his officers for the occasion, whom we found waiting, outside of the wall, to receive his private fee for the service. We mounted the long, barren hill west of the plain, and at the summit, near the tomb of a Moslem shekh, turned to take a last long look at the bowery plain, and the minarets of the city, glittering through the blue morning vapor.

A few paces further on the rocky road, a different scene presented itself to us. There lay, to the westward, a long stretch of naked yellow mountains, basking in the hot glare of the sun, and through the centre, deep down in the heart of the arid landscape, a winding line of living green showed the course of the Barrada. We followed the river, until the path reached an impassable gorge, which occasioned a detour of two or three hours. We then descended to the bed of the dell, where the vegetation, owing to the radiated heat from the mountains and the fertilizing stimulus of the water below, was even richer than on the plain of Damascus. The trees were plethoric with an overplus of life. The boughs of the mulberries were weighed down with the burden of the leaves ; pomegranates were in a violent eruption of blossoms ; and the foliage of the fig and poplar was of so deep a hue that it shone black in the sun.

Passing through a gateway of rock, so narrow that we were often obliged to ride in the bed of the stream, we reached a little meadow, beyond which was a small hamlet, almost hidden in the leaves. Here the mountains again approached each other, and from the side of that on the right hand, the main body of the Barrada, or Pharpar, gushed forth in one full stream. The fountain is nearly double the volume of that of the Jordan at Banias, and much more beautiful. The foundations of an ancient building, probably a temple, overhang it, and tall poplars and sycamores cover it with impenetrable shade. From the low aperture, where it bursts into the light, its waters, white with foam, bound away flashing in the chance rays of sunshine, until they are lost to sight in the dense, dark foliage. We sat an hour on the ruined walls, listening to the roar and rush of the flood, and enjoying the shade of the walnuts and sycamores. Soon after leaving, our path crossed a small stream, which comes down to the Barrada from the upper valleys of the Anti-Lebanon, and entered a wild pass, faced with cliffs of perpendicular rock. An old bridge, of one arch, spanned the chasm, out of which we climbed to a tract of high meadow land. In the pass there were some fragments of ancient columns, traces of an aqueduct, and inscriptions on the rocks, among which Mr. H. found the name of Antoninus The place is not mentioned in any book of travel I have seen, as it is not on the usual road from Damascus to Baalbec.

As we were emerging from the pass, we saw a company of twelve armed men seated in the grass, near the roadside. They were wild-looking characters, and eyed us somewhat sharply as we passed. We greeted them with the usual "salaam aleikoom!" which they did not return. The same evening, as we encamped at the village of Zebdeni, about three hours further up the valley, we were startled by a great noise and outcry, with the firing of pistols. It happened, as we learned on inquiring the cause of all this confusion, that the men we saw in the pass were rebel Druses, who were then lying in wait for the Shekh of Zebdeni, whom, with his son, they had taken captive soon after we passed. The news had by some means been conveyed to the village, and a company of about two hundred persons was then marching out to the rescue. The noise they made was probably to give the Druses intimation of their coming, and thus avoid a fight. I do not believe that any of the mountaineers of Lebanon would willingly take part against the Druses, who, in fact, are not fighting so much against the institution of the conscription law, as its abuse. The law ordains that the conscript shall serve for five years; but since its establishment, as I have been informed, there has not been a single instance of discharge. It amounts, therefore, to lifelong servitude, and there is little wonder that these independent sons of the mountains, as well as the tribes inhabiting the Syrian Desert, should rebel rather than submit.

The next day, we crossed a pass in the Anti-Lebanon beyond Zebdeni, descended a beautiful valley on the western side, under a ridge which was still dotted with patches of snow, and after travelling for some hours over a wide, barren height, the last of the range, saw below us the plain of Baalbec. The grand ridge of Lebanon opposite, crowned with glittering fields of snow, shone out clearly through the pure air, and the hoary head of Hermon, far in the south, lost something of its grandeur by the comparison. Though there is a "divide," or watershed, between Husbeiya, at the foot of Mount Hermon, and Baalbec, whose springs join the Orontes, which flows northward to Antioch, the great natural separation of the two chains continues unbroken to the Gulf of Akaba, in the Red Sea. A little beyond Baalbec, the Anti-Lebanon terminates, sinking into the Syrian plain, while the Lebanon, though its name and general features are lost, about twenty miles further to the north is succeeded by other ranges, which, though broken at intervals, form a regular series, connecting with the Taurus, in Asia Minor.

On leaving Damascus, the Demon of Hasheesh still maintained a partial control over me. I was weak in body and at times confused in my perceptions, wandering away from the scenes about me to some unknown sphere beyond the moon. But the healing balm of my sleep at Zebdeni, and the purity of the morning air among the mountains, completed my cure. As I rode along the valley, with the towering, snow-sprinkled ridge of the Anti-Lebanon on my right, a cloudless heaven above my head, and meads enamelled with the asphodel and scarlet anemone stretching before me, I felt that the last shadow had rolled away from my brain. My mind was now as clear as that sky—my heart as free and joyful as the elastic morning air. The sun never shone so brightly to my eyes; the fair forms of Nature were never penetrated with so perfect a spirit of beauty. I was again master of myself, and the world glowed as if new-created in the light of my joy and gratitude. I thanked God, who had led me out of a darkness more terrible than that of the Valley of the Shadow of Death, and while my feet strayed among the flowery meadows of Lebanon, my heart walked on the Delectable Hills of His Mercy.

By the middle of the afternoon, we reached Baalbec. The distant view of the temple, on descending the last slope of the Anti-Lebanon, is not calculated to raise one's expectations. On the green plain at the foot of the mountain, you see a large square platform of masonry, upon which stand six columns, the body of the temple, and a quantity of ruined walls. As a feature in the landscape, it has a fine effect, but you find yourself pronouncing the speedy judgment, that "Baalbec, without

Lebanon, would be rather a poor show." Having come to this conclusion, you ride down the hill with comfortable feelings of indifference. There are a number of quarries on the left hand; you glance at them with an expression which merely says: "Ah! I suppose they got the stones here," and so you saunter on, cross a little stream that flows down from the modern village, pass a mill, return the stare of the quaint Arab miller who comes to the door to see you, and your horse is climbing a difficult path among the broken columns and friezes, before you think it worth while to lift your eyes to the pile above you. Now re-assert your judgment, if you dare! This is Baalbec: what have you to say? Nothing; but you amazedly measure the torsos of great columns which lie piled across one another in magnificent wreck; vast pieces which have dropped from the entablature, beautiful Corinthian capitals, bereft of the last graceful curves of their acanthus leaves, and blocks whose edges are so worn away that they resemble enormous natural boulders left by the Deluge, till at last you look up to the six glorious pillars, towering nigh a hundred feet above your head, and there is a sensation in your brain which would be a shout, if you could give it utterance, of faultless symmetry and majesty, such as no conception of yours and no other creation of art, can surpass.

I know of nothing so beautiful in all remains of ancient Art as these six columns, except the colonnade of the Memnonium, at Thebes, which is of much smaller proportions. From every position, and with all lights of the day or night, they are equally perfect, and carry your eyes continually away from the peristyle of the smaller temple, which is better preserved, and from the exquisite architecture of the outer courts and pavi lions. The two temples of Baalbec stand on an artificial platform of masonry, a thousand feet in length, and from fifteen to thirty feet (according to the depression of the soil) in height. The larger one, which is supposed to have been a Pantheon, occupies the whole length of this platform. The entrance was at the north, by a grand flight of steps, now broken away, between two lofty and elegant pavilions which are still nearly entire. Then followed a spacious hexagonal court, and three grand halls, parts of which, with niches for statues, adorned with cornices and pediments of elaborate design, still remain entire to the roof. This magnificent series of chambers was terminated at the southern extremity of the platform by the main temple, which had originally twenty columns on a side, similar to the six now standing.

The Temple of the Sun stands on a smaller and lower platform, which appears to have been subsequently added to the greater one. The cella, or body of the temple, is complete except the roof, and of the colonnade surrounding it, nearly one-half of its pillars are still standing, upholding the frieze, entablature, and cornice, which altogether form probably the most ornate specimen of the Corinthian order of architecture now extant. Only four pillars of the superb portico remain, and the Saracens have nearly ruined these by building a sort of watch-tower upon the architrave. The same unscrupulous race completely shut up the portal of the temple with a blank wall, formed of the fragments they had hurled down, and one is obliged to creep through a narrow hole in order to reach the interior. Here the original doorway faces you—and I know not how to describe the wonderful design of its elaborate sculptured mouldings and cornices. The genius of Greek art seems to have exhausted itself in inventing ornaments, which, while they should heighten the gorgeous effect of the work, must yet harmonize with the grand design of the temple. The enormous keystone over the entrance has slipped down, no doubt from the shock of an earthquake, and hangs within six inches of the bottom of the two blocks which uphold it on either side. When it falls, the whole entablature of the portal will be destroyed. On its lower side is an eagle with outspread wings, and on the side-stones a genius with garlands of flowers, exquisitely sculptured in bas relief. Hidden among the wreaths of vines which adorn the jambs are the laughing heads of fauns. This portal was a continual study to me, every visit revealing new refinements of ornament, which I had not before observed. The interior of the temple, with its rich Corinthian pilasters, its niches for statues, surmounted by pediments of elegant design, and its elaborate cornice, needs little aid of the imagination to restore it to its original perfection. Like that of Dendera, in Egypt, the Temple of the Sun leaves upon the mind an impression of completeness which makes you forget far grander remains.

But the most wonderful thing at Baalbec is the foundation platform upon which the temples stand. Even the colossal fabrics of Ancient Egypt dwindle before this superhuman masonry. The platform itself, 1,000 feet long, and averaging twenty feet in height, suggests a vast mass of stones, but when you come to examine the single blocks of which it is composed, you are crushed with their incredible bulk. On the western side is a row of eleven foundation stones, each of which is thirty-two feet in length, twelve in height, and ten in thickness, forming a wall three hundred and fifty-two feet long! But while you are walking on, thinking of the art which cut and raised these enormous blocks, you turn the southern corner and come upon *three* stones, the united length of which is *one hundred and eighty-seven feet*—two of them being sixty-two and the other sixty-three feet in length! There they are, cut with faultless exactness, and so smoothly joined to each other, that you cannot force a cambric needle into the crevice. There is one joint so perfect that it can only be discerned by the minutest search; it is not even so perceptible as the junction of two pieces of paper which have been pasted together. In the quarry, there still lies a finished block, ready for transportation, which is sixty-seven feet in length. The weight of one of these masses has been reckoned at near 9,000 tons, yet they do not form the base of the foundation, but are raised upon other courses, fifteen feet from the ground. It is considered by some antiquarians that they are of a date greatly anterior to that of the temples, and were intended as the basement of a different edifice.

In the village of Baalbec there is a small circular Corinthian temple of very elegant design. It is not more than thirty feet in diameter, and may have been intended as a tomb. A spacious mosque, now roofless and deserted, was constructed almost entirely out of the remains of the temples. Adjoining the court-yard and fountain are five rows of ancient pillars, forty (the sacred number) in all, supporting light Saracenic arches. Some of them are marble, with Corinthian capitals, and eighteen are single shafts of red Egyptian granite. Beside the fountain lies a small broken pillar of porphyry, of a dark violet hue, and of so fine a grain that the stone has the soft rich lustre of velvet. This fragment is the only thing I would carry away if I had the power.

After a day's sojourn, we left Baalbec at noon, and took the road for the Cedars, which lie on the other side of Lebanon, in the direction of Tripoli. Our English fellow-travellers chose the direct road to Beyrout. We crossed the plain in three hours, to the village of Dayr el-Ahmar, and then commenced ascending the lowest slopes of the great range, whose topmost ridge, a dazzling parapet of snow, rose high above us. For several hours, our path led up and down stony ridges, covered with thickets of oak and holly, and with wild cherry, pear, and olive-trees. Just as the sun threw the shadows of the highest Lebanon over us, we came upon a narrow, rocky glen at his very base. Streams that still kept the color and the coolness of the snow-fields from which they oozed, foamed over the stones into the chasm at the bottom. The glen descended into a mountain basin, in which lay the lake of Yemouni, cold and green under the evening shadows. But just opposite us, on a little shelf of soil, there was a rude mill, and a group of superb walnut-trees, overhanging the brink of the largest torrent. We had sent our baggage before us, and the men, with an eye to the picturesque which I should not have suspected in Arabs, had pitched our tents under those trees, where the stream poured its snow-cold beakers beside us, and the tent-door looked down on the plain of Baalbec and across to the Anti-Lebanon. The miller and two or three peasants, who were living in this lonely spot, were Christians.

The next morning we commenced ascending the Lebanon. We had slept just below the snow-line, for the long hollows with which the ridge is cloven were filled up to within a short distance of the glen, out of which we came. The path was very steep, continually ascending, now around the barren shoulder of the mountain, now up some ravine, where the holly and olive still flourished, and the wild rhubarb-plant spread its large, succulent leaves over the soil. We had taken a guide, the day before, at the village of Dayr el-Ahmar, but as the way was plain before us, and he demanded an exorbitant sum, we dismissed him. We had not climbed far, however, before he returned, professing to be content with whatever we might give him, and took us into another road, the first, he said, being impracticable. Up and up we toiled, and the long hollows of snow lay below us, and the wind came cold from the topmost peaks, which began to show near at hand. But now the road, as we had surmised, turned towards that we had first taken, and on reaching the next height we saw the latter at a short distance from us. It was not only a better, but a shorter road, the rascal of a guide having led us out of it in order to give the greater effect to his services. In order to return to it, as was necessary, there were several dangerous snow-fields to be passed. The angle of their descent was so great that a single false step would have hurled our animals, baggage and all, many hundred feet below. The snow was melting, and the crust frozen over the streams below was so thin in places that the animals broke through and sank to their bellies.

It were needless to state the number and character of the anathemas bestowed upon the guide. The impassive Dervish raved ; Mustapha stormed ; François broke out in a frightful eruption of Greek and Turkish oaths, and the two travellers, though not (as I hope and believe) profanely inclined, could not avoid using a few terse Saxon expressions. When the general indignation had found vent, the men went to work, and by taking each animal separately, succeeded, at imminent hazard, in getting them all over the snow. We then dismissed the guide, who, far from being abashed by the discovery of his trickery, had the impudence to follow us for some time, claiming his pay. A few more steep pulls, over deep beds of snow and patches of barren stone, and at length the summit ridge—a sharp, white wall, shining against the intense black-blue of the zenith—stood before us. We climbed a toilsome zig-zag through the snow, hurried over the stones cumbering the top, and all at once the mountains fell away, ridge below ridge, gashed with tremendous chasms, whose bottoms were lost in blue vapor, till the last heights, crowned with white Maronite convents, hung above the sea, whose misty round bounded the vision. I have seen many grander mountain views, but few so sublimely rugged and broken in their features. The sides of the ridges dropped off in all directions into sheer precipices, and the few villages we could see were built like eagles' nests on the brinks. In a little hollow at our feet was the sacred Forest of Cedars, appearing like a patch of stunted junipers. It is the highest speck of vegetation on Lebanon, and in winter cannot be visited, on account of the snow. The summit on which we stood was about nine thousand feet above the sea, but there were peaks on each side at least a thousand feet higher.

We descended by a very steep path, over occasional beds of snow, and reached the Cedars in an hour and a half. Not until we were within a hundred yards of the trees, and below their level, was I at all impressed with their size and venerable aspect. But, once entered into the heart of the little wood, walking over its miniature hills and valleys, and breathing the pure, balsamic exhalations of the trees, all the disappointment rising to my mind was charmed away in an instant There are about three hundred trees, in all, many of which are of the last century's growth, but at least fifty of them would be considered grand in any forest. The patriarchs are five in number, and are undoubtedly as old as the Christian Era, if not the Age of Solomon. The cypresses in the Garden of Montezuma, at Chapultepec, are even older and grander trees, but they are as entire and shapely as ever, whereas these are gnarled and twisted into wonderful forms by the storms of twenty centuries, and shivered in some places by lightning. The hoary father of them all, nine feet in diameter, stands in the centre of the grove, on a little knoll, and spreads his ponderous arms, each a tree in itself, over the heads of the many generations that have grown up below, as if giving his last benediction before decay. He is scarred less with storm and lightning, than with the knives of travellers, and the marble crags of Lebanon do not more firmly retain their inscriptions than his stony trunk. Dates of the last century are abundant, and I recollect a tablet inscribed : "Souard, 1670," around which the newer wood has grown to the height of three or four inches. The seclusion of the grove, shut in by peaks of barren snow, is complete. Only the voice of the nightingale, singing here by daylight in the solemn shadows, breaks the silence. The Maronite monk, who has charge of a little stone chapel standing in the midst, moves about like a shade, and, not before you are ready to leave, brings his book for you to register your name therein. I was surprised to find how few of the crowd that annually overrun Syria reach the Cedars, which, after Baalbec, are the finest remains of antiquity in the whole country.

After a stay of three hours, we rode on to Eden, whither our men had already gone with the baggage. Our road led along the brink of a tremendous gorge, a thousand feet deep, the bottom of which was only accessible here and there by hazardous foot-paths. On either side, a long shelf of cultivated land sloped down to the top, and the mountain streams, after watering a multitude of orchards and grain-fields, tumbled over the cliffs in long, sparkling cascades, to join the roaring flood below. This is the Christian region of Lebanon, inhabited almost wholly by Maronites, who still retain a portion of their former independence, and are the most thrifty, industrious, honest, and happy people in Syria. Their villages are not concrete masses of picturesque filth, as are those of the Moslems, but are loosely scattered among orchards of mulberry, poplar, and vine, washed by fresh rills, and have an air of comparative neatness and comfort. Each has its two or three chapels, with their little belfries, which toll the hours of prayer. Sad and poetic as is the call from the minaret, it never touched me as when I heard the sweet tongues of those Christian bells, chiming vespers far and near on the sides of Lebanon.

Eden merits its name. It is a mountain paradise, inhabited by people so kind and simple-hearted, that assuredly no vengeful angel will ever drive them out with his flaming sword. It hangs above the gorge, which is here nearly two thousand feet deep, and overlooks a grand wilderness of mountain-piles, crowded on and over each other, from the sea that gleams below, to the topmost heights that keep off the morning sun. The houses are all built of hewn stone, and grouped in clusters under the shade of large walnut-trees. In walking among them, we received kind greetings everywhere, and every one who was seated rose and remained standing as we passed. The women are beautiful, with sprightly, intelligent faces, quite different from the stupid Mahometan females.

The children were charming creatures, and some of the girls of ten or twelve years were lovely as angels. They came timidly to our tent (which the men had pitched as before, under two superb trees, beside a fountain), and offered us roses and branches of fragrant white jasmine. They expected some return, of course, but did not ask it, and the delicate grace with which the offering was made was beyond all pay. It was Sunday, and the men and boys, having nothing better to do, all came to see and talk with us. I shall not soon forget the circle of gay and laughing villagers, in which we sat that evening, while the dark purple shadows gradually filled up the gorges, and broad golden lights poured over the shoulders of the hills. The men had much sport in inducing the smaller boys to come up and salute us. There was one whom they called "the Consul," who eluded them for some time, but was finally caught and placed in the ring before us. "Peace be with you, O Consul," I said, making him a profound inclination, "may your days be propitious! may your shadow be increased!" but I then saw, from the vacant expression on the boy's face, that he was one of those harmless, witless creatures, whom yet one cannot quite call idiots. "He is an unfortunate; he knows nothing; he has no protector but God," said the men, crossing themselves devoutly. The boy took off his cap, crept up and kissed my hand, as I gave him some money, which he no sooner grasped, than he sprang up like a startled gazelle, and was out of sight in an instant.

In descending from Eden to the sea-coast, we were obliged

to cross the great gorge of which I spoke. Further down, its sides are less steep, and clothed even to the very bottom with magnificent orchards of mulberry, fig, olive, orange, and pomegranate trees. We were three hours in reaching the opposite side, although the breadth across the top is not more than a mile. The path was exceedingly perilous; we walked down, leading our horses, and once were obliged to unload our mules to get them past a tree, which would have forced them off the brink of a chasm several hundred feet deep. The view from the bottom was wonderful. We were shut in by steeps of foliage and blossoms from two to three thousand feet high, broken by crags of white marble, and towering almost precipitously to the very clouds. I doubt if Melville saw anything grander in the tropical gorges of Typee. After reaching the other side, we had still a journey of eight hours to the sea, through a wild and broken, yet highly cultivated country.

Beyrout was now thirteen hours distant, but by making a forced march we reached it in a day, travelling along the shore, past the towns of Jebeil, the ancient Byblus, and Joonieh. The hills about Jebeil produce the celebrated tobacco known in Egypt as the *Jebelee*, or "mountain" tobacco, which is even superior to the Latakiyeh.

Near Beyrout, the mulberry and olive are in the ascendant. The latter tree bears the finest fruit in all the Levant, and might drive all other oils out of the market, if any one had enterprise enough to erect proper manufactories. Instead of this the oil of the country is badly prepared, rancid from the skins in which it is kept, and the wealthy natives import from France and Italy in preference to using it. In the bottoms near the sea, I saw several fields of the taro-plant, the cultivation of which I had supposed was exclusively confined to the Islands of the Pacific. There would be no end to the wealth of Syria were the country in proper hands.

CHAPTER XIII.

PIPES AND COFFEE

——— "the kind nymph to Bacchus born
By Morpheus' daughter, she that seems
Gifted upon her natal morn
By him with fire, by her with dreams—
Nicotia, dearer to the Muse
Than all the grape's bewildering juice." LOWELL.

In painting the picture of an Oriental, the pipe and the coffee-cup are indispensable accessories. There is scarce a Turk, or Arab, or Persian—unless he be a Dervish of peculiar sanctity—but breathes his daily incense to the milder Bacchus of the moderns. The custom has become so thoroughly naturalized in the East, that we are apt to forget its comparatively recent introduction, and to wonder that no mention is made of the pipe in the Arabian Nights. The practice of smoking harmonizes so thoroughly with the character of Oriental life, that it is difficult for us to imagine a time when it never existed. It has become a part of that supreme patience, that wonderful repose, which forms so strong a contrast to the over-active life of the New World—the enjoyment of which no one can taste, to whom the pipe is not familiar. Howl, ye Reformers! but I solemnly declare unto you, that he who travels through the East without smoking, does not know the East.

It is strange that our Continent, where the meaning of Rest

is unknown, should have given to the world this great agent of Rest. There is nothing more remarkable in history than the colonization of Tobacco over the whole Earth. Not three centuries have elapsed since knightly Raleigh puffed its fumes into the astonished eyes of Spenser and Shakspeare; and now, find me any corner of the world, from Nova Zembla to the Mountains of the Moon, where the use of the plant is unknown! Tarshish (if India was Tarshish) is less distinguished by its "apes, ivory, and peacocks," than by its hookahs; the valleys of Luzon, beyond Ternate and Tidore, send us more cheroots than spices; the Gardens of Shiraz produce more velvety *toombek* than roses, and the only fountains which bubble in Samarcand are those of the narghilehs: Lebanon is no longer "excellent with the Cedars," as in the days of Solomon, but most excellent with its fields of Jebelee and Latakiyeh. On the unvisited plains of Central Africa, the table-lands of Tartary, and in the valleys of Japan, the wonderful plant has found a home. The naked negro, "panting at the Line," inhales it under the palms, and the Lapp and Samoyed on the shores of the Frozen Sea.

It is idle for those who object to the use of Tobacco to attribute these phenomena wholly to a perverted taste. The fact that the custom was at once adopted by all the races of men, whatever their geographical position and degree of civilization, proves that there must be a reason for it in the physical constitution of man. Its effect, when habitually used, is slightly narcotic and sedative, not stimulating—or if so, at times, it stimulates only the imagination and the social faculties. It lulls to sleep the combative and destructive propensities, and hence—so far as a material agent may operate—it exercises a humanizing and refining influence. A profound student of Man, whose name is well known to the world, once informed me that he saw in the eagerness with which savage tribes adopt the use of Tobacco, a spontaneous movement of Nature towards Civilization.

I will not pursue these speculations further, for the narghileh (bubbling softly at my elbow, as I write) is the promoter of repose and the begetter of agreeable reverie. As I inhale its cool, fragrant breath, and partly yield myself to the sensation of healthy rest which wraps my limbs as with a velvet mantle, I marvel how the poets and artists and scholars of olden times nursed those dreams which the world calls indolence, but which are the seeds that germinate into great achievements. How did Plato philosophize without the pipe? How did gray Homer, sitting on the temple-steps in the Grecian twilights, drive from his heart the bitterness of beggary and blindness? How did Phidias charm the Cerberus of his animal nature to sleep, while his soul entered the Elysian Fields and beheld the forms of heroes? For, in the higher world of Art, Body and Soul are sworn enemies, and the pipe holds an opiate more potent than all the drowsy syrups of the East, to drug the former into submission. Milton knew this, as he smoked his evening pipe at Chalfont, wandering, the while, among the palms of Paradise.

But it is also our loss, that Tobacco was unknown to the Greeks. They would else have given us, in verse and in marble, another divinity in their glorious Pantheon—a god less drowsy than Morpheus and Somnus, less riotous than Bacchus, less radiant than Apollo, but with something of the spirit of each: a figure, beautiful with youth, every muscle in perfect repose, and the vague expression of dreams in his half-closed eyes. His temple would have been built in a grove of Southern pines, on the borders of a land-locked gulf, sheltered from the surges that buffet without, where service would have been rendered him in the late hours of the afternoon, or in the evening twilight. From his oracular tripod words of wisdom would have been spoken, and the fanes of Delphi and Dodona would have been deserted for his.

Oh, non-smoking friends, who read these lines with pain and incredulity—and you, ladies, who turn pale at the thought of a pipe—let me tell you that you are familiar only with the vulgar form of tobacco, and have never passed between the wind and its gentility. The word conveys no idea to you but that of "long nines," and pig-tail, and cavendish. Forget these for a moment, and look upon this dark-brown cake of dried leaves and blossoms, which exhales an odor of pressed flowers. These are the tender tops of the *Jebelee*, plucked as the buds begin to expand, and carefully dried in the shade. In order to be used, it is moistened with rose-scented water, and cut to the necessary degree of fineness. The test of true Jebelee is, that it burns with a slow, hidden fire, like tinder, and causes no irritation to the eye when held under it. The smoke, drawn through a long cherry-stick pipe and amber mouth-piece, is pure, cool, and sweet, with an aromatic flavor, which is very pleasant in the mouth. It excites no salivation, and leaves behind it no unpleasant, stale odor.

The narghileh (still bubbling beside me) is an institution known only in the East. It requires a peculiar kind of tobacco, which grows to perfection in the southern provinces of Persia The smoke, after passing through water (rose-flavored, if you choose), is inhaled through a long, flexible tube directly into the lungs. It occasions not the slightest irritation or oppression, but in a few minutes produces a delicious sense of rest, which is felt even in the finger-ends. The pure physical sensation of rest is one of strength also, and of perfect contentment. Many an impatient thought, many an angry word, have I avoided by a resort to the pipe. Among our aborigines the pipe was the emblem of Peace, and I strongly recommend the Peace Society to print their tracts upon papers of smoking tobacco (Turkish, if possible), and distribute pipes with them.

I know of nothing more refreshing, after the fatigue of a long day's journey, than a well-prepared narghileh. That slight feverish and excitable feeling which is the result of fatigue yields at once to its potency. The blood loses its heat and the pulse its rapidity; the muscles relax, the nerves are soothed into quiet, and the frame passes into a condition similar to sleep, except that the mind is awake and active. By the time one has finished his pipe, he is refreshed for the remainder of the day, and his nightly sleep is sound and healthy. Such are some of the physical effects of the pipe, in Eastern lands. Morally and psychologically, it works still greater transformations; but to describe them now, with the mouth-piece at my lips, would require an active self-consciousness which the habit does not allow.

A servant enters with a steamy cup of coffee, seated in a silver *zerf*, or cup-holder. His thumb and fore-finger are clasped firmly upon the bottom of the zerf, which I inclose near the top with my own thumb and finger, so that the transfer is accomplished without his hand having touched mine.

After draining the thick brown liquid, which must be done with due deliberation and a pause of satisfaction between each sip, I return the zerf, holding it in the middle, while the attendant places a palm of each hand upon the top and bottom and carries it off without contact. The beverage is made of the berries of Mocha, slightly roasted, pulverized in a mortar, and heated to a foam, without the addition of cream or sugar. Sometimes, however, it is flavored with the extract of roses or violets. When skilfully made, each cup is prepared separately, and the quantity of water and coffee carefully measured.

Coffee is a true child of the East, and its original home was among the hills of Yemen, the Arabia Felix of the ancients. Fortunately for Mussulmen, its use was unknown in the days of Mahomet, or it would probably have fallen under the same prohibition as wine. The word *Kahweh* (whence *café*) is an old Arabic term for wine. The discovery of the properties of coffee is attributed to a dervish, who, for some misdemeanor, was carried into the mountains of Yemen by his brethren and there left to perish by starvation. In order to appease the pangs of hunger he gathered the ripe berries from the wild coffee-trees, roasted and ate them. The nourishment they contained, with water from the springs, sustained his life, and after two or three months he returned in good condition to his brethren, who considered his preservation as a miracle, and ever afterwards looked upon him as a pattern of holiness. He taught the use of the miraculous fruit, and the demand for it soon became so great as to render the cultivation of the tree necessary. It was a long time, however, before coffee was introduced into Europe. As late as the beginning of the seventeenth century, Sandys, the quaint old traveller, describes the appearance and taste of the beverage, which he calls "Coffa," and sagely asks: "Why not that black broth which the Lacedemonians used?"

On account of the excellence of the material, and the skilful manner of its preparation, the Coffee of the East is the finest in the world. I have found it so grateful and refreshing a drink, that I can readily pardon the pleasant exaggeration of the Arabic poet, Abd-el Kader Anazari Djezeri Hanbali, the son of Mahomet, who thus celebrates its virtues. After such an exalted eulogy, my own praises would sound dull and tame; and I therefore resume my pipe, commending Abd-el Kader to the reader.

"O Coffee! thou dispellest the cares of the great; thou bringest back those who wander from the paths of knowledge. Coffee is the beverage of the people of God, and the cordial of his servants who thirst for wisdom. When coffee is infused into the bowl, it exhales the odor of musk, and is of the color of ink. The truth is not known except to the wise, who drink it from the foaming coffee-cup. God has deprived fools of coffee, who, with invincible obstinacy, condemn it as injurious.

"Coffee is our gold; and in the place of its libations we are in the enjoyment of the best and noblest society. Coffee is even as innocent a drink as the purest milk, from which it is distinguished only by its color. Tarry with thy coffee in the place of its preparation, and the good God will hover over thee and participate in his feast. There the graces of the saloon, the luxury of life, the society of friends, all furnish a picture of the abode of happiness.

"Every care vanishes when the cup-bearer presents the delicious chalice. It will circulate fleetly through thy veins, and will not rankle there : if thou doubtest this, contemplate the youth and beauty of those who drink it. Grief cannot exist where it grows ; sorrow humbles itself in obedience before its powers.

"Coffee is the drink of God's people ; in it is health. Let this be the answer to those who doubt its qualities. In it we will drown our adversities, and in its fire consume our sorrows. Whoever has once seen the blissful chalice, will scorn the wine-cup. Glorious drink ! thy color is the seal of purity, and reason proclaims it genuine. Drink with confidence, and regard not the prattle of fools, who condemn without foundation."

CHAPTER XIV.

JOURNEY TO ANTIOCH AND ALEPPO.

Change of Plans—Routes to Baghdad—Asia Minor—We sail from Beyrout—Yachting on the Syrian Coast—Tartus and Latakiyeh—The Coasts of Syria—The Bay of Suediah—The Mouth of the Orontes—Landing—The Garden of Syria—Ride to Antioch—The Modern City—The Plains of the Orontes—Remains of the Greek Empire—The Ancient Road—The Plain of Keftin—Approach to Aleppo.

"The chain is loosed, the sails are spread,
The living breath is fresh behind,
As, with dews and sunrise fed,
Comes the laughing morning wind."

SHELLEY.

ALEPPO, *Friday*, *June* 4, 1852.

A TRAVELLER in the East, who has not unbounded time and an extensive fortune at his disposal, is never certain where and how far he shall go, until his journey is finished. With but a limited portion of both these necessaries, I have so far carried out my original plan with scarcely a variation; but at present I am obliged to make a material change of route. My farthest East is here at Aleppo. At Damascus, I was told by everybody that it was too late in the season to visit either Baghdad or Mosul, and that, on account of the terrible summer heats and the fevers which prevail along the Tigris, it would be imprudent to undertake it. Notwithstanding this, I should probably have gone (being now so thoroughly acclimated that I have nothing to fear from the heat), had I not met with a friend of Col. Rawlinson, the companion of Layard, and the sharer in his discoveries at Nineveh. This gentleman, who met Col. R. not long since in Constantinople, on his way to Baghdad (where he resides as British Consul), informed me that since the departure of Mr. Layard from Mosul, the most interesting excavations have been filled up, in order to preserve the sculptures. Unless one was able to make a new exhumation, he would be by no means repaid for so long and arduous a journey. The ruins of Nineveh are all below the surface of the earth, and the little of them that is now left exposed, is less complete and interesting than the specimens in the British Museum.

There is a route from Damascus to Baghdad, across the Desert, by way of Palmyra, but it is rarely travelled, even by the natives, except when the caravans are sufficiently strong to withstand the attacks of the Bedouins. The traveller is obliged to go in Arab costume, to leave his baggage behind, except a meagre scrip for the journey, and to pay from $300 to $500 for the camels and escort. The more usual route is to come northward to this city, then cross to Mosul and descend the Tigris—a journey of four or five weeks. After weighing all the advantages and disadvantages of undertaking a tour of such length as it would be necessary to make before reaching Constantinople, I decided at Beyrout to give up the fascinating fields of travel in Media, Assyria and Armenia, and take a rather shorter and perhaps equally interesting route from Aleppo to Constantinople, by way of Tarsus, Konia (Iconium), and the ancient countries of Phrygia, Bithynia, and Mysia. The interior of Asia Minor is even less known to us than the Persian side of Asiatic Turkey, which has of late received more attention from travellers ; and, as I shall traverse it in its whole length, from Syria to the Bosphorus, I may find it replete with "green fields and pastures new," which shall repay me for relinquishing the first and more ambitious undertaking. At least, I have so much reason to be grateful for the uninterrupted good health and good luck I have enjoyed during seven months in Africa and the Orient, that I cannot be otherwise than content with the prospect before me.

I left Beyrout on the night of the 28th of May, with Mr. Harrison, who has decided to keep me company as far as Constantinople. François, our classic dragoman, whose great delight is to recite Homer by the sea-side, is retained for the whole tour, as we have found no reason to doubt his honesty or ability. Our first thought was to proceed to Aleppo by land, by way of Homs and Hamah, whence there might be a chance of reaching Palmyra ; but as we found an opportunity of engaging an American yacht for the voyage up the coast, it was thought preferable to take her, and save time. She was a neat little craft, called the "American Eagle," brought out by Mr. Smith, our Consul at Beyrout. So, one fine moonlit night, we slowly crept out of the harbor, and after returning a volley of salutes from our friends at Demetri's Hotel, ran into the heart of a thunder-storm, which poured down more rain than all I had seen for eight months before. But our raïs, Assad (the Lion), was worthy of his name, and had two good Christian sailors at his command, so we lay in the cramped little cabin, and heard the floods washing our deck, without fear.

In the morning, we were off Tripoli, which is even more deeply buried than Beyrout in its orange and mulberry groves, and slowly wafted along the bold mountain-coast, in the afternoon reached Tartus, the Ancient Tortosa. A mile from shore is the rocky island of Aradus, entirely covered by a town. There were a dozen vessels lying in the harbor. The remains of a large fortress and ancient mole prove it to have been a place of considerable importance. Tartus is a small old place on the sea-shore—not so large nor so important in appearance as its island-port. The country behind is green and hilly, though but partially cultivated, and rises into Djebel Ansairiyeh, which divides the valley of the Orontes from the sea. It is a lovely coast, especially under the flying lights and shadows of such a breezy day as we had. The wind fell at sunset ; but by the next morning, we had passed the tobacco-fields of Latakiyeh, and were in sight of the southern cape of the Bay of Suediah. The mountains forming this cape culminate in a grand conical peak, about 5,000 feet in height, called Djebel Okrab. At ten o'clock, wafted along by a slow wind, we turned the point and entered the Bay of Suediah, formed by the embouchure of the River Orontes. The mountain headland of Akma Dagh, forming the portal of the Gulf of Scanderoon, loomed grandly in front of us across the bay ; and far beyond it, we could just distinguish the coast of Karamania, the snow-capped range of Taurus.

The Coasts of Syria might be divided, like those of Guinea, according to the nature of their productions. The northern division is bold and bare, yet flocks of sheep graze on the slopes of its mountains ; and the inland plains behind them are covered with orchards of pistachio-trees. Silk is cultivated in the neighborhood of Suediah, but forms only a small portion of the exports. This region may be called the Wool and Pistachio Coast. Southward, from Latakiyeh to Tartus and the northern limit of Lebanon, extends the Tobacco Coast, whose undulating hills are now clothed with the pale-green leaves of the renowned plant. From Tripoli to Tyre, embracing all the western slope of Lebanon, and the deep, rich valleys lying between his knees, the mulberry predominates, and the land is covered with the houses of thatch and matting which shelter the busy worms. This is the Silk Coast. The palmy plains of Jaffa, and beyond, until Syria meets the African sands between Gaza and El-Arish, constitute the Orange Coast. The vine, the olive, and the fig flourish everywhere.

We were all day getting up the bay, and it seemed as if we should never pass Djebel Okrab, whose pointed top rose high above a long belt of fleecy clouds that girdled his waist. At sunset we made the mouth of the Orontes. Our lion of a Captain tried to run into the river, but the channel was very narrow, and when within three hundred yards of the shore the yacht struck. We had all sail set, and had the wind been a little stronger, we should have capsized in an instant. The lion went manfully to work, and by dint of hard poling, shoved us off, and came to anchor in deep water. Not until the danger was past did he open his batteries on the unlucky helmsman, and then the explosion of Arabic oaths was equal to a broadside of twenty-four pounders. We lay all night rocking on the swells, and the next morning, by firing a number of signal guns, brought out a boat, which took us off. We entered the mouth of the Orontes, and sailed nearly a mile between rich wheat meadows before reaching the landing-place of Suediah—two or three uninhabited stone huts, with three or four small Turkish craft, and a health officer. The town lies a mile or two inland, scattered along the hill-side amid gardens so luxuriant as almost to conceal it from view.

This part of the coast is ignorant of travellers, and we were obliged to wait half a day before we could find a sufficient number of horses to take us to Antioch, twenty miles distant. When they came, they were solid farmers' horses, with the rudest gear imaginable. I was obliged to mount astride of a broad pack-saddle, with my legs suspended in coils of rope. Leaving the meadows, we entered a lane of the wildest, richest and loveliest bloom and foliage. Our way was overhung with hedges of pomegranate, myrtle, oleander, and white rose, in blossom, and occasionally with quince, fig, and carob trees, laced together with grape vines in fragrant bloom. Sometimes this wilderness of color and odor met above our heads and made a twilight ; then it opened into long, dazzling, sun-bright vistas, where the hues of the oleander, pomegranate and white rose made the eye wink with their gorgeous profusion. The mountains we crossed were covered with thickets of myrtle, mastic, daphne, and arbutus, and all the valleys and sloping meads waved with fig, mulberry, and olive trees. Looking towards the sea, the valley broadened out between mountain ranges whose summits were lost in the clouds. Though the soil was not so rich as in Palestine, the general aspect of the country was much wilder and more luxuriant.

So, by this glorious lane, over the myrtled hills and down into valleys, whose bed was one hue of rose from the blossoming oleanders, we travelled for five hours, crossing the low ranges of hills through which the Orontes forces his way to the sea. At last we reached a height overlooking the valley of the river, and saw in the east, at the foot of the mountain chain, the long lines of barracks built by Ibrahim Pasha for the defence of Antioch. Behind them the ancient wall of the city clomb the mountains, whose crest it followed to the last peak of the chain. From the next hill we saw the city—a large extent of one-story houses with tiled roofs, surrounded with gardens, and half buried in the foliage of sycamores. It extends from the River Orontes, which washes its walls, up the slope of the mountain to the crags of gray rock which overhang it. We crossed the river by a massive old bridge, and entered the town. Riding along the rills of filth which traverse the streets, forming their central avenues, we passed through several lines of bazaars to a large and dreary-looking khan, the keeper of which gave us the best vacant chamber—a narrow place, full of fleas.

Antioch presents not even a shadow of its former splendor. Except the great walls, ten to fifteen miles in circuit, which the Turks have done their best to destroy, every vestige of the old city has disappeared. The houses are all of one story, on account of earthquakes, from which Antioch has suffered more than any other city in the world. At one time, during the Middle Ages, it lost 120,000 inhabitants in one day. Its situation is magnificent, and the modern town, notwithstanding its filth, wears a bright and busy aspect. Situated at the base of a lofty mountain, it overlooks, towards the east, a plain thirty or forty miles in length, producing the most abundant harvests. A great number of the inhabitants are workers in wood and leather, and very thrifty and cheerful people they appear to be.

We remained until the next day at noon, by which time a gray-bearded scamp, the chief of the *mukkairees*, or muleteers, succeeded in getting us five miserable beasts for the journey to Aleppo. On leaving the city, we travelled along a former street of Antioch, part of the ancient pavement still remaining, and after two miles came to the old wall of circuit, which we passed by a massive gateway, of Roman time. It is now called *Bab Boulos*, or St. Paul's Gate. Christianity, it will be remembered, was planted in Antioch by Paul and Barnabas, and the Apostle Peter was the first bishop of the city. We now entered the great plain of the Orontes—a level sea, rioting in the wealth of its ripening harvests. The river, lined with luxuriant thickets, meandered through the centre of this glorious picture. We crossed it during the afternoon, and keeping on our eastward course, encamped at night in a meadow near the tents of some wandering Turcomans, who furnished us with butter and milk from their herds.

Leaving the plain the next morning, we travelled due east all day, over long stony ranges of mountains, inclosing only one valley, which bore evidence of great fertility. It was circular, about ten miles in its greater diameter, and bounded on the north by the broad peak of Djebel Saman, or Mount St. Simon. In the morning we passed a ruined castle, standing in a dry, treeless dell, among the hot hills. The muleteers called it the Maiden's Palace, and said that it was built long ago by a powerful Sultan, as a prison for his daughter. For several hours thereafter, our road was lined with remains of buildings, apparently dating from the time of the Greek Empire. There were tombs, temples of massive masonry, though in a bad style of architecture, and long rows of arched chambers, which resembled store-houses. They were all more or less shattered by earthquakes, but in one place I noticed twenty such arches, each of at least twenty feet span. All the hills, on either hand, as far as we could see, were covered with the remains of buildings. In the plain of St. Simon, I saw two superb pillars, apparently part of a portico, or gateway, and the village of Dana is formed almost entirely of churches and convents, of the Lower Empire. There were but few inscriptions, and these I could not read ; but the whole of this region would, no doubt, richly repay an antiquarian research. I am told here that the entire chain of hills, which extends southward for more than a hundred miles, abounds with similar remains, and that, in many places, whole cities stand almost entire, as if recently deserted by their inhabitants.

During the afternoon, we came upon a portion of the ancient road from Antioch to Aleppo, which is still as perfect as when first constructed. It crossed a very stony ridge, and is much the finest specimen of road-making I ever saw, quite putting to shame the Appian and Flaminian Ways at Rome. It is twenty feet wide, and laid with blocks of white marble, from two to four feet square. It was apparently raised upon a more ancient road, which diverges here and there from the line, showing the deeply-cut traces of the Roman chariot-wheels. In the barren depths of the mountains we found every hour cisterns cut in the rock and filled with water left by the winter rains. Many of them, however, are fast drying up, and a month later this will be a desert road.

Towards night we descended from the hills upon the Plain of Keftin, which stretches south-westward from Aleppo, till the mountain-streams which fertilize it are dried up, when it is merged into the Syrian Desert. Its northern edge, along which we travelled, is covered with fields of wheat, cotton, and castor-beans. We stopped all night at a village called Taireb, planted at the foot of a tumulus, older than tradition. The people were in great dread of the Aneyzeh Arabs, who come in from the Desert to destroy their harvests and carry off their cattle. They wanted us to take a guard, but after our experience on the Anti-Lebanon, we felt safer without one.

Yesterday we travelled for seven hours over a wide, rolling country, now waste and barren, but formerly covered with wealth and supporting an abundant population, evidences of which are found in the buildings everywhere scattered over the hills. On and on we toiled in the heat, over this inhospitable wilderness, and though we knew Aleppo must be very near, yet we could see neither sign of cultivation nor inhabitants. Finally, about three o'clock, the top of a line of shattered wall and the points of some minarets issued out of the earth, several miles in front of us, and on climbing a glaring chalky ridge, the renowned city burst at once upon our view. It filled a wide hollow or basin among the white hills, against which its whiter houses and domes glimmered for miles, in the dead, dreary heat of the afternoon, scarcely relieved by the narrow belt of gardens on the nearer side, or the orchards of pistachio trees beyond. In the centre of the city rose a steep, abrupt mound, crowned with the remains of the ancient citadel, and shining minarets shot up, singly or in clusters, around its base. The prevailing hue of the landscape was a whitish-gray, and the long, stately city and long, monotonous hills, gleamed with equal brilliancy under a sky of cloudless and intense blue. This singular monotony of coloring gave a wonderful effect to the view, which is one of the most remarkable in all the Orient.

CHAPTER XV.

LIFE IN ALEPPO.

Our Entry into Aleppo--We are conducted to a House—Our Unexpected Welcome—The Mystery Explained--Aleppo—Its Name—Its Situation—The Trade of Aleppo—The Christians—The Revolt of 1850—Present Appearance of the City—Visit to Osman Pasha—The Citadel—View from the Battlements—Society in Aleppo—Etiquette and Costume—Jewish Marriage Festivities—A Christian Marriage Procession—Ride around the Town—Nightingales—The Aleppo Button—A Hospital for Cats—Ferhat Pasha.

ALEPPO, *Tuesday*, *June* 8, 1852.

OUR entry into Aleppo was a fitting preliminary to our experiences during the five days we have spent here. After passing a blackamoor, who acted as an advanced guard of the Custom House, at a ragged tent outside of the city, and bribing him with two piastres, we crossed the narrow line of gardens on the western side, and entered the streets. There were many coffee-houses, filled with smokers, nearly all of whom accosted us in Turkish, though Arabic is the prevailing language here. Ignorance made us discourteous, and we slighted every attempt to open a conversation. Out of the narrow streets of the suburbs, we advanced to the bazaars, in order to find a khan where we could obtain lodgings. All the best khans, however, were filled, and we were about to take a very inferior room, when a respectable individual came up to François and said: "The house is ready for the travellers, and I will show you the way." We were a little surprised at this address, but followed him to a neat, quiet and pleasant street near the bazaars, where we were ushered into a spacious court-yard, with a row of apartments opening upon it, and told to make ourselves at home.

The place had evidently been recently inhabited, for the rooms were well furnished, with not only divans, but beds in the Frank style. A lean kitten was scratching at one of the windows, to the great danger of overturning a pair of narghilehs, a tame sea-gull was walking about the court, and two sheep bleated in a stable at the further end. In the kitchen we not only found a variety of utensils, but eggs, salt, pepper, and other condiments. Our guide had left, and the only information we could get, from a dyeing establishment next door, was that the occupants had gone into the country. "Take the good the gods provide thee," is my rule in such cases, and as we were very hungry, we set François to work at preparing dinner. We arranged a divan in the open air, had a table brought out, and by the aid of the bakers in the bazaar, and the stores which the kitchen supplied, soon rejoiced over a very palatable meal. The romantic character of our reception made the dinner a merry one. It was a chapter out of the Arabian Nights, and be he genie or afrite, caliph or merchant of Bassora, into whose hands we had fallen, we resolved to let the adventure take its course. We were just finishing a nondescript pastry which François found at a baker's, and which, for want of a better name, he called *méringues à la Khorassan*, when there was a loud knock at the street door. We felt at first some little trepidation, but determined to maintain our places, and gravely invite the real master to join us.

It was a female servant, however, who, to our great amazement, made a profound salutation, and seemed delighted to see us. "My master did not expect your Excellencies to-day; he has gone into the gardens, but will soon return. Will your Excellencies take coffee after your dinner?" and coffee was forthwith served. The old woman was unremitting in her attentions; and her son, a boy of eight years, and the most venerable child I ever saw, entertained us with the description of a horse which his master had just bought—a horse which had cost two thousand piastres, and was ninety years old. Well, this Aleppo is an extraordinary place, was my first impression, and the inhabitants are remarkable people; but I waited the master's arrival, as the only means of solving the mystery. About dusk, there was another rap at the door. A lady dressed in white, with an Indian handkerchief bound over her black hair, arrived. "Pray excuse us," said she; "we thought you would not reach here before to-morrow; but my brother will come directly." In fact, the brother did come soon afterwards, and greeted us with a still warmer welcome. "Before leaving the gardens," he said, "I heard of your arrival, and have come in a full gallop the whole way." In order to put an end to this comedy of errors, I declared at once that he was mistaken; nobody in Aleppo could possibly know of our coming, and we were, perhaps, transgressing on his hospitality. But no: he would not be convinced. He was a dragoman to the English Consulate; his master had told him we would be here the next day, and he must be prepared to receive us. Besides, the janissary of the Consulate had showed us the way to his house. We, therefore, let the matter rest until next morning, when we called on Mr. Very, the Consul, who informed us that the janissary had mistaken us for two gentlemen we had met in Damascus, the travelling companions of Lord Dalkeith. As they had not arrived, he begged us to remain in the quarters which had been prepared for them. We have every reason to be glad of this mistake, as it has made us acquainted with one of the most courteous and hospitable gentlemen in the East.

Aleppo lies so far out of the usual routes of travel, that it is rarely visited by Europeans. One is not, therefore, as in the case of Damascus, prepared beforehand by volumes of description, which preclude all possibility of mistake or surprise. For my part, I only knew that Aleppo had once been the greatest commercial city of the Orient, though its power had long since passed into other hands. But there were certain stately associations lingering around the name, which drew me towards it, and obliged me to include it, at all hazards, in my Asiatic tour. The scanty description of Captains Irby and Mangles, the only one I had read, gave me no distinct idea of its position or appearance; and when, the other day, I first saw it looming grand and gray among the gray hills, more like a vast natural crystallization than the product of human art, I revelled in the novelty of that startling first impression.

The tradition of the city's name is curious, and worth relating. It is called, in Arabic, *Haleb el-Shahba*—Aleppo, the Gray—which most persons suppose to refer to the prevailing color of the soil. The legend, however, goes much farther. *Haleb*, which the Venetians and Genoese softened into Aleppo, means literally: "has milked." According to Arab tradition, the patriarch Abraham once lived here: his tent being pitched near the mound now occupied by the citadel. He had a certain gray cow (*el-shahba*) which was milked every morning for the benefit of the poor. When, therefore, it was proclaimed: "*Ibrahim haleb el-shahba*" (Abraham has milked the gray cow), all the poor of the tribe came up to receive their share. The repetition of this morning call attached itself to the spot, and became the name of the city which was afterwards founded.

Aleppo is built on the eastern slope of a shallow upland basin, through which flows the little River Koweik. There are low hills to the north and south, between which the country falls into a wide, monotonous plain, extending unbroken to the Euphrates. The city is from eight to ten miles in circuit, and, though not so thickly populated, covers a greater extent of space than Damascus. The population is estimated at 100,000. In the excellence (not the elegance) of its architecture, it surpasses any Oriental city I have yet seen. The houses are all of hewn stone, frequently three and even four stories in height, and built in a most massive and durable style, on account of the frequency of earthquakes. The streets are well paved, clean, with narrow sidewalks, and less tortuous and intricate than the bewildering alleys of Damascus. A large part of the town is occupied with bazaars, attesting the splendor of its former commerce. These establishments are covered with lofty vaults of stone, lighted from the top; and one may walk for miles beneath the spacious roofs. The shops exhibit all the stuffs of the East, especially of Persia and India. There is also an extensive display of European fabrics, as the eastern provinces of Asiatic Turkey, as far as Baghdad, are supplied entirely from Aleppo and Trebizond.

Within ten years—in fact, since the Allied Powers drove

Ibrahim Pasha out of Syria—the trade of Aleppo has increased, at the expense of Damascus. The tribes of the Desert, who were held in check during the Egyptian occupancy, are now so unruly that much of the commerce between the latter place and Baghdad goes northward to Mosul, and thence by a safer road to this city. The khans, of which there are a great number, built on a scale according with the former magnificence of Aleppo, are nearly all filled, and Persian, Georgian, and Armenian merchants again make their appearance in the bazaars. The principal manufactures carried on are the making of shoes (which, indeed, is a prominent branch in every Turkish city), and the weaving of silk and golden tissues. Two long bazaars are entirely occupied with shoe-shops, and there is nearly a quarter of a mile of confectionery, embracing more varieties than I ever saw, or imagined possible. I saw yesterday the operation of weaving silk and gold, which is a very slow process. The warp and the body of the woof were of purple silk. The loom only differed from the old hand-looms in general use in having some thirty or forty contrivances for lifting the threads of the warp, so as to form, by variation, certain patterns. The gold threads by which the pattern was worked were contained in twenty small shuttles, thrust by hand under the different parcels of the warp, as they were raised by a boy trained for that purpose, who sat on the top of the loom. The fabric was very brilliant in its appearance, and sells, as the weavers informed me, at 100 piastres per *pik*—about $7 per yard.

We had letters to Mr. Ford, an American Missionary established here, and Signor di Picciotto, who acts as American Vice-Consul. Both gentlemen have been very cordial in their offers of service, and by their aid we have been enabled to see something of Aleppo life and society. Mr. Ford, who has been here four years, has a pleasant residence at Jedaida, a Christian suburb of the city. His congregation numbers some fifty or sixty proselytes, who are mostly from the schismatic sects of the Armenians. Dr. Smith, who established the mission at Ain-tab (two days' journey north of this), where he died last year, was very successful among these sects, and the congregation there amounts to nine hundred. The Sultan, a year ago, issued a firman, permitting his Christian subjects to erect houses of worship ; but, although this was proclaimed in Constantinople and much lauded in Europe as an act of great generosity and tolerance, there has been no official promulgation of it here. So of the aid which the Turkish Government was said to have afforded to its destitute Christian subjects, whose houses were sacked during the fanatical rebellion of 1850. The world praised the Sultan's charity and love of justice, while the sufferers, to this day, lack the first experience of it. But for the spontaneous relief contributed in Europe and among the Christian communities of the Levant, the amount of misery would have been frightful.

To Feridj Pasha, who is at present the commander of the forces here, is mainly due the credit of having put down the rebels with a strong hand. There were but few troops in the city at the time of the outbreak, and as the insurgents, who were composed of the Turkish and Arab population, were in league with the Aneyzehs of the Desert, the least faltering or delay would have led to a universal massacre of the Christians. Fortunately, the troops were divided into two portions, one occupying the barracks on a hill north of the city, and the other, a mere corporal's guard of a dozen men, posted in the citadel. The leaders of the outbreak went to the latter and offered him a large sum of money (the spoils of Christian houses) to give up the fortress. With a loyalty to his duty truly miraculous among the Turks, he ordered his men to fire upon them, and they beat a hasty retreat. The quarter of the insurgents lay precisely between the barracks and the citadel, and by order of Feridj Pasha a cannonade was immediately opened on it from both points. It was not, however, until many houses had been battered down, and a still larger number destroyed by fire, that the rebels were brought to submission Their allies, the Aneyzehs, appeared on the hill east of Aleppo, to the number of five or six thousand, but a few well-directed cannon-balls told them what they might expect, and they speedily retreated. Two or three hundred Christian families lost nearly all of their property during the sack, and many were left entirely destitute. The house in which Mr. Ford lives was plundered of jewels and furniture to the amount of 400,000 piastres ($20,000). The robbers, it is said, were amazed at the amount of spoil they found. The Government made some feeble efforts to recover it, but the greater part was already sold and scattered through a thousand hands, and the unfortunate Christians have only received about seven per cent. of their loss.

The burnt quarter has since been rebuilt, and I noticed several Christians occupying shops in various parts ot it. But many families, who fled at the time, still remain in various parts of Syria, afraid to return to their homes. The Aneyzehs and other Desert tribes have latterly become more daring than ever. Even in the immediate neighborhood of the city, the inhabitants are so fearful of them that all the grain is brought up to the very walls to be threshed. The burying-grounds on both sides are now turned into threshing-floors, and all day long the Turkish peasants drive their heavy sleds around among the tomb-stones.

On the second day after our arrival, we paid a visit to Osman Pasha, Governor of the City and Province of Aleppo. We went in state, accompanied by the Consul, with two janissaries in front, bearing silver maces, and a dragoman behind. The *serai*, or palace, is a large, plain wooden building, and a group of soldiers about the door, with a shabby carriage in the court, were the only tokens of its character. We were ushered at once into the presence of the Pasha, who is a man of about seventy years, with a good-humored, though shrewd face. He was quite cordial in his manners, complimenting us on our Turkish costume, and vaunting his skill in physiognomy, which at once revealed to him that we belonged to the highest class of American nobility. In fact, in the firman which he has since sent us, we are mentioned as "nobles." He invited us to pass a day or two with him, saying that he should derive much benefit from our superior knowledge. We replied that such an intercourse could only benefit ourselves, as his greater experience, and the distinguished wisdom which had made his name long since familiar to our ears, precluded the hope of our being of any service to him. After half an hour's stay, during which we were regaled with jewelled pipes, exquisite Mocha coffee, and sherbet breathing of the gardens of Gülistan, we took our leave.

The Pasha sent an officer to show us the citadel. We passed around the moat to the entrance on the western side, consisting of a bridge and double gateway. The fortress, as I have already stated, occupies the crest of an elliptical mound, about one thousand feet by six hundred, and two hundred feet in height. It is entirely encompassed by the city and forms a prominent and picturesque feature in the distant view thereof. Formerly, it was thickly inhabited, and at the time of the great earthquake of 1822, there were three hundred families living within the walls, nearly all of whom perished. The outer walls were very much shattered on that occasion, but the enormous towers and the gateway, the grandest specimen of Saracenic architecture in the East, still remain entire. This gateway, by which we entered, is colossal in its proportions. The outer entrance, through walls ten feet thick, admitted us into a lofty vestibule lined with marble, and containing many ancient inscriptions in mosaic. Over the main portal, which is adorned with sculptured lions' heads, there is a tablet stating that the fortress was built by El Melek el Ashraf (the Holiest of Kings), after which follows: "Prosperity to the True Believers—Death to the Infidels!" A second tablet shows that it was afterwards repaired by Mohammed ebn-Berkook, who, I believe, was one of the Fatimite Caliphs. The shekh of the citadel, who accompanied us, stated the age of the structure at nine hundred years, which, as nearly as I can recollect the Saracenic chronology, is correct. He called our attention to numbers of iron arrow-heads sticking in the solid masonry—the marks of ancient sieges. Before leaving, we were presented with a bundle of arrows from the armory—undoubted relics of Saracen warfare.

The citadel is now a mass of ruins, having been deserted since the earthquake. Grass is growing on the ramparts, and the caper plant, with its white-and-purple blossoms, flourishes among the piles of rubbish. Since the late rebellion, however, a small military barrack has been built, and two companies of soldiers are stationed there. We walked around the walls, which command a magnificent view of the city and the wide plains to the south and east. It well deserves to rank with the panorama of Cairo from the citadel, and that of Damascus from the Anti-Lebanon, in extent, picturesqueness and rich oriental character. Out of the gray ring of the city, which incloses the mound, rise the great white domes and the whiter minarets of its numerous mosques, many of which are grand and imposing structures. The course of the river through the centre of the picture is marked by a belt of the greenest verdure, beyond which, to the west, rises a chain of naked red hills, and still further, fading on the horizon, the blue summit of Mt. St. Simon, and the coast range of Akma Dagh. Eastward, over vast orchards of pistachio trees, the barren plain of the Euphrates fades away to a glimmering, hot horizon. Looking downwards on the heart of the city, I was surprised to see a number of open, grassy tracts, out of which, here and there, small trees were growing. But, perceiving what appeared to be subterranean entrances at various points, I found that these tracts were upon the roofs of the houses and bazaars, verifying what I had frequently heard, that in Aleppo the inhabitants visit their friends in different parts of the city, by passing over the roofs of the houses. Previous to the earthquake of 1822, these vast roof-plains were cultivated as gardens, and presented an extent of airy bowers as large, if not as magnificent, as the renowned Hanging Gardens of ancient Babylon.

Accompanied by Signor di Picciotto, we spent two or three

days in visiting the houses of the principal Jewish and Christian families in Aleppo. We found, it is true, no such splendor as in Damascus, but more solid and durable architecture, and a more chastened elegance of taste. The buildings are all of hewn stone, the court-yards paved with marble, and the walls rich with gilding and carved wood. Some of the larger dwellings have small but beautiful gardens attached to them. We were everywhere received with the greatest hospitality, and the visits were considered as a favor rather than an intrusion. Indeed, I was frequently obliged to run the risk of giving offence, by declining the refreshments which were offered us. Each round of visits was a feat of strength, and we were obliged to desist from sheer inability to support more coffee, rose-water, pipes, and aromatic sweetmeats. The character of society in Aleppo is singular; its very life and essence is etiquette. The laws which govern it are more inviolable than those of the Medes and Persians. The question of precedence among the different families is adjusted by the most delicate scale, and rigorously adhered to in the most trifling matters. Even we, humble voyagers as we are, have been obliged to regulate our conduct according to it. After our having visited certain families, certain others would have been deeply mortified had we neglected to call upon them. Formerly, when a traveller arrived here, he was expected to call upon the different Consuls, in the order of their established precedence: the Austrian first, English second, French third, &c. After this, he was obliged to stay at home several days, to give the Consuls an opportunity of returning the visits, which they made in the same order. There was a diplomatic importance about all his movements, and the least violation of etiquette, through ignorance or neglect, was the town talk for days.

This peculiarity in society is evidently a relic of the formal times, when Aleppo was a semi-Venetian city, and the opulent seat of Eastern commerce. Many of the inhabitants are descended from the traders of those times, and they all speak the *lingua franca*, or Levantine Italian. The women wear a costume partly Turkish and partly European, combining the graces of both ; it is, in my eyes, the most beautiful dress in the world. They wear a rich scarf of some dark color on the head, which, on festive occasions, is almost concealed by their jewels, and the heavy scarlet pomegranate blossoms which adorn their dark hair. A Turkish vest and sleeves of embroidered silk, open in front, and a skirt of white or some light color, completes the costume. The Jewesses wear in addition a short Turkish *caftan*, and full trousers gathered at the ankles. At a ball given by Mr. Very, the English Consul, which we attended, all the Christian beauties of Aleppo were present. There was a fine display of diamonds, many of the ladies wearing several thousand dollars' worth on their heads. The peculiar etiquette of the place was again illustrated on this occasion. The custom is, that the music must be heard for at least one hour before the guests come. The hour appointed was eight, but when we went there, at nine, nobody had arrived. As it was generally supposed that the ball was given on our account, several of the families had servants in the neighborhood to watch our arrival ; and, accordingly, we had not been there five minutes before the guests crowded through the door in large numbers. When the first dance (an Arab dance, performed by two ladies at a time) was proposed, the wives of the

French and Spanish Consuls were first led, or rather dragged, out. When a lady is asked to dance, she invariably refuses. She is asked a second and a third time ; and if the gentleman does not solicit most earnestly, and use some gentle force in getting her upon the floor, she never forgives him.

At one of the Jewish houses which we visited, the wedding festivities of one of the daughters were being celebrated. We were welcomed with great cordiality, and immediately ushered into the room of state, an elegant apartment, overlooking the gardens below the city wall. Half the room was occupied by a raised platform, with a divan of blue silk cushions. Here the ladies reclined, in superb dresses of blue, pink, and gold, while the gentlemen were ranged on the floor below. They all rose at our entrance, and we were conducted to seats among the ladies. Pipes and perfumed drinks were served, and the bridal cake, made of twenty-six different fruits, was presented on a golden salver. Our fair neighbors, some of whom literally blazed with jewels, were strikingly beautiful. Presently the bride appeared at the door, and we all rose and remained standing, as she advanced, supported on each side by the two *shebeeniyeh*, or bridesmaids. She was about sixteen, slight and graceful in appearance, though not decidedly beautiful, and was attired with the utmost elegance. Her dress was a pale blue silk, heavy with gold embroidery; and over her long dark hair, her neck, bosom, and wrists, played a thousand rainbow gleams from the jewels which covered them. The Jewish musicians, seated at the bottom of the hall, struck up a loud, rejoicing harmony on their violins, guitars, and dulcimers, and the women servants, grouped at the door, uttered in chorus that wild, shrill cry, which accompanies all such festivals in the East.

The bride was careful to preserve the decorum expected of her, by speaking no word, nor losing the sad, resigned expression of her countenance. She ascended to the divan, bowed to each of us with a low, reverential inclination, and seated herself on the cushions. The music and dances lasted some time, accompanied by the *zughàreet*, or cry of the women, which was repeated with double force when we rose to take leave. The whole company waited on us to the street door, and one of the servants, stationed in the court, shouted some long, sing-song phrases after us as we passed out. I could not learn the words, but was told that it was an invocation of prosperity upon us, in return for the honor which our visit had conferred.

In the evening I went to view a Christian marriage procession, which, about midnight, conveyed the bride to the house of the bridegroom. The house, it appeared, was too small to receive all the friends of the family, and I joined a large number of them, who repaired to the terrace of the English Consulate, to greet the procession as it passed. The first persons who appeared were a company of buffoons; after them four janissaries, carrying silver maces; then the male friends, bearing colored lanterns and perfumed torches, raised on gilded poles; then the females, among whom I saw some beautiful Madonna faces in the torchlight; and finally the bride herself, covered from head to foot with a veil of cloth of gold, and urged along by two maidens: for it is the etiquette of such occasions that the bride should resist being taken, and must be forced every step of the way, so that she is frequently three hours in going the distance of a mile. We watched the procession a long time, winding away through the streets—a line of torches, and songs, and incense, and noisy jubilee—under the sweet starlit heaven.

The other evening, Signor di Picciotto mounted us from his fine Arabian stud, and we rode around the city, outside of the suburbs. The sun was low, and a pale yellow lustre touched the clusters of minarets that rose out of the stately masses of buildings, and the bare, chalky hills to the north. After leaving the gardens on the banks of the Koweik, we came upon a dreary waste of ruins, among which the antiquarian finds traces of the ancient Aleppo of the Greeks, the Mongolian conquerors of the Middle Ages, and the Saracens who succeeded them. There are many mosques and tombs, which were once imposing specimens of Saracenic art; but now, split and shivered by wars and earthquakes, are slowly tumbling into utter decay. On the south-eastern side of the city, its chalk foundations have been hollowed into vast, arched caverns, which extend deep into the earth. Pillars have been left at regular intervals, to support the masses above, and their huge, dim labyrinths resemble the crypts of some great cathedral. They are now used as rope-walks, and filled with cheerful workmen.

Our last excursion was to a country-house of Signor di Picciotto, in the Gardens of Babala, about four miles from Aleppo. We set out in the afternoon on our Arabians, with our host's son on a large white donkey of the Baghdad breed. Passing the Turkish cemetery, where we stopped to view the tomb of General Bem, we loosened rein and sped away at full gallop over the hot, white hills. In dashing down a stony rise, the ambitious donkey, who was doing his best to keep up with the horses, fell, hurling Master Picciotto over his head. The boy was bruised a little, but set his teeth together and showed no sign of pain, mounted again, and followed us. The Gardens of Babala are a wilderness of fruit-trees, like those of Damascus. Signor P.'s country-house is buried in a wild grove of apricot, fig, orange, and pomegranate-trees. A large marble tank, in front of the open, arched *liwan*, supplies it with water. We mounted to the flat roof, and watched the sunset fade from the beautiful landscape. Beyond the bowers of dazzling greenness which surrounded us, stretched the wide, gray hills; the minarets of Aleppo, and the walls of its castled mount shone rosily in the last rays of the sun; an old palace of the Pashas, with the long, low barracks of the soldiery, crowned the top of a hill to the north; dark, spiry cypresses betrayed the place of tombs; and, to the west, beyond the bare red peak of Mount St. Simon, rose the faint blue outline of Giaour Dagh, whose mural chain divides Syria from the plains of Cilicia. As the twilight deepened over the scene, there came a long, melodious cry of passion and of sorrow from the heart of a starry-flowered pomegranate tree in the garden. Other voices answered it from the gardens around, until not one, but fifty nightingales charmed the repose of the hour. They vied with each other in their bursts of passionate music. Each strain soared over the last, or united with others, near and far, in a chorus of the divinest pathos—an expression of sweet, unutterable, unquenchable longing. It was an ecstasy, yet a pain, to listen. "Away!" said Jean Paul to Music: "thou tellest me of that which I have not, and never can have—which I forever seek, and never find!"

But space fails me to describe half the incidents of our stay in Aleppo. There are two things peculiar to the city, however, which I must not omit mentioning. One is the Aleppo

Button, a singular ulcer, which attacks every person born in the city, and every stranger who spends more than a month there. It can neither be prevented nor cured, and always lasts for a year. The inhabitants almost invariably have it on the face—either on the cheek, forehead, or tip of the nose—where it often leaves an indelible and disfiguring scar. Strangers, on the contrary, have it on one of the joints, either the elbow, wrist, knee, or ankle. So strictly is its visitation confined to the city proper, that in none of the neighboring villages, nor even in a distant suburb, is it known. Physicians have vainly attempted to prevent it by inoculation, and are at a loss to what cause to ascribe it. We are liable to have it, even after five days' stay; but I hope it will postpone its appearance until after I reach home.

The other remarkable thing here is the Hospital for Cats. This was founded long ago by a rich, cat-loving Mussulman, and is one of the best endowed institutions in the city. An old mosque is appropriated to the purpose, under the charge of several directors; and here sick cats are nursed, homeless cats find shelter, and decrepit cats gratefully purr away their declining years. The whole category embraces several hundreds, and it is quite a sight to behold the court, the corridors, and terraces of the mosque swarming with them. Here, one with a bruised limb is receiving a cataplasm; there, a cataleptic patient is tenderly cared for; and so on, through the long concatenation of feline diseases. Aleppo, moreover, rejoices in a greater number of cats than even Jerusalem. At a rough guess, I should thus state the population of the city: Turks and Arabs, 70,000; Christians of all denominations, 15,000; Jews, 10,000; dogs, 12,000; and cats, 8,000.

Among other persons whom I have met here, is Ferhat Pasha, formerly General Stein, Hungarian Minister of War, and Governor of Transylvania. He accepted Moslemism with Bem and others, and now rejoices in his circumcision and 7,000 piastres a month. He is a fat, companionable sort of man, who, by his own confession, never labored very zealously for the independence of Hungary, being an Austrian by birth. He conversed with me for several hours on the scenes in which he had participated, and attributed the failure of the Hungarians to the want of material means. General Bem, who died here, is spoken of with the utmost respect, both by Turks and Christians. The former have honored him with a large tomb, or mausoleum, covered with a dome.

But I must close, leaving half unsaid. Suffice it to say that no Oriental city has interested me so profoundly as Aleppo, and in none have I received such universal and cordial hospitality. We leave to-morrow for Asia Minor, having engaged men and horses for the whole route to Constantinople.

CHAPTER XVI.

THROUGH THE SYRIAN GATES.

An Inauspicious Departure—The Ruined Church of St. Simon—The Plain of Antioch—A Turcoman Encampment—Climbing Akma Dagh—The Syrian Gates—Scanderoon—An American Captain—Revolt of the Koords—We take a Guard—The Field of Issus—The Robber-Chief, Kutchuk Ali—A Deserted Town—A Land of Gardens.

"Mountains, on whose barren breast
The lab'ring clouds do often rest."
MILTON.

IN QUARANTINE (Adana, Asia Minor), *Tuesday, June* 15, 1852.

WE left Aleppo on the morning of the 9th, under circumstances not the most promising for the harmony of our journey. We had engaged horses and baggage-mules from the *capidji*, or chief of the muleteers, and in order to be certain of having animals that would not break down on the way, made a particular selection from a number that were brought us. When about leaving the city, however, we discovered that one of the horses had been changed. Signor di Picciotto, who accompanied us past the Custom-House barriers, immediately dispatched the delinquent muleteer to bring back the true horse, and the latter made a farce of trying to find him, leading the Consul and the capidji (who, I believe, was at the bottom of the cheat) a wild-goose chase over the hills around Aleppo, where of course, the animal was not to be seen. When, at length, we had waited three hours, and had wandered about four miles from the city, we gave up the search, took leave of the Consul and went on with the new horse. Our proper plan would have been to pitch the tent and refuse to move till the matter was settled. The animal, as we discovered during the first day's journey, was hopelessly lame, and we only added to the difficulty by taking him.

We rode westward all day over barren and stony hills, meeting with abundant traces of the power and prosperity of this region during the times of the Greek Emperors. The nevastation wrought by earthquakes has been terrible ; there is scarcely a wall or arch standing, which does not bear marks of having been violently shaken. The walls inclosing the fig-orchards near the villages contain many stones with Greek inscriptions, and fragments of cornices. We encamped the first night on the plain at the foot of Mount St. Simon, and not far from the ruins of the celebrated Church of the same name. The building stands in a stony wilderness at the foot of the mountain. It is about a hundred feet long and thirty in height, with two lofty square towers in front. The pavement of the interior is entirely concealed by the masses of pillars, capitals, and hewn blocks that lie heaped upon it. The windows, which are of the tall, narrow, arched form, common in Byzantine Churches, have a common moulding which falls like a mantle over and between them. The general effect of the Church is very fine, though there is much inelegance in the sculptured details. At the extremity is a half-dome of massive stone, over the place of the altar, and just in front of this formerly stood the pedestal whereon, according to tradition, St. Simeon Stylites commenced his pillar-life. I found a recent excavation at the spot, but no pedestal, which has probably been carried off by the Greek monks. Beside the Church stands a large building, with an upper and lower balcony, supported by square stone pillars, around three sides. There is also a paved court-yard, a large cistern cut in the rock and numerous out-buildings, all going to confirm the supposition of its having been a monastery. The main building is three stories high, with pointed gables, and bears a strong resemblance to an American summer hotel, with verandas. Several ancient fig and walnut trees are growing among the ruins, and add to their picturesque appearance.

The next day we crossed a broad chain of hills to the Plain of Antioch, which we reached near its northern extremity. In one of the valleys through which the road lay, we saw a number of hot sulphur springs, some of them of a considerable volume of water. Not far from them was a beautiful fountain of fresh and cold water gushing from the foot of a high rock. Soon after reaching the plain, we crossed the stream of Kara Su, which feeds the Lake of Antioch. This part of the plain is low and swampy, and the streams are literally alive with fish. While passing over the bridge I saw many hundreds, from one to two feet in length. We wandered through the marshy meadows for two or three hours, and towards sunset reached a Turcoman encampment, where the ground was dry enough to pitch our tents. The rude tribe received us hospitably, and sent us milk and cheese in abundance. I visited the tent of the Shekh, who was very courteous, but as he knew no language but Turkish, our conversation was restricted to signs. The tent was of camel's-hair cloth, spacious, and open at the sides. A rug was spread for me, and the Shekh's wife brought me a pipe of tolerable tobacco. The household were seated upon the ground, chatting pleasantly with one another, and apparently not in the least disturbed by my presence. One of the Shekh's sons, who was deaf and dumb, came and sat before me, and described by very expressive signs the character of the road to Scanderoon. He gave me to understand that there were robbers in the mountains, with many grim gestures descriptive of stabbing and firing muskets.

The mosquitoes were so thick during the night that we were obliged to fill the tent with smoke in order to sleep. When morning came, we fancied there would be a relief for us, but it only brought a worse pest, in the shape of swarms of black gnats, similar to those which so tormented me in Nubia. I know of no infliction so terrible as these gnats, which you cannot drive away, and which assail ears, eyes, and nostrils in such quantities that you become mad and desperate in your efforts to eject them. Through glens filled with oleander, we ascended the first slopes of Akma Dagh, the mountain range which divides the Gulf of Scanderoon from the Plain of Antioch. Then, passing a natural terrace, covered with groves of oak, our road took the mountain side, climbing upwards in the shadow of pine and wild olive trees, and between banks of blooming lavender and myrtle. We saw two or three companies of armed guards, stationed by the road-side, for the mountain is infested with robbers, and a caravan had been plundered only three days before. The view, looking backward, took in the whole plain, with the Lake of Antioch glittering in the centre, the valley of the Orontes in the south, and the lofty cone of Djebel Okrab far to the west. As we approached the summit, violent gusts of wind blew through the pass with such force as almost to overturn our horses. Here the road from Antioch joins that from Aleppo, and both for some distance retain the ancient pavement.

From the western side we saw the sea once more, and went down through the *Pylæ Syriæ*, or Syrian Gates, as this defile was called by the Romans. It is very narrow and rugged, with an abrupt descent. In an hour from the summit we came upon an aqueduct of a triple row of arches, crossing the gorge. It is still used to carry water to the town of Beilan, which hangs over the mouth of the pass, half a mile below. This is one of the most picturesque spots in Syria. The houses cling to the sides and cluster on the summits of precipitous crags, and every shelf of soil, every crevice where a tree can thrust its roots, upholds a mass of brilliant vegetation. Water is the life of the place. It gushes into the street from exhaustless fountains ; it trickles from the terraces in showers of misty drops ; it tumbles into the gorge in sparkling streams ; and everywhere it nourishes a life as bright and beautiful as its own. The fruit trees are of enormous size, and the crags are curtained with a magnificent drapery of vines. This green gateway opens suddenly upon another, cut through a glittering mass of micaceous rock, whence one looks down on the town and Gulf of Scanderoon, the coast of Karamania beyond, and the distant snows of the Taurus. We descended through groves of pine and oak, and in three hours more reached the shore.

Scanderoon is the most unhealthy place on the Syrian Coast, owing to the malaria from a marsh behind it. The inhabitants are a wretched pallid set, who are visited every year with devastating fevers. The marsh was partly drained some forty years ago by the Turkish government, and a few thousand dollars would be sufficient to remove it entirely, and make the place—which is of some importance as the seaport of Aleppo—healthy and habitable. At present, there are not five hundred inhabitants, and half of these consist of the Turkish garrison and the persons attached to the different Vice-Consulates. The streets are depositories of filth, and pools of stagnant water, on all sides, exhale the most fetid odors. Near the town are the ruins of a castle built by Godfrey of Bouillon. We marched directly down to the sea-shore, and pitched our tent close beside the waves, as the place most free from malaria. There were a dozen vessels at anchor in the road, and one of them proved to be the American bark Columbia, Capt. Taylor. We took a skiff and went on board, where we were cordially welcomed by the mate. In the evening, the captain came to our tent, quite surprised to find two wandering Americans in such a lonely corner of the world. Soon afterwards, with true seaman-like generosity, he returned, bringing a jar of fine Spanish olives and a large bottle of pickles, which he insisted on adding to our supplies. The olives have the choicest Andalusian flavor, and the pickles lose none of their relish from having been put up in New York.

The road from Scanderoon to this place lies mostly along the shore of the gulf, at the foot of Akma Dagh, and is reckoned dangerous on account of the marauding bands of Koords who infest the mountains. These people, like the Druses, have rebelled against the conscription, and will probably hold their ground with equal success, though the Turks talk loudly of invading their strongholds. Two weeks ago, the post was robbed, about ten miles from Scanderoon, and a government vessel, now lying at anchor in the bay, opened a cannonade on the plunderers, before they could be secured. In consequence of the warnings of danger in everybody's mouth, we decided to take an escort, and therefore waited upon the commander of the forces, with the firman of the Pasha of Aleppo. A convoy of two soldiers was at once promised us; and at sunrise, next morning, they took the lead of our caravan.

In order to appear more formidable, in case we should meet with robbers, we put on our Frank pantaloons, which had no other effect than to make the heat more intolerable. But we formed rather a fierce cavalcade, six armed men in all. Our road followed the shore of the bay, having a narrow, uninhabited flat, covered with thickets of myrtle and mastic, between us and the mountains. The two soldiers, more valiant than the guard of Banias, rode in advance, and showed no signs of fear as we approached the suspicious places. The morning was delightfully clear, and the snow-crowned range of Taurus shone through the soft vapors hanging over the gulf. In one place, we skirted the shore for some distance, under a bank twenty feet in height, and so completely mantled with shrubbery, that a small army might have hidden in it. There were gulleys at intervals, opening suddenly on our path, and we looked up them, expecting every moment to see the gleam of a Koordish gun-barrel, or a Turcoman spear, above the tops of the myrtles.

Crossing a promontory which makes out from the mountains, we came upon the renowned plain of Issus, where Darius lost his kingdom to Alexander. On a low cliff overhanging the sea, there are the remains of a single tower of gray stone.

The people in Scanderoon call it "Jonah's Pillar," and say that it marks the spot where the Ninevite was cast ashore by the whale. [This makes three places on the Syrian coast where Jonah was vomited forth.] The plain of Issus is from two to three miles long, but not more than half a mile wide. It is traversed by a little river, supposed to be the Pinarus, which comes down through a tremendous cleft in the Akma Dagh. The ground seems too small for the battle-field of such armies as were engaged on the occasion. It is bounded on the north by a low hill, separating it from the plain of Baïas, and it is possible that Alexander may have made choice of this position, leaving the unwieldy forces of Darius to attack him from the plain. His advantage would be greater, on account of the long, narrow form of the ground, which would prevent him from being engaged with more than a small portion of the Persian army, at one time. The plain is now roseate with blooming oleanders, but almost entirely uncultivated. About midway there are the remains of an ancient quay jutting into the sea.

Soon after leaving the field of Issus, we reached the town of Baïas, which is pleasantly situated on the shore, at the mouth of a river whose course through the plain is marked with rows of tall poplar trees. The walls of the town, and the white dome and minaret of its mosque, rose dazzlingly against the dark blue of the sea, and the purple stretch of the mountains of Karamania. A single palm lifted its crest in the foreground. We dismounted for breakfast under the shade of an old bridge which crosses the river. It was a charming spot, the banks above and below being overhung with oleander, white rose, honeysuckle and clematis. The two guardsmen finished the remaining half of our Turcoman cheese, and almost exhausted our supply of bread. I gave one of them a cigar, which he was at a loss how to smoke, until our muleteer showed him.

Baïas was celebrated fifty years ago, as the residence of the robber chief, Kutchuk Ali, who, for a long time, braved the authority of the Porte itself. He was in the habit of levying a yearly tribute on the caravan to Mecca, and the better to enforce his claims, often suspended two or three of his captives at the gates of the town, a day or two before the caravan arrived. Several expeditions were sent against him, but he always succeeded in bribing the commanders, who, on their return to Constantinople, made such representations that Kutchuk Ali, instead of being punished, received one dignity after another, until finally he attained the rank of a Pasha of two tails. This emboldened him to commit enormities too great to be overlooked, and in 1812 Baïas was taken, and the atrocious nest of land-pirates broken up.

I knew that the town had been sacked on this occasion, but was not prepared to find such a complete picture of desolation. The place is surrounded with a substantial wall, with two gateways, on the north and south. A bazaar, covered with a lofty vaulted roof of stone, runs directly through from gate to gate; and there was still a smell of spices in the air, on entering. The massive shops on either hand, with their open doors, invited possession, and might readily be made habitable again. The great iron gates leading from the bazaar into the khans and courts, still swing on their rusty hinges. We rode into the court of the mosque, which is surrounded with a light and elegant corridor, supported by pillars. The grass has as yet but partially invaded the marble pavement, and a stone drinking-trough still stands in the centre. I urged my horse up the steps and into the door of the mosque. It is in the form of a Greek cross, with a dome in the centre, resting on four very elegant pointed arches. There is an elaborately gilded and painted gallery of wood over the entrance, and the pulpit opposite is as well preserved as if the *mollah* had just left it. Out of the mosque we passed into a second court, and then over a narrow bridge into the fortress. The moat is perfect, and the walls as complete as if just erected. Only the bottom is dry, and now covered with a thicket of wild pomegranate trees. The heavy iron doors of the fortress swung half open, as we entered unchallenged. The interior is almost entire, and some of the cannon still lie buried in the springing grass. The plan of the little town, which appears to have been all built at one time, is most admirable. The walls of circuit, including the fortress, cannot be more than 300 yards square, and yet none of the characteristics of a large Oriental city are omitted.

Leaving Baïas, we travelled northward, over a waste, though fertile plain. The mountains on our right made a grand appearance, with their feet mantled in myrtle, and their tops plumed with pine. They rise from the sea with a long, bold sweep, but each peak falls off in a precipice on the opposite side, as if the chain were the barrier of the world and there was nothing but space beyond. In the afternoon we left the plain for a belt of glorious garden land, made by streams that came down from the mountains. We entered a lane embowered in pomegranate, white rose, clematis, and other flowering vines and shrubs, and overarched by superb plane, lime, and beech trees, chained together with giant grape vines. On either side were fields of ripe wheat and barley, mulberry orchards and groves of fruit trees, under the shade of which the Turkish families sat or slept during the hot hours of the day. Birds sang in the boughs, and the gurgling of water made a cool undertone to their music. Out of fairyland where shall I see again such lovely bowers? We were glad when the soldiers announced that it was necessary to encamp there; as we should find no other habitations for more than twenty miles.

Our tent was pitched under a grand sycamore, beside a swift mountain stream which almost made the circuit of our camp. Beyond the tops of the elm, beech, and fig groves, we saw the picturesque green summits of the lower ranges of Giaour Dagh, in the north-east, while over the southern meadows a golden gleam of sunshine lay upon the Gulf of Scanderoon. The village near us was Chaya, where there is a military station. The guards we had brought from Scanderoon here left us; but the commanding officer advised us to take others on the morrow, as the road was still considered unsafe.

CHAPTER XVII.

ADANA AND TARSUS.

The Black Gate—The Plain of Cilicia—A Koord Village—Missis—Cilician Scenery—Arrival at Adana—Three days in Quarantine—We receive Pratique—A Landscape—The Plain of Tarsus—The River Cydnus—A Vision of Cleopatra—Tarsus and its Environs—The *Duniktash*—The Moon of Ramazan.

"Paul said, I am a man which am a Jew of Tarsus, a city in Cilicia, a citizen of no mean city."—ACTS, xxi. 39.

KHAN ON MT. TAURUS, *Saturday*, *June* 19, 1852.

WE left our camp at Chaya at dawn, with an escort of three soldiers, which we borrowed from the guard stationed at that place. The path led along the shore, through clumps of myrtle beaten inland by the wind, and rounded as smoothly as if they had been clipped by a gardener's shears. As we approached the head of the gulf, the peaked summits of Giaour Dagh, 10,000 feet in height, appeared in the north-east. The streams we forded swarmed with immense trout. A brown hedgehog ran across our road, but when I touched him with the end of my pipe, rolled himself into an impervious ball of prickles. Soon after turning the head of the gulf, the road swerved off to the west, and entered a narrow pass, between hills covered with thick copse-wood. Here we came upon an ancient gateway of black lava stone, which bears marks of great antiquity It is now called *Kara Kapu*, the "Black Gate," and some suppose it to have been one of the ancient gates of Cilicia.

Beyond this, our road led over high, grassy hills, without a sign of human habitation, to the ruined khan of Koord Koolak. We dismounted and unloaded our baggage in the spacious stone archway, and drove our beasts into the dark, vaulted halls behind. The building was originally intended for a magazine of supplies, and from the ruined mosque near it, I suspect it was formerly one of the caravan stations for the pilgrims from Constantinople to Mecca. The weather was intensely hot and sultry, and our animals were almost crazy from the attacks of a large yellow gad-fly. After the noonday heat was over we descended to the first Cilician plain, which is bounded on the west by the range of Durdun Dagh. As we had now passed the most dangerous part of the road, we dismissed the three soldiers and took but a single man with us. The entire plain is covered with wild fennel, six to eight feet in height, and literally blazing with its bloomy yellow tops. Riding through it, I could barely look over them, and far and wide, on all sides, spread a golden sea, out of which the long violet hills rose with the loveliest effect. Brown, shining serpents, from four to six feet in length, frequently slid across our path. The plain, which must be sixty miles in circumference, is wholly uncultivated, though no land could possibly be richer.

Out of the region of fennel we passed into one of red and white clover, timothy grass and wild oats. The thistles were so large as to resemble young palm-trees, and the salsify of our gardens grew rank and wild. At length we dipped into the evening shadow of Durdun Dagh, and reached the village of Koord Keui, on his lower slope. As there was no place for our tent on the rank grass of the plain or the steep side of the hill, we took forcible possession of the winnowing-floor, a flat terrace built up under two sycamores, and still covered with the chaff of the last threshing. The Koords took the whole thing as a matter of course, and even brought us a felt carpet to rest upon. They came and seated themselves around us, chatting sociably, while we lay in the tent-door, smoking the pipe of refreshment. The view over the wide golden plain, and the hills beyond, to the distant, snow-tipped peaks of Akma Dagh, was superb, as the shadow of the mountain behind us slowly lengthened over it, blotting out the mellow lights of sunset. There were many fragments of pillars and capitals of white marble built up in the houses, showing that they occupied the site of some ancient village or temple.

The next morning, we crossed Durdun Dagh, and entered the great plain of Cilicia. The range, after we had passed it, presented a grand, bold, broken outline, blue in the morning vapor, and wreathed with shifting belts of cloud. A stately castle, called the Palace of Serpents, on the summit of an isolated peak to the north, stood out clear and high, in the midst of a circle of fog, like a phantom picture of the air. The River Jyhoon, the ancient Pyramus, which rises on the borders of Armenia, sweeps the western base of the mountains. It is a larger stream than the Orontes, with a deep, rapid current, flowing at the bottom of a bed lower than the level of the plain. In three hours, we reached Missis, the ancient Mopsuestia, on the right bank of the river. There are extensive ruins on the left bank, which were probably those of the former city. The soil for some distance around is scattered with broken pillars, capitals, and hewn stones. The ancient bridge still crosses the river, but the central arch having been broken away, is replaced with a wooden platform. The modern town is a forlorn place, and all the glorious plain around it is uncultivated. The view over this plain was magnificent: unbounded towards the sea, but on the north girdled by the sublime range of Taurus, whose great snow-fields gleamed in the sun. In the afternoon, we reached the old bridge over the Jyhoon, at Adana. The eastern bank is occupied with the graves of the former inhabitants, and there are at least fifteen acres of tombstones, as thickly planted as the graves can be dug. The fields of wheat and barley along the river are very rich, and at present the natives are busily occupied in drawing the sheaves on large sleds to the open threshing-floors.

The city is built over a low eminence, and its four tall minarets, with a number of palm-trees rising from the mass of brown brick walls, reminded me of Egypt. At the end of the bridge, we were met by one of the Quarantine officers, who preceded us, taking care that we touched nobody in the streets, to the Quarantine building. This land quarantine, between Syria and Asia Minor, when the former country is free from any epidemic, seems a most absurd thing. We were detained at Adana three days and a half, to be purified, before proceeding further. Lately, the whole town was placed in quarantine for five days, because a Turkish Bey, who lives near Baïas, entered the gates without being noticed, and was found in the bazaars. The Quarantine building was once a palace of the Pashas of Adana, but is now in a half-ruined condition. The rooms are large and airy, and there is a spacious open divan which affords ample shade and a cool breeze throughout the whole day. Fortunately for us, there were only three persons in Quarantine, who occupied a room distant from ours. The Inspector was a very obliging person, and procured us a table and two chairs. The only table to be had in the whole place—a town of 15,000 inhabitants—belonged to an Italian merchant, who kindly gave it for our use. We employed a messenger to purchase provisions in the bazaars; and our days passed quietly in writing, smoking, and gazing indolently from our windows upon the flowery plains beyond the town. Our nights, however, were tormented by small white gnats, which stung us unmercifully. The physician of Quarantine, Dr. Spagnolo, is a Venetian refugee, and formerly editor of *La Lega Italiana*, a paper published in Venice during the revolution. He informed us that, except the Princess Belgioioso, who passed through Adana on her way to Jerusalem, we were the only travellers he had seen for eleven months.

After three days and four nights of grateful, because involuntary, indolence, Dr. Spagnolo gave us *pratique*, and we lost no time in getting under weigh again. We were the only occupants of Quarantine; and as we moved out of the portal of the old seraï, at sunrise, no one was guarding it. The Inspector and Mustapha, the messenger, took their backsheeshes with silent gratitude. The plain on the west side of the town is well cultivated; and as we rode along towards Tarsus, I was charmed with the rich pastoral air of the scenery. It was like one of the midland landscapes of England, bathed in Southern sunshine. The beautiful level, stretching away to the mountains, stood golden with the fields of wheat which the reapers were cutting. It was no longer bare, but dotted with orange groves, clumps of holly, and a number of magnificent terebinth-trees, whose dark, rounded masses of foliage remind one of the Northern oak. Cattle were grazing in the stubble, and horses, almost buried under loads of fresh grass, met us as they passed to the city. The sheaves were drawn to the threshing-floor on sleds, and we could see the husbandmen in the distance treading out and winnowing the grain. Over these bright, busy scenes, rose the lesser heights of the Taurus, and beyond them, mingled in white clouds, the snows of the crowning range.

The road to Tarsus, which is eight hours distant, lies over an unbroken plain. Towards the sea, there are two tumuli, resembling those on the plains east of Antioch. Stone wells, with troughs for watering horses, occur at intervals of three or four miles; but there is little cultivation after leaving the vicinity of Adana. The sun poured down an intense summer heat, and hundreds of large gad-flies, swarming around us, drove the horses wild with their stings. Towards noon, we stopped at a little village for breakfast. We took possession of a shop, which the good-natured merchant offered us, and were about to spread our provisions upon the counter, when the gnats and mosquitoes fairly drove us away. We at once went forward in search of a better place, which gave occasion to our chief mukkairee, Hadji Youssuf, for a violent remonstrance. The terms of the agreement at Aleppo gave the entire control of the journey into our own hands, and the Hadji now sought to violate it. He protested against our travelling more than six hours a day, and conducted himself so insolently, that we threatened to take him before the Pasha of Tarsus. This silenced him for the time; but we hate him so cordially since then, that I foresee we shall have more trouble. In the afternoon, a gust, sweeping along the sides of Taurus, cooled the air and afforded us a little relief.

By three o'clock we reached the River Cydnus, which is bare of trees on its eastern side, but flows between banks covered with grass and shrubs. It is still spanned by the ancient bridge, and the mules now step in the hollow ruts worn long ago by Roman and Byzantine chariot wheels. The stream is not more than thirty yards broad, but has a very full and rapid current of a bluish-white color, from the snows which feed it. I rode down to the brink and drank a cup of the water. It was exceedingly cold, and I do not wonder that a bath in it should have killed the Emperor Barbarossa. From the top of the bridge, there is a lovely view, down the stream, where it washes a fringe of willows and heavy fruit-trees on its western bank, and then winds away through the grassy plain, to the sea. For once, my fancy ran parallel with the inspiration of the scene. I could think of nothing but the galley of Cleopatra slowly stemming the current of the stream, its silken sails filled with the sea-breeze, its gilded oars keeping time to the flutes, whose voluptuous melodies floated far out over the vernal meadows. Tarsus was probably almost hidden then, as now, by its gardens, except just where it touched the river; and the dazzling vision of the Egyptian Queen, as she came up conquering and to conquer, must have been all the more bewildering, from the lovely bowers through which she sailed.

From the bridge an ancient road still leads to the old Byzantine gate of Tarsus. Part of the town is encompassed by a wall, built by the Caliph Haroun Al-Raschid, and there is a ruined fortress, which is attributed to Sultan Bajazet

Small streams, brought from the Cydnus, traverse the environs, and, with such a fertile soil, the luxuriance of the gardens in which the city lies buried is almost incredible. In our rambles in search of a place to pitch the tent, we entered a superb orange-orchard, the foliage of which made a perpetual twilight. Many of the trunks were two feet in diameter. The houses are mostly of one story, and the materials are almost wholly borrowed from the ancient city. Pillars, capitals, fragments of cornices and entablatures abound. I noticed here, as in Adana, a high wooden frame on the top of every house, raised a few steps above the roof, and covered with light muslin, like a portable bathing-house. Here the people put up their beds in the evening, sleep, and come down to the roofs in the morning—an excellent plan for getting better air in these malarious plains and escaping from fleas and mosquitoes. In our search for the Armenian Church, which is said to have been founded by St. Paul ("Saul of Tarsus"), we came upon a mosque, which had been originally a Christian Church, of Greek times.

From the top of a mound, whereupon stand the remains of an ancient circular edifice, we obtained a fine view of the city and plain of Tarsus. A few houses or clusters of houses stood here and there like reefs amid the billowy green, and the minarets—one of them with a nest of young storks on its very summit—rose like the masts of sunken ships. Some palms lifted their tufted heads from the gardens, beyond which the great plain extended from the mountains to the sea. The tumulus near Mersyn, the port of Tarsus, was plainly visible. Two hours from Mersyn are the ruins of Pompeiopolis, the name given by Pompey to the town of Soli, after his conquest of the Cilician pirates. From Soli, on account of the bad

Greek spoken by its inhabitants, came the term "solecism." The ruins of Pompeiopolis consist of a theatre, temples, and a number of houses, still in good preservation. The whole coast, as far as Aleya, three hundred miles west of this, is said to abound with ruined cities, and I regret exceedingly that time will not permit me to explore it.

While searching for the antiquities about Tarsus, I accosted a man in a Frank dress, who proved to be the Neapolitan Consul. He told us that the most remarkable relic was the *Duniktash* (the Round Stone), and procured us a guide. It lies in a garden near the city, and is certainly one of the most remarkable monuments in the East. It consists of a square inclosure of solid masonry, 350 feet long by 150 feet wide, the walls of which are eighteen feet in thickness and twenty feet high. It appears to have been originally a solid mass, without entrance, but a passage has been broken in one place, and in another there is a split or fissure, evidently produced by an earthquake. The material is rough stone, brick and mortar. Inside of the inclosure are two detached square masses of masonry, of equal height, and probably eighty feet on a side, without opening of any kind. One of them has been pierced at the bottom, a steep passage leading to a pit or well, but the sides of the passage thus broken indicate that the whole structure is one solid mass. It is generally supposed that they were intended as tombs: but of whom? There is no sign by which they may be recognized, and, what is more singular, no tradition concerning them.

The day we reached Tarsus was the first of the Turkish fast-month of Ramazan, the inhabitants having seen the new moon the night before. At Adana, where they did not keep such a close look-out, the fast had not commenced. During its continuance, which is from twenty-eight to twenty-nine days, no Mussulman dares eat, drink, or smoke, from an hour before sunrise till half an hour after sunset. The Mohammedan months are lunar, and each month makes the whole round of the seasons, once in thirty-three years. When, therefore, the Ramazan comes in midsummer, as at present, the fulfilment of this fast is a great trial, even to the strongest and most devout. Eighteen hours without meat or drink, and what is still worse to a genuine Turk, without a pipe, is a rigid test of faith. The rich do the best they can to avoid it, by feasting all night and sleeping all day, but the poor, who must perform their daily avocations, as usual, suffer exceedingly. In walking through Tarsus I saw many wretched faces in the bazaars, and the guide who accompanied us had a painfully famished air. Fortunately the Koran expressly permits invalids, children, and travellers to disregard the fast, so that although we eat and drink when we like, we are none the less looked upon as good Mussulmans. About dark a gun is fired and a rocket sent up from the mosque, announcing the termination of the day's fast. The meals are already prepared, the pipes filled, the coffee smokes in the *finjans*, and the echoes have not died away nor the last sparks of the rocket become extinct, before half the inhabitants are satisfying their hunger, thirst and smoke-lust.

We left Tarsus this morning, and are now encamped among the pines of Mount Taurus. The last flush of sunset is fading from his eternal snows, and I drop my pen to enjoy the silence of twilight in this mountain solitude.

CHAPTER XVIII.

THE PASS OF MOUNT TAURUS.

We enter the Taurus—Turcomans—Forest Scenery—the Palace of Pan—Khan Mezarluk—Morning among the Mountains—The Gorge of the Cydnus—The Crag of the Fortress—The Cilician Gate—Deserted Forts—A Sublime Landscape—The Gorge of the Sihoon—The Second Gate—Camp in the Defile—Sunrise—Journey up the Sihoon—A Change of Scenery—A Pastoral Valley—Kolü Kushla—A Deserted Khan—A Guest in Ramazan—Flowers—The Plain of Karamania—Barren Hills—The Town of Eregli—The Hadji again.

"Lo! where the pass expands
Its stony jaws, the abrupt mountain breaks,
And seems, with its accumulated crags,
To overhang the world." SHELLEY.

EREGLI, *in Karamania, June* 22, 1852.

STRIKING our tent in the gardens of Tarsus, we again crossed the Cydnus, and took a northern course across the plain. The long line of Taurus rose before us, seemingly divided into four successive ranges, the highest of which was folded in clouds; only the long streaks of snow, filling the ravines, being visible. The outlines of these ranges were very fine, the waving line of the summits cut here and there by precipitous gorges—the gateways of rivers that came down to the plain. In about twc hours, we entered the lower hills. They are barren and stony, with a white, chalky soil; but the valleys were filled with myrtle, oleander, and lauristinus in bloom, and lavender grew in great profusion on the hill-sides. The flowers of the oleander gave out a delicate, almond-like fragrance, and grew in such dense clusters as frequently to hide the foliage. I amused myself with finding a derivation of the name of this beautiful plant, which may answer until somebody discovers a better one. Hero, when the corpse of her lover was cast ashore by the waves, buried him under an oleander bush, where she was accustomed to sit daily, and lament over his untimely fate. Now, a foreign horticulturist, happening to pass by when the shrub was in blossom, was much struck with its beauty, and asked Hero what it was called. But she, absorbed in grief, and thinking only of her lover, clasped her hands, and sighed out: "O Leander! O Leander!" which the horticulturist immediately entered in his note-book as the name of the shrub; and by that name it is known, to the present time.

For two or three hours, the scenery was rather tame, the higher summits being obscured with a thunder-cloud. Towards noon, however, we passed the first chain, and saw, across a strip of rolling land intervening, the grand ramparts of the second, looming dark and large under the clouds. A circular watch-tower of white stone, standing on the summit of a promontory at the mouth of a gorge on our right, flashed out boldly against the storm. We stopped under an oak-tree to take breakfast; but there was no water; and two Turks, who were resting while their horses grazed in the meadow, told us we should find a good spring half a mile further. We ascended a long slope, covered with wheat-fields, where numbers of Turcoman reapers were busy at work, passed their black tents, surrounded with droves of sheep and goats, and reached a rude stone fountain of good water, where two companies of these people had stopped to rest, on their way to the mountains. It was the time of noon prayer, and they went through their devotions with great solemnity. We nestled deep in a bed of myrtles, while we breakfasted; for the sky was clouded, and the wind blew cool and fresh from the region of rain above us. Some of the Turcomans asked us for bread, and were very grateful when we gave it to them.

In the afternoon, we came into a higher and wilder region, where the road led through thickets of wild olive. holly, oak, and lauristinus, with occasional groves of pine. What a joy I felt in hearing, once more, the grand song of my favorite tree! Our way was a woodland road; a storm had passed over the region in the morning; the earth was still fresh and moist, and there was an aromatic smell of leaves in the air. We turned westward into the entrance of a deep valley, over which hung a perpendicular cliff of gray and red rock, fashioned by nature so as to resemble a vast fortress, with windows, portals and projecting bastions. François displayed his knowledge of mythology, by declaring it to be the Palace of Pan. While we were carrying out the idea, by making chambers for the Fauns and Nymphs in the basement story of the precipice, the path wound around the shoulder of the mountain, and the glen spread away before us, branching up into loftier ranges, disclosing through its gateway of cliffs, rising out of the steeps of pine forest, a sublime vista of blue mountain peaks, climbing to the topmost snows. It was a magnificent Alpine landscape, more glowing and rich than Switzerland, yet equalling it in all the loftier characteristics of mountain scenery. Another and greater precipice towered over us on the right, and the black eagles which had made their eyries in its niched and caverned vaults, were wheeling around its crest. A branch of the Cydnus foamed along the bottom of the gorge, and some Turcoman boys were tending their herds on its banks.

Further up the glen, we found a fountain of delicious water, beside the deserted Khan of Mezarluk, and there encamped for the night. Our tent was pitched on the mountain side, near a fountain of the coolest, clearest and sweetest water I have seen in all the East. There was perfect silence among the mountains, and the place was as lonely as it was sublime. The night was cool and fresh; but I could not sleep until towards morning. When I opened my belated eyes, the tall peaks on the opposite side of the glen were girdled below their waists with the flood of a sparkling sunrise. The sky was pure as crystal, except a soft white fleece that veiled the snowy pinnacles of Taurus, folding and unfolding, rising and sinking, as if to make their beauty still more attractive by the partial concealment. The morning air was almost cold, but so pure and bracing—so aromatic with the healthy breath of the pines—that I took it down in the fullest possible draughts.

We rode up the glen, following the course of the Cydnus, through scenery of the wildest and most romantic character. The bases of the mountains were completely enveloped in forests of pine, but their summits rose in precipitous crags, many hundreds of feet in height, hanging above our very heads. Even after the sun was five hours high, their shadows fell upon us from the opposite side of the glen. Mixed with the pine were occasional oaks, an undergrowth of hawthorn in bloom, and shrubs covered with yellow and white flowers. Over these the wild grape threw its rich festoons, filling the air with exquisite fragrance.

Out of this glen, we passed into another, still narrower and wilder. The road was the old Roman way, and in tolerable condition, though it had evidently not been mended for many centuries. In half an hour, the pass opened, disclosing an enormous peak in front of us, crowned with the ruins of an ancient fortress of considerable extent. The position was almost impregnable, the mountain dropping on one side into a precipice five hundred feet in perpendicular height. Under the cliffs of the loftiest ridge, there was a terrace planted with walnut-trees: a charming little hamlet in the wilderness. Wild sycamore-trees, with white trunks and bright green foliage, shaded the foamy twists of the Cydnus, as it plunged down its difficult bed. The pine thrust its roots into the naked precipices, and from their summits hung out over the great abysses below. I thought of Œnone's

> ——" tall, dark pines, that fringed the craggy ledge
> High over the blue gorge, and all between
> The snowy peak and snow-white cataract
> Fostered the callow eaglet ;"

and certainly she had on Mount Ida no more beautiful trees than these.

We had doubled the Crag of the Fortress, when the pass closed before us, shut in by two immense precipices of sheer, barren rock, more than a thousand feet in height. Vast fragments, fallen from above, choked up the entrance, whence the Cydnus, spouting forth in foam, leaped into the defile. The ancient road was completely destroyed, but traces of it were to be seen on the rocks, ten feet above the present bed of the stream, and on the broken masses which had been hurled below.

The path wound with difficulty among these wrecks, and then merged into the stream itself, as we entered the gateway. A violent wind blew in our faces as we rode through the strait, which is not ten yards in breadth, while its walls rise to the region of the clouds. In a few minutes we had traversed it, and stood looking back on the enormous gap. There were several Greek tablets cut in the rock above the old road, but so defaced as to be illegible. This is undoubtedly the principal gate of the Taurus, and the pass through which the armies of Cyrus and Alexander entered Cilicia.

Beyond the gate the mountains retreated, and we climbed up a little dell, past two or three Turcoman houses, to the top of a hill, whence opened a view of the principal range, now close at hand. The mountains in front were clothed with dark cedars to their very tops, and the snow-fields behind them seemed dazzlingly bright and near. Our course for several miles now lay through a more open valley, drained by the upper waters of the Cydnus. On two opposing terraces of the mountain chains are two fortresses, built by Ibraham Pasha, but now wholly deserted. They are large and well-constructed works of stone, and surrounded by ruins of stables, ovens, and the rude houses of the soldiery. Passing between these, we ascended to the shelf dividing the waters of the Cydnus and the Sihoon. From the point where the slope descends to the latter river, there opened before me one of the most glorious landscapes I ever beheld. I stood at the extremity of a long hollow or depression between the two ranges of the Taurus—not a valley, for it was divided by deep cloven chasms, hemmed in by steeps overgrown with cedars. On my right rose a sublime chain, soaring far out of the region of trees, and lifting its peaked summits of gray rock into the sky. Another chain, nearly as lofty, but not so broken, nor with such large, imposing features, overhung me on the left; and far in front, filling up the magnificent vista—filling up all between the lower steeps, crowned with pine, and the round white clouds hanging on the verge of heaven—were the shining snows of the Taurus. Great God, how shall I describe the grandeur of that view! How draw the wonderful outlines of those mountains! How paint the airy hue of violet-gray, the soft white lights, the thousandfold pencillings of mellow shadow, the height, the depth, the far-reaching vastness of the landscape!

In the middle distance, a great blue gorge passed transversely across the two ranges and the region between. This, as I rightly conjectured, was the bed of the Sihoon. Our road led downward through groves of fragrant cedars, and we travelled thus for two hours before reaching the river. Taking a northward course up his banks, we reached the second of the *Pylæ Ciliciæ* before sunset. It is on a grander scale than the first gate, though not so startling and violent in its features. The bare walls on either side fall sheer to the water, and the road, crossing the Sihoon by a lofty bridge of a single arch, is cut along the face of the rock. Near the bridge a subterranean stream, almost as large as the river, bursts forth from the solid heart of the mountain. On either side gigantic masses of rock, with here and there a pine to adorn their sterility, tower to the height of 6,000 feet, in some places almost perpendicular from summit to base. They are worn and broken into all fantastic forms. There are pyramids, towers, bastions, minarets, and long, sharp spires, splintered and jagged as the turrets of an iceberg. I have seen higher mountains, but I have never seen any which looked so high as these. We camped on a narrow plot of ground, in the very heart of the tremendous gorge. A soldier, passing along at dusk, told us that a merchant and his servant were murdered in the same place last winter, and advised us to keep watch. But we slept safely all night, while the stars sparkled over the chasm, and slips of misty cloud hung low on the thousand pinnacles of rock

When I awoke, the gorge lay in deep shadow; but high up on the western mountain, above the enormous black pyramids that arose from the river, the topmost pinnacles of rock sparkled like molten silver, in the full gush of sunrise. The great mountain, blocking up the gorge behind us, was bathed almost to its foot in the rays, and, seen through such a dark vista, was glorified beyond all other mountains of Earth. The air was piercingly cold and keen, and I could scarcely bear the water of the Sihoon on my sun-inflamed face. There was a little spring not far off, from which we obtained sufficient water to drink, the river being too muddy. The spring was but a thread oozing from the soil; but the Hadji collected it in handfuls, which he emptied into his water-skin, and then brought to us.

The morning light gave a still finer effect to the manifold forms of the mountains than that of the afternoon sun. The soft gray hue of the rocks shone clearly against the cloudless sky, fretted all over with the shadows thrown by their innumerable spires and jutting points, and by the natural arches scooped out under the cliffs. After travelling less than an hour, we passed the riven walls of the mighty gateway, and rode again under the shade of pine forests. The height of the mountains now gradually diminished, and their sides, covered with pine and cedar, became less broken and abrupt. The summits, nevertheless, still retained the same rocky spine, shooting up into tall, single towers, or long lines of even parapets Occasionally, through gaps between, we caught glimpses of the snow-fields, dazzlingly high and white.

After travelling eight or nine miles, we emerged from the pass, and left the Sihoon at a place called Chiftlik Khan—a stone building, with a small fort adjoining, wherein fifteen splendid bronze cannon lay neglected on their broken and rotting carriages. As we crossed the stone bridge over the river, a valley opened suddenly on the left, disclosing the whole range of the Taurus, which we now saw on its northern side, a vast stretch of rocky spires, with sparkling snow-fields between, and long ravines filled with snow, extending far down between the dark blue cliffs and the dark green plumage of the cedars.

Immediately after passing the central chain of the Taurus, the character of the scenery changed. The heights were rounded, the rocky strata only appearing on the higher peaks, and the slopes of loose soil were deeply cut and scarred by the rains of ages. Both in appearance, especially in the scattered growth of trees dotted over the dark red soil, and in their formation, these mountains strongly resemble the middle ranges of the Californian Sierra Nevada. We climbed a long, winding glen, until we had attained a considerable height, when the road reached a dividing ridge, giving us a view of a deep valley, beyond which a chain of barren mountains rose to the height of some five thousand feet. As we descended the rocky path, a little caravan of asses and mules clambered up to meet us, along the brinks of steep gulfs. The narrow strip of bottom land along the stream was planted with rye, now in head, and rolling in silvery waves before the wind.

After our noonday halt, we went over the hills to another stream, which came from the north-west. Its valley was broader and greener than that we had left, and the hills inclosing it had soft and undulating outlines. They were bare of trees, but colored a pale green by their thin clothing of grass and herbs. In this valley the season was so late, owing to its height above the sea, that the early spring-flowers were yet in bloom. Poppies flamed among the wheat, and the banks of the stream were brilliant with patches of a creeping plant, with a bright purple blossom. The asphodel grew in great profusion, and an ivy-leaved shrub, covered with flakes of white bloom, made the air faint with its fragrance. Still further up, we came to orchards of walnut and plum trees, and vineyards There were no houses, but the innabitants, who were mostly Turcomans, live in villages during the winter, and in summer pitch their tents on the mountains where they pasture their flocks. Directly over this quiet pastoral vale towered the Taurus, and I looked at once on its secluded loveliness and on the wintry heights, whose bleak and sublime heads were mantled in clouds. From no point is there a more imposing view of the whole snowy range. Near the head of the valley we passed a large Turcoman encampment, surrounded with herds of sheep and cattle.

We halted for the evening at a place called Kolü-Kushla—an immense fortress-village, resembling Baïas, and like it, wholly deserted. Near it there is a small town of very neat houses, which is also deserted, the inhabitants having gone into the mountains with their flocks. I walked through the fortress, which is a massive building of stone, about 500 feet square, erected by Sultan Murad as a resting-place for the caravans to Mecca. It has two spacious portals, in which the iron doors are still hanging, connected by a vaulted passage, twenty feet high and forty wide, with bazaars on each side. Side gateways open into large courts, surrounded with arched chambers. There is a mosque entire, with its pulpit and galleries, and the gilded crescent still glittering over its dome. Behind it is a bath, containing an entrance hall and half a dozen chambers, in which the water-pipes and stone tanks still remain. With a little alteration, the building would make a capital Phalanstery, where the Fourierites might try their experiment without contact with Society. There is no field for them equal to Asia Minor—a glorious region, abounding in natural wealth, almost depopulated, and containing a great number of Phalansteries ready built.

We succeeded in getting some eggs, fowls, and milk from an old Turcoman who had charge of the village. A man who rode by on a donkey sold us a bag of *yaourt* (sour milk-curds), which was delicious, notwithstanding the suspicious appearance of the bag. It was made before the cream had been removed, and was very rich and nourishing. The old Turcoman sat down and watched us while we ate, but would not join us, as these wandering tribes are very strict in keeping Ramazan. When we had reached our dessert—a plate of fine cherries—another white-bearded and dignified gentleman visited us. We handed him the cherries, expecting that he would take a few and politely return the dish : but no such thing. He coolly produced his handkerchief, emptied everything into it, and marched off. He also did not venture to eat, although we pointed to the Taurus, on whose upper snows the last gleam of daylight was just melting away.

We arose this morning in a dark, cloudy dawn. There was a heavy black storm hanging low in the west, and another was gathering its forces along the mountains behind us. A cold wind blew down the valley, and long peals of thunder rolled grandly among the gorges of Taurus. An isolated hill, crowned with a shattered crag which bore a striking resemblance to a ruined fortress, stood out black and sharp against the far, misty, sunlit peaks. As far as the springs were yet undried, the land was covered with flowers. In one place I saw a large square plot of the most brilliant crimson hue, burning amid the green wheat-fields, as if some Tyrian mantle had been flung there. The long, harmonious slopes and rounded summits of the hills were covered with drifts of a beautiful purple clover, and a diminutive variety of the *achillea*, or yarrow, with glowing yellow blossoms. The leaves had a pleasant aromatic odor, and filled the air with their refreshing breath, as they were crushed under the hoofs of our horses.

We had now reached the highest ridge of the hilly country along the northern base of Taurus, and saw, far and wide before us, the great central plain of Karamania. Two isolated mountains, at forty or fifty miles distance, broke the monotony of the desert-like level: Kara Dagh in the west, and the snow-capped summits of Hassan Dagh in the north-east. Beyond the latter, we tried to catch a glimpse of the famous Mons Argæus, at the base of which is Kaisariyeh, the ancient Cæsarea of Cappadocia. This mountain, which is 13,000 feet high, is the loftiest peak of Asia Minor. The clouds hung low on the horizon, and the rains were falling, veiling it from our sight.

Our road, for the remainder of the day, was over barren hills, covered with scanty herbage. The sun shone out intensely hot, and the glare of the white soil was exceedingly painful to my eyes. The locality of Eregli was betrayed, some time before we reached it, by its dark-green belt of fruit trees. It stands in the mouth of a narrow valley which winds down from the Taurus, and is watered by a large rapid stream that finally loses itself in the lakes and morasses of the plain. There had been a heavy black thunder-cloud gathering, and as we reached our camping-ground, under some fine walnut-trees near the stream, a sudden blast of cold wind swept over the town, filling the air with dust. We pitched the tent in all haste, expecting a storm, but the rain finally passed to the northward. We then took a walk through the town, which is a forlorn place. A spacious khan, built apparently for the Mecca pilgrims, is in ruins, but the mosque has an exquisite minaret, eighty feet high, and still bearing traces of the devices, in blue tiles, which once covered it. The shops were mostly closed, and in those which were still open the owners lay at full length on their bellies, their faces gaunt with fasting. They seemed annoyed at our troubling them, even with purchases. One would have thought that some fearful pestilence had fallen upon the town. The cobblers only, who somewhat languidly plied their implements, seemed to retain a little life. The few Jews and Armenians smoked their pipes in a tantalizing manner, in the very faces of the poor Mussulmans. We bought an oka of excellent cherries, which we were cruel enough to taste in the streets, before the hungry eyes of the suffering merchants.

This evening the asses belonging to the place were driven in from pasture—four or five hundred in all ; and such a show of curious asinine specimens as I never before beheld. A Dervish, who was with us in Quarantine, at Adana, has just arrived. He had lost his *teskeré* (passport), and on issuing forth purified, was cast into prison. Finally he found some one who knew him, and procured his release. He had come on foot to this place in five days, suffering many privations, having been forty-eight hours without food. He is bound to Konia, on a pilgrimage to the tomb of Hazret Mevlana, the founder of the sect of dancing Dervishes. We gave him food, in return for which he taught me the formula of his prayers. He tells me I should always pronounce the name of Allah when my horse stumbles, or I see a man in danger of his life, as the word has a saving power. Hadji Youssuf, who has just been begging for an advance of twenty piastres to buy grain for his horses, swore "by the pardon of God" that he would sell the lame horse at Konia and get a better one. We have lost all confidence in the old villain's promises, but the poor beasts shall not suffer for his delinquencies.

Our tent is in a charming spot, and, from without, makes a picture to be remembered. The yellow illumination from within strikes on the under sides of the walnut boughs, while the moonlight silvers them from above. Beyond gardens where the nightingales are singing, the tall minaret of Eregli stands revealed in the vapory glow. The night is too sweet and balmy for sleep, and yet I must close my eyes upon it, for the hot plains of Karamania await us to-morrow.

CHAPTER XIX.

THE PLAINS OF KARAMANIA.

The Plains of Karamania—Afternoon Heat—A Well—Volcanic Phenomena—Karabounar—A Grand Ruined Khan—Moonlight Picture—A Landscape of the Plains—Mirages—A Short Interview—The Village of Ismil—Third Day on the Plains—Approach to Konia.

"A weary waste, expanding to the skies."—GOLDSMITH.

KONIA, Capital of Karamania, *Friday, June* 25, 1854.

FRANÇOIS awoke us at the break of day, at Eregli, as we had a journey of twelve hours before us. Passing through the town, we traversed a narrow belt of garden and orchard land, and entered the great plain of Karamania. Our road led at first northward towards a range called Karadja Dagh, and then skirted its base westward. After three hours' travel we passed a village of neat, whitewashed houses, which were entirely deserted, all the inhabitants having gone off to the mountains. There were some herds scattered over the plain, near the village. As the day wore on, the wind, which had been chill in the morning, ceased, and the air became hot and sultry. The glare from the white soil was so painful that I was obliged to close my eyes, and so ran a continual risk of falling asleep and tumbling from my horse. Thus, drowsy and half unconscious of my whereabouts, I rode on in the heat and arid silence of the plain until noon, when we reached a well. It was a shaft, sunk about thirty feet deep, with a long, sloping gallery slanting off to the surface. The well was nearly dry, but by descending the gallery we obtained a sufficient supply of cold, pure water. We breakfasted in the shaded doorway, sharing our provisions with a Turcoman boy, who was accompanying his father to Eregli with a load of salt.

Our road now crossed a long, barren pass, between two parts of Karadja Dagh. Near the northern side there was a salt lake of one hundred yards in diameter, sunk in a deep natural basin. The water was intensely saline. On the other side of the road, and a quarter of a mile distant, is an extinct volcano, the crater of which, near two hundred feet deep, is a salt lake, with a trachytic cone three hundred feet high rising from the centre. From the slope of the mountain we overlooked another and somewhat deeper plain, extending to the north and west. It was bounded by broken peaks, all of which betrayed a volcanic origin. Far before us we saw the tower on the hill of Kara-bounar, our resting-place for the night. The road thither was over a barren plain, cheered here and there by patches of a cushion-like plant, which was covered with pink blossoms. Mr. Harrison scared up some coveys of the frankolin, a large bird resembling the pheasant, and enriched our larder with a dozen starlings.

Kara-bounar is built on the slope of a mound, at the foot of which stands a spacious mosque, visible far over the plain. It has a dome, and two tall, pencil-like towers, similar to those of the Citadel-mosque of Cairo. Near it are the remains of a magnificent khan-fortress, said to have been built by the eunuch of one of the former Sultans. As there was no water in the wells outside of the town, we entered the khan and pitched the tent in its grass-grown court. Six square pillars of hewn stone made an aisle to our door, and the lofty, roofless walls of the court, 100 by 150 feet, inclosed us. Another court, of similar size, communicated with it by a broad portal, and the remains of baths and bazaars lay beyond. A handsome stone fountain, with two streams of running water, stood in front of the khan. We were royally lodged, but almost starved in our splendor, as only two or three Turcomans remained out of two thousand (who had gone off with their herds to the mountains), and they were unable to furnish us with provisions. But for our frankolins and starlings we should have gone fasting.

The mosque was a beautiful structure of white limestone, and the galleries of its minarets were adorned with rich arabesque ornaments. While the muezzin was crying his sunset-call to prayer, I entered the portico and looked into the interior, which was so bare as to appear incomplete. As we sat in our palace-court, after dinner, the moon arose, lighting up the niches in the walls, the clusters of windows in the immense eastern gable, and the rows of massive columns. The large dimensions of the building gave it a truly grand effect, and but for the whine of a distant jackal I could have believed that we were sitting in the aisles of a roofless Gothic cathedral, in the heart of Europe. François was somewhat fearful of thieves, but the peace and repose of the place were so perfect that I would not allow any such apprehensions to disturb me. In two minutes after I touched my bed I was insensible, and I did not move a limb until sunrise.

Beyond Kara-bounar, there is a low, barren ridge, climbing which, we overlooked an immense plain, uncultivated, apparently unfertile, and without a sign of life as far as the eye could reach. Kara Dagh, in the south, lifted nearer us its cluster of dark summits; to the north, the long ridge of Üsedjik Dagh (the Pigmy Mountain) stretched like a cape into the plain; Hassan Dagh, wrapped in a soft white cloud, receded behind us, and the snows of Taurus seemed almost as distant as when we first beheld them from the Syrian Gates. We rode for four hours over the dead level, the only objects that met our eyes being an occasional herd of camels in the distance. About noon, we reached a well, similar to that of the previous day, but of recent construction. A long, steep gallery led down to the water, which was very cold, but had a villainous taste of lime, salt, and sulphur.

After an hour's halt, we started again. The sun was intensely hot, and for hours we jogged on over the dead level, the bare white soil blinding our eyes with its glare. The distant hills were lifted above the horizon by a mirage. Long sheets of blue water were spread along their bases, islanding the isolated peaks, and turning into ships and boats the black specks of camels far away. But the phenomena were by no means on so grand a scale as I had seen in the Nubian Desert. On the south-western horizon, we discerned the summits of the Karaman range of Taurus, covered with snow. In the middle of the afternoon, we saw a solitary tent upon the plain, from which an individual advanced to meet us. As he drew nearer, we noticed that he wore white Frank pantaloons, similar to the Turkish soldiery, with a jacket of brown cloth, and a heavy sabre. When he was within convenient speaking distance, he cried out: "Stop! why are you running away from me?" "What do you call running away?" rejoined Francois; "we are going on our journey." "Where do you come from?" he then asked. "From there," said François, pointing behind us. "Where are you going?" "There!" and the provoking Greek simply pointed forwards. "You have neither faith nor religion!" said the man, indignantly; then, turning upon his heel, he strode back across the plain.

About four o'clock, we saw a long line of objects rising before us, but so distorted by the mirage that it was impossible to know what they were. After a while, however, we decided that they were houses interspersed with trees; but the trees proved to be stacks of hay and lentils, heaped on the flat roofs. This was Ismil, our halting-place. The houses were miserable mud huts; but the village was large, and, unlike most of those we have seen this side of Taurus, inhabited. The people are Turcomans, and their possessions appear to be almost entirely in their herds. Immense numbers of sheep and goats were pasturing on the plain. There were several wells in the place, provided with buckets attached to long swing-poles; the water was very cold, but brackish. Our tent was pitched on the plain, on a hard, gravelly strip of soil. A crowd of wild-haired Turcoman boys gathered in front, to stare at us, and the shepherds quarrelled at the wells, as to which should take his turn at watering his flocks. In the evening a handsome old Turk visited us, and, finding that we were bound to Constantinople, requested François to take a letter to his son, who was settled there.

François aroused us this morning before the dawn, as we had a journey of thirty-five miles before us. He was in a bad humor; for a man, whom he had requested to keep watch over his tent, while he went into the village, had stolen a fork and spoon. The old Turk, who had returned as soon as we were stirring, went out to hunt the thief, but did not succeed in finding him. The inhabitants of the village were up long before sunrise, and driving away in their wooden-wheeled carts to the meadows where they cut grass. The old Turk accom panied us some distance, in order to show us a nearer way, avoiding a marshy spot. Our road lay over a vast plain, seemingly boundless, for the lofty mountain-ranges that surrounded it on all sides were so distant and cloud-like, and so lifted from the horizon by the deceptive mirage, that the eye did not recognize their connection with it. The wind blew strongly from the north-west, and was so cold that I dismounted and walked ahead for two or three hours.

Before noon, we passed two villages of mud huts, partly inhabited, and with some wheat-fields around them. We breakfasted at another well, which furnished us with a drink that tasted like iced sea-water. Thence we rode forth again into the heat, for the wind had fallen by this time, and the sun shone out with great force. There was ever the same dead level, and we rode directly towards the mountains, which, to my eyes, seemed nearly as distant as ever At last, there was a dark glimmer through the mirage, at their base, and a half-hour's ride showed it to be a line of trees. In another hour, we could distinguish a minaret or two, and finally, walls and the stately domes of mosques. This was Konia, the ancient Iconium, one of the most renowned cities of Asia Minor.

CHAPTER XX.

SCENES IN KONIA.

Approach to Konia—Tomb of Hazret Mevlana—Lodgings in a Khan—An American Luxury—A Night-Scene in Ramazan—Prayers in the Mosque—Remains of the Ancient City—View from the Mosque—The Interior—A Leaning Minaret—The Diverting History of the Muleteers.

"But they shook off the dust of their feet, and came unto Iconium."—ACTS, XIII. 51.

KONIA (Ancient Iconium), *June* 27, 1852.

THE view of Konia from the plain is not striking until one has approached within a mile of the suburbs, when the group of mosques, with their heavy central domes lifted on clusters of smaller ones, and their tall, light, glittering minarets, rising above the foliage of the gardens, against the background of airy hills, has a very pleasing effect. We approached through a long line of dirty suburbs, which looked still more forlorn on account of the Ramazan. Some Turkish officials, in shabby Frank dresses, followed us to satisfy their curiosity by talking with our *Katurjees*, or muleteers. Outside the city walls, we passed some very large barracks for cavalry, built by Ibrahim Pasha. On the plain north-east of the city, the battle between him and the forces of the Sultan, resulting in the defeat of the latter, was fought.

We next came upon two magnificent mosques, built of white

limestone, with a multitude of leaden domes and lofty minarets, adorned with galleries rich in arabesque ornaments. Attached to one of them is the tomb of Hazret Mevlana, the founder of the sect of Mevlevi Dervishes, which is reputed one of the most sacred places in the East. The tomb is surmounted by a dome, upon which stands a tall cylindrical tower, reeded, with channels between each projection, and terminating in a long, tapering cone. This tower is made of glazed tiles, of the most brilliant sea-blue color, and sparkles in the sun like a vast pillar of icy spar in some Polar grotto. It is a most striking and fantastic object, surrounded by a cluster of minarets and several cypress-trees, amid which it seems placed as the central ornament and crown of the group.

The aspect of the city was so filthy and uninviting that we preferred pitching our tent; but it was impossible to find a place without going back upon the plain; so we turned into the bazaar, and asked the way to a khan. There was a tolerable crowd in the street, although many of the shops were shut. The first khan we visited was too filthy to enter; but the second, though most unpromising in appearance, turned out to be better than it looked. The *oda-bashi* (master of the rooms) thoroughly swept and sprinkled the narrow little chamber he gave us, laid clean mats upon the floor, and, when our carpets and beds were placed within, its walls of mud looked somewhat comfortable. Its single window, with an iron grating in lieu of glass, looked upon an oblong court, on the second story, surrounded by the rooms of Armenian merchants. The main court (the gate of which is always closed at sunset) is two stories in height, with a rough wooden balcony running around it, and a well of muddy water in the centre.

The oda-bashi lent us a Turkish table and supplied us with dinner from his own kitchen; kibabs, stewed beans, and cucumber salad. Mr. H. and I, forgetting the Ramazan, went out to hunt for an iced sherbet; but all the coffee-shops were closed until sunset. The people stared at our Egyptian costumes, and a fellow in official dress demanded my *teskeré*. Soon after we returned, François appeared with a splendid lump of ice in a basin and some lemons. The ice, so the *khangee* said, is taken from a lake among the mountains, which in winter freezes to the thickness of a foot. Behind the lake is a natural cavern, which the people fill with ice, and then close up. At this season they take it out, day by day, and bring it down to the city. It is very pure and thick, and justifies the Turkish proverb in regard to Konia, which is celebrated for three excellent things: "*dooz, booz, küz*"—salt, ice, and girls.

Soon after sunset, a cannon announced the close of the fast. We waited an hour or two longer, to allow the people time to eat, and then sallied out into the streets. Every minaret in the city blazed with a crown of lighted lamps around its upper gallery, while the long shafts below, and the tapering cones above, topped with brazen crescents, shone fair in the moonlight. It was a strange, brilliant spectacle. In the square before the principal mosque we found a crowd of persons frolicking around the fountain, in the light of a number of torches on poles planted in the ground. Mats were spread on the stones, and rows of Turks of all classes sat thereon, smoking their pipes. Large earthen water-jars stood here and there, and the people drank so often and so long that they seemed determined to provide against the morrow. The boys were having their amusement in wrestling, shouting and firing off squibs, which they threw into the crowd. We kicked off our slippers, sat down among the Turks, smoked a narghileh, drank a cup of coffee and an iced sherbet of raisin juice, and so enjoyed the Ramazan as well as the best of them.

Numbers of True Believers were drinking and washing themselves at the picturesque fountain, and just as we rose to depart, the voice of a boy-muezzin, on one of the tallest minarets, sent down a musical call to prayer. Immediately the boys left off their sports and started on a run for the great mosque, and the grave, gray-bearded Turks got up from the mats, shoved on their slippers, and marched after them. We followed, getting a glimpse of the illuminated interior of the building, as we passed; but the oda-bashi conducted us still further, to a smaller though more beautiful mosque, surrounded with a garden-court. It was a truly magical picture. We entered the gate, and passed on by a marble pavement, under trees and arbors of vines that almost shut out the moonlight, to a paved space, in the centre whereof was a beautiful fountain, in the purest Saracenic style. Its heavy, projecting cornices and tall pyramidal roof rested on a circle of elegant arches, surrounding a marble structure, whence the water gushed forth in a dozen sparkling streams. On three sides it was inclosed by the moonlit trees and arbors; on the fourth by the outer corridor of the mosque, the door of entrance being exactly opposite.

Large numbers of persons were washing their hands and feet at the fountain, after which they entered and knelt on the floor. We stood unobserved in the corridor, and looked in on the splendidly illuminated interior and the crowd at prayer, all bending their bodies to the earth at regular intervals and mur-

muring the name of Allah. They resembled a plain of reeds bending before the gusts of wind which precede a storm. When all had entered and were united in solemn prayer, we returned, passing the grand mosque. I stole up to the door, lifted the heavy carpet that hung before it, and looked in. There was a Mevlevi Dervish standing in the entrance, but his eyes were lifted in heavenly abstraction, and he did not see me. The interior was brilliantly lit by white and colored lamps, suspended from the walls and the great central dome. It was an imposing structure, simple in form, yet grand from its dimensions. The floor was covered with kneeling figures, and a deep voice, coming from the other end of the mosque, was uttering pious phrases in a kind of chant. I satisfied my curiosity quickly, and we then returned to the khan.

Yesterday afternoon I made a more thorough examination of the city. Passing through the bazaars, I reached the Serai, or Pasha's Palace, which stands on the site of that of the Sultans of Iconium. It is a long, wooden building, with no pretensions to architectural beauty. Near it there is a large and ancient mosque, with a minaret of singular elegance. It is about 120 feet high, with two hanging galleries; the whole built of blue and red bricks, the latter projecting so as to form quaint patterns or designs. Several ancient buildings near this mosque are surmounted with pyramidal towers, resembling Pagodas of India. Following the long, crooked lanes between mud buildings, we passed these curious structures and reached the ancient wall of the city. In one of the streets lay a marble lion, badly executed, and apparently of the time of the Lower Empire. In the wall were inserted many similar figures, with fragments of friezes and cornices. This is the work of the Seljook Kings, who, in build ing the wall, took great pains to exhibit the fragments of the ancient city. The number of altars they have preserved is quite remarkable. On the square towers are sunken tablets, containing long Arabic inscriptions.

The high walls of a ruined building in the southern part of the city attracted us, and on going thither we found it to be an ancient mosque, standing on an eminence formed apparently of the debris of other buildings. Part of the wall was also ancient, and in some places showed the marks of an earthquake. A long flight of steps led up to the door of the mosque, and as we ascended we were rewarded by the most charming view of the city and the grand plain. Konia lay at our feet—a wide, straggling array of low mud dwellings, dotted all over with patches of garden verdure, while its three superb mosques, with the many smaller tombs and places of worship, appeared like buildings left from some former and more magnificent capital. Outside of this circle ran a belt of garden land, adorned with groves and long lines of fruit trees; still further, the plain, a sea of faded green, flecked with the softest cloud-shadows, and beyond all, the beautiful outlines and dreamy tints of the different mountain chains. It was in every respect a lovely landscape, and the city is unworthy such surroundings. The sky, which in this region is of a pale, soft, delicious blue, was dotted with scattered fleeces of white clouds, and there was an exquisite play of light and shade over the hills.

There were half a dozen men and boys about the door, amusing themselves with bursting percussion caps on the stone. They addressed us as "*hadji!*" (pilgrims), begging for more caps. I told them I was not a Turk, but an Arab, which they believed at once, and requested me to enter the mosque. The interior had a remarkably fine effect. It was a maze of arches, supported by columns of polished black marble, forty in number. In form it was nearly square, and covered with a flat, wooden roof. The floor was covered with a carpet, whereon several persons were lying at full length, while an old man, seated in one of the most remote corners, was reading in a loud, solemn voice. It is a peculiar structure, which I should be glad to examine more in detail.

Not far from this eminence is a remarkable leaning minaret, more than a hundred feet in height, while in diameter it cannot be more than fifteen feet. In design it is light and elegant, and the effect is not injured by its deviation from the perpendicular, which I should judge to be about six feet. From the mosque we walked over the mounds of old Iconium to the eastern wall, passing another mosque, wholly in ruin, but which must have once been more splendid than any now standing. The portal is the richest specimen of Saracenic sculpture I have ever seen : a very labyrinth of intricate ornaments. The artist must have seen the great portal of the Temple of the Sun at Baalbec. The minarets have tumbled down, the roof has fallen in, but the walls are still covered with white and blue tiles, of the finest workmanship, resembling a mosaic of ivory and lapis lazuli. Some of the chambers seem to be inhabited, for two old men with white beards lay in the shade, and were not a little startled by our sudden appearance.

We returned to the great mosque, which we had visited on the evening of our arrival, and listened for some time to the voice of a mollah who was preaching an afternoon sermon to a small and hungry congregation. We then entered the court before the tomb of Hazret Mevlana. It was apparently forbidden ground to Christians, but as the Dervishes did not seem to suspect us we walked about boldly, and were about to enter, when an indiscretion of my companion frustrated our plans. Forgetting his assumed character, he went to the fountain and drank, although it was no later than the *asser*, or afternoon prayer. The Dervishes were shocked and scandalized by this violation of the fast, in the very court-yard of their holiest mosque, and we judged it best to retire by degrees. We sent this morning to request an interview with the Pasha, but he had gone to pass the day in a country palace, about three hours distant. It is a still, hot, bright afternoon, and the silence of the famished populace disposes us to repose. Our view is bounded by the mud walls of the khan, and I already long for the freedom of the great Karamanian Plain. Here, in the heart of Asia Minor, all life seems to stagnate. There is sleep everywhere, and I feel that a wide barrier separates me from the living world.

We have been detained here a whole day, through a chain of accidents, all resulting from the rascality of our muleteers on leaving Aleppo. The lame horse they palmed upon us was unable to go further, so we obliged them to buy another animal, which they succeeded in getting for 350 piastres. We advanced the money, although they were still in our debt, hoping to work our way through with the new horse, and thus avoid the risk of loss or delay. But this morning at sunrise Hadji Youssuf comes with a woeful face to say that the new horse has been stolen in the night, and we, who are ready to start, must sit down and wait till he is recovered. I suspected another trick, but when, after the lapse of three hours, François found the hadji sitting on the ground, weeping, and Achmet beating his breast, it seemed probable that the story was true. All search for the horse being vain, François went with them to the shekh of the horses, who promised, in case it should hereafter be found, to place it in the general pen, where they would be sure to get it on their return. The man who sold them the horse offered them another for the lame one and 150 piastres, and there was no other alternative but to accept it. But *we* must advance the 150 piastres, and so, in mid-journey, we have already paid them to the end, with the risk of their horses breaking down, or they, horses and all, absconding from us. But the knavish varlets are hardly bold enough for such a climax of villany.

CHAPTER XXI.

THE HEART OF ASIA MINOR.

Scenery of the Hills—Ladik, the Ancient Laodicea—The Plague of Gad-Flies—Camp at Ilgün—A Natural Warm Bath—The Gad-Flies Again—A Summer Landscape—Ak-Sheher—The Base of Sultan Dagh—The Fountain of Midas—A Drowsy Journey—The Town of Bolawadün.

"By the forests, lakes, and fountains,
Though the many-folded mountains." SHELLEY.

BOLAWADUN, *July* 1, 1852.

OUR men brought all the beasts into the court-yard of the khan at Konia, the evening before our departure, so that no more were stolen during the night. The oda-bashi, indefatigable to the last in his attention to us, not only helped load the mules, but accompanied us some distance on our way. All the merchants in the khan collected in the gallery to see us start, and we made our exit in some state. The morning was clear, fresh, and delightful. Turning away from the city walls, we soon emerged from the lines of fruit-trees and interminable fields of tomb-stones, and came out upon the great bare plain of Karamania. A ride of three hours brought us to a long, sloping hill, which gave us a view of the whole plain, and its circuit of mountains. A dark line in the distance marked the gardens of Konia. On the right, near the centre of the plain, the lake, now contracted to very narrow limits, glimmered in the sun. Notwithstanding the waste and unfertile appearance of the country, the soft, sweet sky that hangs over it, the pure, transparent air, the grand sweep of the plain, and the varied forms of the different mountain chains that encompass it, make our journey an inspiring one. A descent of the hills soon shut out the view ; and the rest of the day's journey lay among them, skirting the eastern base of Allah Dagh.

The country improved in character, as we advanced. The bottoms of the dry glens were covered with wheat, and shrubbery began to make its appearance on the mountain-sides In the afternoon, we crossed a watershed, dividing Karamania from the great central plain of Asia Minor, and descended to a village called Ladik, occupying the site of the ancient Laodicea, at the foot of Allah Dagh. The plain upon which we came was greener and more flourishing than that we had left. Trees were scattered here and there in clumps, and the grassy wastes, stretching beyond the grain-fields, were dotted with herds of cattle. Emir Dagh stood in the north-west, blue and distant, while, towards the north and north-east, the plain extended to the horizon—a horizon fifty miles distant—without a break. In that direction lay the great salt lake of Yüzler, and the strings of camels we met on the road, laden with salt, were returning from it. Ladik is surrounded with poppy-fields, brilliant with white and purple blossoms. When the petals have fallen, the natives go carefully over the whole field and make incisions in every stalk, whence the opium exudes.

We pitched our tent under a large walnut tree, which we found standing in a deserted inclosure. The graveyard of the village is studded with relics of the ancient town. There are pillars, cornices, entablatures, jambs, altars, mullions and sculptured tablets, all of white marble, and many of them in an excellent state of preservation. They appear to date from the early time of the Lower Empire, and the cross has not yet been effaced from some which serve as head-stones for the True Believers. I was particularly struck with the abundance of altars, some of which contained entire and legible inscriptions. In the town there is the same abundance of ruins. The lid of a sarcophagus, formed of a single block of marble, now serves as a water-trough, and the fountain is constructed of ancient tablets. The town stands on a mound which appears to be composed entirely of the debris of the former place, and near the summit there are many holes which the inhabitants have dug in their search for rings, seals and other relics.

The next day we made a journey of nine hours over a hilly country lying between the ranges of Allah Dagh and Emir Dagh. There were wells of excellent water along the road, at intervals of an hour or two. The day was excessively hot and sultry during the noon hours, and the flies were so bad as to give great inconvenience to our horses. The animal I bestrode kicked so incessantly that I could scarcely keep my seat. His belly was swollen and covered with clotted blood, from their bites. The hadji's mule began to show symptoms of illness, and we had great difficulty in keeping it on its legs. Mr. Harrison bled it in the mouth, as a last resource, and during the afternoon it partly recovered.

An hour before sunset we reached Ilgün, a town on the plain, at the foot of one of the spurs of Emir Dagh. To the west of it there is a lake of considerable size, which receives the streams that flow through the town and water its fertile gardens. We passed through the town and pitched our tent upon a beautiful grassy meadow. Our customary pipe of refreshment was never more heartily enjoyed than at this place. Behind us was a barren hill, at the foot of which was a natural hot bath, wherein a number of women and children were amusing themselves. The afternoon heat had passed away, the air was calm, sweet, and tempered with the freshness of coming evening, and the long shadows of the hills, creeping over the meadows, had almost reached the town. Beyond the line of sycamore, poplar and fig-trees that shaded the gardens of Ilgün, rose the distant chain of Allah Dagh, and in the pale-blue sky, not far above it, the dim face of the gibbous moon showed like the ghost of a planet. Our horses were feeding on the green meadow; an old Turk sat beside us, silent with fasting, and there was no sound but the shouts of the children in the bath. Such hours as these, after a day's journey made in the drowsy heat of an Eastern summer, are indescribably grateful.

After the women had retired from the bath, we were allowed to enter. The interior consisted of a single chamber, thirty feet high, vaulted and almost dark. In the centre was a large basin of hot water, filled by four streams which poured into it A ledge ran around the sides, and niches in the wall supplied places for our clothes. The bath-keeper furnished us with towels, and we undressed and plunged in. The water was agreeably warm (about 90°), had a sweet taste, and a very slight sulphury smell. The vaulted hall redoubled the slightest noise, and a shaven Turk, who kept us company, sang in his delight, that he might hear the echo of his own voice. When we went back to the tent we found our visitor lying on the ground, trying to stay his hunger. It was rather too bad in us to light our pipes, make a sherbet, and drink and smoke in his face, while we joked him about the Ramazan ; and he at last got up and walked off, the picture of distress.

We made an early start the next morning, and rode on briskly over the rolling, grassy hills. A beautiful lake, with an island in it, lay at the foot of Emir Dagh. After two hours we reached a guard-house, where our *teskerés* were demanded, and the lazy guardsman invited us in to take coffee, that he might establish a right to the backsheesh which he could not demand. He had seen us afar off, and the coffee was smoking in the *finjans* when we arrived. The sun was already terribly hot, and the large, green gad-flies came in such quantities that I seemed to be riding in the midst of a swarm of bees. My horse suffered very much, and struck out his hind feet so violently, in his endeavors to get rid of them, that he racked every joint in my body. They were not content with sucking his blood, but settling on the small segment of my calf, exposed between the big Tartar boot and the flowing trowsers, bit through my stockings with fierce bills. I killed hundreds of them, to no purpose, and at last, to relieve my horse, tied a bunch of hawthorn to a string, by which I swung it under his belly and against the inner side of his flanks. In this way I gave him some relief—a service which he acknowledged by a grateful motion of his head.

As we descended towards Ak-Sheher the country became exceedingly rich and luxuriant. The range of Sultan Dagh (the Mountain of the Sultan) rose on our left, its sides covered with a thick screen of shrubbery, and its highest peak dotted with patches of snow; opposite, the lower range of Emir Dagh (the Mountain of the Prince) lay blue and bare in the sun shine. The base of Sultan Dagh was girdled with groves of fruit-trees, stretching out in long lines on the plain, with fields of ripening wheat between. In the distance the large lake of Ak-Sheher glittered in the sun. Towards the north-west, the plain stretched away for fifty miles before reaching the hills. It is evidently on a much lower level than the plain of Konia; the heat was not only greater, but the season was further advanced. Wheat was nearly ready for cutting, and the poppy-fields where, the day previous, the men were making their first incisions for opium, here had yielded their harvest and were fast ripening their seed. Ak-Sheher is beautifully situated at the entrance of a deep gorge in the mountains. It is so buried in its embowered gardens that little, except the mosque, is seen as you approach it. It is a large place, and boasts a fine mosque, but contains nothing worth seeing. The bazaar, after that of Konia, was the largest we had seen since leaving Tarsus. The greater part of the shopkeepers lay at full length, dozing, sleeping, or staying their appetites till the sunset gun. We found some superb cherries, and plenty of snow, which is brought down from the mountain. The natives were very friendly and good-humored, but seemed surprised at Mr. Harrison tasting the cherries, although I told them we were upon a journey. Our tent was pitched under a splendid walnut tree, outside of the town. The green mountain rose between us and the fading sunset, and the yellow moon was hanging in the east, as we took our dinner at the tent-door. Turks were riding homewards on donkeys, with loads of grass which they had been cutting in the meadows. The gun was fired, and the shouts of the children announced the close of the day's fast, while the sweet, melancholy voice of a boy muezzin called us to sunset prayer, from the minaret.

Leaving Ak-Sheher this morning, we rode along the base of Sultan Dagh. The plain which we overlooked was magnificent. The wilderness of shrubbery which fringed the slopes of the mountain gave place to great orchards and gardens, interspersed with fields of grain, which extended far out on the plain, to the wild thickets and wastes of reeds surrounding the lake. The sides of Sultan Dagh were terraced and cultivated wherever it was practicable, and I saw some fields of wheat high up on the mountain. There were many people in the road or laboring in the fields; and during the forenoon we passed several large villages. The country is more thickly inhabited, and has a more thrifty and prosperous air than any part of Asia Minor which I have seen. The people are better clad, have more open, honest, cheerful and intelligent faces, and exhibit a genuine courtesy and good-will in their demeanor towards us. I never felt more perfectly secure, or more certain of being among people whom I could trust.

We passed under the summit of Sultan Dagh, which shone out so clear and distinct in the morning sun, that I could scarcely realize its actual height above the plain. From a tremendous gorge, cleft between the two higher peaks, issued a large stream, which, divided into a hundred channels, fertilizes a wide extent of plain. About two hours from Ak-Sheher we passed a splendid fountain of crystal water, gushing up beside the road. I believe it is the same called by some travellers the Fountain of Midas, but am ignorant wherefore the name is given it. We rode for several hours through a succession of grand, rich landscapes. A smaller lake succeeded to that of

Ak-Sheher, Emir Dagh rose higher in the pale-blue sky, and Sultan Dagh showed other peaks, broken and striped with snow ; but around us were the same glorious orchards and gardens, the same golden-green wheat and rustling phalanxes of poppies—armies of vegetable Round heads, beside the bristling and bearded Cavaliers. The sun was intensely hot during the afternoon, as we crossed the plain, and I became so drowsed that it required an agony of exertion to keep from tumbling off my horse. We here left the great post-road to Constantinople, and took a less frequented track. The plain gradually became a meadow, covered with shrub cypress, flags, reeds, and wild water-plants. There were vast wastes of luxuriant grass, whereon thousands of black buffaloes were feeding. A stone causeway, containing many elegant fragments of ancient sculpture, extended across this part of the plain, but we took a summer path beside it, through beds of iris in bloom —a fragile snowy blossom, with a lip of the clearest golden hue. The causeway led to a bare salt plain, beyond which we came to the town of Bolawadün, and terminated our day's journey of forty miles.

Bolawadün is a collection of mud houses, about a mile long, situated on an eminence at the western base of Emir Dagh. I went into the bazaar, which was a small place, and not very well supplied, though, as it was near sunset, there was quite a crowd of people, and the bakers were shovelling out their fresh bread at a brisk rate. Every one took me for a good Egyptian Mohammedan, and I was jostled right and left among the turbans, in a manner that certainly would not have happened me had I not also worn one. Mr. H., who had fallen behind the caravan, came up after we had encamped, and might have wandered a long time without finding us, but for the good-natured efforts of the inhabitants to set him aright. This evening he knocked over a hedgehog, mistaking it for a cat. The poor creature was severely hurt, and its sobs of distress, precisely like those of a little child, were to painful to hear, that we were obliged to have it removed from the vicinity of the tent.

CHAPTER XXII.

THE FORESTS OF PHRYGIA.

The Frontier of Phrygia—Ancient Quarries and Tombs—We Enter the Pine Forests—A Guard-House—Encampments of the Turcomans—Pastoral Scenery—A Summer Village—The Valley of the Tombs—Rock Sepulchres of the Phrygian Kings—The Titan's Camp—The Valley of Kümbeh—A Land of Flowers—Turcoman Hospitality—The Exiled Effendis—The Old Turcoman—A Glimpse of Arcadia—A Landscape—Interested Friendship—The Valley of the Pursek—Arrival at Kiutahya.

"And round us all the thicket rang
To many a flute of Arcady." TENNYSON.

KIUTAHYA, *July* 5, 1852.

WE had now passed through the ancient provinces of Cilicia, Cappadocia, and Lycaonia, and reached the confines of Phrygia—a rude mountain region, which was never wholly penetrated by the light of Grecian civilization. It is still comparatively a wilderness, pierced but by a single high-road, and almost unvisited by travellers, yet inclosing in its depths many curious relics of antiquity. Leaving Bolawadün in the morning, we ascended a long, treeless mountain-slope, and in three or four hours reached the dividing ridge—the watershed of Asia Minor, dividing the affluents of the Mediterranean and the central lakes from the streams that flow to the Black Sea. Looking back, Sultan Dagh, along whose base we had travelled the previous day, lay high and blue in the background, streaked with shining snow, and far away behind it arose a still higher peak, hoary with the lingering winter. We descended into a grassy plain, shut in by a range of broken mountains, covered to their summits with dark-green shrubbery, through which the strata of marble rock gleamed like patches of snow. The hills in front were scarred with old quarries, once worked for the celebrated Phrygian marble. There was neither a habitation nor a human being to be seen, and the landscape had a singularly wild, lonely, and picturesque air.

Turning westward, we crossed a high rolling tract, and entered a valley entirely covered with dwarf oaks and cedars. In spite of the dusty road, the heat, and the multitude of gadflies, the journey presented an agreeable contrast to the great plains over which we had been travelling for many days. The opposite side of the glen was crowned with a tall crest of shattered rock, in which were many old Phrygian tombs. They were mostly simple chambers, with square apertures. There were traces of many more, the rock having been blown up or quarried down—the tombs, instead of protecting it, only furnishing one facility the more for destruction. After an hour's rest at a fountain, we threaded the windings of the glen to a lower plain, quite shut in by the hills, whose ribs of marble showed through the forests of oak, holly, cedar, and pine, which dotted them. We were now fully entered into the hill-country, and our road passed over heights and through hollows covered with picturesque clumps of foliage. It resembled some of the wild western downs of America, and, but for the Phrygian tombs, whose doorways stared at us from every rock, seemed as little familiar with the presence of Man.

Hadji Youssuf, in stopping to arrange some of the baggage, lost his hold of his mule, and in spite of every effort to secure her, the provoking beast kept her liberty for the rest of the day. In vain did we head her off, chase her, coax her, set traps for her: she was too cunning to be taken in, and marched along at her ease, running into every field of grain, stopping to crop the choicest bunches of grass, or walking demurely in the caravan, allowing the hadji to come within arm's length before she kicked up her heels and dashed away again. We had a long chase through the clumps of oak and holly, but all to no purpose. The great green gad-flies swarmed around us, biting myself as well as my horse. Hecatombs, crushed by my whip, dropped dead in the dust, but the ranks were immediately filled from some invisible reserve. The soil was no longer bare, but entirely covered with grass and flowers. In one of the valleys I saw a large patch of the crimson larkspur, so thick as to resemble a pool of blood. While crossing a long, hot hill, we came upon a little arbor of stones, covered with pine branches. It inclosed an ancient sarcophagus of marble, nearly filled with water. Beside it stood a square cup, with a handle, rudely hewn out of a piece of pine wood. This was a charitable provision for travellers, and constantly supplied by the Turcomans who lived in the vicinity.

The last two hours of our journey that day were through a glorious forest of pines. The road lay in a winding glen, green and grassy, and covered to the summits on both sides with beautiful pine trees, intermixed with cedar. The air had the true northern aroma, and was more grateful than wine. Every turn of the glen disclosed a charming woodland view. It was a wild valley of the northern hills, filled with the burning lustre of a summer sun, and canopied by the brilliant blue of a summer sky. There were signs of the woodman's axe, and the charred embers of forest camp-fires. I thought of the lovely *cañadas* in the pine forests behind Monterey, and could really have imagined myself there. Towards evening we reached a solitary guard-house, on the edge of the forest. The glen here opened a little, and a stone fountain of delicious water furnished all that we wanted for a camping-place. The house was inhabited by three soldiers ; sturdy, good-humored fellows, who immediately spread a mat in the shade for us and made us some excellent coffee. A Turcoman encampment in the neighborhood supplied us with milk and eggs.

The guardsmen were good Mussulmans, and took us for the same. One of them asked me to let him know when the sun was down, and I prolonged his fast until it was quite dark, when I gave him permission to eat. They all had tolerable stallions for their service, and seemed to live pleasantly enough, in their wild way. The fat, stumpy corporal, with his enormously broad pantaloons and automaton legs, went down to the fountain with his musket, and after taking a rest and sighting full five minutes, fired at a dove without hitting it. He afterwards joined us in a social pipe, and we sat on a carpet at the door of the guard-house, watching the splendid moonrise through the pine boughs. When the pipes had burned out I went to bed, and slept a long, sweet sleep until dawn.

We knew that the tombs of the Phrygian Kings could not be far off, and, on making inquiries of the corporal, found that he knew the place. It was not four hours distant, by a by-road and as it would be impossible to reach it without a guide, he would give us one of his men, in consideration of a fee of twenty piastres. The difficulty was evident, in a hilly, wooded country like this, traversed by a labyrinth of valleys and ravines, and so we accepted the soldier. As we were about leaving, an old Turcoman, whose beard was dyed a bright red, came up, saying that he knew Mr. H. was a physician, and could cure him of his deafness. The morning air was sweet with the breath of cedar and pine, and we rode on through the woods and over the open turfy glades, in high spirits. We were in the heart of a mountainous country, clothed with ever-green forests, except some open upland tracts, which showed a thick green turf, dotted all over with park-like clumps, and single great trees. The pines were noble trunks, often sixty to eighty feet high, and with boughs disposed in all possible picturesqueness of form. The cedar frequently showed a solid white bole, three feet in diameter.

We took a winding footpath, often a mere track, striking across the hills in a northern direction. Everywhere we met the Turks of the plain, who are now encamped in the mountains, to tend their flocks through the summer months. Herds of sheep and goats were scattered over the green pasture-slopes, and the idle herd-boys basked in the morning sun, playing lively airs on a reed flute, resembling the Arabic *zumarra.* Here and there was a woodman, busy at a recently felled tree, and we met several of the creaking carts of the country, hauling logs. All that we saw had a pleasant rural air, a smack of primitive and unsophisticated life. From the higher ridges over which we passed, we could see, far to the east and west, other ranges of pine-covered mountains, and in the distance the cloudy lines of loftier chains. The trunks of the pines were nearly all charred, and many of the smaller trees dead, from the fires which, later in the year, rage in these forests.

After four hours of varied and most inspiring travel, we reached a district covered for the most part with oak woods—a more open though still mountainous region. There was a summer village of Turks scattered over the nearest slope—probably fifty houses in all, almost perfect counterparts of Western log-cabins. They were built of pine logs, laid crosswise, and covered with rough boards. These, as we were told, were the dwellings of the people who inhabit the village of Khosref Pasha Khan during the winter. Great numbers of sheep and goats were browsing over the hills or lying around the doors of the houses. The latter were beautiful creatures, with heavy, curved horns, and long, white, silky hair, that entirely hid their eyes. We stopped at a house for water, which the man brought out in a little cask. He at first proposed giving us *yaourt*, and his wife suggested *kaïmak* (sweet curds), which we agreed to take, but it proved to be only boiled milk.

Leaving the village, we took a path leading westward, mounted a long hill, and again entered the pine forests. Before long, we came to a well-built country-house, somewhat resembling a Swiss cottage. It was two stories high, and there was an upper balcony, with cushioned divans, overlooking a thriving garden-patch and some fruit-trees. Three or four men were weeding in the garden, and the owner came up and welcomed us. A fountain of ice-cold water gushed into a stone trough at the door, making a tempting spot for our breakfast, but we were bent on reaching the tombs. There were convenient out-houses for fowls, sheep, and cattle. The herds were out, grazing along the edges of the forest, and we heard the shrill, joyous melodies of the flutes blown by the herd-boys.

We now reached a ridge, whence we looked down through the forest upon a long valley, nearly half a mile wide, and bordered on the opposite side by ranges of broken sandstone crags. This was the place we sought—the Valley of the Phrygian Tombs. Already we could distinguish the hewn faces of the rocks, and the dark apertures to the chambers within. The bottom of the valley was a bed of glorious grass, blazoned with flowers, and redolent of all vernal smells. Several peasants, finding it too hot to mow, had thrown their scythes along the swarths, and were lying in the shade of an oak. We rode over the new-cut hay, up the opposite side, and dismounted at the face of the crags. As we approached them, the number of chambers hewn in the rock, the doors and niches now open to the day, surmounted by shattered spires and turrets, gave the whole mass the appearance of a grand fortress in ruins. The crags, which are of a very soft, reddish-gray sandstone, rise a hundred and fifty feet from their base, and their summits are worn by the weather into the most remarkable forms.

The principal monument is a broad, projecting cliff, one side of which has been cut so as to resemble the façade of a temple. The sculptured part is about sixty feet high by sixty in breadth, and represents a solid wall with two pilasters at the ends, upholding an architrave and pediment, which is surmounted by two large volutes. The whole face of the wall is covered with ornaments resembling panel-work, not in regular squares, but a labyrinth of intricate designs. In the centre, at the bottom, is a shallow square recess, surrounded by an elegant, though plain moulding, but there is no appearance of an entrance to the sepulchral chamber, which may be hidden in the heart of the rock. There is an inscription in Greek running up one side, but it is of a later date than the work itself. On one of the tombs there is an inscription: "To King Midas." These relics are supposed to date from the period of the Gordian Dynasty, about seven centuries before Christ.

A little in front of a headland, formed by the summit walls of two meeting valleys, rises a mass of rocks one hundred feet high, cut into sepulchral chambers, story above story, with the traces of steps between them, leading to others still higher. The whole rock, which may be a hundred and fifty feet long by fifty feet broad, has been scooped out, leaving but narrow partitions to separate the chambers of the dead. These chambers are all plain, but some are of very elegant proportions, with arched or pyramidal roofs, and arched recesses at the sides, containing sarcophagi hewn in the solid stone. There are also many niches for cinerary urns. The principal tomb had a portico, supported by columns, but the front is now entirely hurled down, and only the elegant panelling and stone joists of the ceiling remain. The entire hill was a succession of tombs. There is not a rock which does not bear traces of them. I might have counted several hundred within a stone's throw. The position of these curious remains in a lonely valley, shut in on all sides by dark, pine-covered mountains—two of which are crowned with a natural acropolis of rock, resembling a fortress—increases the interest with which they inspire the beholder. The valley on the western side, with its bed of ripe wheat in the bottom, its tall walls, towers, and pinnacles of rock, and its distant vista of mountain and forest, is the most picturesque in Phrygia.

The Turcoman reapers, who came up to see us and talk with us, said that there were the remains of walls on the summit of the principal acropolis opposite us, and that, further up the valley, there was a chamber with two columns in front. Mr. Harrison and I saddled and rode off, passing along a wall of fantastic rock-turrets, at the base of which was a natural column, about ten feet high, and five in diameter, almost perfectly round, and upholding an immense rock, shaped like a cocked hat. In crossing the meadow we saw a Turk sitting in the sun beside a spring, and busily engaged in knitting a stocking. After a ride of two miles we found the chamber, hewn like the façade of a temple in an isolated rock, overlooking two valleys of wild meadow-land. The pediment and cornice were simple and beautiful, but the columns had been broken away. The chambers were perfectly plain, but the panel-work on the ceiling of the portico was entire.

After passing three hours in examining these tombs, we took the track which our guide pointed out as the road to Kiutahya. We rode two hours through the forest, and came out upon a wooded height, overlooking a grand, open valley, rich in grain-fields and pasture land. While I was contemplatting this lovely view, the road turned a corner of the ridge, and lo! before me there appeared (as I thought), above the tops of the pines, high up on the mountain side, a line of enormous tents. Those snow-white cones, uprearing their sharp spires, and spreading out their broad bases—what could they be but an encampment of monster tents? Yet no; they were pinnacles of white rock—perfect cones, from thirty to one hundred feet in height, twelve in all, and ranged side by side along the edge of the cliff, with the precision of a military camp. They were snow-white, perfectly smooth and full, and their bases touched. What made the spectacle more singular, there was no other appearance of the same rock on the mountain. All around them was the dark-green of the pines, out of which they rose like drifted horns of unbroken snow. I named this singular phenomenon—which seems to have escaped the notice of travellers—The Titan's Camp.

In another hour we reached a fountain near the village of Kümbeh, and pitched our tents for the night. The village, which is half a mile in length, is built upon a singular crag, which shoots up abruptly from the centre of the valley, rising at one extremity to a height of more than a hundred feet. It was entirely deserted, the inhabitants having all gone off to the mountains with their herds. The solitary muezzin, who cried the *mughreb* at the close of the fast, and lighted the lamps on his minaret, went through with his work in most unclerical haste, now that there was no one to notice him. We sent Achmet, the *katurgee*, to the mountain camp of the villagers, to procure a supply of fowls and barley.

We rose very early yesterday morning, shivering in the cold air of the mountains, and just as the sun, bursting through the pines, looked down the little hollow where our tents were pitched, set the caravan in motion. The ride down the valley was charming. The land was naturally rich and highly cultivated, which made its desertion the more singular. Leagues of wheat, rye and poppies spread around us, left for the summer warmth to do its silent work. The dew sparkled on the fields as we rode through them, and the splendor of the flowers in blossom was equal to that of the plains of Palestine. There were purple, white and scarlet poppies ; the rich crimson larkspur ; the red anemone ; the golden daisy ; the pink convolvulus ; and a host of smaller blooms, so intensely bright and dazzling in their hues, that the meadows were richer than a pavement of precious jewels. To look towards the sun, over a field of scarlet poppies, was like looking on a bed of live coals ; the light, striking through the petals, made them burn as with an inward fire. Out of this wilderness of gorgeous color, rose the tall spires of a larger plant, covered with great yellow flowers, while here and there the snowy blossoms of a clump of hawthorn sweetened the morning air.

A short distance beyond Kümbeh, we passed another group of ancient tombs, one of which was of curious design. An isolated rock, thirty feet in height by twenty in diameter, was cut so as to resemble a triangular tower, with the apex bevelled. A chamber, containing a sarcophagus, was hewn out of the interior. The entrance was ornamented with double columns in bas-relief, and a pediment. There was another arched chamber, cut directly through the base of the triangle, with a niche on each side, hollowed out at the bottom so as to form a sarcophagus.

Leaving these, the last of the Phrygian tombs, we struck across the valley and ascended a high range of hills, covered with pine, to an upland, wooded region. Here we found a summer village of log cabins, scattered over a grassy slope The people regarded us with some curiosity, and the women hastily concealed their faces. Mr. H. rode up to a large new house, and peeped in between the logs. There were several women inside, who started up in great confusion and threw over their heads whatever article was most convenient. An old man, with a long white beard, neatly dressed in a green jacket and shawl turban, came out and welcomed us. I asked for *kaïmak*, which he promised, and immediately brought out a carpet and spread it on the ground. Then followed a large basin of kaïmak, with wooden spoons, three loaves of bread, and a plate of cheese. We seated ourselves on the carpet, and delved in with the spoons, while the old man retired lest his appetite should be provoked. The milk was excellent, nor were the bread and cheese to be despised.

While we were eating, the Khowagee, or schoolmaster of the community, a genteel little man in a round white turban, came up to inquire of François who we were. "That effendi in the blue dress," said he, "is the Bey, is he not?" "Yes," said F. "And the other, with the striped shirt and white turban, is a writer?" [Here he was not far wrong.] "But how is it that the effendis do not speak Turkish?" he persisted. "Because," said François, "their fathers were exiled by Sultan Mahmoud when they were small children. They have grown up in Aleppo like Arabs, and have not yet learned Turkish; but God grant that the Sultan may not turn his face away from them, and that they may regain the rank their fathers once had in Stamboul." "God grant it!" replied the Khowagee, greatly interested in the story. By this time we had eaten our full share of the kaïmak, which was finished by François and the katurgees. The old man now came up, mounted on a dun mare, stating that he was bound for Kiutahya, and was delighted with the prospect of travelling in such good company. I gave one of his young children some money, as the kaïmak was tendered out of pure hospitality, and so we rode off.

Our new companion was armed to the teeth, having a long gun with a heavy wooden stock and nondescript lock, and a sword of excellent metal. It was, in fact, a weapon of the old Greek empire, and the cross was still enamelled in gold at the root of the blade, in spite of all his efforts to scratch it out. He was something of a *fakeer*, having made a pilgrimage to Mecca and Jerusalem. He was very inquisitive, plying François with questions about the government. The latter answered that we were not connected with the government, but the old fellow shrewdly hinted that he knew better—we were persons of rank, travelling incognito. He was very attentive to us, offering us water at every fountain, although he believed us to be good Mussulmans. We found him of some service as a guide, shortening our road by taking by-paths through the woods.

For several hours we traversed a beautifully wooded region of hills. Graceful clumps of pine shaded the grassy knolls, where the sheep and silky-haired goats were basking at rest, and the air was filled with a warm, summer smell, blown from the banks of golden broom. Now and then, from the thickets of laurel and arbutus, a shrill shepherd's reed piped some joyous woodland melody. Was it a Faun, astray among the hills? Green dells, open to the sunshine, and beautiful as dreams of Arcady, divided the groves of pine. The sky overhead was pure and cloudless, clasping the landscape with its belt of peace and silence. Oh, that delightful region, haunted by all the bright spirits of the immortal Grecian Song! Chased away from the rest of the earth, here they have found a home

—here secret altars remain to them from the times that are departed!

Out of these woods, we passed into a lonely plain, inclosed by piny hills that brightened in the thin, pure ether. In the distance were some shepherds' tents, and musical goat-bells tinkled along the edges of the woods. From the crest of a lofty ridge beyond this plain, we looked back over the wild solitudes wherein we had been travelling for two days—long ranges of dark hills, fading away behind each other, with a perspective that hinted of the hidden gulfs between. From the western slope, a still more extensive prospect opened before us. Over ridges covered with forests of oak and pine, we saw the valley of the Pursek, the ancient Thymbrius, stretching far away to the misty line of Keshish Dagh. The mountains behind Kiutahya loomed up high and grand, making a fine feature in the middle distance. We caught but fleeting glimpses of the view through the trees; and then, plunging into the forest again, descended to a cultivated slope, whereon there was a little village, now deserted. The grave-yard beside it was shaded with large cedar-trees, and near it there was a fountain of excellent water. "Here," said the old man, "you can wash and pray, and then rest awhile under the trees." François excused us by saying that, while on a journey, we always bathed before praying; but, not to slight his faith entirely, I washed my hands and face before sitting down to our scanty breakfast of bread and water.

Our path now led down through long, winding glens, overgrown with oaks, from which the wild yellow honeysuckles fell in a shower of blossoms. As we drew near the valley, the old man began to hint that his presence had been of great service to us, and deserved recompense. "God knows," said he to François, "in what corner of the mountains you might now be, if I had not accompanied you." "Oh," replied François, "there are always plenty of people among the woods, who would have been equally as kind as yourself in showing us the way." He then spoke of the robbers in the neighborhood, and pointed out some graves by the road-side, as those of persons who had been murdered. "But," he added, "everybody in these parts knows me, and whoever is in company with me is always safe." The Greek assured him that we always depended on ourselves for our safety. Defeated on these tacks, he boldly affirmed that his services were worthy of payment. "But," said François, "you told us at the village that you had business in Kiutahya, and would be glad to join us for the sake of having company on the road." "Well, then," rejoined the old fellow, making a last effort, "I leave the matter to your politeness. "Certainly," replied the imperturbable dragoman, "we could not be so impolite as to offer money to a man of your wealth and station; we could not insult you by giving you alms." The old Turcoman thereupon gave a shrug and a grunt, made a sullen good-by salutation, and left us.

It was nearly six o'clock when we reached the Pursek. There was no sign of the city, but we could barely discern an old fortress on the lofty cliff which commands the town. A long stone bridge crossed the river, which here separates into half a dozen channels. The waters are swift and clear, and wind away in devious mazes through the broad green meadows. We hurried on, thinking we saw minarets in the distance, but they proved to be poplars. The sun sank lower and lower, and finally went down before there was any token of our being in the vicinity of the city. Soon, however, a line of tiled roofs appeared along the slope of a hill on our left, and turning its base, we saw the city before us, filling the mouth of a deep valley or gorge, which opened from the mountains.

But the horses are saddled, and François tells me it is time to put up my pen. We are off, over the mountains, to the old Greek city of Œzani, in the valley of the Rhyndacus.

CHAPTER XXIII.

KIUTAHYA AND THE RUINS OF ŒZANI.

Entrance into Kiutahya—The New Khan—An Unpleasant Discovery—Kiutahya—The Citadel—Panorama from the Walls—The Gorge of the Mountains—Camp in a Meadow—The Valley of the Rhyndacus—Chavdür—The Ruins of Œzani—The Acropolis and Temple—The Theatre and Stadium—Ride down the Valley—Camp at Daghje Köi.

"There is a temple in ruin stands,
Fashioned by long-forgotten hands;
Two or three columns and many a stone,
Marble and granite, with grass o'ergrown!
Out upon Time! it will leave no more
Of the things to come than the things before!"

DAGHJE KÖI, on the Rhyndacus, *July* 6, 1852.

ON entering Kiutahya, we passed the barracks, which were the residence of Kossuth and his companions in exile. Beyond them, we came to a broad street, down which flowed the vilest stream of filth of which even a Turkish city could ever boast. The houses on either side were two stories high, the upper part of wood, with hanging balconies, over which shot the eaves of the tiled roofs. The welcome cannon had just sounded, announcing the close of the day's fast. The coffee-shops were already crowded with lean and hungry customers, the pipes were filled and lighted, and the coffee smoked in the finjans. In half a minute such whiffs arose on all sides as it would have cheered the heart of a genuine smoker to behold.

Out of these cheerful places we passed into other streets which were entirely deserted, the inhabitants being at dinner. It had a weird, uncomfortable effect to ride through streets where the clatter of our horses' hoofs was the only sound of life. At last we reached the entrance to a bazaar, and near it a khan—a new khan, very neatly built, and with a spare room so much better than we expected, that we congratulated ourselves heartily. We unpacked in a hurry, and François ran off to the bazaar, from which he speedily returned with some roast kid, cucumbers, and cherries. We lighted two lamps, I borrowed the oda-bashi's narghileh, and François, learning that it was our national anniversary, procured us a flask of Greek wine, that we might do it honor. The beverage, however, resembled a mixture of vinegar and sealing-wax, and we contented ourselves with drinking patriotic toasts, in two finjans of excellent coffee. But in the midst of our enjoyment, happening to cast my eye on the walls, I saw a sight that turned all our honey into gall. Scores on scores—nay, hundreds on hundreds—of enormous bed-bugs swarmed on the plaster, and were already descending to our beds and baggage. To sleep there was impossible, but we succeeded in getting possession of one of the outside balconies, where we made our beds, after searching them thoroughly.

In the evening a merchant, who spoke a little Arabic, came up to me and asked: "Is not your Excellency's friend the *hakim pasha?*" (chief physican). I did not venture to assent, but replied: "No; he is a *sowakh.*" This was beyond his comprehension, and he went away with the impression that Mr. H. was much greater than a *hakim pasha*. I slept soundly on my out-doors bed, but was awakened towards morning by two tremendous claps of thunder, echoing in the gorge, and the rattling of rain on the roof of the khan.

I spent two or three hours next morning in taking a survey of Kiutahya. The town is much larger than I had supposed : I should judge it to contain from fifty to sixty thousand inhabitants. The situation is remarkable, and gives a picturesque effect to the place when seen from above, which makes one forget its internal filth. It is built in the mouth of a gorge, and around the bases of the hills on either side. The lofty mountains which rise behind it supply it with perpetual springs of pure water. At every dozen steps you come upon a fountain, and every large street has a brook in the centre. The houses are all two and many of them three stories high, with hanging balconies, which remind me much of Switzerland. The bazaars are very extensive, covering all the base of the hill on which stands the ancient citadel. The goods displayed were mostly European cotton fabrics, *quincaillerie*, boots and slippers, pipe-sticks and silks. In the parts devoted to the produce of the country, I saw very fine cherries, cucumbers and lettuce, and bundles of magnificent clover, three to four feet high.

We climbed a steep path to the citadel, which covers the snmmit of an abrupt, isolated hill, connected by a shoulder with the great range. The walls are nearly a mile in circuit, consisting almost wholly of immense circular buttresses, placed so near each other that they almost touch. The connecting walls are broken down on the northern side, so that from below the buttresses have the appearance of enormous shattered columns. They are built of rough stones, with regular layers of flat, burnt bricks. On the highest part of the hill stands the fortress, or stronghold, a place which must have been almost impregnable before the invention of cannon. The structure probably dates from the ninth or tenth century, but is built on the foundations of more ancient edifices. The old Greek city of Cotyæum (whence Kiutahya) probably stood upon this hill. Within the citadel is an upper town, containing about a hundred houses, the residence, apparently of poor families.

From the circuit of the walls, on every side, there are grand views over the plain, the city, and the gorges of the mountains behind. The valley of the Pursek, freshened by the last night's shower, spread out a sheet of vivid green, to the pine-covered mountains which bounded it on all sides. Around the city it was adorned with groves and gardens, and, in the direction of Brousa, white roads went winding away to other gardens and villages in the distance. The mountains of Phrygia, through which we had passed, were the loftiest in the circle that inclosed the valley. The city at our feet presented a thick array of red-tiled roofs, out of which rose here and there the taper shaft of a minaret, or the dome of a mosque or bath. From the southern side of the citadel, we looked down into the gorge which supplies Kiutahya with water—a wild, desert landscape of white crags and shattered peaks of gray rock, hanging over a narrow winding bed of the greenest foliage.

Instead of taking the direct road to Brousa, we decided to make a detour of two days, in order to visit the ruins of the old Greek city of Œzani, which are thirty-six miles south of Kiutahya. Leaving at noon, we ascended the gorge behind the city, by delightfully embowered paths, at first under the eaves of superb walnut-trees, and then through wild thickets of willow, hazel, privet, and other shrubs, tangled together with the odorous white honeysuckle. Near the city, the mountain-sides were bare white masses of gypsum and other rock, in many places with the purest chrome-yellow hue; but as we advanced, they were clothed to the summit with copsewood. The streams that foamed down these perennial heights were led into buried channels, to come to light again in sparkling fountains, pouring into ever-full stone basins. The day was cool and cloudy, and the heavy shadows which hung on the great sides of the mountain gateway, heightened, by contrast, the glory of the sunlit plain seen through them.

After passing the summit ridge, probably 5,000 feet above the sea, we came upon a wooded, hilly region, stretching away in long misty lines to Murad Dagh, whose head was spotted with snow. There were patches of wheat and rye in the hollows, and the bells of distant herds tinkled occasionally among the trees. There was no village on the road, and we were on the way to one which we saw in the distance, when we came upon a meadow of good grass, with a small stream running through it. Here we encamped, sending Achmet, the katurgee, to the village for milk and eggs. The ewes had just been milked for the suppers of their owners, but they went over the flock again, stripping their udders, which greatly improved the quality of the milk. The night was so cold that I could scarcely sleep during the morning hours. There was a chill, heavy dew on the meadow; but when François awoke me at sunrise, the sky was splendidly clear and pure, and the early beams had a little warmth in them. Our coffee, before starting, made with sheep's milk, was the richest I ever drank.

After riding for two hours across broad, wild ridges, covered with cedar, we reached a height overlooking the valley of the Rhyndacus, or rather the plain whence he draws his sources—a circular level, ten or twelve miles in diameter, and contracting towards the west into a narrow dell, through which his waters find outlet; several villages, each embowered in gardens, were scattered along the bases of the hills that inclose it We took the wrong road, but were set aright by a herdsman, and after threading a lane between thriving grain-fields, were cheered by the sight of the Temple of Œzani, lifted on its acropolis above the orchards of Chavdür, and standing out sharp and clear against the purple ot the hills.

Our approach to the city was marked by the blocks of sculptured marble that lined the way: elegant mouldings, cornices, and entablatures, thrown together with common stone to make walls between the fields. The village is built on both sides of the Rhyndacus; it is an ordinary Turkish hamlet, with tiled roofs and chimneys, and exhibits very few of the remains of the old city in its composition. This, I suspect, is owing to the great size of the hewn blocks, especially of the pillars, cornices, and entablatures, nearly all of which are from twelve to fifteen feet long. It is from the size and number of these scattered blocks, rather than from the buildings which still partially exist, that one obtains an idea of the size and splendor of the ancient Œzani. The place is filled with fragments, especially of columns, of which there are several hundred, nearly all finely fluted. The Rhyndacus is still spanned by an ancient bridge of three arches, and both banks are lined with piers of hewn stone. Tall poplars and massy walnuts of the richest green shade the clear waters, and there are many picturesque combinations of foliage and ruin—death and life—

which would charm a painter's eye. Near the bridge we stopped to examine a pile of immense fragments which have been thrown together by the Turks—pillars, cornices, altars, pieces of a frieze, with bulls' heads bound together by hanging garlands, and a large square block, with a legible tablet. It resembled an altar in form, and, from the word "*Artemidoron*," appeared to have belonged to some temple to Diana.

Passing through the village we came to a grand artificial platform on its western side, called the Acropolis. It is of solid masonry, five hundred feet square, and averaging ten feet in height. On the eastern side it is supported on rude though massive arches, resembling Etruscan workmanship. On the top and around the edges of this platform lie great numbers of fluted columns, and immense fragments of cornice and architrave. In the centre, on a foundation platform about eight feet high, stands a beautiful Ionic temple, one hundred feet in length. On approaching, it appeared nearly perfect, except the roof, and so many of the columns remain standing that its ruined condition scarcely injures the effect. There are seventeen columns on the side and eight at the end, Ionic in style, fluted, and fifty feet in height. About half the cella remains, with an elegant frieze and cornice along the top, and a series of tablets, set in panels of ornamental sculpture, running along the sides. The front of the cella includes a small open peristyle, with two composite Corinthian columns at the entrance, making, with those of the outer colonnade, eighteen columns standing. The tablets contain Greek inscriptions, perfectly legible, where the stone has not been shattered. Under the temple there are large vaults, which we found filled up with young kids, who had gone in there to escape the heat of the sun. The portico was occupied by sheep, which at first refused to make room for us, and gave strong olfactory evidence of their partiality for the temple as a resting-place.

On the side of a hill, about three hundred yards to the north, are the remains of a theatre. Crossing some patches of barley and lentils, we entered a stadium, forming an extension of the theatre—that is, it took the same breadth and direction, so that the two might be considered as one grand work, more than one thousand feet long by nearly four hundred wide. The walls of the stadium are hurled down, except an entrance of five arches of massive masonry, on the western side. We rode up the artificial valley, between high, grassy hills, completely covered with what at a distance resembled loose boards, but which were actually the long marble seats of the stadium. Urging our horses over piles of loose blocks, we reached the base of the theatre, climbed the fragments that cumber the main entrance, and looked on the spacious arena and galleries within. Although greatly ruined, the materials of the whole structure remain, and might be put together again. It is a grand wreck; the colossal fragments which have tumbled from the arched proscenium fill the arena, and the rows of seats, though broken and disjointed, still retain their original order. It is somewhat more than a semicircle, the radius being about one hundred and eighty feet. The original height was upwards of fifty feet, and there were fifty rows of seats in all, each row capable of seating two hundred persons, so that the number of spectators who could be accommodated was eight thousand.

The fragments cumbering the arena were enormous, and highly interesting from their character. There were rich blocks of cornice, ten feet long; fluted and reeded pillars; great arcs of heavily-carved sculpture, which appeared to have served as architraves from pillar to pillar, along the face of the proscenium, where there was every trace of having been a colonnade; and other blocks sculptured with figures of animals in alto-relievo. There were generally two figures on each block, and among those which could be recognized were the dog and the lion. Doors opened from the proscenium into the retiring-rooms of the actors, under which were the vaults where the beasts were kept. A young fox or jackal started from his siesta as we entered the theatre, and took refuge under the loose blocks. Looking backwards through the stadium from the seats of the theatre, we had a lovely view of the temple, standing out clear and bright in the midst of the summer plain, with the snow-streaked summits of Murad Dagh in the distance. It was a picture which I shall long remember. The desolation of the magnificent ruins was made all the more impressive by the silent, solitary air of the region around them.

Leaving Chavdür in the afternoon, we struck northward, down the valley of the Rhyndacus, over tracts of rolling land, interspersed with groves of cedar and pine. There were so many branch roads and crossings that we could not fail to go wrong; and after two or three hours found ourselves in the midst of a forest, on the broad top of a mountain, without any road at all. There were some herdsmen tending their flocks near at hand, but they could give us no satisfactory direction. We thereupon took our own course, and soon brought up on the brink of a precipice, overhanging a deep valley. Away to the eastward we caught a glimpse of the

Rhyndacus, and the wooden minaret of a little village on his banks. Following the edge of the precipice, we came at last to a glen, down which ran a rough footpath that finally conducted us, by a long road through the forests, to the village of Daghje Köi, where we are now encamped.

The place seems to be devoted to the making of flints, and the streets are filled with piles of the chipped fragments. Our tent is pitched on the bank of the river, in a barren meadow. The people tell us that the whole region round about has just been visited by a plague of grasshoppers, which have destroyed their crops. Our beasts have wandered off to the hills, in search for grass, and the disconsolate Hadji is hunting them. Achmet, the katurgee, lies near the fire, sick ; Mr. Harrison complains of fever, and François moves about languidly, with a dismal countenance. So here we are in the solitudes of Bithynia, but there is no God but God, and that which is destined comes to pass.

CHAPTER XXIV.

THE MYSIAN OLYMPUS.

Journey Down the Valley—The Plague of Grasshoppers—A Defile—The Town of Taushanlü—The Camp of Famine—We leave the Rhyndacus—The Base of Olympus—Primeval Forests—The Guard-House—Scenery of the Summit—Forests of Beech—Saw-Mills—Descent of the Mountain—The View of Olympus—Morning—The Land of Harvest—Aineghiöl—A Showery Ride—The Plain of Brousa—The Structure of Olympus—We reach Brousa—The Tent is Furled.

"I looked yet farther and higher, and saw in the heavens a silvery cloud that stood fast, and still against the breeze; * * * * and so it was as a sign and a testimony—almost as a call from the neglected gods, that I now saw and acknowledged the snowy crown of the Mysian Olympus!" KINGLAKE.

BROUSA, *July* 9, 1852.

FROM Daghje Köi, there were two roads to Taushanlü, but the people informed us that the one which led across the mountains was difficult to find, and almost impracticable. We therefore took the river road, which we found picturesque in the highest degree. The narrow dell of the Rhyndacus wound through a labyrinth of mountains, sometimes turning at sharp angles between craggy buttresses, covered with forests, and sometimes broadening out into a sweep of valley, where the villagers were working in companies among the grain and poppy fields. The banks of the stream were lined with oak, willow and sycamore, and forests of pine, descending from the mountains, frequently overhung the road. We met numbers of peasants, going to and from the fields, and once a company of some twenty women, who, on seeing us, clustered together like a flock of frightened sheep, and threw their mantles over their heads. They had curiosity enough, however, to peep at us as we went by, and I made them a salutation, which they returned, and then burst into a chorus of hearty laughter. All this region was ravaged by a plague of grasshoppers. The earth was black with them in many places, and our horses ploughed up a living spray, as they drove forward through the meadows. Every spear of grass was destroyed, and the wheat and rye fields were terribly cut up. We passed a large crag where myriads of starlings had built their nests, and every starling had a grasshopper in his mouth.

We crossed the river, in order to pass a narrow defile, by which it forces its way through the rocky heights of Dumanidj Dagh. Soon after passing the ridge, a broad and beautiful valley expanded before us. It was about ten miles in breadth, nearly level, and surrounded by picturesque ranges of wooded mountains. It was well cultivated, principally in rye and poppies, and more thickly populated than almost any part of Europe. The tinned tops of the minarets of Taushanlü shone over the top of a hill in front, and there was a large town nearly opposite, on the other bank of the Rhyndacus, and seven small villages scattered about in various directions. Most of the latter, however, were merely the winter habitations of the herdsmen, who are now living in tents on the mountain tops. All over the valley, the peasants were at work in the harvest-fields, cutting and binding grain, gathering opium from the poppies, or weeding the young tobacco. In the south, over the rim of the hills that shut in this pastoral solitude, rose the long blue summits of Urus Dagh. We rode into Taushanlü, which is a long town, filling up a hollow between two stony hills. The houses are all of stone, two stories high, with tiled roofs and chimneys, so that, but for the clapboarded and shingled minarets, it would answer for a North-German village.

The streets were nearly deserted, and even in the bazaars, which are of some extent, we found but few persons. Those few, however, showed a laudable curiosity with regard to us, clustering about us whenever we stopped, and staring at us with provoking pertinacity. We had some difficulty in procuring information concerning the road, the directions being so contradictory that we were as much in the dark as ever. We lost half an hour in wandering among the hills; and, after travelling four hours over piny uplands, without finding the village of Kara Köi, encamped on a dry plain, on the western bank of the river. There was not a spear of grass for the beasts, everything being eaten up by the grasshoppers, and there were no Turcomans near who could supply us with food. So we dined on hard bread and black coffee, and our forlorn beasts walked languidly about, cropping the dry stalks of weeds and the juiceless roots of the dead grass.

We crossed the river next morning, and took a road following its course, and shaded with willows and sycamores. The lofty, wooded ranges of the Mysian Olympus lay before us, and our day's work was to pass them. After passing the village of Kara Köi, we left the valley of the Rhyndacus, and commenced ascending one of the long, projecting spurs thrust out from the main chain of Olympus. At first we rode through thickets of scrubby cedar, but soon came to magnificent pine forests, that grew taller and sturdier the higher we clomb. A superb mountain landscape opened behind us. The valleys sank deeper and deeper, and at last disappeared behind the great ridges that heaved themselves out of the wilderness of smaller hills. All these ridges were covered with forests; and as we looked backwards out of the tremendous gulf up the sides of which we were climbing, the scenery was wholly wild and uncultivated. Our path hung on the imminent side of a chasm so steep that one slip might have been destruction to both horse and rider. Far below us, at the bottom of the chasm, roared an invisible torrent. The opposite side, vapory from its depth, rose like an immense wall against Heaven. The pines were even grander than those in the woods of Phrygia. Here they grew taller and more dense, hanging their cloudy boughs over the giddy depths, and clutching with desperate roots to the almost perpendicular sides of the gorges. In many places they were the primeval forests of Olympus, and the Hamadryads were not yet frightened from their haunts.

Thus, slowly toiling up through the sublime wilderness, breathing the cold, pure air of those lofty regions, we came at last to a little stream, slowly trickling down the bed of the gorge. It was shaded, not by the pine, but by the Northern beech, with its white trunk and close, confidential boughs, made for the talks of lovers and the meditations of poets. Here we stopped to breakfast, but there was nothing for the poor beasts to eat, and they waited for us droopingly, with their heads thrust together. While we sat there three camels descended to the stream, and after them a guard with a long gun. He was a well-made man, with a brown face, keen, black eye, and piratical air, and would have made a good hero of modern romance. Higher up we came to a guard house, on a little cleared space, surrounded by beech forests. It was a rough stone hut, with a white flag planted on a pole before it, and a miniature water-wheel, running a miniature saw at a most destructive rate, beside the door.

Continuing our way, we entered on a region such as I had no idea could be found in Asia. The mountains, from the bottoms of the gorges to their topmost summits, were covered with the most superb forests of beech I ever saw—masses of impenetrable foliage, of the most brilliant green, touched here and there by the darker top of a pine. Our road was through a deep, dark shade, and on either side, up and down, we saw but a cool, shadowy solitude, sprinkled with dots of emerald light, and redolent with the odor of damp earth, moss, and dead leaves. It was a forest, the counterpart of which could only be found in America—such primeval magnitude of growth, such wild luxuriance, such complete solitude and silence! Through the shafts of the pines we had caught glorious glimpses of the blue mountain world below us; but now the beech folded us in its arms, and whispered in our ears the legends of our Northern home. There, on the ridges of the Mysian Olympus, sacred to the bright gods of Grecian song, I found the inspiration of our darker and colder clime and age. "*O gloriosi spiriti degli boschi!*"

I could scarcely contain myself, from surprise and joy. François failed to find French adjectives sufficient for his admiration, and even our cheating katurgees were touched by the spirit of the scene. On either side, whenever a glimpse could be had through the boughs, we looked upon leaning walls of trees, whose tall, rounded tops basked in the sunshine, while their bases were wrapped in the shadows cast by themselves. Thus, folded over each other like scales, or feathers on a falcon's wing, they clad the mountain. The trees were taller, and had a darker and more glossy leaf than the American beech. By and by patches of blue shone between the boughs before us, a sign that the summit was near, and before one o'clock we stood upon the narrow ridge forming the crest of the mountain. Here, although we were between five and six thousand feet above the sea, the woods of beech were a hundred feet in height, and shut out all view. On the northern side the forest scenery is even grander than on the southern. The beeches are magnificent trees, straight as an arrow, and from a hundred to a hundred and fifty feet in height. Only now and then could we get any view beyond the shadowy depths sinking below us, and then it was only to see similar mountain ranges, buried in foliage, and rolling far behind each other into the distance. Twice, in the depth of the gorge, we saw a saw-mill, turned by the snow-cold torrents. Piles of pine and beechen boards were heaped around them, and the sawyers were busily plying their lonely business. The axe of the woodman echoed but rarely through the gulfs, though many large trees lay felled by the roadside. The rock, which occasionally cropped out of the soil, was white marble, and there was a shining precipice of it, three hundred feet high, on the opposite side of the gorge.

After four hours of steady descent, during the last hour of which we passed into a forest entirely of oaks, we reached the first terrace at the base of the mountain. Here, as I was riding in advance of the caravan, I met a company of Turkish officers, who saluted me with an inclination of the most profound reverence. I replied with due Oriental gravity, which seemed to justify their respect, for when they met François, who is everywhere looked upon as a Turkish janissary, they asked: "Is not your master a *Shekh el-Islam?*" "You are right: he is," answered the unscrupulous Greek. A Shekh el-Islam is a sort of high-priest, corresponding in dignity to a Cardinal in the Roman Catholic Church. It is rather singular that I am generally taken for a Secretary of some kind, or a Moslem priest, while my companion, who, by this time, has assumed the Oriental expression, is supposed to be either medical or military.

We had no sooner left the forests and entered the copsewood which followed, than the blue bulk of Olympus suddenly appeared in the west, towering far into the sky. It is a magnificent mountain, with a broad though broken summit, streaked with snow. Before us, stretching away almost to his base, lay a grand mountain slope, covered with orchards and golden harvest-fields. Through lanes of hawthorn and chestnut trees in blossom, which were overgrown with snowy clematis and made a shady roof above our heads, we reached the little village of Orta Köi, and encamped in a grove of pear-trees. There was grass for our beasts, who were on the brink of starvation, and fowls and cucumbers for ourselves, who had been limited to bread and coffee for two days. But as one necessity was restored, another disappeared. We had smoked the last of our delicious Aleppo tobacco, and that which the villagers gave us was of very inferior quality. Nevertheless, the pipe which we smoked with them in the twilight, beside the marble fountain, promoted that peace of mind which is the sweetest preparative of slumber.

François was determined to finish our journey to-day. He had a presentiment that we should reach Brousa, although I expected nothing of the kind. He called us long before the lovely pastoral valley in which we lay had a suspicion of the sun, but just in time to see the first rays strike the high head of Olympus. The long lines of snow blushed with an opaline radiance against the dark-blue of the morning sky, and all the forests and fields below lay still, and cool, and dewy, lapped in dreams yet unrecalled by the fading moon. I bathed my face in the cold well that perpetually poured over its full brim, drank the coffee which François had already prepared, sprang into the saddle, and began the last day of our long pilgrimage. The tent was folded, alas! for the last time; and now farewell to the freedom of our wandering life! Shall I ever feel it again?

The dew glistened on the chestnuts and the walnuts, on the wild grape-vines and wild roses, that shaded our road, as we followed the course of an Olympian stream through a charming dell, into the great plain below. Everywhere the same bountiful soil, the same superb orchards, the same ripe fields of wheat and barley, and silver rye. The peasants were at work, men and women, cutting the grain with rude scythes, binding it into sheaves, and stacking it in the fields. As we rode over the plain, the boys came running out to us with handfuls of grain, saluting us from afar, bidding us welcome as pilgrims, wishing us as many years of prosperity as there were kernels in their sheaves, and kissing the hands that gave them the harvest-toll. The whole landscape had an air of plenty, peace, and contentment. The people all greeted us cordially; and once a Mevlevi Dervish and a stately Turk, riding in company, saluted me so respectfully, stopping to speak with me, that I quite regretted being obliged to assume an air of dignified reserve, and ride away from them.

Ere long, we saw the two white minarets of Aineghiöl, above the line of orchards in front of us, and, in three hours after starting, reached the place. It is a small town, not particularly clean, but with brisk-looking bazaars. In one of the houses, I saw half-a-dozen pairs of superb antlers, the spoils of Olympian stags. The bazaar is covered with a trellised roof, overgrown with grape-vines, which hang enormous bunches of young grapes over the shop-boards. We were cheered by the news that Brousa was only eight hours distant, and I now began to hope that we might reach it. We jogged on as fast as we could urge our weary horses, passed another belt of orchard land, paid more harvest-tolls to the reapers, and commenced ascending a chain of low hills which divides the plain of Aineghiöl from that of Brousa.

At a fountain called the "mid-day *konnàk*," we met some travellers coming from Brousa, who informed us that we could get there by the time of *asser* prayer. Rounding the north-eastern base of Olympus, we now saw before us the long head-land which forms his south-western extremity. A storm was arising from the sea of Marmora, and heavy white clouds settled on the topmost summits of the mountain. The wind began to blow fresh and cool, and when we had reached a height overlooking the deep valley, in the bottom of which lies the picturesque village of Ak-su, there were long showery lines coming up from the sea, and a filmy sheet of gray rain descended between us and Olympus, throwing his vast bulk far into the background. At Ak-su, the first shower met us, pouring so fast and thick that we were obliged to put on our capotes, and halt under a walnut-tree for shelter. But it soon passed over, laying the dust, for the time, and making the air sweet and cool.

We pushed forward over heights covered with young forests of oak, which are protected by the government, in order that they may furnish ship-timber. On the right, we looked down into magnificent valleys, opening towards the west into the the plain of Brousa; but when, in the middle of the afternoon, we reached the last height, and saw the great plain itself, the climax was attained. It was the crown of all that we had yet seen. This superb plain or valley, thirty miles long, by five in breadth, spread away to the westward, between the mighty mass of Olympus on the one side, and a range of lofty mountains on the other, the sides of which presented a charming mixture of forest and cultivated land. Olympus, covered with woods of beech and oak, towered to the clouds that concealed his snowy head; and far in advance, under the last cape he threw out towards the sea, the hundred minarets of Brousa stretched in a white and glittering line, like the masts of a navy, whose hulls were buried in the leafy sea. No words can describe the beauty of the valley, the blending of the richest cultivation with the wildest natural luxuriance. Here were gardens and orchards; there groves of superb chestnut-trees in blossom; here, fields of golden grain or green pasture-land; there, Arcadian thickets overgrown with clematis and wild rose; here, lofty poplars growing beside the streams; there, spiry cypresses looking down from the slopes: and all blended in one whole, so rich, so grand, so gorgeous, that I scarcely breathed when it first burst upon me.

And now we descended to its level, and rode westward along the base of Olympus, grandest of Asian mountains. This after-storm view, although his head was shrouded, was sublime. His base is a vast sloping terrace, leagues in length, resembling the flights of steps by which the ancient temples were approached. From this foundation rise four mighty pyramids, two thousand feet in height, and completely mantled with forests. They are very nearly regular in their form and size, and are flanked to the east and west by headlands, or abutments, the slopes of which are longer and more gradual, as if to strengthen the great structure. Piled upon the four pyramids are others nearly as large, above whose green pinnacles appear still other and higher ones, bare and bleak, and clustering thickly together, to uphold the great central dome of snow. Between the bases of the lowest, the streams which drain the gorges of the mountain issue forth, cutting their way through the foundation terrace, and widening their beds downwards to the plain, like the throats of bugles, where, in winter rains, they pour forth the hoarse, grand monotone of their Olympian music. These broad beds are now dry and stony tracts, dotted all over with clumps of dwarfed sycamores and threaded by the summer streams, shrunken in bulk, but still swift, cold, and clear as ever.

We reached the city before night, and François is glad to find his presentiment fulfilled. We have safely passed through the untravelled heart of Asia Minor, and are now almost in sight of Europe. The camp-fire is extinguished ; the tent is furled. We are no longer happy nomads, masquerading in Moslem garb. We shall soon become prosaic Christians, and meekly hold out our wrists for the handcuffs of Civilization.

Ah, prate as we will of the progress of thè race, we are but forging additional fetters, unless we preserve that healthy physical development, those pure pleasures of mere animal existence, which are now only to be found among our semi-barbaric brethren. Our progress is nervous, when it should be muscular.

CHAPTER XXV.

BROUSA AND THE SEA OF MARMORA.

The City of Brousa—Return to Civilization—Storm—The Kalputcha Hammam—A Hot Bath—A Foretaste of Paradise—The Streets and Bazaars of Brousa—The Mosque—The Tombs of the Ottoman Sultans—Disappearance of the Katurgees—We start for Moudania—The Sea of Marmora—Moudania—Passport Difficulties—A Greek Caïque—Breakfast with the Fishermen—A Torrid Voyage—The Princes' Islands—Prinkipo—Distant View of Constantinople—We enter the Golden Horn.

"And we glode fast o'er a pellucid plain
Of waters, azure with the noontide ray.
Ethereal mountains shone around—a fane
Stood in the midst, beyond green isles which lay
On the blue, sunny deep, resplendent far away."

SHELLEY.

CONSTANTINOPLE, *Monday*, *July* 12, 1852.

BEFORE entering Brousa, we passed the whole length of the town, which is built on the side of Olympus, and on three bluffs or spurs which project from it. The situation is more picturesque than that of Damascus, and from the remarkable number of its white domes and minarets, shooting upward from the groves of chestnut, walnut, and cypress-trees, the city is even more beautiful. There are large mosques on all the most prominent points, and, near the centre of the city, the ruins of an ancient castle, built upon a crag. The place, as we rode along, presented a shifting diorama of delightful views. The hotel is at the extreme western end of the city, not far from its celebrated hot baths. It is a new building, in European style, and being built high on the slope, commands one of the most glorious prospects I ever enjoyed from windows made with hands. What a comfort it was to go up stairs into a clean, bright, cheerful room; to drop at full length on a broad divan; to eat a Christian meal; to smoke a narghileh of the softest Persian tobacco; and finally, most exquisite of all luxuries, to creep between cool, clean sheets, on a curtained bed, and find it impossible to sleep on account of the delicious novelty of the sensation!

At night, another storm came up from the Sea of Marmora. Tremendous peals of thunder echoed in the gorges of Olympus and sharp, broad flashes of lightning gave us blinding glimpses of the glorious plain below. The rain fell in heavy showers, but our tent-life was just closed, and we sat securely at our windows and enjoyed the sublime scene.

The sun, rising over the distant mountains of Isnik, shone full in my face, awaking me to a morning view of the valley, which, freshened by the night's thunder-storm, shone wonderfully bright and clear. After coffee, we went to see the baths, which are on the side of the mountain, a mile from the hotel. The finest one, called the Kalputcha Hammam, is at the base of the hill. The entrance hall is very large, and covered by two lofty domes. In the centre is a large marble urn-shaped fountain, pouring out an abundant flood of cold water. Out of this, we passed into an immense rotunda, filled with steam and traversed by long pencils of light, falling from holes in the roof. A small but very beautiful marble fountain cast up a jet of cold water in the centre. Beyond this was still another hall, of the same size, but with a circular basin, twenty-five feet in diameter, in the centre. The floor was marble mosaic, and the basin was lined with brilliantly-colored tiles. It was kept constantly full by the natural hot streams of the mountain. There were a number of persons in the pool, but the atmosphere was so hot that we did not long disturb them by our curiosity.

We then ascended to the Armenian bath, which is the neatest of all, but it was given up to the women, and we were therefore obliged to go to a Turkish one adjoining. The room into which we were taken was so hot that a violent perspiration immediately broke out all over my body, and by the time the *dellèks* were ready to rasp me, I was as limp as a wet towel, and as plastic as a piece of putty. The man who took me was sweated away almost to nothing; his very bones appeared to have become soft and pliable. The water was slightly sulphureous, and the pailfuls which he dashed over my head were so hot that they produced the effect of a chill—a violent nervous shudder. The temperature of the springs is 180° Fahrenheit, and I suppose the tank into which he afterwards plunged me must have been nearly up to the mark. When, at last, I was laid on the couch, my body was so parboiled that I perspired at all pores for full an hour—a feeling too warm and unpleasant at first, but presently merging into a mood which was wholly rapturous and heavenly. I was like a soft white cloud, that rests all of a summer afternoon on the peak of a distant mountain. I felt the couch on which I lay no more than the cloud might feel the cliffs on which it lingers so airily. I saw nothing but peaceful, glorious sights; spaces of clear blue sky; stretches of quiet lawns; lovely valleys threaded by the gentlest of streams; azure lakes, unruffled by a breath; calms far out on mid-ocean, and Alpine peaks bathed in the flush of an autumnal sunset. My mind retraced all our journey from Aleppo, and there was a halo over every spot I had visited. I dwelt with rapture on the piny hills of Phrygia, on the gorges of Taurus, on the beechen solitudes of Olympus. Would to heaven that I might describe those scenes as I then felt them! All was revealed to me: the heart of Nature lay bare, and I read the meaning and knew the inspiration of her every mood. Then, as my frame grew cooler, and the fragrant clouds of the narghileh, which had helped my dreams, diminished, I was like that same summer cloud, when it feels a gentle breeze and is lifted above the hills, floating along independent of Earth, but for its shadow.

Brousa is a very long, straggling place, extending for three or four miles along the side of the mountain, but presenting a very picturesque appearance from every point. The houses are nearly all three stories high, built of wood and unburnt bricks, and each story projects over the other, after the manner of German towns of the Middle Ages. They have not the hanging balconies which I have found so quaint and pleasing in Kiutahya. But, especially in the Greek quarter, many of them are plastered and painted of some bright color, which gives a gay, cheerful appearance to the streets. Besides, Brousa is the cleanest Turkish town I have seen. The mountain streams traverse most of the streets, and every heavy rain washes them out thoroughly. The whole city has a brisk, active air, and the workmen appear both more skilful and more industrious than in the other parts of Asia Minor. I noticed a great many workers in copper, iron, and wood, and an extensive manufactory of shoes and saddles. Brousa, however, is principally noted for its silks, which are produced in this valley, and others to the South and East. The manufactories are near the city. I looked over some of the fabrics in the bazaars, but found them nearly all imitations of European stuffs, woven in mixed silk and cotton, and even more costly than the silks of Damascus.

We passed the whole length of the bazaars, and then, turning up one of the side streets on our right, crossed a deep ravine by a high stone bridge. Above and below us there were other bridges, under which a stream flowed down from the mountains. Thence we ascended the height, whereon stands the largest and one of the oldest mosques in Brousa. The position is remarkably fine, commanding a view of nearly the whole city and the plain below it. We entered the court-yard boldly, François taking the precaution to speak to me only in Arabic, as there was a Turk within. Mr. H. went to the fountain, washed his hands and face, but did not dare to swallow a drop, putting on a most dolorous expression of countenance, as if perishing with thirst. The mosque was a plain, square building, with a large dome and two minarets. The door was a rich and curious specimen of the *stalactitic* style, so frequent in Saracenic buildings. We peeped into the windows, and, although the mosque, which does not appear to be in common use, was darkened, saw enough to show that the interior was quite plain.

Just above this edifice stands a large octagonal tomb, surmounted by a dome, and richly adorned with arabesque cornices and coatings of green and blue tiles. It stood in a small garden inclosure, and there was a sort of porter's lodge at the entrance. As we approached, an old gray-bearded man in a green turban came out, and, on François requesting entrance for us, took a key and conducted us to the building. He had not the slightest idea of our being Christians. We took off our slippers before touching the lintel of the door, as the place was particularly holy. Then, throwing open the door, the old man lingered a few moments after we entered, so as not to disturb our prayers—a mark of great respect. We advanced to the edge of the parapet, turned our faces towards Mecca, and imitated the usual Mohammedan prayer on entering a mosque, by holding both arms outspread for a few moments, then bringing the hands together and bowing the face upon them. This done, we leisurely examined the building, and the old man was ready enough to satisfy our curiosity. It was a rich and elegant structure, lighted from the dome. The walls were lined with brilliant tiles, and had an elaborate cornice, with Arabic inscriptions in gold. The floor was covered with a carpet, whereon stood eight or ten ancient coffins, surrounding a larger one which occupied a raised platform in the centre. They were all of wood, heavily carved, and many of them entirely covered with gilded inscriptions. These, according to the old man, were the coffins of the Ottoman Sultans, who had reigned at Brousa previous to the taking of Constantinople, with some members of their families. There were four Sultans, among whom were Mahomet I., and a certain Achmet. Orchan, the founder of the Ottoman dynasty, is buried somewhere in Brousa, and the great central coffin may have been his. François and I talked entirely in Arabic, and the old man asked: "Who are these Hadjis?" whereupon F. immediately answered: "They are Effendis from Baghdad."

We had intended making the ascent of Olympus, but the summit was too thickly covered with clouds. On the morning of the second day, therefore, we determined to take up the line of march for Constantinople. The last scene of our strange, eventful history with the katurgees had just transpired, by their deserting us, being two hundred piastres in our debt. They left their khan on the afternoon after our arrival, ostensibly for the purpose of taking their beasts out to pasture, and were never heard of more. We let them go, thankful that they had not played the trick sooner. We engaged fresh horses for Moudania, on the Sea of Marmora, and dispatched François in advance, to procure a caïque for Constantinople, while we waited to have our passports signed. But after waiting an hour, as there was no appearance of the precious documents, we started the baggage also, under the charge of a *surroudjee*, and remained alone. Another hour passed by, and yet another, and the Bey was still occupied in sleeping off his hunger. Mr. Harrison, in desperation, went to the office, and after some delay, received the passports with a visè, but not, as we afterwards discovered, the necessary one.

It was four o'clock by the time we left Brousa. Our horses were stiff, clumsy pack-beasts ; but, by dint of whips and the sharp shovel-stirrups, we forced them into a trot and made them keep it. The road was well travelled, and by asking everybody we met : "*Bou yôl Moudania yedermi ?*" ("Is this the way to Moudania?"), we had no difficulty in finding it. The plain in many places is marshy, and traversed by several streams. A low range of hills stretches across, and nearly closes it, the united waters finding their outlet by a narrow valley to the north. From the top of the hill we had a grand view, looking back over the plain, with the long line of Brousa's minarets glittering through the interminable groves at the foot of the mountain Olympus now showed a superb outline ; the clouds hung about his shoulders, but his snowy head was bare. Before us lay a broad, rich valley, extending in front to the mountains of Moudania. The country was well cultivated, with large farming establishments here and there.

The sun was setting as we reached the summit ridge, where stood a little guard-house. As we rode over the crest, Olympus disappeared, and the Sea of Marmora lay before us, spreading out from the Gulf of Moudania, which was deep and blue among the hills, to an open line against the sunset. Beyond that misty line lay Europe, which I had not seen for nearly nine months, and the gulf below me was the bound of my tent and saddle life. But one hour more, old horse ! Have patience with my Ethiopian thong, and the sharp corners of my Turkish stirrups : but one hour more, and I promise never to molest you again ! Our path was downward, and I marvel that the poor brute did not sometimes tumble headlong with me. He had been too long used to the pack, however, and his habits were as settled as a Turk's. We passed a beautiful village in a valley on the right, and came into olive groves and vineyards, as the dusk was creeping on. It was a lovely country of orchards and gardens, with fountains spouting by the wayside, and country houses perched on the steeps. In another hour, we reached the sea-shore. It was now nearly dark, but we could see the tower of Moudania some distance to the west.

Still in a continual trot, we rode on ; and as we drew near, Mr. H. fired his gun to announce our approach. At the entrance of the town, we found the sourrudjee waiting to conduct us. We clattered through the rough streets for what seemed an endless length of time. The Ramazan gun had just fired, the minarets were illuminated, and the coffee-houses were filled with people. Finally, François, who had been almost in despair at our non-appearance, hailed us with the welcome news that he had engaged a caïque, and that our baggage was already embarked. We only needed the visès of the authorities, in order to leave. He took our teskerés to get them, and we went upon the balcony of a coffee-house overhanging the sea, and smoked a narghileh.

But here there was another history. The teskerés had not been properly visèd at Brousa, and the Governor at first decided to send us back. Taking François, however, for a Turk, and finding that we had regularly passed quarantine, he signed them after a delay of an hour and a half, and we left the shore, weary, impatient, and wolfish with twelve hours' fasting. A cup of Brousan beer and a piece of bread brought us into a better mood, and I, who began to feel sick from the rolling of the caïque, lay down on my bed, which was spread at the bottom, and found a kind of uneasy sleep. The sail was hoisted at first, to get us across the mouth of the Gulf, but soon the Greeks took to their oars. They were silent, however, and though I only slept by fits, the night wore away rapidly. As the dawn was deepening, we ran into a little bight in the northern side of a promontory, where a picturesque Greek village stood at the foot of the mountains. The houses were of wood, with balconies overgrown with grape-vines, and there was a fountain of cold, excellent water on the very beach. Some Greek boatmen were smoking in the portico of a café on shore, and two fishermen, who had been out before dawn to catch sardines, were emptying their nets of the spoil. Our men kindled a fire on the sand, and roasted us a dish of the fish. Some of the last night's hunger remained, and the meal had enough of that seasoning to be delicious.

After giving our men an hour's rest, we set off for the Princes' Islands, which now appeared to the north, over the glassy plain of the sea. The Gulf of Iskmid, or Nicomedia, opened away to the east, between two mountain headlands. The morning was intensely hot and sultry, and but for the protection of an umbrella, we should have suffered greatly. There was a fiery blue vapor on the sea, and a thunder-cloud hid the shores of Thrace. Now and then came a light puff of wind, whereupon the men would ship the little mast, and crowd on an enormous quantity of sail. So, sailing and rowing, we neared the islands with the storm, but it advanced slowly enough to allow a sight of the mosques of St. Sophia and Sultan Achmed, gleaming far and white, like icebergs astray on a torrid sea. Another cloud was pouring its rain over the Asian shore, and we made haste to get to the landing at Prinkipo before it could reach us. From the south, the group of islands is not remarkable for beauty. Only four of them—Prinkipo, Chalki, Prote, and Antigone—are inhabited, the other five being merely barren rocks.

There is an ancient convent on the summit of Prinkipo, where the Empress Irene—the contemporary of Charlemagne—is buried. The town is on the northern side of the island, and consists mostly of the summer residences of Greek and Armenian merchants. Many of these are large and stately houses, surrounded with handsome gardens. The streets are shaded with sycamores, and the number of coffee-houses shows that the place is much frequented on festal days. A company of drunken Greeks were singing in violation of all metre and harmony—a discord the more remarkable, since nothing could be more affectionate than their conduct towards each other. Nearly everybody was in Frank costume, and our Oriental habits, especially the red Tartar boots, attracted much observation. I began to feel awkward and absurd, and longed to show myself a Christian once more.

Leaving Prinkipo, we made for Constantinople, whose long array of marble domes and gilded spires gleamed like a far mirage over the waveless sea. It was too faint and distant and dazzling to be substantial. It was like one of those imaginary cities which we build in a cloud fused in the light of the setting sun. But as we neared the point of Chalcedon, running along the Asian shore, those airy piles gathered form and substance. The pinnacles of the Seraglio shot up from the midst of cypress groves ; fantastic kiosks lined the shore ; the minarets of St. Sophia and Sultan Achmed rose more clearly against the sky; and a fleet of steamers and men-of-war, gay with flags, marked the entrance of the Golden Horn. We passed the little bay where St. Chrysostom was buried, the point of Chalcedon, and now, looking up the renowned Bosphorus, saw the Maiden's Tower, opposite Scutari. An enormous pile, the barracks of the Anatolian soldiery, hangs over the high bank, and, as we row abreast of it, a fresh breeze comes up from the Sea of Marmora. The prow of the caïque is turned across the stream, the sail is set, and we glide rapidly and noiselessly over the Bosphorus and into the Golden Horn, between the banks of the Frank and Moslem—Pera and Stamboul. Where on the earth shall we find a panorama more magnificent ?

The air was filled with the shouts and noises of the great

Oriental metropolis; the water was alive with caïques and little steamers; and all the world of work and trade, which had grown almost to be a fable, welcomed us back to its restless heart. We threaded our rather perilous way over the populous waves, and landed in a throng of Custom-House officers and porters, on the wharf at Galata

CHAPTER XXVI.

THE NIGHT OF PREDESTINATION.

Constantinople in Ramazan—The Origin of the Fast—Nightly Illuminations—The Night of Predestination—The Golden Horn at Night—Illumination of the Shores—The Cannon of Constantinople—A Fiery Panorama—The Sultan's Caïque—Close of the Celebration—A Turkish Mob—The Dancing Dervishes.

"Skies full of splendid moons and shooting stars,
And spouting exhalations, diamond fires." KEATS.

CONSTANTINOPLE, *Wednesday*, *July* 14, 1852.

CONSTANTINOPLE, during the month of Ramazan, presents a very different aspect from Constantinople at other times. The city, it is true, is much more stern and serious during the day; there is none of that gay, careless life of the Orient which you see in Smyrna, Cairo, and Damascus; but when once the sunset gun has fired, and the painful fast is at an end, the picture changes as if by magic. In all the outward symbols of their religion, the Mussulmans show their joy at being relieved from what they consider a sacred duty. During the day, it is quite a science to keep the appetite dormant, and the people not only abstain from eating and drinking, but as much as possible from the sight of food. In the bazaars, you see the famished merchants either sitting, propped back against their cushions, with the shawl about their stomachs, tightened so as to prevent the void under it from being so sensibly felt, or lying at full length in the vain attempt to sleep. It is whispered here that many of the Turks will both eat and smoke, when there is no chance of detection, but no one would dare infringe the fast in public. Most of the mechanics and porters are Armenians, and the boatmen are Greeks.

I have endeavored to ascertain the origin of this fast month. The Syrian Christians say that it is a mere imitation of an incident which happened to Mahomet. The Prophet, having lost his camels, went day after day seeking them in the Desert, taking no nourishment from the time of his departure in the morning until his return at sunset. After having sought them thus daily, for the period of one entire moon, he found them, and in token of joy, gave a three days' feast to the tribe, now imitated in the festival of Bairam, which lasts for three days after the close of Ramazan. This reason, however, seems too trifling for such a rigid fast, and the Turkish tradition, that the Koran was sent down from heaven during this month, offers a more probable explanation. During the fast, the Mussulmans, as is quite natural, are much more fanatical than at other times. They are obliged to attend prayers at the mosque every night, or to have a *mollah* read the Koran to them at their own houses. All the prominent features of their religion are kept constantly before their eyes, and their natural aversion to the Giaour, or Infidel, is increased tenfold. I have heard of several recent instances in which strangers have been exposed to insults and indignities.

At dusk the minarets are illuminated ; a peal of cannon from the Arsenal, echoed by others from the forts along the Bosphorus, relieves the suffering followers of the Prophet, and after an hour of silence, during which they are all at home, feasting, the streets are filled with noisy crowds, and every coffee-shop is thronged. Every night there are illuminations along the water, which, added to the crowns of light sparkling on the hundred minarets and domes, give a magical effect to the night view of the city. Towards midnight there is again a season of comparative quiet, most of the inhabitants having retired to rest ; but, about two hours afterwards a watchman comes along with a big drum, which he beats lustily before the doors of the Faithful, in order to arouse them in time to eat again before the daylight-gun, which announces the commencement of another day's fast.

Last night was the holiest night of Islam, being the twenty-fifth of the fast. It is called the *Leilet-el-Kadr*, or Night of the Predestination, the anniversary of that on which the Koran was miraculously communicated to the Prophet. On this night the Sultan, accompanied by his whole suite, attends service at the mosque, and on his return to the Seraglio, the Sultana Valide, or Sultana-Mother, presents him with a virgin from one of the noble families of Constantinople. Formerly, St. Sophia was the theatre of this celebration, but this year the Sultan chose the Mosque of Tophaneh, which stands on the shore—probably as being nearer to his imperial palace at Beshiktashe, on the Bosphorus. I consider myself fortunate in having reached Constantinople in season to witness this ceremony, and the illumination of the Golden Horn, which accompanies it.

After sunset the mosques crowning the hills of Stamboul, the mosque of Tophaneh, on this side of the water, and the Turkish men-of-war and steamers afloat at the mouth of the Golden Horn, began to blaze with more than their usual brilliance. The outlines of the minarets and domes were drawn in light on the deepening gloom, and the masts and yards of the vessel were hung with colored lanterns. From the battery in front of the mosque and arsenal of Tophaneh a blaze of intense light streamed out over the water, illuminating the gliding forms of a thousand caïques, and the dark hulls of the vessels lying at anchor. The water is the best place from which to view the illumination, and a party of us descended to the landing-place. The streets of Tophaneh were crowded with swarms of Turks, Greeks and Armenians. The square around the fountain was brilliantly lighted, and venders of sherbet and kaimak were ranged along the sidewalks. In the neighborhood of the mosque the crowd was so dense that we could with difficulty make our way through. All the open space next the water was filled up with the clumsy *arabas*, or carriages of the Turks, in which sat the wives of the Pashas and other dignitaries.

We took a caïque, and were soon pulled out into the midst of a multitude of other caïques, swarming all over the surface of the Golden Horn. The view from this point was strange, fantastic, yet inconceivably gorgeous. In front, three or four large Turkish frigates lay in the Bosphorus, their hulls and spars outlined in fire against the dark hills and distant twinkling lights of Asia. Looking to the west, the shores of the Golden Horn were equally traced by the multitude of lamps that covered them, and on either side, the hills on which the city is built rose from the water—masses of dark buildings, dotted all over with shafts and domes of the most brilliant light. The gateway on Seraglio Point was illuminated, as well as the quay in front of the mosque of Tophaneh, all the cannons of the battery being covered with lamps. The commonest objects shared in the splendor, even a large lever used for hoisting goods being hung with lanterns from top to bottom. The mosque was a mass of light, and between the tall minarets flanking it, burned the inscription, in Arabic characters, "Long life to you, O our Sovereign!"

The discharge of a cannon announced the Sultan's departure from his palace, and immediately the guns on the frigates and the batteries on both shores took up the salute, till the grand echoes, filling the hollow throat of the Golden Horn, crashed from side to side, striking the hills of Scutari and the point of Chalcedon, and finally dying away among the summits of the Princes' Islands, out on the Sea of Marmora. The hulls of the frigates were now lighted up with intense chemical fires, and an abundance of rockets were spouted from their decks. A large Drummond light on Seraglio Point, and another at the Battery of Tophaneh, poured their rival streams across the Golden Horn, revealing the thousands of caïques jostling each other from shore to shore, and the endless variety of gay costumes with which they were filled. The smoke of the cannon hanging in the air, increased the effect of this illumination, and became a screen of auroral brightness, through which the superb spectacle loomed with large and unreal features. It was a picture of air—a phantasmagoric spectacle, built of luminous vapor and meteoric fires, and hanging in the dark round of space. In spite of ourselves, we became eager and excited, half fearing that the whole pageant would dissolve the next moment, and leave no trace behind.

Meanwhile, the cannon thundered from a dozen batteries, and the rockets burst into glittering rain over our heads. Grander discharges I never heard; the earth shook and trembled under the mighty bursts of sound, and the reverberation which rattled along the hill of Galata, broken by the scattered buildings into innumerable fragments of sound, resembled the crash of a thousand falling houses. The distant echoes from Asia and the islands in the sea filled up the pauses between the nearer peals, and we seemed to be in the midst of some great naval engagement. But now the caïque of the Sultan is discerned, approaching from the Bosphorus. A signal is given, and a sunrise of intense rosy and golden radiance suddenly lights up the long arsenal and stately mosque of Tophaneh, plays over the tall buildings on the hill of Pera, and falls with a fainter lustre on the Genoese watch-tower that overlooks Galata. It is impossible to describe the effect of this magical illumination. The mosque, with its taper minarets, its airy galleries, and its great central dome, is built of compact, transparent flame, and in the shifting of the red and yellow fires, seems to flicker and waver in the air. It is as lofty, and gorgeous, and unsubstantial as the cloudy palace in Cole's picture of "Youth." The long white front of the arsenal is fused in crimson heat, and burns against the dark as if it were one mass of living coal. And over all hangs the luminous canopy of smoke, redoubling its lustre on the waters of the Golden Horn, and mingling with the phosphorescent gleams that play around the oars of the caïques.

A long barge, propelled by sixteen oars, glides around the dark corner of Tophaneh, and shoots into the clear, brilliant space in front of the mosque. It is not lighted, and passes with great swiftness towards the brilliant landing-place. There are several persons seated under a canopy in the stern, and we are trying to decide which is the Sultan, when a second boat, driven by twenty-four oarsmen, comes in sight. The men rise up at each stroke, and the long, sharp craft flies over the surface of the water, rather than forces its way through it. A gilded crown surmounts the long, curved prow, and a light though superb canopy covers the stern. Under this, we catch a glimpse of the Sultan and Grand Vizier, as they appear for an instant like black silhouettes against the burst of light on shore.

After the Sultan had entered the mosque, the fires diminished and the cannon ceased, though the illuminated masts, minarets and gateways still threw a brilliant gleam over the scene. After more than an hour spent in devotion, he again entered his caïque and sped away to greet his new wife, amid a fresh discharge from the frigates and the batteries on both shores, and a new dawn of auroral splendor. We made haste to reach the landing-place, in order to avoid the crowd of caïques ; but, although we were among the first, we came near being precipitated into the water, in the struggle to get ashore. The market-place at Tophaneh was so crowded that nothing but main force brought us through, and some of our party had their pockets picked. A number of Turkish soldiers and policemen were mixed up in the melée, and they were not sparing of blows when they came in contact with a Giaour. In making my way through, I found that a collision with one of the soldiers was inevitable, but I managed to plump against him with such force as to take the breath out of his body, and was out of his reach before he had recovered himself. I saw several Turkish women striking right and left in their endeavors to escape, and place their hands against the faces of those who opposed them, pushing them aside. This crowd was contrived by thieves, for the purpose of plunder, and, from what I have since learned, must have been very successful.

I visited to-day the College of the Mevlevi Dervishes at Pera, and witnessed their peculiar ceremonies. They assemble in a large hall, where they take their seats in a semi-circle, facing the shekh. After going through several times with the usual Moslem prayer, they move in slow march around the room, while a choir in the gallery chants Arabic phrases in a manner very similar to the mass in Catholic churches. I could distinguish the sentences "God is great," "Praise be to God," and other similar ejaculations. The chant was accompanied with a drum and flute, and had not lasted long before the Dervishes set themselves in a rotary motion, spinning slowly around the shekh, who stood in the centre. They stretched both arms out, dropped their heads on one side, and glided around with a steady, regular motion, their long white gowns spread out and floating on the air. Their steps were very similar to those of the modern waltz, which, it is possible, may have been derived from the dance of the Mevlevis. Baron Von Hammer finds in this ceremony an imitation of the dance of the spheres, in the ancient Samothracian Mysteries ; but I see no reason tc go so far back for its origin. The dance lasted for about twenty minutes, and the Dervishes appeared very much exhausted at the close, as they are obliged to observe the fast very strictly.

CHAPTER XXVII.

THE SOLEMNITIES OF BAIRAM

The Appearance of the New Moon—The Festival of Bairam—The Interior of the Seraglio—The Pomp of the Sultan's Court—Reschid Pasha—The Sultan's Dwarf—Arabian Stallions—The Imperial Guard—Appearance of the Sultan—The Inner Court—Return of the Procession—The Sultan on his Throne—The Homage of the Pashas—An Oriental Picture—Kissing the Scarf—The Shekh el-Islam—The Descendant of the Caliphs—Bairam Commences.

CONSTANTINOPLE, *Monday, July* 19, 1852.

SATURDAY was the last day of the fast-month of Ramazan, and yesterday the celebration of the solemn festival of Bairam took place. The moon changed on Friday morning at 11 o'clock, but as the Turks have no faith in astronomy, and do not believe the moon has actually changed until they see it, all good Mussulmen were obliged to fast an additional day. Had Saturday been cloudy, and the new moon invisible, I am not sure but the fast would have been still further prolonged. A good look-out was kept, however, and about four o'clock on Saturday afternoon some sharp eyes saw the young crescent above the sun. There is a hill near Gemlik, on the Gulf of Moudania, about fifty miles from here, whence the Turks believe the new moon can be first seen. The families who live on this hill are exempted from taxation, in consideration of their keeping a watch for the moon, at the close of Ramazan

A series of signals, from hill to hill, is in readiness, and the news is transmitted to Constantinople in a very short time Then, when the muezzin proclaims the *asser*, or prayer two hours before sunset, he proclaims also the close of Ramazan. All the batteries fire a salute, and the big guns along the water announce the joyful news to all parts of the city. The forts on the Bosphorus take up the tale, and both shores, from the Black Sea to the Propontis, shake with the burden of their rejoicing. At night the mosques are illuminated for the last time, for it is only during Ramazan that they are lighted, or open for night service.

After Ramazan, comes the festival of Bairam, which lasts three days, and is a season of unbounded rejoicing. The bazaars are closed, no Turk does any work, but all, clothed in their best dresses, or in an entire new suit if they can afford it, pass the time in feasting, in paying visits, or in making excursions to the shores of the Bosphorus, or other favorite spots around Constantinople. The festival is inaugurated by a solemn state ceremony, at the Seraglio and the mosque of Sultan Achmed, whither the Sultan goes in procession, accompanied by all the officers of the Government. This is the last remaining pageant which has been spared to the Ottoman monarchs by the rigorous reforming measures of Sultan Mahmoud, and shorn as it is of much of its former splendor, it probably surpasses in brilliant effect any spectacle which any other European Court can present. The ceremonies which take place inside of the Seraglio were, until within three or four years, prohibited to Frank eyes, and travellers were obliged to content themselves with a view of the procession, as it passed to the mosque. Through the kindness of Mr. Brown, of the

American Embassy, I was enabled to witness the entire solemnity, in all its details.

As the procession leaves the Seraglio at sunrise, we rose with the first streak of dawn, descended to Tophaneh, and crossed to Seraglio Point, where the cavass of the Embassy was in waiting for us. He conducted us through the guards, into the garden of the Seraglio, and up the hill to the Palace. The Capudan Pasha, or Lord High Admiral, had just arrived in a splendid caïque, and pranced up the hill before us on a magnificent stallion, whose trappings blazed with jewels and gold lace. The rich uniforms of the different officers of the army and marine glittered far and near under the dense shadows of the cypress trees, and down the dark alleys where the morning twilight had not penetrated. We were ushered into the great outer court-yard of the Seraglio, leading to the Sublime Porte. A double row of marines, in scarlet jackets and white trowsers, extended from one gate to the other, and a very excellent brass band played "*Suoni la tromba*" with much spirit. The groups of Pashas and other officers of high rank, with their attendants, gave the scene a brilliant character of festivity. The costumes, except those of the secretaries and servants, were after the European model, but covered with a lavish profusion of gold lace. The horses were all of the choicest Eastern breeds, and the broad housings of their saddles of blue, green, purple, and crimson cloth, were enriched with gold lace, rubies, emeralds and turquoises.

The cavass took us into a chamber near the gate, and commanding a view of the whole court. There we found Mr. Brown and his lady, with several officers from the U. S. steamer San Jacinto. At this moment the sun, appearing above the hill of Bulgurlu, behind Scutari, threw his earliest rays upon the gilded pinnacles of the Seraglio. The commotion in the long court-yard below increased. The marines were formed into exact line, the horses of the officers clattered on the rough pavement as they dashed about to expedite the arrangements, the crowd pressed closer to the line of the procession, and in five minutes the grand pageant was set in motion. As the first Pasha made his appearance under the dark archway of the interior gate, the band struck up the *Marseillaise* (which is a favorite air among the Turks), and the soldiers presented arms. The court-yard was near two hundred yards long, and the line of Pashas, each surrounded with the officers of his staff, made a most dazzling show. The lowest in rank came first. I cannot recollect the precise order, nor the names of all of them, which, in fact, are of little consequence, while power and place are such uncertain matters in Turkey

Each Pasha wore the red fez on his head, a frock-coat of blue cloth, the breast of which was entirely covered with gold lace, while a broad band of the same decorated the skirts, and white pantaloons. One of the Ministers, Mehemet Ali Pasha, the brother-in-law of the Sultan, was formerly a cooper's apprentice, but taken, when a boy, by the late Sultan Mahmoud, to be a playmate for his son, on account of his extraordinary beauty. Reschid Pasha, the Grand Vizier, is a man of about sixty years of age. He is frequently called Giaour, or Infidel, by the Turks, on account of his liberal policy, which has made him many enemies. The expression of his face denotes intelligence, but lacks the energy necessary to accomplish great reforms. His son, a boy of about seventeen, already possesses the rank of Pasha, and is affianced to the Sultan's daughter, a child of ten or twelve years old. He is a fat, handsome youth, with a sprightly face, and acted his part in the ceremonies with a nonchalance which made him appear graceful beside his stiff, dignified elders.

After the Pashas came the entire household of the Sultan, including even his eunuchs, cooks, and constables. The Kislar Aga, or Chief Eunuch, a tall African in resplendent costume, is one of the most important personages connected with the Court. The Sultan's favorite dwarf, a little man about forty years old and three feet high, bestrode his horse with as consequential an air as any of them. A few years ago, this man took a notion to marry, and applied to the Sultan for a wife. The latter gave him permission to go into his harem and take the one whom he could kiss. The dwarf, like all short men, was ambitious to have a long wife. While the Sultan's five hundred women, who knew the terms according to which the dwarf was permitted to choose, were laughing at the amorous mannikin, he went up to one of the tallest and handsomest of them, and struck her a sudden blow on the stomach. She collapsed with the pain, and before she could recover he caught her by the neck and gave her the dreaded kiss. The Sultan kept his word, and the tall beauty is now the mother of the dwarf's children.

The procession grows more brilliant as it advances, and the profound inclination made by the soldiers at the further end of the court, announces the approach of the Sultan himself. First come three led horses, of the noblest Arabian blood—glorious creatures, worthy to represent

"The horse that guide the golden eye of heaven,
And snort the morning from their nostrils,
Making their fiery gait above the glades."

Their eyes were more keen and lustrous than the diamonds which studded their head-stalls, and the wealth of emeralds, rubies, and sapphires that gleamed on their trappings would have bought the possessions of a German Prince. After them came the Sultan's body-guard, a company of tall, strong men, in crimson tunics and white trousers, with lofty plumes of peacock feathers in their hats. Some of them carried crests of green feathers, fastened upon long staves. These superb horses and showy guards are the only relics of that barbaric pomp which characterized all State processions during the time of the Janissaries. In the centre of a hollow square of plume-bearing guards rode Abdul-Medjid himself, on a snow-white steed. Every one bowed profoundly as he passed along, but he neither looked to the right or left, nor made the slightest acknowledgment of the salutations. Turkish etiquette exacts the most rigid indifference on the part of the Sovereign, who, on all public occasions, never makes a greeting. Formerly, before the change of costume, the Sultan's turbans were carried before him in the processions, and the servants who bore them inclined them to one side and the other, in answer to the salutations of the crowd.

Sultan Abdul-Medjid is a man of about thirty, though he looks older. He has a mild, amiable, weak face, dark eyes, a prominent nose, and short, dark brown mustaches and beard. His face is thin, and wrinkles are already making their appearance about the corners of his mouth and eyes. But for a certain vacancy of expression, he would be called a handsome man. He sits on his horse with much ease and grace, though there is a slight stoop in his shoulders. His legs are crooked, owing to which cause he appears awkward when on his feet, though he wears a long cloak to conceal the deformity. Sensual indulgence has weakened a constitution not naturally strong, and increased that mildness which has now become a defect in his character. He is not stern enough to be just, and his subjects are less fortunate under his easy rule than under the rod of his savage father, Mahmoud. He was dressed in a style of the utmost richness and elegance. He wore a red Turkish fez, with an immense rosette of brilliants, and a long, floating plume of bird-of-paradise feathers. The diamond in the centre of the rosette is of unusual size; it was picked up some years ago in the Hippodrome, and probably belonged to the treasury of the Greek Emperors. The breast and collar of his coat were one mass of diamonds, and sparkled in the early sun with a thousand rainbow gleams. His mantle of dark-blue cloth hung to his knees, concealing the deformity of his legs. He wore white pantaloons, white kid gloves, and patent leather boots, thrust into his golden stirrups.

A few officers of the Imperial household followed behind the Sultan, and the procession then terminated. Including the soldiers, it contained from two to three thousand persons. The marines lined the way to the mosque of Sultan Achmed, and a great crowd of spectators filled up the streets and the square of the Hippodrome. Coffee was served to us, after which we were all conducted into the inner court of the Seraglio, to await the return of the cortège. This court is not more than half the size of the outer one, but is shaded with large sycamores, embellished with fountains, and surrounded with light and elegant galleries, in pure Saracenic style. The picture which it presented was therefore far richer and more characteristic of the Orient than the outer court, where the architecture is almost wholly after Italian models. The portals at either end rested on slender pillars, over which projected broad eaves, decorated with elaborate carved and gilded work, and above all rose a dome, surmounted by the Crescent. On the right, the tall chimneys of the Imperial kitchens towered above the walls. The sycamores threw their broad, cool shadows over the court, and groups of servants, in gala dresses, loitered about the corridors.

After waiting nearly half an hour, the sound of music and the appearance of the Sultan's body-guard proclaimed the return of the procession. It came in reversed order, headed by the Sultan, after whom followed the Grand Vizier and other Ministers of the Imperial Council, and the Pashas, each surrounded by his staff of officers. The Sultan dismounted at the entrance to the Seraglio, and disappeared through the door. He was absent for more than half an hour, during which time he received the congratulations of his family, his wives, and the principal personages of his household, all of whom came to kiss his feet. Meanwhile, the Pashas ranged themselves in a semicircle around the arched and gilded portico. The servants of the Seraglio brought out a large Persian carpet, which they spread on the marble pavement. The throne, a large square seat, richly carved and covered with gilding, was placed in the centre, and a dazzling piece of cloth-of-gold thrown over the back of it. When the Sultan re-appeared, he took his seat thereon, placing his feet on a small footstool. The ceremony of kissing his feet now commenced. The first who had this honor was the Chief of the Emirs, an old man in a green robe, embroidered with pearls. He advanced to the throne, knelt, kissed the Sultan's patent-leather boot, and retired backward from the presence.

The Ministers and Pashas followed in single file, and, after they had made the salutation, took their stations on the right hand of the throne. Most of them were fat, and their glittering frock-coats were buttoned so tightly that they seemed ready to burst. It required a great effort for them to rise from their knees. During all this time, the band was playing operatic airs, and as each Pasha knelt, a marshal, or master of ceremonies, with a silver wand, gave the signal to the Imperial Guard, who shouted at the top of their voices: "Prosperity to our Sovereign! May he live a thousand years!" This part of the ceremony was really grand and imposing. All the adjuncts were in keeping: the portico, wrought in rich arabesque designs; the swelling domes and sunlit crescents above; the sycamores and cypresses shading the court; the red tunics and peacock plumes of the guard; the monarch himself, radiant with jewels, as he sat in his chair of gold—all these features combined to form a stately picture of the lost Orient, and for the time Abdul-Medjid seemed the true representative of Caliph Haroun Al-Raschid.

After the Pashas had finished, the inferior officers of the Army, Navy, and Civil Service followed, to the number of at least a thousand. They were not considered worthy to touch the Sultan's person, but kissed his golden scarf, which was held out to them by a Pasha, who stood on the left of the throne. The Grand Vizier had his place on the right, and the Chief of the Eunuchs stood behind him. The kissing of the scarf occupied an hour. The Sultan sat quietly during all this time, his face expressing a total indifference to all that was going on. The most skilful physiognomist could not have found in it the shadow of an expression. If this was the etiquette prescribed for him, he certainly acted it with marvellous skill and success.

The long line of officers at length came to an end, and I fancied that the solemnities were now over ; but after a pause appeared the *Shekh el-Islàm*, or High Priest of the Mahometan religion. His authority in religious matters transcends that of the Sultan, and is final and irrevocable. He was a very venerable man, of perhaps seventy-five years of age, and his tottering steps were supported by two mollahs. He was dressed in a long green robe, embroidered with gold and pearls, over which his white beard flowed below his waist. In his turban of white cambric was twisted a scarf of cloth-of-gold. He kissed the border of the Sultan's mantle, which salutation was also made by a long line of the chief priests of the mosques of Constantinople, who followed him. These priests were dressed in long robes of white, green, blue, and violet, many of them with collars of pearls and golden scarfs wound about their turbans, the rich fringes falling on their shoulders. They were grave, stately men, with long gray beards, and the wisdom of age and study in their deep-set eyes.

Among the last who came was the most important personage of all. This was the Governor of Mecca (as I believe he is called), the nearest descendant of the Prophet, and the successor to the Caliphate, in case the family of Othman becomes extinct. Sultan Mahmoud, on his accession to the throne, was the last descendant of Orchan, the founder of the Ottoman Dynasty, the throne being inherited only by the male heirs. He left two sons, who are both living, Abdul-Medjid having departed from the practice of his predecessors, each of whom slew his brothers, in order to make his own sovereignty secure

He has one son, Muzad, who is about ten years old, so that there are now three males of the family of Orchan. In case of their death, the Governor of Mecca would become Caliph, and the sovereignty would be established in his family. He is a swarthy Arab, of about fifty, with a bold, fierce face. He wore a superb dress of green, the sacred color, and was followed by his two sons, young men of twenty and twenty-two. As he advanced to the throne, and was about to kneel and kiss the Sultan's robe, the latter prevented him, and asked politely after his health—the highest mark of respect in his power to show. The old Arab's face gleamed with such a sudden gush of pride and satisfaction, that no flash of lightning could have illumined it more vividly.

The sacred writers, or transcribers of the Koran, closed the procession, after which the Sultan rose and entered the Seraglio. The crowd slowly dispersed, and in a few minutes the grand reports of the cannon on Seraglio Point announced the departure of the Sultan for his palace on the Bosphorus. The festival of Bairam was now fairly inaugurated, and all Stamboul was given up to festivity. There was no Turk so poor that he did not in some sort share in the rejoicing. Our Fourth could scarcely show more flags, let off more big guns or send forth greater crowds of excursionists than this Moslem holiday.

CHAPTER XXVIII.

THE MOSQUES OF CONSTANTINOPLE.

Sojourn at Constantinople—Semi-European Character of the City—The Mosque—Procuring a Firman—The Seraglio—The Library—The Ancient Throne-Room—Admittance to St. Sophia—Magnificence of the Interior—The Marvellous Dome—The Mosque of Sultan Achmed—The Sulemanye—Great Conflagrations—Political Meaning of the Fires—Turkish Progress—Decay of the Ottoman Power.

> "*Is that indeed Sophia's far-famed dome,*
> Where first the Faith was led in triumph home,
> Like some high bride, with banner and bright sign,
> And melody, and flowers?" AUBREY DE VERE.

CONSTANTINOPLE, *Tuesday*, *August* 3, 1852.

THE length of my stay in Constantinople has enabled me to visit many interesting spots in its vicinity, as well as to familiarize myself with the peculiar features of the great capital. I have seen the beautiful Bosphorus from steamers and caïques; ridden up the valley of Buyukdere, and through the chestnut woods of Belgrade; bathed in the Black Sea, under the lee of the Symplegades, where the marble altar to Apollo still invites an oblation from passing mariners; walked over the flowery meadows beside the "Heavenly Waters of Asia;" galloped around the ivy-grown walls where Dandolo and Mahomet II. conquered, and the last of the Palæologi fell; and dreamed away many an afternoon-hour under the funereal cypresses of Pera, and beside the Delphian tripod in the Hippodrome. The historic interest of these spots is familiar to all, nor, with one exception, have their natural beauties been exaggerated by travellers. This exception is the village of Belgrade, over which Mary Montague went into raptures, and set the fashion for tourists ever since. I must confess to having been wofully disappointed. The village is a miserable cluster of rickety houses, on an open piece of barren land, surrounded by the forests, or rather thickets, which keep alive the springs that supply Constantinople with water. We reached there with appetites sharpened by our morning's ride, expecting to find at least a vender of *kibabs* (bits of fried meat) in so renowned a place; but the only things to be had were raw salt mackerel, and bread which belonged to the primitive geological formation.

The general features of Constantinople and the Bosphorus are so well known, that I am spared the dangerous task of painting scenes which have been colored by abler pencils. Von Hammer, Lamartine, Willis, Miss Pardoe, Albert Smith, and thou, most inimitable Thackeray! have made Pera and Scutari, the Bazaars and Baths, the Seraglio and the Golden Horn, as familiar to our ears as Cornhill and Wall street. Besides, Constantinople is not the true Orient, which is to be found rather in Cairo, in Aleppo, and brightest and most vital, in Damascus. Here, we tread European soil; the Franks are fast crowding out the followers of the Prophet, and Stamboul itself, were its mosques and Seraglio removed, would differ little in outward appearance from a third-rate Italian town. The Sultan lives in a palace with a Grecian portico; the pointed Saracenic arch, the arabesque sculptures, the latticed balconies, give place to clumsy imitations of Palladio, and every fire that sweeps away a recollection of the palmy times of Ottoman rule, sweeps it away forever.

But the Mosque—that blossom of Oriental architecture, with its crowning domes, like the inverted bells of the lotus, and its reed-like minarets, its fountains and marble courts—can only perish with the faith it typifies. I, for one, rejoice that, so long as the religion of Islam exists (and yet, may its time be short!), no Christian model can shape its houses of worship. The minaret must still lift its airy tower for the muezzin; the dome must rise like a gilded heaven above the prayers of the Faithful, with its starry lamps and emblazoned phrases; the fountain must continue to pour its waters of purification. A reformation of the Moslem faith is impossible. When it begins to give way, the whole fabric must fall. Its ceremonies, as well as its creed, rest entirely on the recognition of Mahomet as the Prophet of God. However the Turks may change in other respects, in all that concerns their religion they must continue the same.

Until within a few years, a visit to the mosques, especially the more sacred ones of St. Sophia and Sultan Achmed, was attended with much difficulty. Miss Pardoe, according to her own account, risked her life in order to see the interior of St. Sophia, which she effected in the disguise of a Turkish Effendi. I accomplished the same thing, a few days since, but without recourse to any such romantic expedient. Mr. Brown, the interpreter of the Legation, procured a firman from the Grand Vizier, on behalf of the officers of the San Jacinto, and kindly invited me, with several other American and English travellers, to join the party. During the month of Ramazan, no firmans are given, and as at this time there are few travellers in Constantinople, we should otherwise have been subjected to a heavy expense. The cost of a firman, including backsheesh to the priests and doorkeepers, is 700 piastres (about $33).

We crossed the Golden Horn in caïques, and first visited the gardens and palaces on Seraglio Point. The Sultan at present resides in his summer palace of Beshiktashe, on the Bosphorus, and only occupies the Serai Bornou, as it is called, during the winter months. The Seraglio covers the extremity of the promontory on which Constantinople is built, and is nearly three miles in circuit. The scattered buildings erected by different Sultans form in themselves a small city, whose domes and pointed turrets rise from amid groves of cypress and pine. The sea-wall is lined with kiosks, from whose cushioned windows there are the loveliest views of the European and Asian shores. The newer portion of the palace, where the Sultan now receives the ambassadors of foreign nations, shows the influence of European taste in its plan and decorations. It is by no means remarkable for splendor, and suffers by contrast with many of the private houses in Damascus and Aleppo. The building is of wood, the walls ornamented with detestable frescoes by modern Greek artists, and except a small but splendid collection of arms, and some wonderful specimens of Arabic chirography, there is nothing to interest the visitor.

In ascending to the ancient Seraglio, which was founded by Mahomet II., on the site of the palace of the Palæologi, we passed the Column of Theodosius, a plain Corinthian shaft, about fifty feet high. The Seraglio is now occupied entirely by the servants and guards, and the greater part of it shows a neglect amounting almost to dilapidation. The Saracenic corridors surrounding its courts are supported by pillars of marble, granite, and porphyry, the spoils of the Christian capital. We were allowed to walk about at leisure, and inspect the different compartments, except the library, which unfortunately was locked. This library was for a long time supposed to contain many lost treasures of ancient literature—among other things, the missing books of Livy—but the recent researches of Logothetos, the Prince of Samos, prove that there is little of value among its manuscripts. Before the door hangs a wooden globe, which is supposed to be efficacious in neutralizing the influence of the Evil Eye. There are many ancient altars and fragments of pillars scattered about the courts, and the Turks have even commenced making a collection of antiquities, which, with the exception of two immense sarcophagi of red porphyry, contains nothing of value. They show, however, one of the brazen heads of the Delphian tripod in the Hippodrome, which, they say, Mahomet the Conqueror struck off with a single blow of his sword, on entering Constantinople.

The most interesting portion of the Seraglio is the ancient throne-room, now no longer used, but still guarded by a company of white eunuchs. The throne is an immense, heavy bedstead, the posts of which are thickly incrusted with rubies, turquoises, emeralds, and sapphires. There is a funnel-shaped chimney-piece in the room, a master-work of Benevenuto Cellini. There, half a century ago, the foreign ambassadors were presented, after having been bathed, fed, and clothed with a rich mantle in the outer apartments. They were ushered into the imperial presence, supported by a Turkish official on either side, in order that they might show no signs of breaking down under the load of awe and reverence they were supposed to feel. In the outer Court, adjoining the Sublime Porte, is the Chapel of the Empress Irene, now converted into an armory, which, for its size, is the most tasteful and picturesque collection of weapons I have ever seen. It is especially rich in Saracenic armor, and contains many superb casques of inlaid gold. In a large glass case in the chancel, one sees the keys of some thirty or forty cities, with the date of their capture. It is not likely that another will ever be added to the list.

We now passed out through the Sublime Porte, and directed our steps to the famous *Aya Sophia*—the temple dedicated by Justinian to the Divine Wisdom. The repairs made to the outer walls by the Turks, and the addition of the four minarets, have entirely changed the character of the building, without injuring its effect. As a Christian Church, it must have been less imposing than in its present form. A priest met us at the entrance, and after reading the firman with a very discontented face, informed us that we could not enter until the midday prayers were concluded. After taking off our shoes, however, we were allowed to ascend to the galleries, whence we looked down on the bowing worshippers. Here the majesty of the renowned edifice, despoiled as it now is, bursts at once upon the eye. The wonderful flat dome, glittering with its golden mosaics, and the sacred phrase from the Koran : *God is the Light of the Heavens and the Earth*," swims in the air, one hundred and eighty feet above the marble pavement. On the eastern and western sides, it rests on two half domes, which again rise from or rest upon a group of three small half-domes, so that the entire roof of the mosque, unsupported by a pillar, seems to have been dropped from above on the walls, rather than to have been built up from them. Around the edifice run an upper and a lower gallery, which alone preserve the peculiarities of the Byzantine style. These galleries are supported by the most precious columns which ancient art could afford: among them eight shafts of green marble, from the Temple of Diana, at Ephesus; eight of porphyry, from the Temple of the Sun, at Baalbek; besides Egyptian granite from the shrines of Isis and Osiris, and Pentelican marble from the sanctuary of Pallas Athena. Almost the whole of the interior has been covered with gilding, but time has softened its brilliancy, and the rich, subdued gleam of the walls is in perfect harmony with the varied coloring of the ancient marbles.

Under the dome, four Christian seraphim, executed in mosaic, have been allowed to remain, but the names of the four archangels of the Moslem faith are inscribed underneath. The bronze doors are still the same, the Turks having taken great pains to obliterate the crosses with which they were adorned. Around the centre of the dome, as on that of Sultan Achmed, may be read, in golden letters, and in all the intricacy of Arabic penmanship, the beautiful verse:—"God is the Light of the Heavens and the Earth. His wisdom is a light on the wall, in which burns a lamp covered with glass. The glass shines like a star, the lamp is lit with the oil of a blessed tree. No Eastern, no Western oil, it shines for whoever wills." After the prayers were over, and we had descended to the floor of the mosque, I spent the rest of my time under the dome, fascinated by its marvellous lightness and beauty. The worshippers present looked at us with curiosity, but without ill-will; and before we left, one of the priests came slyly with some fragments of the ancient gilded mosaic, which he was heathen enough to sell, and we to buy.

From St. Sophia we went to Sultan Achmed, which faces

the Hippodrome, and is one of the stateliest piles of Constantinople. It is avowedly an imitation of St. Sophia, and the Turks consider it a more wonderful work, because the dome is seven feet higher. It has six minarets, exceeding in this respect all the mosques of Asia. The dome rests on four immense pillars, the bulk of which quite oppresses the light galleries running around the walls. This, and the uniform white color of the interior, impairs the effect which its bold style and imposing dimensions would otherwise produce. The outside view, with the group of domes swelling grandly above the rows of broad-armed sycamores, is much more satisfactory. In the tomb of Sultan Achmed, in one corner of the court, we saw his coffin, turban, sword, and jewelled harness. I had just been reading old Sandys' account of his visit to Constantinople, in 1610, during this Sultan's reign, and could only think of him as Sandys represents him, in the title-page to his book, as a fat man, with bloated cheeks, in a long gown and big turban, and the words underneath :—"*Achmed, sive Tyrannus.*"

The other noted mosques of Constantinople are the *Yeni Djami*, or Mosque of the Sultana Valide, on the shore of the Golden Horn, at the end of the bridge to Galata ; that of Sultan Bajazet ; of Mahomet II., the Conqueror, and of his son, Suleyman the Magnificent, whose superb mosque well deserves this title. I regret exceedingly that our time did not allow us to view the interior, for outwardly it not only surpasses St Sophia, and all other mosques in the city, but is undoubtedly one of the purest specimens of Oriental architecture extant. It stands on a broad terrace, on one of the seven hills of Stamboul, and its exquisitely proportioned domes and minarets shine as if crystalized in the blue of the air. It is a type of Oriental, as the Parthenon is of Grecian, and the Cologne Cathedral of Gothic art. As I saw it the other night, lit by the flames of a conflagration, standing out red and clear against the darkness, I felt inclined to place it on a level with either of those renowned structures. It is a product of the rich fancy of the East, splendidly ornate, and not without a high degree of symmetry—yet here the symmetry is that of ornament alone, and not the pure, absolute proportion of forms, which we find in Grecian Art. It requires a certain degree of enthusiasm—nay, a slight inebriation of the imaginative faculties—in order to feel the sentiment of this Oriental Architecture. If I rightly express all that it says to me, I touch the verge of rapsody. The East, in almost all its aspects, is so essentially poetic, that a true picture of it must be poetic in spirit, if not in form.

Constantinople has been terribly ravaged by fires, no less than fifteen having occurred during the past two weeks Almost every night the sky has been reddened by burning houses, and the minarets of the seven hills lighted with an illumination brighter than that of the Bairam. All the space from the Hippodrome to the Sea of Marmora has been swept away ; the lard, honey, and oil magazines on the Golden Horn, with the bazaars adjoining ; several large blocks on the hill of Galata, with the College of the Dancing Dervishes ; a part of Scutari, and the College of the Howling Dervishes, all have disappeared ; and to-day, the ruins of 3,700 houses, which were destroyed last night, stand smoking in the Greek quarter, behind the aqueduct of Valens. The entire amount of buildings consumed in these two weeks is estimated at between *five and six thousand !* The fire on the hill of Galata threatened to destroy a great part of the suburb of Pera. It came, sweeping over the brow of the hill, towards my hotel, turning the tall cypresses in the burial ground into shafts of angry flame, and eating away the crackling dwellings of hordes of hapless Turks. I was in bed, from a sudden attack of fever, but seeing the other guests packing up their effects and preparing to leave, I was obliged to do the same; and this, in my weak state, brought on such a perspiration that the ailment left me. The officers of the United States steamer *San Jacinto*, and the French frigate *Charlemagne*, came to the rescue with their men and fire-engines, and the flames were finally quelled. The proceedings of the Americans, who cut holes in the roofs and played through them upon the fires within, were watched by the Turks with stupid amazement. "Máshallah!" said a fat Bimbashi, as he stood sweltering in the heat; "The Franks are a wonderful people."

To those initiated into the mysteries of Turkish politics, these fires are more than accidental; they have a most weighty significance. They indicate either a general discontent with the existing state of affairs, or else a powerful plot against the Sultan and his Ministry. Setting fire to houses is, in fact, the Turkish method of holding an "indignation meeting," and from the rate with which they are increasing, the political crisis must be near at hand. The Sultan, with his usual kindness of heart, has sent large quantities of tents and other supplies to the guiltless sufferers; but no amount of kindness can soften the rancor of these Turkish intrigues. Reschid Pasha, the present Grand Vizier, and the leader of the party of Progress, is the person against whom this storm of opposition is now gathering.

In spite of all efforts, the Ottoman Power is rapidly wasting away. The life of the Orient is nerveless and effete; the native strength of the race has died out, and all attempts to resuscitate it by the adoption of European institutions produce mere galvanic spasms, which leave it more exhausted than before. The rosy-colored accounts we have had of Turkish Progress are for the most part mere delusions. The Sultan is a well-meaning but weak man, and tyrannical through his very weakness. Had he strength enough to break through the meshes of falsehood and venality which are woven so close about him, he might accomplish some solid good. But Turkish rule, from his ministers down to the lowest *cadi*, is a monstrous system of deceit and corruption. These people have not the most remote conception of the true aims of government; they only seek to enrich themselves and their parasites, at the expense of the people and the national treasury. When we add to this the conscript system, which is draining the provinces of their best Moslem subjects, to the advantage of the Christians and Jews, and the blindness of the Revenue Laws, which impose on domestic manufactures double the duty levied on foreign products, it will easily be foreseen that the next half-century, or less, will completely drain the Turkish Empire of its last lingering energies.

Already, in effect, Turkey exists only through the jealousy of the European nations. The treaty of Unkiar-iskelessi, in 1833, threw her into the hands of Russia, although the influence of England has of late years reigned almost exclusively in her councils. These are the two powers who are lowering at each other with sleepless eyes, in the Dardanelles and the Bosphorus. The people, and most probably the government, is strongly preposessed in favor of the English ; but the Russian Bear has a heavy paw, and when he puts it into the scale, all other weights kick the beam. It will be a long and wary struggle, and no man can prophecy the result. The Turks are a people easy to govern, were even the imperfect laws, now in existence, fairly administered. They would thrive and improve under a better state of things ; but I cannot avoid the conviction that the regeneration of the East will never be effected at their hands.

CHAPTER XXIX.

FAREWELL TO THE ORIENT—MALTA.

Embarcation—Farewell to the Orient—Leaving Constantinople—A Wreck—The Dardanelles—Homeric Scenery—Smyrna Revisited—The Grecian Isles—Voyage to Malta—Detention—La Valetta—The Maltese—The Climate—A Boat for Sicily.

"Farewell, ye mountains,
By glory crowned·
Ye sacred fountains
Of Gods renowned;
Ye woods and highlands,
Where heroes dwell;
Ye seas and islands,
Farewell! Farewell!"

FRITHIOF'S SAGA.

IN THE DARDANELLES, *Saturday, August* 7, 1852.

AT last, behold me fairly embarked for Christian Europe, to which I bade adieu in October last, eager for the unknown wonders of the Orient. Since then, nearly ten months have passed away, and those wonders are now familiar as every-day experiences. I set out, determined to be satisfied with no slight taste of Eastern life, but to drain to the bottom its beaker of mingled sunshine and sleep. All this has been accomplished; and if I have not wandered so far, nor enriched myself with such varied knowledge of the relics of ancient history, as I might have purposed or wished, I have at least learned to know the Turk and the Arab, been soothed by the patience inspired by their fatalism, and warmed by the gorgeous gleams of fancy that animate their poetry and religion.

These ten months of my life form an episode which seems to belong to a separate existence. Just refined enough to be poetic, and just barbaric enough to be freed from all conventional fetters, it is as grateful to brain and soul, as an Eastern bath to the body. While I look forward, not without pleasure, to the luxuries and conveniences of Europe, I relinquish with a sigh the refreshing indolence of Asia.

We have passed between the Castles of the two Continents, guarding the mouth of the Dardanelles, and are now entering the Grecian Sea. To-morrow, we shall touch, for a few hours, at Smyrna, and then turn westward, on the track of Ulysses and St. Paul. Farewell, then, perhaps forever, to the bright Orient! Farewell to the gay gardens, the spicy bazaars, to the plash of fountains and the gleam of golden-tipped minarets! Farewell to the perfect morns, the balmy twilights, the still heat of the blue noons, the splendor of moon and stars! Farewell to the glare of the white crags, the tawny wastes of dead sand, the valleys of oleander, the hills of myrtle and spices! Farewell to the bath, agent of purity and peace, and parent of delicious dreams—to the shebook, whose fragrant fumes are breathed from the lips of patience and contentment—to the narghileh, crowned with that blessed plant which grows in the gardens of Shiraz, while a fountain more delightful than those of Samarcand bubbles in its crystal bosom! Farewell to the red cap and slippers, to the big turban, the flowing trousers, and the gaudy shawl—to squatting on broad divans, to sipping black coffee in acorn cups, to grave faces and *salaam aleikooms*, and touching of the lips and forehead! Farewell to the evening meal in the tent door, to the couch on the friendly earth, to the yells of the muleteers, to the deliberate marches of the plodding horse, and the endless rocking of the dromedary that knoweth his master! Farewell, finally, to annoyance without anger, delay without vexation, indolence without ennui, endurance without fatigue, appetite without intemperance, enjoyment without pall!

La Valetta, Malta, *Saturday, August* 14, 1852.

My last view of Stamboul was that of the mosques of St. Sophia and Sultan Achmed, shining faintly in the moonlight, as we steamed down the Sea of Marmora. The *Caire* left at nine o'clock, freighted with the news of Reschid Pasha's deposition, and there were no signs of conflagration in all the long miles of the city that lay behind us. So we speculated no more on the exciting topics of the day, but went below and took a vapor bath in our berths; for I need not assure you that the nights on the Mediterranean at this season are anything but chilly. And here I must note the fact, that the French steamers, while dearer than the Austrian, are more cramped in their accommodations, and filled with a set of most uncivil servants. The table is good, and this is the only thing to be commended. In all other respects, I prefer the Lloyd vessels.

Early next morning, we passed the promontory of Cyzicus, and the Island of Marmora, the marble quarries of which give name to the sea. As we were approaching the entrance to the Dardanelles, we noticed an Austrian brig drifting in the current, the whiff of her flag indicating distress. Her rudder was entirely gone, and she was floating helplessly towards the Thracian coast. A boat was immediately lowered and a hawser carried to her bows, by which we towed her a short distance;

but our steam engine did not like this drudgery, and snapped the rope repeatedly, so that at last we were obliged to leave her to her fate. The lift we gave, however, had its effect, and by dexterous manœuvering with the sails, the captain brought her safely into the harbor of Gallipoli, where she dropped anchor beside us.

Beyond Gallipoli, the Dardanelles contract, and the opposing continents rise into lofty and barren hills. In point of natural beauty, this strait is greatly inferior to the Bosphorus. It lacks the streams and wooded valleys which open upon the latter. The country is but partially cultivated, except around the town of Dardanelles, near the mouth of the strait. The site of the bridge of Xerxes is easily recognized, the conformation of the different shores seconding the decision of antiquarians. Here, too, are Sestos and Abydos, of passionate and poetic memory. But as the sun dipped towards the sea, we passed out of the narrow gateway. On our left lay the plain of Troy, backed by the blue range of Mount Ida. The tumulus of Patroclus crowned a low bluff looking on the sea. On the right appeared the long, irregular island of Imbros, and the peaks of misty Samothrace over and beyond it. Tenedos was before us. The red flush of sunset tinged the grand Homeric landscape, and lingered and lingered on the summit of Ida, as if loth to depart. I paced the deck until long after it was too dark to distinguish it any more.

The next morning we dropped anchor in the harbor of Smyrna, where we remained five hours. I engaged a donkey, and rode out to the Caravan Bridge, where the Greek driver and I smoked narghilehs and drank coffee in the shade of the acacias. I contrasted my impressions with those of my first visit to Smyrna last October—my first glimpse of Oriental ground. Then, every dog barked at me, and all the horde of human creatures who prey upon innocent travellers ran at my heels, but now, with my brown face and Turkish aspect of grave indifference, I was suffered to pass as quietly as my donkey-driver himself. Nor did the latter, nor the ready *cafidji*, who filled our pipes on the banks of the Meles, attempt to overcharge me—a sure sign that the Orient had left its seal on my face. Returning through the city, the same mishap befel me which travellers usually experience on their first arrival. My donkey, while dashing at full speed through a crowd of Smyrniotes in their Sunday dresses, slipped up in a little pool of black mud, and came down with a crash. I flew over his head and alighted firmly on my feet, but the spruce young Greeks, whose snowy fustanelles were terribly bespattered, came off much worse. The donkey shied back, levelled his ears and twisted his head on one side, awaiting a beating, but his bleeding legs saved him.

We left at two o'clock, touched at Scio in the evening, and the next morning at sunrise lay-to in the harbor of Syra. The Piræus was only twelve hours distant; but after my visitation of fever in Constantinople, I feared to encounter the pestilential summer heats of Athens. Besides, I had reasons for hastening with all speed to Italy and Germany. At ten o'clock we weighed anchor again and steered southwards, between the groups of the Cyclades, under a cloudless sky and over a sea of the brightest blue. The days were endurable under the canvas awning of our quarter-deck, but the nights in our berths were sweat-baths, which left us so limp and exhausted that we were almost fit to vanish, like ghosts, at daybreak.

Our last glimpse of the Morea—Cape Matapan—faded away in the moonlight, and for two days we travelled westward over the burning sea. On the evening of the 11th, the long, low outline of Malta rose gradually against the last flush of sunset, and in two hours thereafter, we came to anchor in Quarantine Harbor. The quarantine for travellers returning from the East, which formerly varied from fourteen to twenty-one days, is now reduced to one day for those arriving from Greece or Turkey, and three days for those from Egypt and Syria. In our case, it was reduced to sixteen hours, by an official courtesy. I had intended proceeding directly to Naples; but by the contemptible trickery of the agents of the French steamers—a long history, which it is unnecessay to recapitulate—am left here to wait ten days for another steamer. It is enough to say that there are six other travellers at the same hotel, some coming from Constantinople, and some from Alexandria, in the same predicament. Because a single ticket to Naples costs some thirty or forty francs less than by dividing the trip into two parts, the agents in those cities refuse to give tickets further than Malta to those who are not keen enough to see through the deception. I made every effort to obtain a second ticket in time to leave by the branch steamer for Italy, but in vain.

La Valetta is, to my eyes, the most beautiful small city in the world. It is a jewel of a place; not a street but is full of picturesque effects, and all the look-outs, which you catch at every turn, let your eyes rest either upon one of the beautiful harbors on each side, or the distant horizon of the sea. The streets are so clean that you might eat your dinner off the pavement; the white balconies and cornices of the houses, all cleanly cut in the soft Maltese stone, stand out in intense relief against the sky, and from the manifold reflections and counter reflections, the shadows (where there are any) become a sort of milder light. The steep sides of the promontory, on which the city is built, are turned into staircases, and it is an inexhaustible pastime to watch the groups, composed of all nations who inhabit the shores of the Mediterranean, ascending and descending. The Auberges of the old Knights, the Palace of the Grand Master, the Church of St. John, and other relics of past time, but more especially the fortifications, invest the place with a romantic interest, and I suspect that, after Venice and Granada, there are few cities where the Middle Ages have left more impressive traces of their history.

The Maltese are contented, and appear to thrive under the English administration. They are a peculiar people, reminding me of the Arab even more than the Italian, while a certain rudeness in their build and motions suggests their Punic ancestry. Their language is a curious compound of Arabic and Italian, the former being the basis. I find that I can understand more than half that is said, the Arabic terminations being applied to Italian words. I believe it has never been successfully reduced to writing, and the restoration of pure Arabic has been proposed, with much reason, as preferable to an attempt to improve or refine it. Italian is the language used in the courts of justice and polite society, and is spoken here with much more purity than either in Naples or Sicily.

The heat has been so great since I landed that I have not ventured outside of the city, except last evening to an amateur theatre, got up by the non-commissioned officers and privates in the garrison. The performances were quite tolerable, except a love-sick young damsel who spoke with a rough masculine voice, and made long strides across the stage when she rushed into her lover's arms. I am at a loss to account for the exhausting character of the heat. The thermometer shows 90° by day, and 80° to 85° by night—a much lower temperature than I have found quite comfortable in Africa and Syria. In the Desert 100° in the shade is rather bracing than otherwise; here, 90° renders all exercise, more severe than smoking a pipe, impossible. Even in a state of complete inertia, a shirt-collar will fall starchless in five minutes.

Rather than waste eight more days in this glimmering half-existence, I have taken passage in a Maltese *speronara*, which sails this evening for Catania, in Sicily, where the grand festival of St. Agatha, which takes place once in a hundred years, will be celebrated next week. The trip promises a new experience, and I shall get a taste, slight though it be, of the golden Trinacria of the ancients. Perhaps, after all, this delay which so vexes me (bear in mind, I am no longer in the Orient!) may be meant solely for my good. At least, Mr. Winthrop, our Consul here, who has been exceedingly kind and courteous to me, thinks it a rare good fortune that I shall see the Catanian festa.

CHAPTER XXX.

THE FESTIVAL OF ST. AGATHA

Departure from Malta—The Speronara—Our Fellow-Passengers—The First Night on Board—Sicily—Scarcity of Provisions—Beating in the Calabrian Channel—The Fourth Morning—The Gulf of Catania—A Sicilian Landscape—The Anchorage—The Suspected List—The Streets of Catania—Biography of St. Agatha—The Illuminations—The Procession of the Veil—The Biscari Palace—The Antiquities of Catania—The Convent of St. Nicola.

"The morn is full of holiday, loud bells
With rival clamors ring from every spire;
Cunningly-stationed music dies and swells
In echoing places; when the winds respire,
Light flags stream out like gauzy tongues of fire."—KEATS.

CATANIA, Sicily, *Friday, August* 20, 1852.

I WENT on board the *speronara* in the harbor of La Valetta at the appointed hour (5 P. M.), and found the remaining sixteen passengers already embarked. The captain made his appearance an hour later, with our bill of health and passports, and as the sun went down behind the brown hills of the island, we passed the wave-worn rocks of the promontory, dividing the two harbors, and slowly moved off towards Sicily.

The Maltese *speronara* resembles the ancient Roman galley more than any modern craft. It has the same high, curved poop and stern, the same short masts and broad, square sails. The hull is too broad for speed, but this adds to the security of the vessel in a gale. With a fair wind, it rarely makes more than eight knots an hour, and in a calm, the sailors (if not too lazy) propel it forward with six long oars. The hull is painted in a fanciful style, generally blue, red, green and white, with bright red masts. The bulwarks are low, and the deck of such a convexity that it is quite impossible to walk it in a heavy sea. Such was the vessel to which I found myself consigned. It was not more than fifty feet long, and of less capacity than a Nile *dahabiyeh*. There was a sort of deck cabin, or crib, with two berths, but most of the passengers slept in the hold. For a passage to Catania I was obliged to pay forty francs, the owner swearing that this was the regular price ; but, as I afterwards discovered, the Maltese only paid thirty-six francs for the whole trip. However, the Captain tried to make up the money's worth in civilities, and was incessant in his attentions to "your Lordships," as he styled myself and my companion, Cæsar di Cagnola, a young Milanese.

The Maltese were tailors and clerks, who were taking a holiday trip to witness the great festival of St. Agatha. With two exceptions, they were a wild and senseless, though good-natured set, and in spite of sea-sickness, which exercised them terribly for the first two days, kept up a constant jabber in their bastard Arabic from morning till night. As is usual in such a company, one of them was obliged to serve as a butt for the rest, and "Maestro Paolo," as they termed him, wore such a profoundly serious face all the while, from his sea-sickness, that the fun never came to an end. As they were going to a religious festival, some of them had brought their breviaries along with them ; but I am obliged to testify that, after the first day, prayers were totally forgotten. The sailors, however, wore linen bags, printed with a figure of the Madonna, around their necks.

The sea was rather rough, but Cæsar and I fortified our stomachs with a bottle of English ale, and as it was dark by this time, sought our resting-places for the night. As we had paid double, *places* were assured us in the coop on deck, but beds were not included in the bargain. The Maltese, who had brought mattresses and spread a large Phalansterian bed in the hold, fared much better. I took one of my carpet bags for a pillow and lay down on the planks, where I succeeded in getting a little sleep between the groans of the helpless land-lubbers. We had the *ponente*, or west-wind, all night, but the speronara moved sluggishly, and in the morning it changed to the *greco-levante*, or north-east. No land was in sight; but towards noon, the sky became clearer, and we saw the southern coast of Sicily—a bold mountain-shore, looming phantom-like in the distance. Cape Passaro was to the east, and the rest of the day was spent in beating up to it. At sunset, we were near enough to see the villages and olive-groves of the beautiful shore, and, far behind the nearer mountains, ninety miles distant, the solitary cone of Etna.

The second night passed like the first, except that our bruised limbs were rather more sensitive to the texture of the planks. We crawled out of our coop at dawn, expecting to behold Catania in the distance; but there was Cape Passaro still staring us in the face. The Maltese were patient, and we did not complain, though Cæsar and I began to make nice calculations as to the probable duration of our two cold fowls and three loaves of bread. The promontory of Syracuse was barely visible forty miles ahead; but the wind was against us, and so another day passed in beating up the eastern coast. At dusk, we overtook another speronara which had left Malta two hours before us, and this was quite a triumph to our captain. All the oars were shipped, the sailors and some of the more courageous passengers took hold, and we shot ahead, scudding rapidly along the dark shores, to the sound of the wild Maltese songs. At length, the promontory was gained, and the restless current, rolling down from Scylla and Charybdis, tossed our little bark from wave to wave with a recklessness that would have made any one nervous but an old sailor like myself.

"To-morrow morning," said the Captain, "we shall sail into Catania;" but after a third night on the planks, which were now a little softer, we rose to find ourselves abreast of Syracuse, with Etna as distant as ever. The wind was light, and what little we made by tacking was swept away by the current, so that, after wasting the whole forenoon, we kept a straight course across the mouth of the channel, and at sunset saw the Calabrian Mountains. This move only lost us more ground, as it happened. Cæsar and I mournfully and silently consumed our last fragment of beef, with the remaining dry crusts of bread, and then sat down doggedly to smoke and see whether the captain would discover our situation. But no; while we were supplied, the whole vessel was at our Lordships' command, and now that we were destitute, he took care to make no rash offers. Cæsar, at last, with an imperial dignity becoming his name, commanded dinner. It came, and the pork and maccaroni, moistened with red Sicilian wine, gave us patience for another day.

The fourth morning dawned, and—Great Neptune be

praised!—we were actually within the Gulf of Catania. Etna loomed up in all his sublime bulk, unobscured by cloud or mist, while a slender jet of smoke, rising from his crater, was slowly curling its wreaths in the clear air, as if happy to receive the first beam of the sun. The towers of Syracuse, which had mocked us all the preceding day, were no longer visible; the land-locked little port of Augusta lay behind us; and, as the wind continued favorable, ere long we saw a faint white mark at the foot of the mountain. This was Catania. The shores of the bay were enlivened with olive-groves and the gleam of the villages, while here and there a single palm dreamed of its brothers across the sea. Etna, of course, had the monarch's place in the landscape, but even his large, magnificent outlines could not usurp all my feeling. The purple peaks to the westward and farther inland, had a beauty of their own, and in the gentle curves with which they leaned towards each other, there was a promise of the flowery meadows of Enna. The smooth blue water was speckled with fishing-boats. We hailed one, inquiring when the *festa* was to commence; but, mistaking our question, they answered: "Anchovies." Thereupon, a waggish Maltese informed them that Maestro Paolo thanked them heartily. All the other boats were hailed in the name of Maestro Paolo, who, having recovered from his sea-sickness, took his bantering good-humoredly.

Catania presented a lovely picture, as we drew near the harbor. Planted at the very foot of Etna, it has a background such as neither Naples nor Genoa can boast. The hills next the sea are covered with gardens and orchards, sprinkled with little villages and the country palaces of the nobles—a rich, cultured landscape, which gradually merges into the forests of oak and chestnut that girdle the waist of the great volcano. But all the wealth of southern vegetation cannot hide the footsteps of that Ruin, which from time to time visits the soil. Half-way up, the mountain-side is dotted with cones of ashes and cinders, some covered with the scanty shrubbery which centuries have called forth, some barren and recent; while two dark, winding streams of sterile lava descend to the very shore, where they stand congealed in ragged needles and pyramids. Part of one of these black floods has swept the town, and, tumbling into the sea, walls one side of the port.

We glided slowly past the mole, and dropped anchor a few yards from the shore. There was a sort of open promenade planted with trees, in front of us, surrounded with high white houses, above which rose the dome of the Cathedral and the spires of other churches. The magnificent palace of Prince Biscari was on our right, and at its foot the Customs and Revenue offices. Every roof, portico, and window was lined with lamps, a triumphal arch spanned the street before the palace, and the landing-place at the offices was festooned with crimson and white drapery, spangled with gold. While we were waiting permission to land, a scene presented itself which recalled the pagan days of Sicily to my mind. A procession came in sight from under the trees, and passed along the shore. In the centre was borne a stately shrine, hung with garlands, and containing an image of St. Agatha. The sound of flutes and cymbals accompanied it, and a band of children, bearing orange and palm branches, danced riotously before. Had the image been Pan instead of St. Agatha, the ceremonies would have been quite as appropriate.

The speronara's boat at last took us to the gorgeous landing-place, where we were carefully counted by a fat Sicilian official, and declared free from quarantine. We were then called into the Passport Office, where the Maltese underwent a searching examination. One of the officers sat with the Black Book, or list of suspected persons of all nations, open before him, and looked for each name as it was called out. Another scanned the faces of the frightened tailors, as if comparing them with certain revolutionary visages in his mind. Terrible was the keen, detective glance of his eye, and it went straight through the poor Maltese, who vanished with great rapidity when they were declared free to enter the city. At last, they all passed the ordeal, but Cæsar and I remained, looking in at the door. "There are still these two Frenchmen," said the captain. "I am no Frenchman," I protested; "I am an American." "And I," said Cæsar, "am an Austrian subject." Thereupon we received a polite invitation to enter; the terrible glance softened into a benign, respectful smile; he of the Black Book ran lightly over the C's and T's, and said, with a courteous inclination: "There is nothing against the signori." I felt quite relieved by this; for, in the Mediterranean, one is never safe from spies, and no person is too insignificant to escape the ban, if once suspected.

Calabria was filled to overflowing with strangers from all parts of the Two Sicilies, and we had some difficulty in finding very bad and dear lodgings. It was the first day of the *festa*, and the streets were filled with peasants, the men in black velvet jackets and breeches, with stockings, and long white cotton caps hanging on the shoulders, and the women with gay silk shawls on their heads, after the manner of the Mexican *reboza*. In all the public squares, the market scene in Masaniello was acted to the life. The Sicilian dialect is harsh and barbarous, and the original Italian is so disguised by the admixture of Arabic, Spanish, French, and Greek words, that even my imperial friend, who was a born Italian, had great difficulty in understanding the people.

I purchased a guide to the festa, which, among other things, contained a biography of St. Agatha. It is a beautiful specimen of pious writing, and I regret that I have not space to translate the whole of it. Agatha was a beautiful Catanian virgin, who secretly embraced Christianity during the reign of Nero. Catania was then governed by a prætor named Quintianus, who, becoming enamored of Agatha, used the most brutal means to compel her to submit to his desires, but without effect. At last, driven to the cruelest extremes, he cut off her breasts, and threw her into prison. But at midnight, St. Peter, accompanied by an angel, appeared to her, restored the maimed parts, and left her more beautiful than ever. Quintianus then ordered a furnace to be heated, and cast her therein. A terrible earthquake shook the city ; the sun was eclipsed ; the sea rolled backwards, and left its bottom dry ; the prætor's palace fell in ruins, and he, pursued by the vengeance of the populace, fled till he reached the river Simeto, where he was drowned in attempting to cross. "The thunders of the vengeance of God," says the biography, "struck him down into the profoundest Hell!" This was in the year 252.

The body was carried to Constantinople in 1040, "although the Catanians wept incessantly at their loss ;" but in 1126, two French knights, named Gilisbert and Goselin, were moved by angelic influences to restore it to its native town, which they accomplished, "and the eyes of the Catanians again burned with joy." The miracles effected by the saint are numberless, and her power is especially efficacious in preventing earthquakes and eruptions of Mount Etna. Nevertheless, Catania has suffered more from these causes than any other town in Sicily. But I would that all saints had as good a claim to canonization as St. Agatha. The honors of such a festival as this are not out of place, when paid to such youth, beauty, and "heavenly chastity," as she typifies.

The guide, which I have already consulted, gives a full account of the festa, in advance, with a description of Catania. The author says: "If thy heart is not inspired by gazing on this lovely city, it is a fatal sign—thou wert not born to feel the sweet impulses of the Beautiful!" Then, in announcing the illuminations and pyrotechnic displays, he exclaims: "Oh, the amazing spectacle! Oh, how happy art thou, that thou beholdest it! What pyramids of lamps! What myriads of rockets! What wonderful temples of flame! The Mountain himself is astonished at such a display." And truly, except the illumination of the Golden Horn on the Night of Predestination, I have seen nothing equal to the spectacle presented by Catania, during the past three nights. The city, which has been built up from her ruins more stately than ever, was in a blaze of light—all her domes, towers, and the long lines of her beautiful palaces revealed in the varying red and golden flames of a hundred thousand lamps and torches. Pyramids of fire, transparencies, and illuminated triumphal arches filled the four principal streets, and the fountain in the Cathedral square gleamed like a jet of molten silver, spinning up from one of the pores of Etna. At ten o'clock, a gorgeous display of fire-works closed the day's festivities, but the lamps remained burning nearly all night.

On the second night, the grand Procession of the Veil took place. I witnessed this imposing spectacle from the balcony of Prince Gessina's palace. Long lines of waxen torches led the way, followed by a military band, and then a company of the highest prelates, in their most brilliant costumes, surrounding the Bishop, who walked under a canopy of silk and gold, bearing the miraculous veil of St. Agatha. I was blessed with a distant view of it, but could see no traces of the rosy hue left upon it by the flames of the Saint's martyrdom. Behind the priests came the *Intendente* of Sicily, Gen. Filangieri, the same who, three years ago, gave up Catania to sack and slaughter. He was followed by the Senate of the City, who have just had the cringing cowardice to offer him a ball on next Sunday night. If ever a man deserved the vengeance of an outraged people, it is this Filangieri, who was first a Liberal, when the cause promised success, and then made himself the scourge of the vilest of kings. As he passed me last night in his carriage of State, while the music pealed in rich rejoicing strains, that solemn chant with which the monks break upon the revellers, in "Lucrezia Borgia," came into my mind:

"La gioja dei profani
'E un fumo passagier'—"

[the rejoicing of the profane is a transitory mist.] I heard, under the din of all these festivities, the voice of that Retribution which even now lies in wait, and will not long be delayed.

To-night Signor Scavo, the American Vice-Consul, took me to the palace of Prince Biscari, overlooking the harbor, in order to behold the grand display of fireworks from the end of the mole. The showers of rockets and colored stars, and the temples of blue and silver fire, were repeated in the dark, quiet bosom of the sea, producing the most dazzling and startling effects. There was a large number of the Catanese nobility present, and among them a Marchesa Gioveni, the descendant of the bloody house of Anjou. Prince Biscari is a benign, courtly old man, and greatly esteemed here. His son is at present in exile, on account of the part he took in the late revolution. During the sack of the city under Filangieri, the palace was plundered of property to the amount of ten thousand dollars. The museum of Greek and Roman antiquities attached to it, and which the house of Biscari has been collecting for many years, is probably the finest in Sicily. The state apartments were thrown open this evening, and when I left, an hour ago, the greater portion of the guests were going through mazy quadrilles on the mosaic pavements.

Among the antiquities of Catania which I have visited, are the Amphitheatre, capable of holding 15,000 persons, the old Greek Theatre, the same in which Alcibiades made his noted harangue to the Catanians, the Odeon, and the ancient Baths. The theatre, which is in tolerable preservation, is built of lava, like many of the modern edifices in the city. The Baths proved to me, what I had supposed, that the Oriental Bath of the present day is identical with that of the Ancients. Why so admirable an institution has never been introduced into Europe (except in the *Bains Chinois* of Paris) is more than I can tell. From the pavement of these baths, which is nearly twenty feet below the surface of the earth, the lava of later eruptions has burst up, in places, in hard black jets. The most wonderful token of that flood which whelmed Catania two hundred years ago, is to be seen at the Grand Benedictine Convent of San Nicola, in the upper part of the city. Here the stream of lava divides itself just before the Convent, and flows past on both sides, leaving the building and gardens untouched. The marble courts, the fountains, the splendid galleries, and the gardens of richest southern bloom and fragrance, stand like an epicurean island in the midst of the terrible stony waves, whose edges bristle with the thorny aloe and cactus. The monks of San Nicola are all chosen from the Sicilian nobility, and live a comfortable life of luxury and vice. Each one has his own carriage, horses, and servants, and each his private chambers outside of the convent walls and his kept concubines. These facts are known and acknowledged by the Catanians, to whom they are a lasting scandal.

It is past midnight, and I must close. Cæsar started this afternoon, alone, for the ascent of Etna. I would have accompanied him, but my only chance of reaching Messina in time for the next steamer to Naples is the diligence which leaves here to-morrow. The mountain has been covered with clouds for the last two days, and I have had no view at all comparable to that of the morning of my arrival. To-morrow the grand procession of the Body of St. Agatha takes place, but I am quite satisfied with three days of processions and horse races, and three nights of illuminations.

I leave in the morning, with a Sicilian passport, my own availing me nothing, after landing.

CHAPTER XXXI.

THE ERUPTION OF MOUNT ETNA

The Mountain Threatens—The Signs Increase—We Leave Catania—Gardens Among the Lava—Etna Labors—Aci Reale—The Groans of Etna—The Eruption—Gigantic Tree of Smoke—Formation of the New Crater—We Lose Sight of the Mountain—Arrival at Messina—Etna is Obscured—Departure.

——— "the shattered side
Of thundering Ætna, whose combustible
And fuel'd entrails thence conceiving fire,
Sublimed with mineral fury, aid the winds,
And leave a singed bottom." MILTON.

MESSINA, Sicily, *Monday, August* 23, 1852.

THE noises of the festival had not ceased when I closed my letter at midnight, on Friday last. I slept soundly through the night, but was awakened before sunrise by my Sicilian landlord. "O, Excellenza! have you heard the Mountain? He is going to break out again; may the holy Santa Agatha protect us!" It is rather ill-timed on the part of the Mountain, was my involuntary first thought, that he should choose for a new eruption precisely the centennial festival of the only Saint who is supposed to have any power over him. It shows a disregard of female influence not at all suited to the present day, and I scarcely believe that he seriously means it. Next came along the jabbering landlady: "I don't like his looks. It was just so the last time. Come, Excellenza, you can see him from the back terrace." The sun was not yet risen, but the east was bright with his coming, and there was not a cloud in the sky All the features of Etna were sharply sculptured in the clear air. From the topmost cone, a thick stream of white smoke was slowly puffed out at short intervals, and rolled lazily down the eastern side. It had a heavy, languid character, and I should have thought nothing of the appearance but for the alarm of my hosts. It was like the slow fire of Earth's incense, burning on that grand mountain altar.

I hurried off to the Post Office, to await the arrival of the diligence from Palermo. The office is in the Strada Etnea, the main street of Catania, which runs straight through the city, from the sea to the base of the mountain, whose peak closes the long vista. The diligence was an hour later than usual, and I passed the time in watching the smoke which continued to increase in volume, and was mingled, from time to time, with jets of inky blackness. The postilion said he had seen fires and heard loud noises during the night. According to his account, the disturbances commenced about midnight. I could not but envy my friend Cæsar, who was probably at that moment on the summit, looking down into the seething fires of the crater.

At last, we rolled out of Catania. There were in the diligence, besides myself, two men and a woman, Sicilians of the secondary class. The road followed the shore, over rugged tracts of lava, the different epochs of which could be distinctly traced in the character of the vegetation. The last great flow (of 1679) stood piled in long ridges of terrible sterility, barely allowing the aloe and cactus to take root in the hollows between. The older deposits were sufficiently decomposed to nourish the olive and vine ; but even here, the orchards were studded with pyramids of the harder fragments, which are laboriously collected by the husbandmen. In the few favored spots which have been untouched for so many ages that a tolerable depth of soil has accumulated, the vegetation has all the richness and brilliancy of tropical lands. The palm, orange, and pomegranate thrive luxuriantly, and the vines almost break under their heavy clusters. The villages are frequent and well built, and the hills are studded, far and near, with the villas of rich proprietors, mostly buildings of one story, with verandahs extending their whole length. Looking up towards Etna, whose base the road encircles, the views are gloriously rich and beautiful. On the other hand is the blue Mediterranean and the irregular outline of the shore, here and there sending forth promontories of lava, cooled by the waves into the most fantastic forms.

We had not proceeded far before a new sign called my attention to the mountain. Not only was there a perceptible jar or vibration in the earth, but a dull, groaning sound, like the muttering of distant thunder, began to be heard. The smoke increased in volume, and, as we advanced further to the eastward, and much nearer to the great cone, I perceived that it consisted of two jets, issuing from different mouths. A broad stream of very dense white smoke still flowed over the lip of the topmost crater and down the eastern side. As its breadth did not vary, and the edges were distinctly defined, it was no doubt the sulphureous vapor rising from a river of molten lava. Perhaps a thousand yards below, a much stronger column of mingled black and white smoke gushed up, in regular beats or pants, from a depression in the mountain side, between two small, extinct cones. All this part of Etna was scarred with deep chasms, and in the bottoms of those nearest the opening, I could see the red gleam of fire. The air was perfectly still, and as yet there was no cloud in the sky.

When we stopped to change horses at the town of Aci Reale, I first felt the violence of the tremor and the awful sternness of the sound. The smoke by this time seemed to be gathering on the side towards Catania, and hung in a dark mass about half-way down the mountain. Groups of the villagers were gathered in the streets which looked upwards to Etna, and discussing the chances of an eruption. "Ah," said an old peasant, "the Mountain knows how to make himself respected. When he talks, everybody listens." The sound was the most awful that ever met my ears. It was a hard, painful moan, now and then fluttering like a suppressed sob, and had, at the same time, an expression of threatening and of agony. It did not come from Etna alone. It had no fixed location; it pervaded all space. It was in the air, in the depths of the sea, in the earth under my feet—everywhere, in fact; and as it continued to increase in violence, I experienced a sensation of positive pain. The people looked anxious and alarmed, although they said it was a good thing for all Sicily; that last year they had been in constant fear from earthquakes, and that an eruption invariably left the island quiet for several years. It is true that, during the past year, parts of Sicily and Calabria have been visited with severe shocks, occasioning much damage to property. A merchant of this city informed me yesterday that his whole family had slept for two months in the vaults of his warehouse, fearing that their residence might be shaken down in the night.

As we rode along from Aci Reale to Taormina, all the rattling of the diligence over the rough road could not drown the awful noise. There was a strong smell of sulphur in the air, and the thick pants of smoke from the lower crater continued to increase in strength. The sun was fierce and hot, and the edges of the sulphureous clouds shone with a dazzling whiteness. A mounted soldier overtook us, and rode beside the diligence, talking with the postillion. He had been up to the mountain, and was taking his report to the Governor of the district. The heat of the day and the continued tremor of the air lulled me into a sort of doze, when I was suddenly aroused by a cry from the soldier and the stopping of the diligence. At the same time, there was a terrific peal of sound, followed by a jar which must have shaken the whole island. We looked up to Etna, which was fortunately in full view before us. An immense mass of snow-white smoke had burst up from the crater and was rising perpendicularly into the air, its rounded volumes rapidly whirling one over the other, yet urged with such impetus that they only rolled outwards after they had ascended to an immense height. It might have been one minute or five—for I was so entranced by this wonderful spectacle that I lost the sense of time—but it seemed instantaneous (so rapid and violent were the effects of the explosion), when there stood in the air, based on the summit of the mountain, a mass of smoke four or five miles high, and shaped precisely like the Italian pine tree.

Words cannot paint the grandeur of this mighty tree. Its trunk of columned smoke, one side of which was silvered by the sun, while the other, in shadow, was lurid with red flame, rose for more than a mile before it sent out its cloudy boughs. Then parting into a thousand streams, each of which again threw out its branching tufts of smoke, rolling and waving in the air, it stood in intense relief against the dark blue of the sky. Its rounded masses of foliage were dazzlingly white on one side, while, in the shadowy depths of the branches, there was a constant play of brown, yellow, and crimson tints, revealing the central shaft of fire. It was like the tree celebrated in the Scandinavian sagas, as seen by the mother of Harold Hardrada—that tree, whose roots pierced through the earth, whose trunk was of the color of blood, and whose branches filled the uttermost corners of the heavens.

This outburst seemed to have relieved the mountain, for the tremors were now less violent, though the terrible noise still droned in the air, and earth, and sea. And now, from the base of the tree, three white streams slowly crept into as many separate chasms, against the walls of which played the flickering glow of the burning lava. The column of smoke and flame was still hurled upwards, and the tree, after standing about ten minutes—a new and awful revelation of the active forces of Nature—gradually rose and spread, lost its form, and, slowly moved by a light wind (the first that disturbed the dead calm of the day), bent over to the eastward. We resumed our course. The vast belt of smoke at last arched over the strait, here about twenty miles wide, and sank towards the distant Calabrian shore. As we drove under it, for some miles of our way, the sun was totally obscured, and the sky presented the singular spectacle of two hemispheres of clear blue, with a broad belt of darkness drawn between them. There was a hot, sulphureous vapor in the air, and showers of white ashes fell, from time to time. We were distant about twelve miles, in a straight line, from the crater; but the air was so clear, even under the shadow of the smoke, that I could distinctly trace the downward movement of the rivers of lava.

This was the eruption, at last, to which all the phenomena of the morning had been only preparatory. For the first time in ten years the depths of Etna had been stirred, and I thanked God for my detention at Malta, and the singular hazard of travel which had brought me here, to his very base, to witness a scene, the impression of which I shall never lose, to my dying day. Although the eruption may continue and the mountain pour forth fiercer fires and broader tides of lava, I cannot but think that the first upheaval, which lets out the long-imprisoned forces, will not be equalled in grandeur by any later spectacle.

After passing Taormina, our road led us under the hills of the coast, and although I occasionally caught glimpses of Etna, and saw the reflection of fires from the lava which was filling up his savage ravines, the smoke at last encircled his waist, and he was then shut out of sight by the intervening mountains. We lost a bolt in a deep valley opening on the sea, and during our stoppage I could still hear the groans of the Mountain, though farther off and less painful to the ear. As evening came on, the beautiful hills of Calabria, with white towns and villages on their sides, gleamed in the purple light of the setting sun. We drove around headland after headland, till the strait opened, and we looked over the harbor of Messina to Capo Faro, and the distant islands of the Tyrrhene Sea.

I leave this afternoon for Naples and Leghorn. I have lost already so much time between Constantinople and this place, that I cannot give up ten days more to Etna. Besides, I am so thoroughly satisfied with what I have seen, that I fear no second view of the eruption could equal it. Etna cannot be seen from here, nor from a nearer point than a mountain six or eight miles distant. I tried last evening to get a horse and ride out to it, in order to see the appearance of the eruption by night; but every horse, mule and donkey in the place was engaged, except a miserable lame mule, for which five dollars was demanded. However, the night happened to be cloudy so that I could have seen nothing.

My passport is finally *en règle*. It has cost the labors of myself and an able-bodied valet-de-place since yesterday morning, and the expenditure of five dollars and a half, to accomplish this great work. I have just been righteously abusing the Neapolitan Government to a native merchant whom, from his name, I took to be a Frenchman, but as I am off in an hour or two, hope to escape arrest. Perdition to all Tyranny!

CHAPTER XXXII.

GIBRALTAR.

Unwritten Links of Travel—Departure from Southampton—The Bay of Biscay—Cintra—Trafalgar—Gibraltar at Midnight—Landing—Search for a Palm-Tree—A Brilliant Morning—The Convexity of the Earth—Sun-Worship—The Rock.

> ——— "to the north-west, Cape St. Vincent died away,
> Sunset ran, a burning blood-red, blushing into Cadiz Bay.
> In the dimmest north-east distance dawned Gibraltar, grand and gray."
>
> BROWNING.

GIBRALTAR, *Saturday, November* 6, 1852.

I LEAVE unrecorded the links of travel which connected Messina and Gibraltar. They were over the well-trodden fields of Europe, where little ground is left that is not familiar. In leaving Sicily I lost the Saracenic trail, which I had been following through the East, and first find it again here, on the rock of Calpe, whose name, *Djebel el-Tarik* (the Mountain of Tarik), still speaks of the fiery race whose rule extended from the unknown ocean of the West to "Ganges and Hydaspes, Indian streams." In Malta and Sicily, I saw their decaying watch-towers, and recognized their sign-manual in the deep, guttural, masculine words and expressions which they have left behind them. I now design following their footsteps through the beautiful *Belàd-el-Andaluz*, which, to the eye of the Melek Abd-er-rahmàn, was only less lovely than the plains of Damascus.

While in Constantinople, I received letters which opened to me wider and richer fields of travel than I had already traversed. I saw a possibility of exploring the far Indian realms, the shores of farthest Cathay and the famed Zipango of Marco Polo. Before entering on this new sphere of experiences, however,. it was necessary for me to visit Italy, Germany, and England. I sailed from Messina to Leghorn, and travelled thence, by way of Florence, Venice, and the Tyrol, to Munich After three happy weeks at Gotha, and among the valleys of the Thüringian Forest, I went to London, where business and the preparation for my new journeys detained me two or three weeks longer. Although the comforts of European civilization were pleasant, as a change, after the wild life of the Orient, the autumnal rains of England soon made me homesick for the sunshine I had left. The weather was cold, dark, and dreary, and the oppressive, sticky atmosphere of the bituminous metropolis weighed upon me like a nightmare. Heartily tired of looking at a sun that could show nothing brighter than a red copper disk, and of breathing an air that peppered my face with particles of soot, I left on the 28th of October. It was one of the dismalest days of autumn; the meadows of Berkshire were flooded with broad, muddy streams, and the woods on the hills of Hampshire looked brown and sodden, as if slowly rotting away. I reached Southampton at dusk, but there the sky was neither warmer nor clearer, so I spent the evening over a coal fire, all impatience for the bright beloved South, towards which my face was turned once more.

The *Madras* left on the next day, at 2 P.M., in the midst of a cheerless rain, which half blotted out the pleasant shores of Southampton Water, and the Isle of Wight. The *Madras* was a singularly appropriate vessel for one bound on such a journey as mine. The surgeon was Dr. Mungo Park, and one of my room-mates was Mr. R. Crusoe. It was a Friday, which boded no good for the voyage; but then my journey commenced with my leaving London the day previous, and Thursday is a lucky day among the Arabs. I caught a watery view of the gray cliffs of the Needles, when dinner was announced, but many were those (and I among them) who commenced that meal, and did not stay to finish it.

Is there any piece of water more unreasonably, distressingly, disgustingly rough and perverse than the British Channel? Yes: there is one, and but one—the Bay of Biscay. And as the latter succeeds the former, without a pause between, and the head-winds never ceased, and the rain continually poured, I leave you to draw the climax of my misery. Four days and four nights in a berth, lying on your back, now dozing dull hour after hour, now making faint endeavors to eat, or reading the feeblest novel ever written, because the mind cannot digest stronger aliment—can there be a greater contrast to the wide-awake life, the fiery inspiration, of the Orient? My blood became so sluggish and my mind so cloudy and befogged, that I despaired of ever thinking clearly or feeling vividly again. "The winds are rude" in Biscay, Byron says. They are, indeed: very rude. They must have been raised in some most disorderly quarter of the globe. They pitched the waves right over our bulwarks, and now and then dashed a bucketful of water down the cabin skylight, swamping the ladies' cabin, and setting scores of bandboxes afloat. Not that there was the least actual danger ; but Mrs. ——— would not be persuaded that we were not on the brink of destruction, and wrote to friends at home a voluminous account of her feelings. There was an Irishman on board, bound to Italy, with his sister. It was his first tour, and when asked why he did not go direct, through France, he replied, with brotherly concern, that he was anxious his sister should see the Bay of Biscay.

This youth's perceptions were of such an emerald hue, that a lot of wicked Englishmen had their own fun out of him. The other day, he was trying to shave, to the great danger of slicing off his nose, as the vessel was rolling fearfully. "Why don't you have the ship headed to the wind?" said one of the Englishmen, who heard his complaints ; "she will then lie steady, and you can shave beautifully." Thereupon the Irishman sent one of the stewards upon deck with a polite message to the captain, begging him to put the vessel about for five minutes.

Towards noon of the fifth day, we saw the dark, rugged mountains that guard the north-western corner of the Spanish Peninsula. We passed the Bay of Corunna, and rounding the bold headland of Finisterre, left the Biscayan billows behind us. But the sea was still rough and the sky clouded, although the next morning the mildness of the air showed the change in our latitude. About noon that day, we made the Burlings, a cluster of rocks forty miles north of Lisbon, and just before sunset, a transient lifting of the clouds revealed the Rock of Cintra, at the mouth of the Tagus. The tall, perpendicular cliffs, and the mountain slopes behind, covered with gardens, orchards, and scattered villas and hamlets, made a grand though dim picture, which was soon hidden from our view.

On the 4th, we were nearly all day crossing the mouth of the Bay of Cadiz, and only at sunset saw Cape Trafalgar afar off, glimmering through the reddish haze. I remained on deck, as there were patches of starlight in the sky. After passing the light-house at Tarifa, the Spanish shore continued to be visible. In another hour, there was a dim, cloudy outline high above the horizon, on our right. This was the Lesser Atlas, in Morocco. And now, right ahead, distinctly visible, though fifteen miles distant, lay a colossal lion, with his head on his outstretched paws, looking towards Africa. If I had been brought to the spot blindfolded, I should have known what it was. The resemblance is certainly very striking, and the light-house on Europa Point seemed to be a lamp held in his paws. The lights of the city and fortifications rose one by one, glittering along the base, and at midnight we dropped anchor before them on the western side.

I landed yesterday morning. The mists, which had followed me from England, had collected behind the Rock, and the sun, still hidden by its huge bulk, shone upwards through them, making a luminous background, against which the lofty walls and jagged ramparts of this tremendous natural fortification were clearly defined. I announced my name, and the length of time I designed remaining, at a little office on the quay, and was then allowed to pass into the city. A number of familiar white turbans met me on entering, and I could not resist the temptation of cordially saluting the owners in their own language. The town is long and narrow, lying steeply against the Rock. The houses are white, yellow and pink, as in Spanish towns, but the streets are clean and well paved. There is a square, about the size of an ordinary building-lot, where a sort of market of dry goods and small articles is held The "Club-House Hotel" occupies one side of it; and, as I look out of my window upon it, I see the topmost cliffs of the Rock above me, threatening to topple down from a height of 1,500 feet

My first walk in Gibraltar was in search of a palm-tree. After threading the whole length of the town, I found two small ones in a garden, in the bottom of the old moat. The sun was shining, and his rays seemed to fall with double warmth on their feathery crests. Three brown Spaniards, bare-armed, were drawing water with a pole and bucket, and filling the little channels which conveyed it to the distant vegetables. The sea glittered blue below; an Indian fig-tree shaded me; but, on the rock behind, an aloe lifted its blossoming stem, some twenty feet high, into the sunshine. To describe what a weight was lifted from my heart would seem foolish to those who do not know on what little things the whole tone of our spirits sometimes depends.

But if an even balance was restored yesterday, the opposite scale kicked the beam this morning. Not a speck of vapor blurred the spotless crystal of the sky, as I walked along the hanging paths of the Alameda. The sea was dazzling ultramarine, with a purple lustre; every crag and notch of the mountains across the bay, every shade of brown or gray, or the green of grassy patches, was drawn and tinted with a pencil so exquisitely delicate as almost to destroy the perspective. The white houses of Algeciras, five miles off, appeared close at hand: a little toy-town, backed by miniature hills. Apes' Hill, the ancient Abyla, in Africa, advanced to meet Calpe, its opposing pillar, and Atlas swept away to the eastward, its blue becoming paler and paler, till the powers of vision finally failed. From the top of the southern point of the Rock, I saw the mountain-shore of Spain, as far as Malaga, and the snowy top of one of the Sierra Nevada. Looking eastward to the horizon line of the Mediterranean, my sight extended so far, in the wonderful clearness of the air, that the convexity of the earth's surface was plainly to be seen. The sea, instead of being a plane, was slightly convex, and the sky, instead of resting upon it at the horizon, curved down beyond it, as the upper side of a horn curves over the lower, when one looks into the mouth. There is none of the many aspects of Nature more grand than this, which is so rarely seen, that I believe the only person who has ever described it is Humboldt, who saw it, looking from the Silla de Caraccas over the Caribbean Sea. It gives you the impression of standing on the edge of the earth, and looking off into space. From the mast-head, the ocean appears either flat or slightly concave, and æronauts declare that this apparent concavity becomes more marked, the higher they ascend. It is only at those rare periods when the air is so miraculously clear as to produce the effect of *no air*—rendering impossible the slightest optical illusion—that our eyes can see things as they really are. So pure was the atmosphere to-day, that, at meridian, the moon, although a thin sickle, three days distant from the sun, shone perfectly white and clear.

As I loitered in the Alameda, between thick hedges of ever-blooming geraniums, clumps of heliotrope three feet high, and luxuriant masses of ivy, around whose warm flowers the bees clustered and hummed, I could only think of the voyage as a hideous dream. The fog and gloom had been in my own eyes and in my own brain, and now the blessed sun, shining full in my face, awoke me. I am a worshipper of the Sun. I took off my hat to him, as I stood there, in a wilderness of white, crimson, and purple flowers, and let him blaze away in my face for a quarter of an hour. And as I walked home with my back to him, I often turned my face from side to side that I might feel his touch on my cheek. How a man can live, who is sentenced to a year's imprisonment, is more than I can understand.

But all this (you will say) gives you no picture of Gibraltar. The Rock is so familiar to all the world, in prints and descriptions, that I find nothing new to say of it, except that it is by no means so barren a rock as the island of Malta, being clothed, in many places, with beautiful groves and the greenest turf; besides, I have not yet seen the rock-galleries, having taken passage for Cadiz this afternoon. When I return—as I hope to do in twenty days, after visiting Seville and Granada—I shall procure permission to view all the fortifications, and likewise to ascend to the summit.

CHAPTER XXXIII.

CADIZ AND SEVILLE.

Voyage to Cadiz—Landing—The City—Its Streets—The Women of Cadiz—Embarkation for Seville—Scenery of the Guadalquivir—Custom House Examination—The Guide—The Streets of Seville—The Giralda—The Cathedral of Seville—The Alcazar—Moorish Architecture—Pilate's House—Morning View from the Giralda—Old Wine—Murillos—My Last Evening in Seville.

"The walls of Cadiz front the shore,
And shimmer o'er the sea." R. H. STODDARD.

"Beautiful Seville!
Of which I've dreamed, until I saw its towers
In every cloud that hid the setting sun." GEORGE H. BOKER.

SEVILLE, *November* 10, 1852.

I LEFT Gibraltar on the evening of the 6th, in the steamer Iberia. The passage to Cadiz was made in nine hours, and we came to anchor in the harbor before day-break. It was a cheerful picture that the rising sun presented to us. The long white front of the city, facing the East, glowed with a bright rosy lustre, on a ground of the clearest blue. The tongue of land on which Cadiz stands is low, but the houses are lifted by the heavy sea-wall which encompasses them. The main-land consists of a range of low but graceful hills, while in the south-east the mountains of Ronda rise at some distance. I went immediately on shore, where my carpet-bag was seized upon by a boy, with the rich brown complexion of one of Murillo's beggars, who trudged off with it to the gate. After some little detention there, I was conducted to a long, deserted, barn-like building, where I waited half an hour before the proper officer came. When the latter had taken his private toll of my contraband cigars, the brown imp conducted me to Blanco's English Hotel, a neat and comfortable house on the Alameda.

Cadiz is soon seen. Notwithstanding its venerable age of three thousand years—having been founded by Hercules, who figures on its coat-of-arms—it is purely a commercial city, and has neither antiquities, nor historic associations that interest any but Englishmen. It is compactly built, and covers a smaller space than accords with my ideas of its former splen-dor. I first walked around the sea-ramparts, enjoying the glorious look-off over the blue waters. The city is almost insulated, the triple line of fortifications on the land side being of but trifling length. A rocky ledge stretches out into the sea from the northern point, and at its extremity rises the massive light-house tower, 170 feet high. The walls toward the sea were covered with companies of idle anglers, fishing with cane rods of enormous length. On the open, waste spaces between the bastions, boys had spread their limed cords to catch singing birds, with chirping decoys placed here and there in wicker cages. Numbers of boatmen and peasants, in their brown jackets, studded with tags and bugles, and those round black caps which resemble smashed bandboxes, loitered about the walls or lounged on the grass in the sun.

Except along the Alameda, which fronts the bay, the exterior of the city has an aspect of neglect and desertion The interior, however, atones for this in the gay and lively air of its streets, which, though narrow, are regular and charmingly clean. The small plazas are neatness itself, and one is too content with this to ask for striking architectural effects. The houses are tall and stately, of the most dazzling whiteness, and though you could point out no one as a pattern of style, the general effect is chaste and harmonious. In fact, there are two or three streets which you would almost pronounce faultless. The numbers of hanging balconies and of court-yards paved with marble and surrounded with elegant corridors, show the influence of Moorish taste. There is not a mean-looking house to be seen, and I have no doubt that Cadiz is the best built city of its size in the world. It lies, white as new-fallen snow, like a cluster of ivory palaces, between sea and sky. Blue and silver are its colors, and, as everybody knows, there can be no more charming contrast.

I visited both the old and new cathedrals, neither of which is particularly interesting. The latter is unfinished, and might have been a fine edifice had the labor and money expended on its construction been directed by taste. The interior, rich as it is in marbles and sculpture, has a heavy, confused effect. The pillars dividing the nave from the side-aisles are enormous composite masses, each one consisting of six Corinthian columns, stuck around and against a central shaft. More satisfactory to me was the Opera-House, which I visited in the evening, and where the dazzling array of dark-eyed Gaditanas put a stop to architectural criticism. The women of Cadiz are noted for their beauty and their graceful gait. Some of them are very beautiful, it is true ; but beauty is not the rule among them. Their gait, however, is the most graceful possible, because it is perfectly free and natural. The commonest serving-maid who walks the streets of Cadiz would put to shame a whole score of our mincing and wriggling belles.

Honest old Blanco prepared me a cup of chocolate by sunrise next morning, and accompanied me down to the quay, to embark for Seville. A furious wind was blowing from the south-east, and the large green waves raced and chased one another incessantly over the surface of the bay. I took a heavy craft, which the boatmen pushed along under cover of the pier, until they reached the end, when the sail was dropped in the face of the wind, and away we shot into the watery tumult. The boat rocked and bounced over the agitated surface, running with one gunwale on the waves, and sheets of briny spray broke over me. I felt considerably relieved when I reached the deck of the steamer, but it was then diversion enough to watch those who followed. The crowd of boats pitching tumultuously around the steamer, jostling against each other, their hulls gleaming with wet, as they rose on the beryl-colored waves, striped with long, curdled lines of wind-blown foam, would have made a fine subject for the pencil of Achenbach.

At last we pushed off, with a crowd of passengers fore and aft, and a pyramid of luggage piled around the smoke-pipe. There was a party of four Englishmen on board, and, on making their acquaintance, I found one of them to be a friend to some of my friends—Sir John Potter, the progressive ex-Mayor of Manchester. The wind being astern, we ran rapidly along the coast, and in two hours entered the mouth of the Guadalquivir. [This name comes from the Arabic *wadi el-kebeer*—literally, the Great Valley.] The shores are a dead flat. The right bank is a dreary forest of stunted pines, abounding with deer and other game ; on the left is the dilapidated town of San Lucar, whence Magellan set sail on his first voyage around the world. A mile further is Bonanza, the port of Xeres, where we touched and took on board a fresh lot of passengers. Thenceforth, for four hours, the scenery of the Guadalquivir had a most distressing sameness. The banks were as flat as a board, with here and there a straggling growth of marshy thickets. Now and then we passed a herdsman's hut, but there were no human beings to be seen, except the peasants who tended the large flocks of sheep and cattle. A sort of breakfast was served in the cabin, but so great was the number of guests that I had much difficulty in getting anything to eat. The waiters were models of calmness and deliberation.

As we approached Seville, some low hills appeared on the left, near the river. Dazzling white villages were planted at their foot, and all the slopes were covered with olive orchards, while the banks of the stream were bordered with silvery birch trees. This gave the landscape, in spite of the African warmth and brightness of the day, a gray and almost wintry aspect. Soon the graceful Giralda, or famous Tower of Seville, arose in the distance ; but, from the windings of the river, we were half an hour in reaching the landing-place. One sees nothing of the far-famed beauty of Seville, on approaching it. The boat stops below the Alameda, where the passengers are received by Custom-House officers, who, in my case, did not verify the stories told of them in Cadiz. I gave my carpet-bag to a boy, who conducted me along the hot and dusty banks to the bridge over the Guadalquivir, where he turned into the city. On passing the gate, two loafer-like guards stopped my baggage, notwithstanding it had already been examined. "What!" said I, "do you examine twice on entering Seville?" "Yes," answered one; "twice, and even three times;" but added in a lower tone, "it depends entirely on yourself." With that he slipped behind me, and let one hand fall beside my pocket. The transfer of a small coin was dexterously made, and I passed on without further stoppage to the Fonda de Madrid.

Sir John Potter engaged Antonio Bailli, the noted guide of Seville, who professes to have been the cicerone of all distinguished travellers, from Lord Byron and Washington Irving down to Owen Jones, and I readily accepted his invitation to join the party. Bailli is recommended by Ford as "fat and good-humored." Fat he certainly is, and very good-humored when speaking of himself, but he has been rather spoiled by popularity, and is much too profuse in his critical remarks on art and architecture. Nevertheless, as my stay in Seville is limited, I have derived no slight advantage from his services.

On the first morning I took an early stroll through the streets. The houses are glaringly white, like those of Cadiz, but are smaller and have not the same stately exteriors. The windows are protected by iron gratings, of florid patterns, and, as many of these are painted green, the general effect is pleasing. Almost every door opens upon a *patio*, or courtyard, paved with black and white marble and adorned with flowers and fountains. Many of these remain from the time of the Moors, and are still surrounded by the delicate arches and brilliant tile-work of that period. The populace in the streets are entirely Spanish—the jaunty *majo* in his queer black cap, sash, and embroidered jacket, and the nut-brown, dark-eyed damsel, swimming along in her mantilla, and armed with the irresistible fan.

We went first to the Cathedral, built on the site of the great mosque of Abou Youssuf Yakoub. The tall Giralda beckoned to us over the tops of the intervening buildings, and finally a turn in the street brought us to the ancient Moorish gateway on the northern side. This is an admirable specimen of the horse-shoe arch, and is covered with elaborate tracery. It originally opened into the court, or *hàram*, of the mosque, which still remains, and is shaded by a grove of orange trees. The Giralda, to my eye, is a more perfect tower than the Campanile of Florence, or that of San Marco, at Venice, which is evidently an idea borrowed from it. The Moorish structure, with a base of fifty feet square, rises to the height of two hundred and fifty feet. It is of a light pink color, and the sides, which are broken here and there by exquisitely proportioned double Saracenic arches, are covered from top to bottom with arabesque tracery, cut in strong relief. Upon this tower, a Spanish architect has placed a tapering spire, one hundred feet high, which fortunately harmonizes with the general design, and gives the crowning grace to the work.

The Cathedral of Seville may rank as one of the grandest Gothic piles in Europe. The nave lacks but five feet of being as high as that of St. Peter's, while the length and breadth of the edifice are on a commensurate scale. The ninety-three windows of stained glass fill the interior with a soft and richly-tinted light, mellower and more gentle than the sombre twilight of the Gothic Cathedrals of Europe. The wealth lavished on the smaller chapels and shrines is prodigious, and the high altar, inclosed within a gilded railing fifty feet high, is probably the most enormous mass of wood-carving in existence. The Cathedral, in fact, is encumbered with its riches. While they bewilder you as monuments of human labor and patience, they detract from the grand simplicity of the building. The great nave, on each side of the transept, is quite blocked up, so that the choir and magnificent royal chapel behind it have almost the effect of detached edifices.

We returned again this morning, remaining two hours, and succeeded in making a thorough survey, including a number of trashy pictures and barbarously rich shrines. Murillo's "Guardian Angel" and the "Vision of St. Antonio" are the only gems. The treasury contains a number of sacred vessels of silver, gold and jewels—among other things, the keys of Moorish Seville, a cross made of the first gold brought from the New-World by Columbus, and another from that robbed in Mexico by Cortez. The Cathedral won my admiration more and more. The placing of the numerous windows, and their rich coloring, produce the most glorious effects of light in the lofty aisles, and one is constantly finding new vistas, new combinations of pillar, arch and shrine. The building is in itself a treasury of the grandest Gothic pictures.

From the Cathedral we went to the Alcazar (*El-Kasr*), or Palace of the Moorish Kings. We entered by a long passage, with round arches on either side, resting on twin pillars, placed at right angles to the line of the arch, as one sees both in Saracenic and Byzantine structures. Finally, old Bailli brought us into a dull, deserted court-yard, where we were surprised by the sight of an entire Moorish façade, with its pointed arches, its projecting roof, its rich sculptured ornaments and its illuminations of red, blue, green and gold. It has been lately restored, and now rivals in freshness and brilliancy any of the rich houses of Damascus. A doorway, entirely too low and mean for the splendor of the walls above it, admitted us into the first court. On each side of the passage are the rooms of the guard and the Moorish nobles. Within, all is pure Saracenic, and absolutely perfect in its grace and richness. It is the realization of an Oriental dream ; it is the poetry and luxury of the East in tangible forms. Where so much depends on the proportion and harmony of the different parts—on those correspondences, the union of which creates that nameless soul of the work, which cannot be expressed in words—it is useless to describe details. From first to last—the chambers of state ; the fringed arches ; the open tracery, light and frail as the frost-stars crystallized on a window-pane ; the courts, fit to be vestibules to Paradise ; the audience-hall, with its wondrous sculptures, its columns and pavement of marble, and its gilded dome ; the garden, gorgeous with its palm, banana, and orange-trees—all were in perfect keeping, all jewels of equal lustre, forming a diadem which still lends a royal dignity to the phantom of Moorish power.

We then passed into the gardens laid out by the Spanish monarchs—trim, mathematical designs, in box and myrtle, with concealed fountains springing up everywhere unawares in the midst of the paven walks ; yet still made beautiful by the roses and jessamines that hung in rank clusters over the marble balustrades, and by the clumps of tall orange trees, bending to earth under the weight of their fruitage. We afterward visited Pilate's House, as it is called—a fine Span ish-Moresco palace, now belonging to the Duke of Medina Cœli. It is very rich and elegant, but stands in the same relation to the Alcazar as a good copy does to the original picture. The grand staircase, nevertheless, is a marvel of tile work, unlike anything else in Seville, and exhibits a genius in the invention of elaborate ornamental patterns, which is truly wonderful. A number of workmen were busy in restoring the palace, to fit it for the residence of the young Duke. The Moorish sculptures are reproduced in plaster, which, at least, has a better effect than the fatal whitewash under which the original tints of the Alcazar are hidden. In the courts stand a number of Roman busts—Spanish antiquities, and therefore not of great merit—singularly out of place in niches surrounded by Arabic devices and sentences from the Koran.

This morning, I climbed the Giralda. The sun had just risen, and the day was fresh and crystal-clear. A little door in the Cathedral, near the foot of the tower, stood open, and I entered. A rather slovenly Sevillaña had just completed her toilet, but two children were still in undress. However, she opened a door in the tower, and I went up without hindrance. The ascent is by easy ramps, and I walked four hundred yards, or nearly a quarter of a mile, before reaching the top of the Moorish part. The panoramic view was superb. To the east and west, the Great Valley made a level line on a far-distant horizon. There were ranges of hills in the north and south, and those rising near the city, clothed in a gray mantle of olive-trees, were picturesquely crowned with villages. The Guadalquivir, winding in the most sinuous mazes, had no longer a turbid hue; he reflected the blue morning sky, and gleamed brightly between his borders of birch and willow. Seville sparkled white and fair under my feet, her painted towers and tiled domes rising thickly out of the mass of buildings. The level sun threw shadows into the numberless courts, permitting the mixture of Spanish and Moorish architecture to be plainly discerned, even at that height. A thin golden vapor softened the features of the landscape, towards the sun, while, on the opposite side, every object stood out in the sharpest and clearest outlines.

On our way to the Muséo, Bailli took us to the house of a friend of his, in order that we might taste real Manzanilla wine. This is a pale, straw-colored vintage, produced in the valley of the Guadalquivir. It is flavored with camomile blossoms, and is said to be a fine tonic for weak stomachs The master then produced a dark-red wine, which he declared to be thirty years old. It was almost a syrup in consistence, and tasted more of sarsaparilla than grapes. None of us relished it, except Bailli, who was so inspired by the draught, that he sang us two Moorish songs and an Andalusian catch, full of fun and drollery.

The Muséo contains a great amount of bad pictures, but it also contains twenty-three of Murillo's works, many of them of his best period. To those who have only seen his tender, spiritual "Conceptions" and "Assumptions," his "Vision of St. Francis" in this gallery reveals a mastery of the higher walks of his art, which they would not have anticipated. But it is in his "Cherubs" and his "Infant Christs" that he excels. No one ever painted infantile grace and beauty with so true a pencil. There is but one Velasquez in the collection, and the only thing that interested me, in two halls filled with rubbish, was a "Conception" by Murillo's mulatto pupil, said by some to have been his slave. Although an imitation of the great master, it is a picture of much sweetness and beauty. There is no other work of the artist in existence, and this, as the only production of the kind by a painter of mixed African blood, ought to belong to the Republic of Liberia.

Among the other guests at the Fonda de Madrid is Mr. Thomas Hobhouse, brother of Byron's friend. We had a pleasant party in the Court this evening, listening to blind Pépé, who sang to his guitar a medley of merry Andalusian refrains. Singing made the old man courageous, and, at the close, he gave us the radical song of Spain, which is now strictly prohibited. The air is charming, but too gay ; one would sooner dance than fight to its measures. It does not bring the hand to the sword, like the glorious Marseillaise.

Adios, beautiful Seville !

CHAPTER XXXIV.

JOURNEY IN A SPANISH DILIGENCE.

Spanish Diligence Lines—Leaving Seville—An Unlucky Start—Alcalà of the Bakers—Dinner at Carmona—A Dehesa—The Mayoral and his Team—Ecija—Night Journey—Cordova—The Cathedral-Mosque—Moorish Architecture—The Sierra Morena—A Rainy Journey—A Chapter of Accidents—Baylen—The Fascination of Spain—Jaen—The Vega of Granada.

GRANADA, *November* 14, 1852.

It is an enviable sensation to feel for the first time that you are in Granada. No amount of travelling can weaken the romantic interest which clings about this storied place, or take away aught from the freshness of that emotion with which you first behold it. I sit almost at the foot of the Alhambra, whose walls I can see from my window, quite satisfied for to-day with being here. It has been raining since I arrived, the thunder is crashing overhead, and the mountains are covered with clouds, so I am kept in-doors, with the luxury of knowing that all the wonders of the place are within my reach. And now let me beguile the dull weather by giving you a sketch of my journey from Seville hither.

There are three lines of stages from Seville to Madrid, and their competition has reduced the fare to $12, which, for a ride of 350 miles, is remarkably cheap. The trip is usually made in three days and a half. A branch line from Baylen—nearly half-way—strikes southward to Granada, and as there is no competition on this part of the road, I was charged $15 for a through seat in the *coupé*. On account of the lateness of the season, and the limited time at my command, this was preferable to taking horses and riding across the country from Seville to Cordova. Accordingly, at an early hour on Thursday morning last, furnished with a travelling ticket inscribed : "Don Valtar de Talor (myself!), I took leave of my English friends at the Fonda de Madrid, got into an immense, lumbering yellow vehicle, drawn by ten mules, and started, trusting to my good luck and bad Spanish to get safely through. The commencement, however, was unpropitious, and very often a stumble at starting makes the whole journey limp. The near mule in the foremost span was a horse, ridden by our postillion, and nothing could prevent that horse from darting into all sorts of streets and alleys where we had no desire to go. As all mules have implicit faith in horses, of course the rest of the animals followed. We were half an hour in getting out of Seville, and when at last we reached the open road and dashed off at full gallop, one of the mules in the traces fell and was dragged in the dust some twenty or thirty yards before we could stop. My companions in the coupé were a young Spanish officer and his pretty Andalusian bride, who was making her first journey from home, and after these mishaps was in a state of constant fear and anxiety.

The first stage across the valley of the Guadalquivir took us to the town of Alcalà, which lies in the lap of the hills above the beautiful little river Guadaira. It is a picturesque spot ; the naked cliffs overhanging the stream have the rich, red hue of cinnabar, and the trees and shrubbery in the meadows, and on the hill-sides are ready grouped to the artist's hand. The town is called Alcalà de los Panadores (of the Bakers) from its hundreds of flour mills and bake-ovens, which supply Seville with those white, fine, delicious twists, of which Spain may be justly proud. They should have been sent to the Exhibition last year, with the Toledo blades and the wooden mosaics. We left the place and its mealy-headed population, and turned eastward into wide, rolling tracts, scattered here and there with gnarled olive trees. The soil was loose and sandy, and hedges of aloes lined the road. The country is thinly populated, and very little of it under cultivation.

About noon we reached Carmona, which was founded by the Romans, as, indeed, were nearly all the towns of Southern Spain. It occupies the crest and northern slope of a high hill, whereon the ancient Moorish castle still stands. The Alcazar, or palace, and the Moorish walls also remain, though in a very ruinous condition. Here we stopped to dinner, for the "Nueva Peninsular," in which I was embarked, has its hotels all along the route, like that of Zurutuza, in Mexico. We were conducted into a small room adjoining the stables, and adorned with colored prints illustrating the history of Don John of Austria. The table-cloths, plates and other appendages were of very ordinary quality, but indisputably clean; we seated ourselves, and presently the dinner appeared. First, a vermicelli *pilaff*, which I found palatable, then the national *olla*, a dish of enormous yellow peas, sprinkled with bits of bacon and flavored with oil; then three successive courses of chicken, boiled, stewed and roasted, but in every case done to rags, and without a particle of the original flavor. This was the usual style of our meals on the road, whether breakfast, dinner or supper, except that kid was sometimes substituted for fowl, and that the oil employed, being more or less rancid, gave different flavors to the dishes. A course of melons, grapes or pomegranates wound up the repast, the price of which varied from ten to twelve reals—a real being about a half-dime. In Seville, at the Fonda de Madrid, the cooking is really excellent; but further in the interior, judging from what I have heard, it is even worse than I have described.

Continuing our journey, we passed around the southern brow of the hill, under the Moorish battlements. Here a superb view opened to the south and east over the wide Vega of Carmona, as far as the mountain chain which separates it from the plain of Granada. The city has for a coat of arms a silver star in an azure field, with the pompous motto : "As Lucifer shines in the morning, so shines Carmona in Andalusia." If it shines at all, it is because it is a city set upon a hill ; for that is the only splendor I could find about the place. The Vega of Carmona is partially cultivated, and now wears a sombre brown hue, from its tracts of ploughed land.

Cultivation soon ceased, however, and we entered on a *dehesa*, a boundless plain of waste land, covered with thickets of palmettos. Flocks of goats and sheep, guarded by shepherds in brown cloaks, wandered here and there, and except their huts and an isolated house, with its group of palm-trees, there was no sign of habitation. The road was a deep, red sand, and our mules toiled along slowly and painfully, urged by the incessant cries of the *mayoral*, or conductor, and his *mozo*. As the mayoral's whip could only reach the second span, the business of the latter was to jump down every ten minutes, run ahead and belabor the flanks of the foremost mules, uttering at the same time a series of sharp howls, which seemed to strike the poor beasts with quite as much severity as his whip. I defy even a Spanish ear to distinguish the import of these cries, and the great wonder was how they could all come out of one small throat. When it came to a hard pull, they cracked and exploded like volleys of musketry, and flew like hail-stones about the ears of the *machos* (he-mules). The postillion, having only the care of the foremost span, is a silent man, but he has contracted a habit of sleeping in the saddle, which I mention for the benefit of timid travellers, as it adds to the interest of a journey by night.

The clouds which had been gathering all day, now settled down upon the plain, and night came on with a dull rain. At eight o'clock we reached the City of Ecija, where we had two hours' halt and supper. It was so dark and rainy that I saw nothing, not even the classic Xenil, the river of Granada, which flows through the city on its way to the Guadalquivir. The night wore slowly away, and while the *mozo* drowsed on his post, I caught snatches of sleep between his cries. As the landscape began to grow distinct in the gray, cloudy dawn, we saw before us Cordova, with the dark range of the Sierra Morena rising behind it. This city, once the glory of Moorish Spain, the capital of the great Abd-er-Rahman, containing, when in its prime, a million of inhabitants, is now a melancholy wreck. It has not a shadow of the art, science, and taste which then distinguished it, and the only interest it now possesses is from these associations, and the despoiled remnant of its renowned Mosque.

We crossed the Guadalquivir on a fine bridge built on Roman foundations, and drove slowly down the one long, rough, crooked street. The diligence stops for an hour, to allow passengers to breakfast, but my first thought was for the Cathedral-mosque, *la Mezquita,* as it is still called. "It is closed," said the ragged crowd that congregated about us; "you cannot get in until eight o'clock." But I remembered that a silver key will open anything in Spain, and taking a mozo as a guide we hurried off as fast as the rough pavements would permit. We had to retrace the whole length of the city, but on reaching the Cathedral, found it open. The exterior is low, and quite plain, though of great extent. A Moorish gateway admitted me into the original court-yard, or *haram,* of the mosque, which is planted with orange trees and contains the fountain, for the ablutions of Moslem worshippers, in the centre. The area of the Mosque proper, exclusive of the court-yard, is about 400 by 350 feet. It was built on the plan of the great Mosque of Damascus, about the end of the eighth century. The materials—including twelve hundred columns of marble, jasper and porphyry, from the ruins of Carthage, and the temples of Asia Minor—belonged to a Christian basilica, of the Gothic domination, which was built upon the foundations of a Roman temple of Janus; so that the three great creeds of the world have here at different times had their seat. The Moors considered this mosque as second in holiness to the Kaaba of Mecca, and made pilgrimages to it from all parts of Moslem Spain and Barbary. Even now, although shorn of much of its glory, it surpasses any Oriental mosque into which I have penetrated, except St. Sophia, which is a Christian edifice.

All the nineteen original entrances—beautiful horse-shoe arches—are closed, except the central one. I entered by a low door, in one corner of the corridor. A wilderness of columns connected by double arches (one springing above the other, with an opening between), spread their dusky aisles before me in the morning twilight. The eight hundred and fifty shafts of this marble forest formed labyrinths and mazes, which at that early hour appeared boundless, for their long vistas disappeared in the shadows. Lamps were burning before distant shrines, and a few worshippers were kneeling silently here and there. The sound of my own footsteps, as I wandered through the ranks of pillars, was all that I heard. In the centre of the wood (for such it seemed) rises the choir, a gaudy and tasteless excrescence added by the Christians. Even Charles V., who laid a merciless hand on the Alhambra, reproved the Bishop of Cordova for this barbarous and unnecessary disfigurement.

The sacristan lighted lamps in order to show me the Moorish chapels. Nothing but the precious materials of which these exquisite structures are composed could have saved them from the holy hands of the Inquisition, which intentionally destroyed all the Roman antiquities of Cordova. Here the fringed arches, the lace-like filigrees, the wreathed inscriptions, and the domes of pendent stalactites which enchant you in the Alcazar of Seville, are repeated, not in stucco, but in purest marble, while the entrance to the "holy of holies" is probably the most glorious piece of mosaic in the world. The pavement of the interior is deeply worn by the knees of the Moslem pilgrims, who compassed it seven times, kneeling, as they now do in the Kaaba, at Mecca. The sides are embroidered with sentences from the Koran, in Cufic characters, and the roof is in the form of a fluted shell, of a single piece of pure white marble, fifteen feet in diameter. The roof of the vestibule is a wonderful piece of workmanship, formed of pointed arches, wreathed and twined through each other, like basket-work. No people ever wrought poetry into stone so perfectly as the Saracens. In looking on these precious relics of an elegant and refined race, I cannot help feeling a strong regret that their kingdom ever passed into other hands.

Leaving Cordova, our road followed the Guadalquivir, along the foot of the Sierra Morena, which rose dark and stern, a barrier to the central table-lands of La Mancha. At Alcolea, we crossed the river on a noble bridge of black marble, out of all keeping with the miserable road. It rained incessantly, and the scenery through which we passed had a wild and gloomy character. The only tree to be seen was the olive, which covered the hills far and near, the profusion of its fruit showing the natural richness of the soil. This part of the road is sometimes infested with robbers, and once, when I saw two individuals waiting for us in a lonely defile, with gun-barrels thrust out from under their black cloaks, I anticipated a recurrence of a former unpleasant experience. But they proved to be members of the *guardia civil*, and therefore our protectors.

The ruts and quagmires, made by the rain, retarded our progress, and it was dark when we reached Andujar, fourteen leagues from Cordova. To Baylen, where I was to quit the diligence, and take another coming down from Madrid to Granada, was four leagues further. We journeyed on in the dark, in a pouring rain, up and down hill for some hours, when all at once the cries of the mozo ceased, and the diligence came to a dead stop. There was some talk between our conductors, and then the mayoral opened the door and invited us to get out. The postillion had fallen asleep, and the mules had taken us into a wrong road. An attempt was made to turn the diligence, but failed, leaving it standing plump against a high bank of mud. We stood, meanwhile, shivering in the cold and wet, and the fair Andalusian shed abundance of tears. Fortunately, Baylen was close at hand, and, after some delay, two men came with lanterns and escorted us to the *posada*, or inn, where we arrived at midnight. The diligence from Madrid, which was due six hours before, had not made its appearance, and we passed the rest of the night in a cold room, fasting, for the meal was only to be served when the other passengers came. At day-break, finally, a single dish of oily meat was vouchsafed to us, and, as it was now certain that some accident had happened, the passengers to Madrid requested the *Administrador* to send them on in an extra conveyance. This he refused, and they began to talk about getting up a pronunciamento, when a messenger arrived with the news that the diligence had broken down at midnight, about two leagues off. Tools were thereupon dispatched, nine hours after the accident happened, and we might hope to be released from our imprisonment in four or five more.

Baylen is a wretched place, celebrated for having the first palm-tree which those see who come from Madrid, and for the victory gained by Castaños over the French forces under Dupont, which occasioned the flight of Joseph Buonaparte from Madrid, and the temporary liberation of Spain from the French yoke. Castaños, who received the title of Duke de

Baylen, and is compared by the Spaniards to Wellington, died about three months ago. The battle-field I passed in the night; the palm-tree I found, but it is now a mere stump, the leaves having been stripped off to protect the houses of the inhabitants from lightning. Our posada had one of them hung at the window. At last, the diligence came, and at three P.M., when I ought to have been in sight of Granada, I left the forlorn walls of Baylen. My fellow-passengers were a young sprig of the Spanish nobility and three chubby-faced nuns.

The rest of the journey that afternoon was through a wide, hilly region, entirely bare of trees and habitations, and but partially cultivated. There was something sublime in its very nakedness and loneliness, and I felt attracted to it as I do towards the Desert. In fact, although I have seen little fine scenery since leaving Seville, have had the worst of weather, and no very pleasant travelling experiences, the country has exercised a fascination over me, which I do not quite understand. I find myself constantly on the point of making a vow to return again. Much to my regret, night set in before we reached Jaen, the capital of the Moorish kingdom of that name. We halted for a short time in the large plaza of the town, where the dash of fountains mingled with the sound of the rain, and the black, jagged outline of a mountain overhanging the place was visible through the storm.

All night we journeyed on through the mountains, sometimes splashing through swollen streams, sometimes coming almost to a halt in beds of deep mud. When this morning dawned, we were ascending through wild, stony hills, overgrown with shrubbery, and the driver said we were six leagues from Granada. Still on, through a lonely country, with now and then a large *venta*, or country inn, by the road-side, and about nine o'clock, as the sky became more clear, I saw in front of us, high up under the clouds, the snow-fields of the Sierra Nevada. An hour afterwards we were riding between gardens, vineyards, and olive orchards, with the magnificent Vega of Granada stretching far away on the right, and the Vermilion Towers of the Alhambra crowning the heights before us.

CHAPTER XXXV.

GRANADA AND THE ALHAMBRA.

Mateo Ximenez, the Younger—The Cathedral of Granada—A Monkish Miracle—Catholic Shrines—Military Cherubs—The Royal Chapel—The Tombs of Ferdinand and Isabella—Chapel of San Juan de Dios—The Albaycin—View of the Vega—The Generalife—The Alhambra—Torra de la Vela—The Walls and Towers—A Visit to Old Mateo—The Court of the Fish-pond—The Halls of the Alhambra—Character of the Architecture—Hall of the Abencerrages—Hall of the Two Sisters—The Moorish Dynasty in Spain.

"Who has not in Granada been,
Verily, he has nothing seen."
Andalusian Proverb.

GRANADA, *Wednesday, Nov.* 17, 1852.

IMMEDIATELY on reaching here, I was set upon by an old gentleman who wanted to act as guide, but the mozo of the hotel put into my hand a card inscribed "Don Mateo Ximenez, Guide to the celebrated Washington Irving," and I dismissed the other applicant. The next morning, as the mozo brought me my chocolate, he said; "Señor, *el chico* is waiting for you." The "little one" turned out to be the son of old Mateo, "honest Mateo," who still lives up in the Alhambra, but is now rather too old to continue his business, except on great occasions. I accepted the young Mateo, who spoke with the greatest enthusiasm of Mr. Irving, avowing that the whole family was devoted to him, in life and death. It was still raining furiously, and the golden Darro, which roars in front of the hotel, was a swollen brown flood. I don't wonder that he sometimes threatens, as the old couplet says, to burst up the Zacatin, and bear it down to his bride, the Xenil.

Towards noon, the clouds broke away a little, and we sallied out. Passing through the gate and square of Vivarrambla (may not this name come from the Arabic *bab er-raml*, the "gate of the sand?"), we soon reached the Cathedral. This massive structure, which makes a good feature in the distant view of Granada, is not at all imposing, near at hand. The interior is a mixture of Gothic and Roman, glaring with whitewash, and broken, like that of Seville, by a wooden choir and two grand organs, blocking up the nave. Some of the side chapels, nevertheless, are splendid masses of carving and gilding. In one of them, there are two full-length portraits of Ferdinand and Isabella, supposed to be by Alonzo Cano. The Cathedral contains some other good pictures by the same master, but all its former treasures were carried off by the French.

We next went to the Picture Gallery, which is in the Franciscan Convent. There are two small Murillos, much damaged, some tolerable Alonzo Canos, a few common-place pictures by Juan de Sevilla, and a hundred or more by authors whose names I did not inquire, for a more hideous collection of trash never met my eye. One of them represents a miracle performed by two saints, who cut off the diseased leg of a sick white man, and replace it by the sound leg of a dead negro, whose body is seen lying beside the bed. Judging from the ghastly face of the patient, the operation is rather painful, though the story goes that the black leg grew fast, and the man recovered. The picture at least illustrates the absence of "prejudice of color" among the Saints.

We went into the adjoining Church of Santo Domingo, which has several very rich shrines of marble and gold. A sort of priestly sacristan opened the Church of the Madonna del Rosario—a glittering mixture of marble, gold, and looking-glasses, which has rather a rich effect. The beautiful yellow and red veined marbles are from the Sierra Nevada. The sacred Madonna—a big doll with staring eyes and pink cheeks—has a dress of silver, shaped like an extinguisher, and encrusted with rubies and other precious stones. The utter absence of taste in most Catholic shrines is an extraordinary thing. It seems remarkable that a Church which has produced so many glorious artists should so constantly and grossly violate the simplest rules of art. The only shrine which I have seen, which was in keeping with the object adored, is that of the Virgin, at Nazareth, where there is neither picture nor image, but only vases of fragrant flowers, and perfumed oil in golden lamps, burning before a tablet of spotless marble.

Among the decorations of the chapel, there are a host of cherubs frescoed on the ceiling, and one of them is represented in the act of firing off a blunderbuss. "Is it true that the angels carry blunderbusses?" I asked the priest. He shrugged his shoulders with a sort of half-smile, and said nothing. In the Cathedral, on the plinths of the columns in the outer aisles, are several notices to the effect that "whoever speaks to women, either in the nave or the aisles, thereby puts himself in danger of excommunication." I could not help laughing, as I read this monkish and yet most *un*monk-like statute.

"Oh," said Mateo, "all that was in the despotic times; it is not so now."

A deluge of rain put a stop to my sight-seeing until the next morning, when I set out with Mateo to visit the Royal Chapel. A murder had been committed in the night, near the entrance of the Zacatin, and the paving-stones were still red with the blood of the victim. A *funcion* of some sort was going on in the Chapel, and we went into the sacristy to wait. The priests and choristers were there, changing their robes; they saluted me good-humoredly, though there was an expression in their faces that plainly said: "a heretic!" When the service was concluded, I went into the chapel and examined the high altar, with its rude wood-carvings, representing the surrender of Granada. The portraits of Ferdinand and Isabella, Cardinal Ximenez, Gonzalvo of Cordova, and King Boabdil, are very curious. Another tablet represents the baptism of the conquered Moors.

In the centre of the chapel stand the monuments erected to Ferdinand and Isabella, and their successors Philip I., and Maria, by Charles V. They are tall catafalques of white marble, superbly sculptured, with the full length effigies of the monarchs upon them. The figures are admirable; that of Isabella, especially, though the features are settled in the repose of death, expresses all the grand and noble traits which belonged to her character. The sacristan removed the matting from a part of the floor, disclosing an iron grating underneath. A damp, mouldly smell, significant of death and decay, came up through the opening. He lighted two long waxen tapers, lifted the grating, and I followed him down the narrow steps into the vault where lie the coffins of the Catholic Sovereigns. They were brought here from the Alhambra, in 1525. The leaden sarcophagi, containing the bodies of Ferdinand and Isabella, lie, side by side, on stone slabs ; and as I stood between the two, resting a hand on each, the sacristan placed the tapers in apertures in the stone, at the head and foot. They sleep, as they wished, in their beloved Granada, and no profane hand has ever disturbed the repose of their ashes.

After visiting the Church of San Jeronimo, founded by Gonzalvo of Cordova, I went to the adjoining Church and Hospital of San Juan de Dios. A fat priest, washing his hands in the sacristy, sent a boy to show me the Chapel of San Juan, and the relics. The remains of the Saint rest in a silver chest, standing in the centre of a richly-adorned chapel. Among the relics is a thorn from the crown of Christ, which, as any botanist may see, must have grown on a different plant from the other thorn they show at Seville ; and neither kind is found in Palestine. The true *spina christi*, the nebbuk, has very small thorns; but nothing could be more cruel, as I found when riding through patches of it near Jericho. The boy also showed me a tooth of San Lorenzo, a crooked brown *bicuspis*, from which I should infer that the saint was rather an ill-favored man. The gilded chapel of San Juan is in singular contrast with one of the garments which he wore when living —a cowl of plaited reeds, looking like an old fish basket— which is kept in a glass case. His portrait is also to be seen · a mild and beautiful face, truly that of one who went about doing good. He was a sort of Spanish John Howard, and deserved canonization, if anybody ever did.

I ascended the street of the Darro to the Albaycin, which

we entered by one of the ancient gates. This suburb is still surrounded by the original fortifications, and undermined by the capacious cisterns of the Moors. It looks down on Granada; and from the crumbling parapets there are superb views over the city, the Vega, and its inclosing mountains. The Alhambra rose opposite, against the dark-red and purple background of the Sierra Nevada, and a canopy of heavy rain-clouds rested on all the heights. A fitful gleam of sunshine now and then broke through and wandered over the plain, touching up white towers and olive groves and reaches of the winding Xenil, with a brilliancy which suggested the splendor of the whole picture, if once thus restored to its proper light. I could see Santa Fé in the distance, toward Loxa; nearer, and more eastward, the Sierra de Elvira, of a deep violet color, with the woods of the Soto de Roma, the Duke of Wellington's estate, at its base; and beyond it the Mountain of Parapanda, the weather-guage of Granada, still covered with clouds. There is an old Granadian proverb which says:—"When Parapanda wears his bonnet, it will rain whether God wills it or no." From the chapel of San Miguel, above the Albaycin, there is a very striking view of the deep gorge of the Darro, at one's feet, with the gardens and white walls of the Generalife rising beyond, and the Silla del Moro and the Mountain of the Sun towering above it. The long, irregular lines of the Alhambra, with the huge red towers rising here and there, reminded me somewhat of a distant view of Karnak; and, like Karnak, the Alhambra is picturesque from whatever point it is viewed.

We descended through wastes of cactus to the Darro, in whose turbid stream a group of men were washing for gold. I watched one of them, as he twirled his bowl in precisely the California style, but got nothing for his pains. Mateo says that they often make a dollar a day, each. Passing under the Tower of Comares and along the battlements of the Alhambra, we climbed up to the Generalife. This charming villa is still in good preservation, though its exquisite filigree and scroll-work have been greatly injured by whitewash. The elegant colonnades surround gardens rich in roses, myrtles and cypresses, and the fountains that lulled the Moorish Kings in their summer idleness still pour their fertilizing streams. In one of the rooms is a small and bad portrait gallery, containing a supposed portrait of Boabdil. It is a mild, amiable face, but wholly lacks strength of character.

To-day I devoted to the Alhambra. The storm, which, as the people say, has not been equalled for several years, showed no signs of breaking up, and in the midst of a driving shower I ascended to the Vermilion Towers, which are supposed to be of Phœnician origin. They stand on the extremity of a long, narrow ledge, which stretches out like an arm from the hill of the Alhambra. The *paseo* lies between, and is shaded by beautiful elms, which the Moors planted.

I entered the Alhambra by the Gate of Justice, which is a fine specimen of Moorish architecture, though of common red brick and mortar. It is singular what a grace the horse-shoe arch gives to the most heavy and lumbering mass of masonry. The round arches of the Christian edifices of Granada seem tame and inelegant, in comparison. Over the arch of the vestibule of this gate is the colossal hand, and over the inner entrance the key, celebrated in the tales of Washington Irving and the superstitions of the people. I first ascended the Torre de la Vela, where the Christian flag was first planted on the 2d of January, 1492. The view of the Vega and City of Granada was even grander than from the Albaycin. Parapanda was still bonneted in clouds, but patches of blue sky began to open above the mountains of Loxa. A little boy accompanied us, to see that I did not pull the bell, the sound of which would call together all the troops in the city. While we stood there, the funeral procession of the man murdered two nights before came up the street of Gomerez, and passed around the hill under the Vermilion Towers.

I made the circuit of the walls before entering the Palace. In the Place of the Cisterns, I stopped to take a drink of the cool water of the Darro, which is brought thither by subterranean channels from the hills. Then, passing the ostentatious pile commenced by Charles V., but which was never finished, and never will be, nor ought to be, we walked along the southern ramparts to the Tower of the Seven Floors, amid the ruins of which I discerned the top of the arch by which the unfortunate Boabdil quitted Granada, and which was thenceforth closed for ever. In the Tower of the Infantas, a number of workmen were busy restoring the interior, which has been cruelly damaged. The brilliant *azulejo*, or tile-work, the delicate arches and filigree sculpture of the walls, still attest its former elegance, and give some color to the tradition that it was the residence of the Moorish Princesses.

As we passed through the little village which still exists among the ruins of the fortress, Mateo invited me to step in and see his father, the genuine "honest Mateo," immortalized in the "Tales of the Alhambra." The old man has taken up the trade of silk-weaving, and had a number of gay-colored ribbons on his loom. He is more than sixty years old and now quite gray-headed, but has the same simple manners, the same honest face that attracted his temporary master. He spoke with great enthusiasm of Mr. Irving, and brought out from a place of safety the "Alhambra" and the "Chronicles of the Conquest," which he has carefully preserved. He then produced an Andalusian sash, the work of his own hands, which he insisted on binding around my waist, to see how it would look. I must next take off my coat and hat, and put on his Sunday jacket and jaunty sombrero. "*Por Dios!*" he exclaimed: "*que buen mozo!* Señor, you are a legitimate Andalusian!" After this, of course, I could do no less than buy the sash. "You must show it to Washington Irving," said he, "and tell him it was made by Mateo's own hands;" which I promised. I must then go into the kitchen, and eat a pomegranate from his garden—a glorious pomegranate, with kernels of crimson, and so full of blood that you could not touch them but it trickled through your fingers. El Marques, a sprightly dog, and a great slate-colored cat, took possession of my legs, and begged for a share of every mouthful I took, while old Mateo sat beside me, rejoicing in the flavor of a Gibraltar cigar which I gave him. But my time was precious, and so I let the "Son of the Alhambra" go back to his loom, and set out for the Palace of the Moorish Kings.

This palace is so hidden behind the ambitious shell of that of Charles V. that I was at a loss where it could be. I thought I had compassed the hill, and yet had seen no indications of the renowned magnificence of the Alhambra. But a little door in a blank wall ushered me into a true Moorish realm, the Court of the Fishpond, or of the Myrtles, as it is sometimes called. Here I saw again the slender pillars, the fringed and embroidered arches, and the perforated, lace-like tracery of the fairy corridors. Here, hedges of roses and myrtles still bloomed around the ancient tank, wherein hundreds of gold-fish disported. The noises of the hill do not penetrate here, and the solitary porter who admitted me went back to his post, and suffered me to wander at will through the enchanted halls.

I passed out of this court by an opposite door, and saw, through the vistas of marble pillars and the wonderful fret-work which seems a thing of air rather than of earth, the Fountain of the Lions. Thence I entered in succession the Hall of the Abencerrages, the Hall of the Two Sisters, the apartments of the Sultanas, the Mosque, and the Hall of the Ambassadors. These places—all that is left of the renowned palace—are now well kept, and carefully guarded. Restorations are going on, here and there, and the place is scrupulously watched, that no foreign Vandal may further injure what the native Goths have done their best to destroy. The rubbish has been cleared away; the rents in the walls have been filled up, and, for the first time since it passed into Spanish hands, there seems a hope that the Alhambra will be allowed to stand. What has been already destroyed we can only partially conjecture; but no one sees what remains without completing the picture in his own imagination, and placing it among the most perfect and marvellous creations of human genius.

Nothing can exceed the richness of invention which, in this series of halls, corridors, and courts, never repeats the same ornaments, but, from the simplest primitive forms and colors, produces a thousand combinations, not one of which is in discord with the grand design. It is useless to attempt a detailed description of this architecture; and it is so unlike anything else in the world, that, like Karnak and Baalbec, those only know the Alhambra who see it. When you can weave stone, and hang your halls with marble tapestry, you may rival it. It is nothing to me that these ornaments are stucco; to sculpture them in marble is only the work of the hands. Their great excellence is in the design, which, like all great things, suggests even more than it gives. If I could create all that the Court of Lions suggested to me for its completion, it would fulfil the dream of King Sheddad, and surpass the palaces of the Moslem Paradise.

The pavilions of the Court of Lions, and the halls which open into it, on either side, approach the nearest to their original perfection. The floors are marble, the wainscoting of painted tiles, the walls of embroidery, still gleaming with the softened lustre of their original tints, and the lofty conical domes seem to be huge sparry crystalizations, hung with dropping stalactites, rather than any work of the human hand. Each of these domes is composed of five thousand separate pieces, and the pendent prismatic blocks, colored and gilded, gradually resolve themselves, as you gaze, into the most intricate and elegant designs. But you must study long ere you have won all the secret of their beauty. To comprehend them, one should spend a whole day, lying on his back, under each one. Mateo spread his cloak for me in the fountain in the Hall of the Abencerrages, over the blood-stains made by the decapitation of those gallant chiefs, and I lay half an hour looking upward: and this is what I made out of the dome. From its central pinnacle hung the chalice of a flower with feathery petals, like the "crape myrtle" of our Southern States Outside of this, branched downward the eight rays of a large star, whose points touched the base of the dome ; yet the star was itself composed of flowers, while between its rays and around its points fell a shower of blossoms, shells, and sparry drops. From the base of the dome hung a gorgeous pattern of lace, with a fringe of bugles, projecting into eight points so as to form a star of drapery, hanging from the points of the flowery star in the dome. The spaces between the angles were filled with masses of stalactites, dropping one below the other, till they tapered into the plain square sides of the hall.

In the Hall of the Two Sisters, I lay likewise for a considerable time, resolving its misty glories into shape. The dome was still more suggestive of flowers. The highest and central piece was a deep trumpet-flower, whose mouth was cleft into eight petals. It hung in the centre of a superb lotus-cup, the leaves of which were exquisitely veined and chased. Still further below swung a mass of mimosa blossoms, intermixed with pods and lance-like leaves, and around the base of the dome opened the bells of sixteen gorgeous tulips. These pictures may not be very intelligible, but I know not how else to paint the effect of this fairy architecture.

In Granada, as in Seville and Cordova, one's sympathies are wholly with the Moors. The few mutilated traces which still remain of their power, taste, and refinement, surpass any of the monuments erected by the race which conquered them. The Moorish Dynasty in Spain was truly, as Irving observes, a splendid exotic, doomed never to take a lasting root in the soil It was choked to death by the native weeds ; and, in place of lands richly cultivated and teeming with plenty, we now have barren and almost depopulated wastes—in place of education, industry, and the cultivation of the arts and sciences, an enslaved, ignorant and degenerate race. Andalusia would be far more prosperous at this day, had she remained in Moslem hands. True, she would not have received that Faith which is yet destined to be the redemption of the world, but the doctrines of Mahomet are more acceptable to God, and more beneficial to Man than those of that Inquisition, which, in Spain alone, has shed ten times as much Christian blood as all the Moslem races together for the last six centuries. It is not from a mere romantic interest that I lament the fate of Boabdil, and the extinction of his dynasty. Had he been a king worthy to reign in those wonderful halls, he never would have left them. Had he perished there, fighting to the last, he would have been freed from forty years of weary exile and an obscure death. Well did Charles V. observe, when speaking of him: "Better a tomb in the Alhambra than a palace in the Alpujarras!"

CHAPTER XXXVI.

THE BRIDLE-ROADS OF ANDALUSIA.

Change of Weather—Napoleon and his Horses—Departure from Granada—My Guide, José Garcia—His Domestic Troubles—The Tragedy of the Umbrella—The Vow againts Aguardiente—Crossing the Vega—The Sierra Nevada—The Baths of Alhama—"Woe is Me, Alhama!"—The Valley of the River Velez—Velez Malaga—The Coast Road—The Fisherman and his Donkey—Malaga—Summer Scenery—The Story of Don Pedro, without Fear and without Care—The Field of Monda—A Lonely Venta.

VENTA DE VILLALON, *November* 20, 1852.

THE clouds broke away before I had been two hours in the Alhambra, and the sunshine fell broad and warm into its courts. They must be roofed with blue sky, in order to give the full impression of their brightness and beauty. Mateo procured me a bottle of *vino rancio*, and we drank it together in the Court of Lions. Six hours had passed away before I knew it, and I reluctantly prepared to leave. The clouds by this time had disappeared; the Vega slept in brilliant sunshine, and the peaks of the Sierra Nevada shone white and cold against the sky.

On reaching the hotel, I found a little man, nicknamed Napoleon, awaiting me. He was desirous to furnish me with horses, and, having a prophetic knowledge of the weather, promised me a bright sky as far as Gibraltar. "I furnish all the señors," said he; "they know me, and never complain of me or my horses;" but, by way of security, on making the bargain, I threatened to put up a card in the hotel at Gibraltar, warning all travellers against him, in case I was not satisfied. My contract was for two horses and a guide, who were to be ready at sunrise the next morning. Napoleon was as good as his word; and before I had finished an early cup of chocolate, there was a little black Andalusian stallion awaiting me. The *alforjas*, or saddle-bags, of the guide were strengthened by a stock of cold provisions, the leathern *bota* hanging beside it was filled with ripe Granada wine; and now behold me ambling over the Vega, accoutred in a gay Andalusian jacket, a sash woven by Mateo Ximenes, and one of those bandboxy sombreros, which I at first thought so ungainly, but now consider quite picturesque and elegant.

My guide, a short but sinewy and well-knit son of the mountains, named José Garcia, set off at a canter down the banks of the Darro. "Don't ride so fast!" cried Napoleon, who watched our setting out, from the door of the fonda; but José was already out of hearing. This guide is a companion to my liking. Although he is only twenty-seven, he has been for a number of years a *correo*, or mail-rider, and a guide for travelling parties. His olive complexion is made still darker by exposure to the sun and wind, and his coal-black eyes shine with Southern heat and fire. He has one of those rare mouths which are born with a broad smile in each corner, and which seem to laugh even in the midst of grief. We had not been two hours together, before I knew his history from beginning to end. He had already been married eight years, and his only trouble was a debt of twenty-four dollars, which the illness of his wife had caused him. This money was owing to the pawnbroker, who kept his best clothes in pledge until he could pay it. "Señor," said he, "if I had ten million dollars, I would rather give them all away than have a sick wife." He had a brother in Puerto Principe, Cuba, who sent over money enough to pay the rent of the house, but he found that children were a great expense. "It is most astonishing," he said, "how much children can eat. From morning till night, the bread is never out of their mouths."

José has recently been travelling with some Spaniards, one of whom made him pay two dollars for an umbrella which was lost on the road. This umbrella is a thorn in his side. At every venta where we stop, the story is repeated, and he is not sparing of his maledictions. The ghost of that umbrella is continually raised, and it will be a long time before he can shut it. "One reason why I like to travel with foreign Señors," said he to me, "is, that when I lose anything, they never make me pay for it." "For all that," I answered, "take care you don't lose my umbrella: it cost three dollars." Since then, nothing can exceed José's attention to that article. He is at his wit's end how to secure it best. It appears sometimes before, sometimes behind him, lashed to the saddle with innumerable cords; now he sticks it into the alforja, now carries it in his hand, and I verily believe that he sleeps with it in his arms. Every evening, as he tells his story to the muleteers, around the kitchen fire, he always winds up by triumphantly appealing to me with: "Well, Señor, have I lost *your* umbrella yet?"

Our bargain is that I shall feed him on the way, and as we travel in the primitive style of the country, we always sit down together to the same dish. To his supervision, the olla is often indebted for an additional flavor, and no "thorough-bred" gentleman could behave at table with more ease and propriety. He is as moderate as a Bedouin in his wants, and never touches the burning aguardiente which the muleteers are accustomed to drink. I asked him the reason of this. "I drink wine, Señor," he replied, "because that, you know, is like meat and bread; but I have made a vow never to drink aguardiente again. Two of us got drunk on it, four or five years ago, in Granada, and we quarrelled. My comrade drew his knife and stabbed me here, in the left shoulder. I was furious and cut him across the breast. We both went to the hospital—I for three months and he for six—and he died in a few days after getting out. It cost my poor father many a thousand reals; and when I was able to go to work, I vowed before the Virgin that I would never touch aguardiente again."

For the first league, our road lay over the rich Vega of Granada, but gradually became wilder and more waste. Passing the long, desert ridge, known as the "Last Sigh of the Moor," we struck across a region of low hills. The road was very deep, from the recent rains, and studded, at short intervals, by rude crosses, erected to persons who had been murdered. José took a grim delight in giving me the history of each. Beyond the village of Lamála, which lies with its salt-pans in a basin of the hills, we ascended the mountain ridge which forms the southern boundary of the Vega. Granada, nearly twenty miles distant, was still visible. The Alhambra was dwindled to a speck, and I took my last view of it and the magnificent landscape which lies spread out before it. The Sierra Nevada, rising to the height of 13,000 feet above the sea, was perfectly free from clouds, and the whole range was visible at one glance. All its chasms were filled with snow, and for nearly half-way down its sides there was not a speck of any other color. Its summits were almost wholly devoid of shadow, and their notched and jagged outlines rested flatly against the sky, like ivory inlaid on a table of lapis-lazuli.

From these waste hills, we descended into the valley of Cacia, whose poplar-fringed river had been so swollen by the rains that the *correo* from Malaga had only succeeded in passing it that morning. We forded it without accident, and, crossing a loftier and bleaker range, came down into the valley of the Marchan. High on a cliff over the stream stood Alhama, my resting-place for the night. The natural warm baths, on account of which this spot was so beloved by the Moors, are still resorted to in the summer. They lie in the bosom of a deep and rugged gorge, half a mile further down the river. The town occupies the crest of a narrow promontory, bounded, on all sides but one, by tremendous precipices. It is one of the most picturesque spots imaginable, and reminded me—to continue the comparison between Syria and Andalusia, which I find so striking—of the gorge of the Barrada, near Damascus. Alhama is now a poor, insignificant town, only visited by artists and muleteers. The population wear long brown cloaks and slouched hats, like the natives of La Mancha.

I found tolerable quarters in a house on the plaza, and took the remaining hour of daylight to view the town. The people looked at me with curiosity, and some boys, walking on the edge of the *tajo*, or precipice, threw over stones that I might see how deep it was. The rock, in some places, quite overhung the bed of the Marchan, which half-girdles its base. The close scrutiny to which I was subjected by the crowd in the plaza called to mind all I had heard of Spanish spies and robbers. At the venta, I was well treated, but received such an exorbitant bill in the morning that I was ready to exclaim, with King Boabdil, "Woe is me, Alhama!" On comparing notes with José, I found that he had been obliged to pay, in addition, for what he received—a discovery which so exasperated that worthy that he folded his hands, bowed his head, made three kisses in the air, and cried out: "I swear before the Virgin that I will never again take a traveller to that inn."

We left Alhama an hour before daybreak, for we had a rough journey of more than forty miles before us. The bridle-path was barely visible in the darkness, but we continued ascending to a height of probably 5,000 feet above the sea, and thus met the sunrise half-way. Crossing the *llano* of Acefaraya, we reached a tremendous natural portal in the mountains, from whence, as from a door, we looked down on all the country lying between us and the sea. The valley of the River Velez, winding among the hills, pointed out the course of our road. On the left towered over us the barren Sierra Tejeda, an isolated group of peaks, about 8,000 feet in height. For miles, the road was a rocky ladder, which we scrambled down on foot, leading our horses. The vegetation gradually became of a warmer and more luxuriant cast; the southern slopes were planted with the vine that produces the famous Malaga raisins, and the orange groves in the sunny depths of the valleys were as yellow as autumnal beeches, with their enormous loads of fruit. As the bells of Vélez Malaga were ringing noon, we emerged from the mountains, near the mouth of the river, and rode into the town to breakfast.

We halted at a queer old inn, more like a Turkish khan than a Christian hostlery. It was kept by a fat landlady, who made us an olla of kid and garlic, which, with some coarse bread and the red Malaga wine, soon took off the sharp edge of our mountain appetites. While I was washing my hands at a well in the court-yard, the *mozo* noticed the pilgrim-seal of Jerusalem, which is stamped indelibly on my left arm. His admiration and reverence were so great that he called the fat landlady, who, on learning that it had been made in Jerusalem, and that I had visited the Holy Sepulchre, summoned her children to see it. "Here, my children!" she said; "cross yourselves, kneel down, and kiss this holy seal; for, as long as you live, you may never see the like of it again." Thus I, a Protestant heretic, became a Catholic shrine. The children knelt and kissed my arm with touching simplicity; and the seal will henceforth be more sacred to me than ever.

The remaining twenty miles or more of the road to Malaga follow the line of the coast, passing headlands crowned by the *atalayas*, or watch-towers, of the Moors. It is a new road, and practicable for carriages, so that, for Spain, it may be considered an important achievement. The late rains have, however, already undermined it in a number of places. Here, as among the mountains, we met crowds of muleteers, all of whom greeted me with: "*Vaya usted con Dios, caballero!*"—("May you go with God, cavalier!") By this time, all my forgotten Spanish had come back again, and a little experience of the simple ways of the people made me quite at home among them. In almost every instance, I was treated precisely as a Spaniard would have been, and less annoyed by the curiosity of the natives than I have been in Germany, and even America.

We were still two leagues from Malaga, at sunset. The fishermen along the coast were hauling in their nets, and we soon began to overtake companies of them, carrying their fish to the city on donkeys. One stout, strapping fellow, with flesh as hard and yellow as a sturgeon's, was seated sideways on a very small donkey, between two immense panniers of fish. As he trotted before us, shouting, and slapping the flanks of the sturdy little beast, José and I began to laugh, whereupon the fellow broke out into the following monologue, addressed to the donkey: "Who laughs at this *burrico?* Who says he's not fine gold from head to foot? What is it that he can't do? If there was a mountain ever so high, he would gallop over it. If there was a river ever so deep, he would swim through it. If he could but speak, I might send him to market alone with the fish, and not a *chavo* of the money would he spend on the way home. Who says he can't go as far as that limping horse? Arrrre, burrico! puñate—ar-r-r-r-e-e!"

We reached Malaga, at last, our horses sorely fagged. At the Fonda de la Alameda, a new and very elegant hotel, I found a bath and a good dinner, both welcome things to a tired traveller. The winter of Malaga is like spring in other lands and on that account it is much visited by invalids, especially English. It is a lively commercial town of about 80,000 inhabitants, and, if the present scheme of railroad communication with Madrid is carried out, must continue to increase in size and importance. A number of manufacturing establishments have lately been started, and in this department it bids fair to rival Barcelona. The harbor is small, but good, and the country around rich in all the productions of temperate and even tropical climates. The city contains little to interest the tourist. I visited the Cathedral, an immense unfinished mass, without a particle of architectural taste outwardly, though the interior has a fine effect from its large dimensions.

At noon to-day, we were again in the saddle, and took the road to the Baths of Caratraca. The tall factory chimneys of Malaga, vomiting forth streams of black smoke, marred the serenity of the sky; but the distant view of the city is very fine. The broad Vega, watered by the Guadaljorce, is rich and well cultivated, and now rejoices in the verdure of spring. The meadows are clothed with fresh grass, butter-cups and daisies are in blossom, and larks sing in the olive-trees. Now and then, we passed a *casa del campo*, with its front half buried in orange-trees, over which towered two or three sentinel palms. After two leagues of this delightful travel, the country became more hilly, and the groups of mountains which inclosed us assumed the most picturesque and enchanting forms. The soft haze in which the distant peaks were bathed, the lovely violet shadows filling up their chasms and gorges, and the fresh meadows, vineyards, and olive groves below, made the landscape one of the most beautiful I have seen in Spain

As we were trotting along through the palmetto thickets, Jose asked me if I should not like to hear an Andalusian story. "Nothing would please me better," I replied. "Ride close beside me, then," said he, "that you may understand every word of it." I complied, and he gave me the following, just as I repeat it: "There was once a very rich man, who had thousands of cattle in the Sierra Nevada, and hundreds of houses in the city. Well: this man put a plate, with his name on it, on the door of the great house in which he lived, and the name was this: Don Pedro, without Fear and without Care. Now, when the King was making his *paséo*, he happened to ride by this house in his carriage, and saw the plate on the door. 'Read me the name on that plate!' said he to his officer. Then the officer read the name: Don Pedro, without Fear and without Care. 'I will see whether Don Pedro is without Fear and without Care,' said the King. The next day came a messenger to the house, and, when he saw Don Pedro, said he to him; 'Don Pedro, without Fear and without Care, the King wants you!' 'What does the King want with me?' said Don Pedro. 'He sends you four questions which you must answer within four days, or he will have you shot; and the questions are:—How can the Sierra Nevada be cleared of snow? How can the sea be made smaller? How many arrobas does the moon weigh? And: How many leagues from here to the Land of Heavenly Glory?' Then Don Pedro without Fear and without Care began to sweat from fright, and knew not what he should do. He called some of his arrieros and loaded twenty mules with money, and went up into the Sierra Nevada, where his herdsmen tended his flocks; for, as I said, he had many thousand cattle. 'God keep you, my master!' said the chief herdsman, who was young, and *buen mozo*, and had as good a head as ever was set on two shoulders. '*Anda, hombre!*' said Don Pedro, 'I am a dead man;' and so he told the herdsman all that the King had said. 'Oh, is that all?' said the knowing mozo. 'I can get you out of the scrape. Let me go and answer the questions in your name, my master!' 'Ah, you fool! what can you do?' said Don Pedro without Fear and without Care, throwing himself upon the earth, and ready to die.

"But, nevertheless, the herdsman dressed himself up as a *caballero*, went down to the city, and, on the fourth day, presented himself at the King's palace. 'What do you want?' said the officers. 'I am Don Pedro without Fear and without Care, come to answer the questions which the King sent to me.' 'Well,' said the King, when he was brought before him, 'let me hear your answers, or I will have you shot this day.' 'Your Majesty,' said the herdsman, 'I think I can do it. If you were to set a million of children to playing among the snow of the Sierra Nevada, they would soon clear it all away; and if you were to dig a ditch as wide and as deep as all Spain, you would make the sea that much smaller.' 'But,' said the King, 'that makes only two questions; there are two more yet.' 'I think I can answer those, also,' said the herdsman: 'the moon contains four quarters, and therefore weighs only one arroba; and as for the last question, it is not even a single league to the Land of Heavenly Glory—for, if your Majesty were to die after breakfast, you would get there before you had an appetite for dinner.' 'Well done!' said the King; and he then made him Count, and Marquez, and I don't know how many other titles. In the meantime, Don Pedro without Fear and without Care had died of his fright; and, as he left no family, the herdsman took possession of all his estates, and, until the day of his death, was called Don Pedro without Fear and without Care."

I write, sitting by the grated window of this lonely inn, looking out on the meadows of the Guadaljorce. The chain of mountains which rises to the west of Malaga is purpled by the light of the setting sun, and the houses and Castle of Cartama hang on its side, in full view. Further to the right, I see the smoke of Monda, where one of the greatest battles of antiquity was fought—that which overthrew the sons of Pompey, and gave the Roman Empire to Cæsar. The mozo of the venta is busy, preparing my kid and rice, and José is at his elbow, gently suggesting ingredients which may give the dish a richer flavor. The landscape is softened by the hush of coming evening; a few birds are still twittering among the bushes, and the half-moon grows whiter and clearer in mid-heaven. The people about me are humble, but appear honest and peaceful, and nothing indicates that I am in the wild *Serrania de Ronda*, the country of robbers, contrabandistas, and assassins.

CHAPTER XXXVII.

THE MOUNTAINS OF RONDA.

Orange Valleys—Climbing the Mountains—José's Hospitality—El Burgo—The Gate of the Wind—The Cliff and Cascades of Ronda—The Mountain Region—Traces of the Moors—Haunts of Robbers—A Stormy Ride—The Inn at Gaucin—Bad News—A Boyish Auxiliary—Descent from the Mountains—The Ford of the Guadiaro—Our Fears Relieved—The Cork Woods—Ride from San Roque to Gibraltar—Parting with José—Travelling in Spain—Conclusion.

GIBRALTAR, *Thursday, November* 25, 1852.

I PASSED an uncomfortable night at the Venta de Villalon, lying upon a bag stuffed with equal quantities of wool and fleas. Starting before dawn, we followed a path which led into the mountains, where herdsmen and boys were taking out their sheep and goats to pasture; then it descended into the valley of a stream, bordered with rich bottom-lands. I never saw the orange in a more flourishing state. We passed several orchards of trees thirty feet high, and every bough and twig so completely laden with fruit, that the foliage was hardly to be seen.

At the Venta del Vicario, we found a number of soldiers just setting out for Ronda. They appeared to be escorting a convoy of goods, for there were twenty or thirty laden mules gathered at the door. We now ascended a most difficult and stony path, winding through bleak wastes of gray rock, till we reached a lofty pass in the mountain range. The wind swept through the narrow gateway with a force that almost unhorsed us. From the other side, a sublime but most desolate landscape opened to my view. Opposite, at ten miles' distance, rose a lofty ridge of naked rock, overhung with clouds. The country between was a chaotic jumble of stony hills, separated by deep chasms, with just a green patch here and there, to show that it was not entirely forsaken by man. Nevertheless, as we descended into it, we found valleys with vineyards and olive groves, which were invisible from above. As we were both getting hungry, José stopped at a ventorillo and ordered two cups of wine, for which he insisted on paying. "If I had as many horses as my master, Napoleon," said he, "I would regale the Señors whenever I travelled with them. I would have *puros*, and sweetmeats, with plenty of Malaga or Valde peñas in the bota, and they should never complain of their fare." Part of our road was studded with gray cork-trees, at a distance hardly to be distinguished from olives, and José dismounted to gather the mast, which was as sweet and palatable as chestnuts, with very little of the bitter quercine flavor. At eleven o'clock, we reached El Burgo, so called, probably, from its ancient Moorish fortress. It is a poor, starved village, built on a barren hill, over a stream which is still spanned by a lofty Moorish bridge of a single arch.

The remaining three leagues to Ronda were exceedingly rough and difficult. Climbing a barren ascent of nearly a league in length, we reached the *Puerto del Viento*, or Gate of the Wind, through which drove such a current that we were obliged to dismount; and even then it required all my strength to move against it. The peaks around, far and near, faced with precipitous cliffs, wore the most savage and forbidding aspect: in fact, this region is almost a counterpart of the wilderness lying between Jerusalem and the Dead Sea. Very soon, we touched the skirt of a cloud, and were enveloped in masses of chill, whirling vapor, through which we travelled for three or four miles to a similar gate on the western side of the chain. Descending again, we emerged into a clearer atmosphere, and saw below us a wide extent of mountain country, but of a more fertile and cheerful character. Olive orchards and wheat-fields now appeared; and, at four o'clock, we rode into the streets of Ronda.

No town can surpass this in the grandeur and picturesqueness of its position. It is built on the edge of a broad shelf of the mountains, which falls away in a sheer precipice of from six to eight hundred feet in height, and, from the windows of many of the houses you can look down the dizzy abyss. This shelf, again, is divided in the centre by a tremendous chasm, three hundred feet wide, and from four to six hundred feet in depth, in the bed of which roars the Guadalvin, boiling in foaming whirlpools or leaping in sparkling cascades, till it reaches the valley below. The town lies on both sides of the chasm, which is spanned by a stone bridge of a single arch, with abutments nearly four hundred feet in height. The view of this wonderful cleft, either from above or below, is one of the finest of its kind in the world. Ronda is as far superior to Tivoli, as Tivoli is to a Dutch village, on the dead levels of Holland. The panorama which it commands is on the grandest scale. The valley below is a garden of fruit and vines; bold yet cultivated hills succeed, and in the distance rise the lofty summits of another chain of the Serrania de Ronda. Were these sublime cliffs, these charming cascades of the Guadalvin, and this daring bridge, in Italy instead of in Spain, they would be sketched and painted every day in the year ; but I have yet to know where a good picture of Ronda may be found

In the bottom of the chasm are a number of corn-mills as old as the time of the Moors. The water, gushing out from the arches of one, drives the wheel of that below, so that a single race supplies them all. I descended by a very steep zig-zag path nearly to the bottom. On a little point or promontory overhanging the black depths, there is a Moorish gateway still standing. The sunset threw a lovely glow over the brown cliffs and the airy town above ; but they were far grander when the cascades glittered in the moonlight, and the gulf out of which they leap was lost in profound shadow. The window of my bed-room hung over the chasm.

Ronda was wrapped in fog, when José awoke me on the morning of the 22d. As we had but about twenty-four miles to ride that day, we did not leave until sunrise. We rode across the bridge, through the old town and down the hill, passing the triple lines of the Moorish walls by the original gateways. The road, stony and rugged beyond measure, now took to the mountains. From the opposite height, there was a fine view of the town, perched like an eagle's nest on the verge of its tremendous cliffs ; but a curtain of rain soon fell before it, and the dense dark clouds settled around us, and filled up the gorges on either hand. Hour after hour, we toiled along the slippery paths, scaling the high ridges by rocky ladders, up which our horses climbed with the greatest difficulty. The scenery, whenever I could obtain a misty glimpse of it, was sublime. Lofty mountain ridges rose on either hand ; bleak, jagged summits of naked rock pierced the clouds, and the deep chasms which separated them sank far below us, dark and indistinct through the rain. Sometimes I caught sight of a little hamlet, hanging on some almost inaccessible ledge, the home of the lawless, semi-Moorish mountaineers who inhabit this wild region. The faces of those we met exhibited marked traces of their Moslem ancestry, especially in the almond-shaped eye and the dusky olive complexion. Their dialect retains many Oriental forms of expression, and I was not a little surprised at finding the Arabic "*eiwa*" (yes) in general use, instead of the Spanish "*si.*"

About eleven o'clock, we reached the rude village of Atajate, where we procured a very good breakfast of kid, eggs, and white Ronda wine. The wind and rain increased, but I had no time to lose, as every hour swelled the mountain floods and made the journey more difficult. This district is in the worst repute of any in Spain ; it is a very nest of robbers and contrabandistas. At the venta in Atajate, they urged us to take a guard, but my valiant José declared that he had never taken one, and yet was never robbed ; so I trusted to his good luck. The weather, however, was our best protection. In such a driving rain, we could bid defiance to the flint locks of their escopettes, if, indeed, any could be found, so fond of their trade, as to ply it in a storm

"Wherein the cub-drawn bear would crouch,
The lion and the belly-pinched wolf
Keep their furs dry."

Nevertheless, I noticed that each of the few convoys of laden mules which we met, had one or more of the *guardia civil* accompanying it. Besides these, the only persons abroad were some wild-looking individuals, armed to the teeth, and muffled in long cloaks, towards whom, as they passed, José would give his head a slight toss, and whisper to me: "more contrabandistas."

We were soon in a condition to defy the weather. The rain beat furiously in our faces, especially when threading the wind-blown passes between the higher peaks. I raised my umbrella as a defence, but the first blast snapped it in twain. The mountain-sides were veined with rills, roaring downward into the hollows, and smaller rills soon began to trickle down my own sides. During the last part of our way, the path was notched along precipitous steeps, where the storm was so thick that we could see nothing either above or below. It was like riding along the outer edge of the world. When once you are thoroughly wet, it is a great satisfaction to know that you can be no wetter; and so José and I went forward in the best possible humor, finding so much diversion in our plight that the dreary leagues were considerably shortened.

At the venta of Gaucin, where we stopped, the people received us kindly. The house consisted of one room—stable, kitchen, and dining-room all in one. There was a small apartment in a windy loft, where a bed (much too short) was prepared for me. A fire of dry heather was made in the wide fire-place, and the ruddy flames, with a change of clothing and a draught of the amber vintage of Estepona, soon thawed out the chill of the journey. But I received news which caused me a great deal of anxiety. The River Guadiaro was so high that nobody could cross, and two forlorn muleteers had been waiting eight days at the inn, for the waters to subside. Augmented by the rain which had fallen, and which seemed to increase as night came on, how could I hope to cross it on the morrow? In two days, the India steamer would be at Gibraltar; my passage was already taken, and I *must* be there. The matter was discussed for some time; it was pronounced impossible to travel by the usual road, but the landlord knew a path among the hills which led to a ferry on the Guadiaro, where there was a boat, and from thence we could make our way to San Roque, which is in sight of Gibraltar. He demanded rather a large fee for accompanying me, but there was nothing else to be done. José and I sat down in great tribulation to our accustomed olla, but neither of us could do justice to it, and the greater part gladdened the landlord's two boys—beautiful little imps, with faces like Murillo's cherubs.

Nevertheless, I passed rather a merry evening, chatting with some of the villagers over a brazier of coals; and one of the aforesaid boys, who, although only eight years old, already performed the duties of mozo, lighted me to my loft. When he had put down the lamp, he tried the door, and asked me: "Have you the key?" "No," said I, "I don't want one; I am not afraid." "But," he rejoined, "perhaps you may get afraid in the night; and if you do, strike on this part of the wall (suiting the action to the word)—*I* sleep on that side." I willingly promised to call him to my aid, if I should get alarmed. I slept but little, for the wind was howling around the tiles over my head, and I was busy with plans for constructing rafts and swimming currents with a rope around my waist. Finally, I found a little oblivion, but it seemed that I had scarcely closed my eyes, when José pushed open the door. "Thanks be to God, señor!" said he, "it begins to dawn, and the sky is clear: we shall certainly get to Gibraltar to-day."

The landlord was ready, so we took some bread and a basket of olives, and set out at once. Leaving Gaucin, we commenced descending the mountain staircase by which the Serrania of Ronda is scaled, on the side towards Gibraltar. "The road," says Mr. Ford, "seems made by the Evil One in a hanging garden of Eden." After four miles of frightfully rugged descent, we reached an orange grove on the banks of the Xenar, and then took a wild path leading along the hills on the right of the stream. We overtook a few muleteers, who were tempted out by the fine weather, and before long the *correo*, or mail-rider from Ronda to San Roque, joined us. After eight miles more of toilsome travel we reached the valley of the Guadiaro. The river was not more than twenty yards wide, flowing with a deep, strong current, between high banks. Two ropes were stretched across, and a large, clumsy boat was moored to the shore. We called to the ferrymen, but they hesitated, saying that nobody had yet been able to cross. However, we all got in, with our horses, and two of the men, with much reluctance, drew us over. The current was very powerful, although the river had fallen a little during the night, but we reached the opposite bank without accident.

We had still another river, the Guargante, to pass, but we were cheered by some peasants whom we met, with the news that the ferry-boat had resumed operations. After this current lay behind us, and there was now nothing but firm land all the way to Gibraltar, José declared with much earnestness that he was quite as glad, for my sake, as if somebody had given him a million of dollars. Our horses, too, seemed to feel that something had been achieved, and showed such a fresh spirit that we loosened the reins and let them gallop to their hearts' content over the green meadows. The mountains were now behind us, and the Moorish castle of Gaucin crested a peak blue with the distance. Over hills covered with broom and heather in blossom, and through hollows grown with oleander, arbutus and the mastic shrub, we rode to the cork-wood forests of San Roque, the sporting-ground of Gibraltar officers. The barking of dogs, the cracking of whips, and now and then a distant halloo, announced that a hunt was in progress, and soon we came upon a company of thirty or forty horsemen, in caps, white gloves and top-boots, scattered along the crest of a hill. I had no desire to stop and witness the sport, for the Mediterranean now lay before me, and the huge gray mass of "The Rock" loomed in the distance.

At San Roque, which occupies the summit of a conical hill, about half-way between Gibraltar and Algeciras, the landlord left us, and immediately started on his return. Having now exchanged the rugged bridle-paths of Ronda for a smooth carriage-road, José and I dashed on at full gallop, to the end of our journey. We were both bespattered with mud from head to foot, and our jackets and sombreros had lost something of their spruce air. We met a great many ruddy, cleanly-shaven Englishmen, who reined up on one side to let us pass, with a look of wonder at our Andalusian impudence. Nothing diverted José more than to see one of these Englishmen rising in his stirrups, as he went by on a trot. "Look, look, Señor!" he exclaimed; "did you ever see the like?"

and then broke into a fresh explosion of laughter. Passing the Spanish Lines, which stretch across the neck of the sandy little peninsula, connecting Gibraltar with the main land, we rode under the terrible batteries which snarl at Spain from this side of the Rock. Row after row of enormous guns bristle the walls, or look out from the galleries hewn in the sides of inaccessible cliffs An artificial moat is cut along the base of the Rock, and a simple bridge-road leads into the fortress and town. After giving up my passport I was allowed to enter, José having already obtained a permit from the Spanish authorities.

I clattered up the long street of the town to the Club House, where I found a company of English friends. In the evening, José made his appearance, to settle our accounts and take his leave of me. While scrambling down the rocky stairway of Gaucin, José had said to me: "Look you, Señor, I am very fond of English beer, and if I get you to Gibraltar to day you must give me a glass of it." When, therefore, he came in the evening, his eyes sparkled at the sight of a bottle of Alsop's Ale, and a handful of good Gibraltar cigars. "Ah, Señor," said he, after our books were squared, and he had pocketed his *gratificacion*, "I am sorry we are going to part; for we are good friends, are we not, Señor?" "Yes, José," said I; "if I ever come to Granada again, I shall take no other guide than José Garcia; and I will have you for a longer journey than this. We shall go over all Spain together, *mi amigo!*" "May God grant it!" responded José, crossing himself; "and now, Señor, I must go. I shall travel back to Granada, *muy triste*, Señor, *muy triste*." The faithful fellow's eyes were full of tears, and, as he lifted my hand twice to his lips, some warm drops fell upon it. God bless his honest heart, wherever he goes !

And now a word as to travelling in Spain, which is not attended with half the difficulties and annoyances I had been led to expect. My experience, of course, is limited to the provinces of Andalusia, but my route included some of the roughest roads and most dangerous robber-districts in the Peninsula. The people with whom I came in contact were invariably friendly and obliging, and I was dealt with much more honestly than I should have been in Italy. With every disposition to serve you, there is nothing like servility among the Spaniards. The native dignity which characterizes their demeanor prepossesses me very strongly in their favor. There is but one dialect of courtesy, and the muleteers and common peasants address each other with the same grave respect as the Dons and Grandees. My friend José was a model of good-breeding.

I had little trouble either with passport-officers or custom-houses. My passport, in fact, was never once demanded, although I took the precaution to have it visèd in all the large cities. In Seville and Malaga, it was signed by the American Consuls, without the usual fee of two dollars—almost the only instances which have come under my observation. The regulations of the American Consular System, which gives the Consuls no salary, but permits them, instead, to get their pay out of travellers, is a disgrace to our government. It amounts, in effect, to *a direct tax on travel*, and falls heavily on the hundreds of young men of limited means, who annually visit Europe for the purpose of completing their education. Every American citizen who travels in Italy pays a passport tax of ten dollars. In all the ports of the Mediterranean, there is an American Vice-Consul, who does not even get the postage paid on his dispatches, and to whom the advent of a traveller is of course a welcome sight. Misled by a false notion of economy, our government is fast becoming proverbial for its meanness. If those of our own citizens who represent us abroad only worked as they are paid, and if the foreigners who act as Vice-Consuls without pay did not derive some petty trading advantages from their position, we should be almost without protection.

With my departure from Spain closes the record of my journey in the Lands of the Saracen; for, although I afterwards beheld more perfect types of Saracenic Art on the banks of the Jumna and the Ganges, they grew up under the great Empire of the descendants of Tamerlane, and were the creations of artists foreign to the soil. It would, no doubt, be interesting to contrast the remains of Oriental civilization and refinement, as they still exist at the extreme eastern and western limits of the Moslem sway, and to show how that Art, which had its birth in the capitals of the Caliphs—Damascus and Baghdad—attained its most perfect development in Spain and India; but my visit to the latter country connects itself naturally with my voyage to China, Loo-Choo, and Japan, forming a separate and distinct field of travel.

On the 27th of November, the Overland Mail Steamer arrived at Gibraltar, and I embarked in her for Alexandria, entering upon another year of even more varied, strange, and adventurous experiences, than that which had closed. I am almost afraid to ask those patient readers, who have accompanied me thus far, to travel with me through another volume; but next to the pleasure of seeing the world, comes the pleasure of telling of it, and I must needs finish my story.

www.ingramcontent.com/pod-product-compliance
Lightning Source LLC
LaVergne TN
LVHW021125110826
845150LV00005B/948

* 9 7 8 1 4 2 5 5 5 1 0 2 5 *